# ON LIBERTY,
# SOCIETY,
# AND POLITICS

*AyN Davis*

*Colorado Springs*
*Dec 1992*

*A Liberty Classics*
*Edition*

WILLIAM GRAHAM SUMNER

# ON LIBERTY,
# SOCIETY,
# AND POLITICS

---

## The Essential Essays of
## William Graham Sumner

---

EDITED BY

ROBERT C. BANNISTER

Liberty Fund
Indianapolis

This is a Liberty Classics Edition published by Liberty Fund, Inc., a foundation established to encourage study of the ideal of a society of free and responsible individuals.

The cuneiform inscription that serves as our logo and as the design motif for our endpapers is the earliest-known written appearance of the word "freedom" (*amagi*), or "liberty." It is taken from a clay document written about 2300 B.C. in the Sumerian city-state of Lagash.

"*Laissez-Faire*" reprinted from *Essays of William Graham Sumner*, eds. A. Keller and M. Davie (2 vols., New Haven: Yale University Press, 1934), vol. II, pp. 468–477. Reprinted by permission of Yale University Press. "Individualism," "Tradition and Progress," "Solidarity of the Human Race," "Mores and Statistics," "Science and Mores," and "On Mores and Progress" reprinted from the William Graham Sumner Papers, Manuscripts and Archives, Yale University Library. Reprinted by permission.

Frontispiece photo courtesy of Yale University Library.

**Library of Congress Cataloging-in-Publication Data**

Sumner, William Graham, 1840–1910.
   On liberty, society, and politics: the essential essays of
William Graham Sumner / edited by Robert C. Bannister.
     p.   cm.
   Includes bibliographical references and index.
   ISBN 0-86597-100-5 (alk. paper). — ISBN 0-86597-101-3 (pbk.:
alk. paper)
   1.  Social sciences.   I.  Bannister, Robert C.   II.  Title.
H35.S9178    1992
330—dc20                            91-36630
                                             CIP

10 9 8 7 6 5 4 3 2 1

# Contents

# Foreword

William Graham Sumner, as his contemporaries testified, was someone you liked a lot or not at all. During his four decades at Yale, undergraduates thronged to his classes. "In my estimation, he was the greatest teacher I have ever known," one of his early students wrote when Sumner died in 1910. Even the radical economist Thorstein Veblen, who attended Yale for graduate studies in the early 1880s, reported that he was "particularly" pleased with Sumner. In the following decades, a loyal band of Sumnerites, led by his protégé Albert G. Keller, kept alive a "Sumner Club" to promote his teachings.

Others were less charitable. Commenting on an anonymous review in the *Nation*, one angry reader guessed that Sumner must have been the author since no one else was "capable of so bigoted a hatred." When he opposed Free Silver in the mid-1890s, one westerner wondered how "such an arrogant jackass . . . can occupy a chair in a college at Yale." When Sumner's *Folkways* appeared in 1906, a disgruntled reader likened it to "a card index." "Now and then are interspersed some general conclusions," he added, "which shock without convincing."

Inevitably, much of the debate about Sumner turned on his politics. To his defenders, he provided an arsenal of arguments against the encroachment of government. To his critics, he was, at worst, a "business hireling" and, at best, the confused spokesman of an older middle class whose day was done. Often conflating the two charges, historians pictured him as the leading "social Darwinist" of his generation, a theorist who appropriated the rhetoric of evolutionism to defend the worst excesses of unregulated capitalism. Despite challenges to this view during the past two decades, he remains the late nineteenth-century thinker American history textbooks most like to hate. Sumner's blunt, uncompromising, and often provocative manner was partly to blame for this situation. "Bluff Billy," as he was called, did not suffer fools easily.

There were other factors at work that contributed to this view of Sumner, not all of which were of his own making. Many critics quoted a few phrases concerning "fittest" and "unfittest" as the sum of his social thought. Focusing on his views of government and the economy, most historians and critics failed to place his work within the broader context of the effort of several generations of American intellectuals to ground morals and public policy in science rather than in Protestant Christianity. As a member of the "generation of 1840" who initiated this movement, Sumner shared in this enterprise with the sociologist Lester Ward and the jurist Oliver Wendell Holmes, Jr., among others, even though he did not share their politics. As these intellectuals debated the meaning of science, the charge of misapplied Darwinism (including the epithet "social Darwinist"), as I have argued in *Social Darwinism: Science and Myth* (1979), was essentially a battle strategy of the opponents of this movement, more caricature than accurate characterization. Critics also assumed that Sumner's ideas remained static throughout his career. Quotations from lectures of the 1870s or from *Folkways* became interchangeable evidence of a monolithic ideology.

The image of Sumner that emerges from these criticisms seriously misrepresents him. He launched his career in a decade with more than its share of corruption and fraud, including the scandals of the Grant presidency and New York's Tweed Ring, the financial buccaneering of Jay Gould, the "corrupt bargain" that gave Rutherford B. Hayes the presidency in 1876. Yet he was as critical of these developments as were the self-styled "reformers" whose proposals, in his view, only compounded the problems. During the 1880s and 1890s, he continued to defend free markets, individual enterprise, and the accumulation of capital. However, he was acutely aware of mounting problems, from the rise of plutocracy (defined broadly as the influence of wealth on politics) to the excesses of consumerism and of democracy. The United States was entering its "glory days," he lamented shortly before his death, referring to the "corruption and extravagance which ultimately have ruined all the republics of the past." In sounding these warnings, he seemed to his admirers to be the epitome of the "old Roman," a defender of the republican tradition of the founders, not the business "hireling" or the spirit of individualism past.

Sumner's "conservatism" was accordingly complex. As he moved from clergyman to sociologist, he struggled to reconcile two contradictory impulses: a desire for organic community, historical continuity, and traditional values as antidote to unfettered individualism and materialistic progress; *and* a commitment to individual freedom that he believed would fuel this progress. Complicating this dilemma was the specter of cultural relativism wherein all truth appeared relative to conditions. In freeing the individual from past custom and tradition, cultural relativism appeared to rule out any common standard for individual behavior or public policy. In his early sermons, Sumner confronted these issues in repeated attempts to balance "tradition" and "progress." In *Folkways,* he discussed them in terms of the relation between the "mores" and "science," the former being the encoded customs and traditions that shape all human activity, and the latter being the objective attitude that allows limited escape from those customs and traditions.

In this quest, Sumner's conception of science was crucial. Since the eighteenth century, science had been seen as a means of freeing humanity from the burdens of the past, while providing for one or another type of social engineering. Inspired by Darwin, many of Sumner's contemporaries found in evolution the basis for an instrumental view of reason that justified governmental activism and a relativism that rejected established institutions and beliefs. Sumner, in contrast, distinguished the "methods" of science from its "speculations," viewing the former in terms of the narrowly inductive procedures of what American intellectuals of his generation termed "Baconian" science (dubiously claiming lineage from the celebrated seventeenth-century English scientist Francis Bacon). Science, so viewed, was not some "ism," but a matter-of-factness that stressed classification over hypothesis.

Although on the surface Sumner shared his generation's faith in science, he diverged from a majority of his fellow social scientists by rejecting the notion that science taught that truth is merely a consensus of trained observers. Sumner's "expert" was not a credentialed member of a social scientific community that drew up social blueprints to meet changing conditions—the model that was increasingly used in American sociology in the decades after Sumner's death. Rather, Sumner's expert was the tough-minded individual who viewed current mores objectively in the light of history. In grasping the essence behind appearance, science, in Sumner's view, provided an absolute standard for individual behavior and social policy, and hence an escape from a debilitating relativism and moral anarchy.

While Sumner defended private property, individual enterprise, and *laissez-faire,* he was not an uncritical apologist for American business. Rather, he joined a tradition of American thinkers who championed republicanism against democracy, hard work and self-denial over material luxury, and public good over individual gratification. Unlike the founding fathers, Sumner did not ground his conservatism in the classical republicanism of Greece or Rome, but in scientific method and an ethos of professionalism that sought the equivalents of public virtue in discipline, denial, and detachment. Although some contradictions remained, he took more seriously than many of his contemporaries the problems of change vs. tradition and cultural relativism vs. common standards that continue to dominate our discourse more than a century later.


## Youth and Education

Born in Paterson, New Jersey, on October 30, 1840, Sumner was the son of recent English immigrants. A mechanic by training, his father Thomas left the low wages and unemployment of Lancashire just in time to feel the sting of the American depression of 1837. He was distantly related by marriage to a prominent free-trader and temperance advocate, whose causes he made his own. However, as his son later recalled, he was also contemptuous of "demagogical arguments," "the notions of labor agitators," and "the entire gospel of gush." After losing an eye in an industrial accident and his health to a lifetime of toil, Thomas died in 1881 almost as poor as he was when he arrived in the New World, remembered only as the "forgotten man" of his son's best-known essay.

As a youth, Sumner enjoyed neither the security of place nor the comforts of the emotional life. After surveying prospects from New York to Ohio, his father moved the family to New Haven and then to Hartford. The death of his mother Sarah in 1848 placed eight-year-old William and his younger brother, Joseph Graham, in the custody of a stepmother whose concern with economy at the expense of affection grieved even her taciturn husband. Still grief-stricken, the brothers even plotted to kill their stepmother, which may have been the last time they thoroughly agreed on anything. Although Sumner never referred to his youthful deprivations and, indeed, rarely mentioned his childhood, these experiences left him with a keen sense of the separation between the inner and outer life, between private and public spheres, and between sentiment and fact. As an adult, Sumner's sternness was legendary. Nevertheless, a tenderness also surfaced with surprising intensity in love letters he wrote to his fiancée and, later, in his fondness for children, an indulgence he once desired from his parents but never received.

Excessively serious, even a bit of a prig, young Sumner compensated for what he was missing at home by throwing himself into his schoolwork. After rigorous training in the public school in Hartford, with the help of money his father made in one of his rare successful ventures, Sumner entered Yale in 1859. There he plodded through the ironclad curriculum that the Yale faculty report of 1828 had prescribed for all of antebellum America: two years of the classics, a third that added physics and some astronomy and chemistry, and a fourth that included lectures in history, politics, and international law. Outside the classroom, Sumner discovered a more vital Yale—in eating clubs, in the Brothers in Unity debating society, in sports (where he was a keen follower of the Yale "Navy"), and finally in Skull and Bones, whose coveted election he received in the spring of his junior year. Fueling this vitality was a markedly changed student body as sons of business magnates from New York, Chicago, and other cities swelled classes previously drawn mostly from New England and settlements of New Englanders throughout the Midwest. Sumner's friend Henry Holt dated the change precisely to 1856 when the first group of New Yorkers entered Yale, bringing with them a "revolutionary quantity of new clothes."

Yale gave Sumner a new identity, replacing the dour William with the more congenial "Graeme," as his fellow Bones men came to call him. Yale also provided Sumner with connections who supplied him with the funds for several years of European study. A fellow Bones man then put Sumner's name forward for a tutorship at Yale, a position he occupied upon his return from Europe.

For the ambitious Yale man, the Civil War was largely an inconvenience. Although some of Sumner's classmates marched in torchlight parades for Abraham Lincoln and responded to the call to enlist after Sumter, enthusiasm soon waned. Less than a third of the class of 1863, including nongraduates, saw any military service. Although Sumner later portrayed the war as a victory for the forces of modernity, he was less optimistic at the time. Distrusting northern leaders, he feared that Lincoln's emergency war measures threatened to create a dictatorship. Within his own family, his postwar lack of enthusiasm for suffrage for the freedmen estranged him from his brother Joe (later a clerk at the New Orleans office of the Freedmen's Bureau), and even brought a reprimand from his father. Feeling no guilt for his failure to enlist, he scurried frantically to salvage his European studies, while his father used a $300 loan from a brother of a friend of Sumner's to arrange a substitute after Sumner was drafted in July 1863. Although one candidate Thomas found "skedaddled" out a hotel window with the money, the government accepted the transaction as meeting the legal requirement. Thus, as Sumner's biographer Donald Bellomy has commented, "No one died (or lived) in Sumner's place."

Although marriage lay in the future, Sumner's interest in the opposite sex also developed during his college years. He knew he was no ladies man. "I am not the sort of man women love," he once confessed, but this realization did not keep him from trying. At several parties, he became jealous when a classmate bested him for the favors of Jeannie Elliott, a pretty relative of a locally prominent family. By the spring of his senior year, he became deeply involved with a young woman from Hartford, only to be devastated when she died shortly before his graduation.

Happily, in the summer of 1869, after several years of studying abroad and another three as classics tutor at Yale, Sumner again met Jeannie Elliott while vacationing in the Catskills. Until their marriage in April 1871, he poured out his yearnings and hopes in letter after letter. When he announced his engagement, friends looked on in disbelief at a Sumner they had not previously known. One colleague wrote, "I still find it difficult to associate so much emotion as an engagement involves with a being whose composition I have hitherto supposed to consist only of *pure thought.*" By this time, still another Sumner had emerged as Episcopalian clergyman, a career for which he had been preparing more or less since entering Yale.

As Sumner entered his twenties, he was headed for success. However, the story of his youth had not quite followed the usual Horatio Alger plot. Although he was the upwardly mobile son of a recent immigrant, he did not pretend or wish to be the legendary self-made man. In a letter to his fiancée, written soon after he left New Haven for New York, he said that many people would say that "I have 'succeeded' & say that I have 'made my way up,' " but they would be wrong. He had never set out to " 'rise in the world,' " he added, echoing Alger's recently published *Ragged Dick* (1868). He later told his students, "the 'self-made man' is, by definition, the first bungling essay of a bad workman."

Nor, given his many debts to community and friends, had his youth provided a homily on "individualism" in the way some nineteenth-century Americans used the term. "Individualism," he told his congregation a few years later, reduces a man to the status of the "wild beast," destroying the "union and organization" that make society possible. In later years, he continued to inveigh against the man "on the make." Sumner's individualism was not a creed of "go-it-alone and devil-take-the hindmost." Rather, it was a code of discipline, duty, and responsibility within the confines of external restraints, whether imposed by Providence, one's profession, or the social norms he later termed "mores." Philosophically, Sumner tried to address the limits of free will, and he wrestled with this issue throughout his career with mixed success. In his personal life, it took the form of a professionalism that linked individual advancement with self-discipline and hard work. For society, it meant finding and obeying the "laws" that alone make freedom possible.

## Preacher

In the spring of 1869, Sumner left Yale and plunged into Anglican church politics, first as editor of *The Living Church* and assistant pastor in New York and New Haven and then as minister of The Church of the Redeemer in Morristown, New Jersey, from 1870 to 1872. At the time, the Episcopalians were torn between a High Church and a Low Church group, the one stressing dogma and tradition, the other emphasizing evangelical conversion. Sumner identified with a third and moderate Broad Church faction that was more open to reason and science. The Broad Church creed was summed up in the title of his journal, *The Living Church*—"living," because it addressed the most vital issues then confronting Christianity, and "church" because the issues could be resolved within this historically evolved institution.

By the late 1860s, Sumner's religious ideas were still in flux. Converted from his parent's Anglicanism to Congregationalism in his youth, he later had come to feel less sympathy with the lingering revivalism of his own congregation than with the anti-revivalist views of Hartford's most famous Congregationalist, Horace Bushnell. While studying in Germany, he had dabbled briefly with the rationalism of the "higher criticism" (the study of biblical writings to determine their literary history and the purpose and meaning of the authors) before being returned to "common sense" by the Oxford Anglicans. At Oxford, he also discovered Richard Hooker's *Of the Laws of Ecclesiastical Polity* (1597–1662), a treatise that combined an attack on excessive reverence for a literal interpretation of the Bible with a celebration of constitutional order and historical continuity. Peer pressure from home pulled Sumner in the direction of the Episcopalians. "We are all of us Episcopalians, Bill, and you must be the same, can't you," wrote friend William Whitney on behalf of the Bones group. Upon returning to Yale, Sumner joined his friends and the Episcopalians.

Although conventions of the pulpit ruled out specific references to current affairs, Sumner used his sermons to tackle the most pressing intellectual and social issues of the day. His sermon titles alone told much of the story: "Ill-Gotten Wealth," "Individualism," "Tradition and

Progress," and "Solidarity of the Human Race." In the Broad Church spirit, he sought in each case a middle ground upon which contending factions could unite.

A case in point was the mounting conflict between religion and science, not a "warfare" of opposing groups (as Cornell president Andrew D. White would soon imply), but a battle over the nature of science itself. Negotiating this thicket, Sumner distinguished science as "method" from the "speculations" of individual scientists. He found "no great fault" with Charles Darwin, Thomas Huxley, or Herbert Spencer in "their original works," he told his New Jersey congregation. "They may be right or wrong in their speculations and theories," but they were "honest, sincere, and industrious" in method. What this method was he was not yet prepared to say, although he was still disposed to the narrowly inductive Baconianism he first learned at Yale.

Sumner also sought compromise on the merits of "tradition" and "progress." "The traditions of centuries have a true *moral* authority," he told his parishioners. "We must begin with the world as we find it, that is, as it is handed down to us from the past." But he also cautioned that the "true use of tradition" should be distinguished from "traditionalism,"—the blind acceptance of "old errors" and "worn-out falsehoods."

The issue was personal as well as theological. During his stay at Oxford, tradition in the form of English class snobbery made Sumner acutely aware of his own humble origins. Like many an American Oxonian in similar circumstances, he accommodated by embracing English tradition with the passion of the half-converted, chiding fellow Americans for their lack of tradition. But the spirit of progress in post-Civil War America proved equally contagious. "When I came back," he later wrote his fiancée, "I saw that the vast body of people here were free, prosperous, free from care, & happy, & that is worth all the elegance it robs us of." This inner tension, as it turned out, dovetailed neatly with the desire of most Anglicans to avoid the excesses of either the High or Low Church positions, as he soon demonstrated in the sermon "Tradition and Progress."

In an age when career patterns remained fluid, Sumner was soon unhappy within the church. Friends showered him with advice concerning alternative careers—in law, perhaps even in commerce. In the spring of 1871, a week before he proposed marriage to Jeannie, he was offered the presidency of the University of Alabama at the princely sum of $5,000 a year. At Yale, friends lobbied on his behalf for a faculty position, the job he really wanted, although in precisely what field remained to be seen. For two years, obstacles delayed the appointment: Jeannie had no wish to be a faculty wife, and the $2,000 his friends were able to raise initially was too little. Finally, in September 1873, he returned to Yale.

Sumner's reasons for leaving the clergy and the legacy of this experience have been the subject of considerable speculation. Denying a crisis of faith, he later quipped that he merely put his beliefs in a drawer, only to find them gone when next he looked. He never officially resigned from the clergy, served as a vestryman, and attended various church functions until his death. At the other extreme, he once remarked cynically to a student that one of two wasted periods in his life was when he was "a parson." (The second one was when he was active politically during the 1870s.)

Sumner's refusal to break cleanly with the church probably reflected a desire not to offend his wife and other family members, perhaps coupled with a reluctance to undermine so powerful a source of social authority. As he grappled with questions of faith and reason, tradition and progress, and solidarity and individualism, Sumner's ideas *did* change. His analysis gradually secularized in tone, a shift already evident in an 1873 revision of an earlier sermon, "The Solidarity of the Human Race." However, this change registered his participation in a broad transformation of western thought rather than any sudden conversion to the ideas of Spencer or Darwin.

The clerical years, nonetheless, left their mark. Affording an opportunity to develop his oratorical skills and prose style, the pulpit allowed Sumner scope to discuss pressing issues, both philosophical and social. If some of the answers changed, the questions remained remarkably the same, notably those concerning tradition and progress. For Sumner, this issue involved two deeply held, but potentially contradictory convictions: a belief in history and institutions as a check on progress, and an instinctive commitment to individual freedom. For someone who would be at once "conservative" and "American," this dilemma admitted no easy solution.

## Educational Reformer, Politician, Polemicist

When Sumner returned to New Haven in 1873, Yale was struggling in its own way with changes then transforming American higher education. Harvard's appointment in 1869 of Charles W. Eliot, the university's first lay president, symbolized an end to clerical domination. Two years later, Noah Porter replaced Theodore Dwight Woolsey as Yale's president. Although a clergyman, Porter also was a moral philosopher of considerable repute and dedicated to his own vision of the modern university.

Woolsey's departure left Porter with the unattractive prospect of teaching single-handedly the senior-year catchall course in mental and moral philosophy they had previously shared. Hoped-for assistance vanished with the resignation of Daniel Coit Gilman of the Sheffield Scientific School, an unannounced presidential candidate and the one person who might have taken over Woolsey's part of the course. The subsequent allotment of funds for a chair in "political and social science" placed Sumner in competition with a well-connected Congregationalist clergyman named Diman, who had been showered with academic offers since his appointment at Brown in 1864 and who was soon the favorite of Yale faculty members who opposed Sumner. A year of vintage academic politics ensued, including attempts to steer Sumner to a less-prestigious (and unendowed) chair in ancient history or to persuade him to withdraw his candidacy altogether. Sumner was finally offered and accepted the new chair in political economy with high hopes that it could be made "most influential on the future of this country."

In most respects, Sumner was the consummate college reformer. Writing in *The Living Church*, he welcomed Eliot's appointment at Harvard, arguing that American colleges could become true universities only by overcoming their sectarian origins. At Yale, he endorsed a recent experiment to divide classes by academic rank rather than alphabetically for recitations, and he even supported attempts to eliminate the tedious recitations altogether. In his own courses, he replaced graded recitations with a single final examination and made attendance optional, causing Porter to warn that he was destroying the program "on which the whole system of discipline and honors is founded."

At the same time, Sumner rejected as worthless one Eliot proposal to bring experts to the university to energize graduate studies. He likewise distrusted extreme demands that the universities "keep up with the times," wanting only to assure that they not become bastions of "mere traditionalism and stagnation." Although admiring the German model, he wanted the United States to build its universities upon the experience and traditions of its colleges. With characteristic bluntness, he identified poor endowment rather than curriculum as the heart of the matter. "It is *money*, or the want of it, which is the root of all evil." As in the Broad Church debates, Sumner again staked out an idealistic as well as practical position, a balance between tradition and progress. As he turned to public affairs, this balance would be more difficult to attain.


During the early Yale years (1873–78), Sumner was best known as scholar-politician and polemicist rather than for any contributions to social theory. "What is needed now," he wrote, "is, not more thorough theoretical discussion of the scholar-in-politics, but that a few more should try it." Sumner launched his career as scholar-in-politics in the fall of 1873 when he ran successfully for New Haven alderman, a position he held for four years. The same year he also became an honorary member of the New Haven Chamber of Congress, which he used as a personal forum for his favored causes. At the national level, he joined the recently founded American Social Science Association (ASSA), where he served on a newly established finance committee until finally resigning in disgust at ASSA's congenital do-goodism. In November 1877, he joined an electoral commission to investigate fraud in New Orleans during the recent presidential election. The following year, he testified before a congressional committee investigating labor unrest.

In politics, Sumner was a Republican less from conviction than from the absence of a viable alternative. The Democrats historically represented the excesses of Jeffersonianism and Jacksonianism he most despised, while the GOP attracted most of the "best men" in the North and, more importantly, in New Haven. Disgusted by the corruption of the Grant years and dismayed by Republican policy on tariffs and the money issue, he shared the outlook of future Mugwumps, as independents in both parties would later be dubbed. In the fall of 1877, he shocked friends and political allies by throwing his support to the Democrat, Samuel Tilden.

As polemicist, Sumner attempted to reach a popular audience by way of public lectures, newspapers, essays, and books. Among public issues, he focused especially on the currency issue, then agitated by calls for the retirement of the Civil War "greenbacks" and later by the establishment of a "bimetal" standard of gold and silver. He also focused on free trade, now apparently doomed by the protective tariffs of the war years. He devoted his first two books—A History of American Currency (1874), and Lectures on the History of Protection (1877)—respectively, to these two issues.

Sumner's own experience with the depreciating value of money through inflation gave him a personal stake in the currency issue. The size of his debt to his friends and his concern over financing further work in Europe or the Far East left a legacy of hatred for paper currency and inflation. Although he paid little attention to the demonetarization of silver in 1873 (a move critics later dubbed the "Crime of '73"), he was distressed as leading economists otherwise within the classicist camp supported international bimetallism, among them his Yale colleague Francis A. Walker. After holding his fire for several years, Sumner attacked bimetallism in 1878, placing himself in open conflict with potential allies.

In his attacks on the protective tariffs, Sumner characteristically combined appeals to the pocketbook and to morality. Tariffs were ostensibly a levy on overseas trade, but Sumner saw them as a tax to benefit some Americans over others. "The victim and the beneficiary are amongst ourselves," he argued, since consumers ultimately paid in higher prices. Worse, the tax was an indirect one, leaving those taxed unaware of their burden.

Although few Americans appeared so well-equipped to raise economic theory to a new level, Sumner sought to popularize rather than to extend classical British theory. More interested in practical problems than theoretical issues, he instead catalogued the dire consequences, past and present, of paper money and high tariffs. After a visit with Sumner in New Haven in 1875, Alfred Marshall, the brilliant British economist, judged him to be a man of "enormous ability," but one lacking "the nature fitted for epoch-making truths."

Disillusionment with politics during 1877, a result both of his personal experience as New Haven alderman and of his assessment of voting fraud in the Hayes-Tilden election, presaged a shift in Sumner's priorities during the next decade. "I found out that I was more likely to do more harm than good in politics than almost any other kind of man," he later wrote of his career as alderman, "because I did not know the rules of the game and did not want to learn them." After an abortive attempt to return to the Republican fold, he repudiated politics as a waste of time, declining even to vote in the 1880 election. Accordingly, during the 1880s, he argued for the necessary separation of politics and economics and for the need to eliminate political corruption through civil service reform.

Meanwhile, developments in the industrial sphere shifted the focus of Sumner's interest to labor and big business and, finally, to Marxism. Responding to the bloody summer of railway strikes in 1877, he penned an angry article meant for but not finally published in the *North American Review*, following it with several other essays on labor and strikes throughout the 1880s. Although the secretive formation of the Standard Oil trust in 1882 heralded a new phase of industrial combination, Sumner, like most of his contemporaries, realized its implications only gradually. In a series in the *Independent* in 1888–89, however, he took direct aim at the emerging "plutocracy," a concept that joined middle-class fear of industrial combination with the patrician dislike of vulgar wealth he had earlier expressed in his sermons. Narrowly defined by Sumner, plutocracy referred to "a political form in which the controlling force is wealth." But more generally it enshrined the "increasing thirst for luxury" and the acquisitive appetites of the man "on the make." He concluded with disgust that "the principle of plutocracy is that money buys whatever the owner of money wants."

He also gradually realized that Karl Marx was not just another socialist. Initially he knew Marx only as the leader of the International who wanted "to carry the war into the arena of scientific economy." But Marx's treatment of "capital" was soon at the center of Sumner's indictment of the entire socialist movement. When the visit of Marx's daughter and son-in-law to the United States in 1886 stimulated new interest in his theories, Sumner took aim at such concepts as "proletariat" and "bourgeoisie." "No American artisan" can understand these terms, he charged. "Such ideas are a part of a foreign dress of a set of ideas which are not yet naturalized."

As Sumner moved from the mugwumpish scholar-in-politics to full-blown controversialist, his prose gained strength and power. His early style, as his biographer Donald Bellomy has written in *The Moulding of an Iconoclast* (1979), was "frequently stilted, often latinate, more than a little long-winded," probably due to his status as a newcomer attempting to use an official rhetoric, but lacking the confidence or experience to do so gracefully. Although his friend Henry Holt finally published the *History of American Currency*, Holt confessed that it never failed to put him to sleep. Only in extemporaneous speeches and student lectures did Sumner display the boldness that would become his hallmark. As he directed his attention from public policy to social theory in the early 1880s, this boldness quickly won national attention.

## Social Theorist

During his early clerical years, Sumner had dipped into Herbert Spencer's *Social Statics* (1850) and *First Principles* (1861), but found both works too "metaphysical" for his taste. During the seventies he displayed only passing rhetorical interest in the Englishman's work. His first recorded use of the phrase "survival of the fittest" in 1872 was in the context of appealing for charity toward the weak. However, he also apparently read the *Study of Sociology* when it appeared in serial form in 1872 and eventually thought enough of it to assign it as a text at Yale. For this decision, he soon earned an undeserved reputation as America's "leading Spencerian."

Until the early 1880s, Sumner's social thought echoed other works he had read. Among these were Harriet Martineau's *Illustrations of Political Economy* (1834), a primer of classical economics by example, and Francis Lieber's *On Civil Liberty and Self-Government* (1853), whose proto-sociological emphasis on customs and institutions informed his later distrust of schemes based on "natural rights." In Woolsey's course at Yale, he read enough of Francis Wayland's *Elements of Political Economy* (1837) to convince him that Martineau was basically right about economic issues. Later he added David Ricardo, Thomas Malthus, and others in the British tradition.

Growing attack on this tradition in the late 1870s first forced Sumner to rethink his basic assumptions. From overseas, this attack was spearheaded by representatives of the German Historical School, the *Kathedersozialisten* ("professorial socialists," as Sumner rendered the term) and their American disciples who founded the American Economic Association in 1884. More popularly, it found voice in Henry George's *Progress and Poverty* (1879), Lawrence Gronlund's *Cooperative Commonwealth* (1883), and Edward Bellamy's *Looking Backward* (1888). All bothered Sumner: George for his attack on Malthus, Gronlund as a homegrown socialist, and Bellamy as the model for the "absurd effort" to plan a better world with "a slate and pencil." In one way or other, George, Gronlund, and Bellamy figured in most of his essays of the eighties. Social scientists seemed little better. He wrote in the late seventies that the social sciences were the stronghold of many "pernicious dogmatisms." The economists, he added with reference to the German school, "instead of holding together and sustaining . . . the scientific authority and the positive truth of their doctrines, break up and run hither and thither."

In a series on "Socialism" and "Sociology" between 1878 and 1882, Sumner defended Malthus in particular, fired in part by Henry George's attack on Malthusianism in *Progress and Poverty*. "Human beings tend to multiply beyond the power of a limited area of land to support life, under a given stage of the arts, and a given standard of living," he wrote in *Scribner's* in 1878, summarizing the Malthusian doctrine on the eve of George's attack. Although technology and emigration had temporarily suspended population pressure, the "struggle for existence" was inescapable. This struggle pitted men against nature, he explained, his model being the individual against the wilderness as pictured in one of Martineau's *Illustrations*. Parallel to the struggle for existence was, according to Sumner, the "competition of life," which set the social rules governing the relation of individuals in society, private property being one example. Although the relationship between the struggle for existence and the competition of life remained vague, Sumner insisted on the distinction between them. Confusing the two, socialists erred in blaming the rules of the competition of life for hardships that were really due to the struggle for existence.

Henry George, in turn, had "wasted his effort" because "the 'Malthusian doctrine' is swallowed up in a great biological law," Sumner wrote in a review. Since Sumner remained virtually ignorant of Darwin's theory, he meant only to assert that the biologist lent support to the general idea of struggle as a starting point for all speculation. But why not carry Darwinism further? Indulging a flair for epigram, Sumner appeared to do precisely this in several speeches and at least one published essay, but only between 1879 and the early 1880s. "The Law of the survival of the fittest was not made by man," the argument went. "We can only, by interfering with it, produce the survival of the unfittest." With this phrasemaking, he ceased to be an academic of modest fame. The specter of "social Darwinist" was soon to haunt him.

Meanwhile, at Yale, a conflict with Noah Porter forced Sumner to think more systematically about science, an issue unresolved in his clerical days. The struggle began in 1879 when President Porter objected to his assigning Herbert Spencer's *The Study of Sociology* in a senior social science class. Although Sumner and Porter attempted to settle the matter privately, both went public after a report on the struggle appeared in the *New York Times* in 1880. Sumner challenged Porter's right to proscribe textbooks, and he threatened to resign in an open letter to the Yale Corporation and faculty in 1881. In the end, both could claim a victory of sorts: Sumner, because he refused to concede the principle; Porter, because Sumner stopped assigning the book.

The major issue in the affair was not so much religion vs. science or even classroom freedom or professionalism. It was the definition of social science itself. Sumner's own convoluted development of this issue revealed how uncertain his own grasp of it was, especially in its social dimensions. "All that we can affirm with certainty is that social phenomena are subject to law, and that the natural laws of the social order are in their entire character like the laws of physics," he noted weakly in an essay on "Sociology."

The writing and reception of *What Social Classes Owe to Each Other* (1884) pushed Sumner further down the road to a narrowly inductive view of science. Ironically, this book would also earn him a reputation as the Gilded Age's leading "social Darwinist." Although the book dealt ostensibly with class relations in industrial society, it owed its central theme and its emotional edge to events in Sumner's personal life during the previous two years, the most important of which was the death of his father in 1881 after a long downhill slide in health and fortune. For the son, as numerous commentators have observed, the death was the occasion to reflect on the enormous debt he owed to the Lancashire mechanic who, despite poor business sense and numerous reverses, asked from life only a fair chance.

Yet there was more to it than that. Thomas Sumner's failures, no less than his principles, provided a lesson in the fruits of irresponsibility. On his death, his son found himself saddled with the emotionally drain-ing business of paying off creditors and untangling his father's botched affairs. Irresponsibility also came home to roost in the reappearance of his brother, Joe, a ne'er-do-well (in Sumner's view), whose wayward ways had never stopped him in the past from rubbing in the fact that he made more money than his "successful" older sibling. Now in financial trouble, Joe regularly nagged his brother for loans through the early 1880s. About this time, Sumner also helped a former housekeeper with money to get married, only to have her return later, a penniless widow with children to support. Added to these burdens was the emotional collapse of Sumner's always-fragile wife Jeannie, which strained his finances and sense of duty to the near-breaking point. If he suggested that charity begins at home, he had his reasons.

In *Social Classes*, Sumner forged these personal experiences and a mounting fear of social unrest into a celebration of the "forgotten man," arriving at the unsettling conclusion that social classes apparently owe nothing to one other. In structure and tone, the work combined pulpit oratory and deductive logic. Sermon-style chapter titles summoned the faithful to the weekly meeting: "That It Is Not Wicked To Be Rich; Nay, Even, That It Is Not Wicked to Be Richer than One's Neighbor." School-book logic captured the essence of all humanitarian schemes: "that A and B decide what C shall do for D" (or X, as in the lecture version reprinted here). The burden always fell on number three (C): the "forgotten man."

Although Sumner invested a good deal in this portrait, the economic and class position of his "forgotten man" was tantalizingly vague. As a victim of protectionism or excise taxes, he was virtually the entire American population. As the victim of legislation, he was all taxpayers except those who initiated taxes and those who benefitted from them. However, the "forgotten man" was not the "ill-fed, ill-clothed, ill-housed" worker, as Franklin Roosevelt implied in appropriating Sumner's phrase five decades later. Rather, politically, the "forgotten man" foreshadowed the newspaper cartoon figure, "John Q. Public," looking puzzled at the antics of elected officials. Economically, he represented that large segment of the American population who would become "middle class" in the mid-twentieth century, but who, like Thomas Sumner, still languished as artisans offering their services to the highest bidder.

In a somewhat incongruous final installment, Sumner explained "Wherefore We Should Love One Another." "Men . . . owe to men, in the chances and perils of this life, aid and sympathy, on account of the common participation in human frailty and folly," he wrote in an attenuated version of his earlier theory of "human solidarity." However, "private and personal" relations were one thing and science another. "There is no injunction, no 'ought' in political economy at all," he intoned. "It does not tell man what he ought to do." Only an apparent step back from his earlier conclusions, this chapter showed Sumner again taking comfort in private-public, heart-head dualisms that he earlier applied to theological problems. The split now, however, was between individual emotion and social science, a harbinger of the "ought-is" distinction of the objectivist, behavioristic sociology his work later inspired.

*Social Classes* invoked neither the names nor the rhetoric of Spencer or Darwin, but its appearance revived charges that Sumner was misusing biology to justify a dog-eat-dog social order. Although the *New York Times* leveled this charge in the spring of 1883 in response to one of his "fittest-unfittest" flourishes in an unpublished speech, Sumner faced it explicitly for the first time in print a year later in an exchange in the *Index*, the journal of the liberal and ecumenical Free Religious Association of Boston. The editor, denying that "fitness" had meaning in any social sense, noted that Sumner's emphasis on human morality and reason seemed to belie the thrust of his closing epigram. Sumner himself equivocated. "Rattlesnakes survive where horses perish," he wrote, conceding his critics' main point. "The 'economic harmonies' are a great subject," he wrote in June 1884 in the last of several apologies on the subject, denying that he held to Darwinian doctrine as charged. Although he promised to "publish [his] notion in proper detail," he instead effectively dropped all use of analogical language, Spencerian or otherwise, and let the subject die.

This change brought another important if subtle shift in emphasis in Sumner's essays of the late 1880s and early 1890s. As he turned his attention to monopoly and Marxism, he escalated his assault on metaphysics, redefining abstract conceptions in terms of hard, irrefutable, material facts. A term such as "proletariat," thus reduced, had virtually no meaning; the real social contest was between the "House of Have and the House of Want." "Monopoly" referred to the natural monopoly inherent in the technology of the railway and telegraph and was in no way a product of "capitalist society." "Capital" was not, as Marx maintained, a product of an exploitative system, but was rather the banked reserves of past effort.

A measure of this change, "The Absurd Effort to Make Over the World" (1894), differed from *Social Classes* in tone and argument. Unlike his earlier appeals to logic or the "laws of nature," he now answered social reformers with an "appeal to the facts," historical facts in particular. "[All] the allegations of general mischief, social corruption, wrong, and evil in our society must be referred back to those who make them for particulars and specifications," he wrote. "As they are offered to us we cannot allow them to stand, because we discern in them faulty observation of facts, or incorrect interpretation of facts, or a construction of facts according to some philosophy, or misunderstanding of phenomena and their relations, or incorrect inferences, or crooked deductions."

But Sumner also tacitly admitted that, in his own way, he himself had been guilty of "the vain fancy that we can make or guide the movement." Although in later years he took up his pen to oppose free silver, condemn American imperialism, and attack the socialist Upton Sinclair in *Collier's* in 1904, he increasingly avoided public controversy. In this sense, "The Absurd Effort" was Sumner's own valedictory after one decade as educational reformer and scholar-in-politics, and a second as social theorist trying to figure out what a science of society should look like.

## Anti-Imperialist to Sociologist

In 1890, Sumner fell victim to what was termed a "nervous illness." His personal problems and poor health could not take the punishing work schedule that had resulted in sixty articles and two books in the previous three years. In December, he set sail for an extended stay in Europe, financed in part by forty-two loyal supporters, among them Henry Holt, Chauncey Depew, and William C. Whitney.

Although Sumner resumed his duties at Yale in the fall of 1892, the collapse took a permanent toll on his energies and output. Between 1876 and 1890, he had published some 108 articles and 7 books. In the five years following his breakdown, he wrote "only" four articles and two books. Although in 1896 he added another dozen articles and a book, he averaged only two articles a year during the rest of his career and left uncompleted his projected "Science of Society," save for the substantial fragment that appeared as *Folkways* (1906). Although ill health alone does not explain the tone and mood of his later work, he judged the world from a bed of pain.

Personal disillusionment, as in the late 1870s, had important implications for Sumner's intellectual development. The growing gap between American ideals and current realities pushed him toward both a thoroughgoing relativism *and* a reification of national folly soon to be termed "folkways" and "mores." For example, the United States historically had one set of principles. However, embarking on a war with Spain in 1898, it found some of these principles inconvenient and dropped them. "There are no dogmatic propositions of political philosophy which are universally and always true," he wrote with new-found resignation. The Spanish-American War also dramatized the difference between "purposes" and "consequences," a distinction that led directly to the behavioristic orientation of *Folkways*.

The blustering Theodore Roosevelt, along with the "fads" and "delusions" of the progressive era, completed this descent into political cynicism. With T.R. at the helm, Sumner feared that America was entering its dangerous "glory days." However, to Sumner the alternative of William Jennings Bryan seemed even worse. "We shall have to vote for Teddy in 1908 in order to ward off Bryan and Hades," Sumner commented in 1906, but, in so doing, we would be "disgraced forever." Although Sumner in fact supported his former student William Howard Taft in 1908, more than a decade of Bryanism left its mark—Sumner judged Bryan's proposals to be not merely passing folly, but significant indicators of changes in the national "mores," a term he first adopted in 1899 when he began to work seriously on his proposed science of society.

In *Folkways*, Sumner molded his disgust at the course of American politics and society into one of the five or six most important books in sociology published in the United States in the years before the First World War. On the surface, the thesis of *Folkways* was beguilingly straightforward—humanity is driven by four basic instincts: hunger, love, vanity, and fear. In all societies, individuals attempt to satisfy these drives as best they can. Through trial and error, one method of satisfying demand becomes customary for all or a significant part of a society. Sumner termed these methods "folkways." Initially experimental, folkways gain a moral sanction through a process of comparison and reflection. The mores are folkways grown moral and reflective. "Good" and "bad" have no meaning outside of the mores. Since those mores that command the support of the most powerful groups survive, "nothing but might has ever made right."

Sumner then complicated things by adding that the mores are sometimes mischievous and even wrong, sometimes shaped by accidents, irrationality, and "pseudo-knowledge." Some folkways are "positively harmful." The results were things he increasingly disliked: "advertisers who exaggerate," "the ways of journalism," "electioneering devices," and "oratorical and dithyrambic extravagances in politics." Although these contemporary horrors were "not properly part of the mores," they were "symptoms of them."

The problem was that the judgment of mores as "bad" and "good" seemed to imply an external standard that, by Sumner's own accounting, existed only *within* the mores. This standard, however, was not a patchwork of youthful assumptions smuggled in through a back door (as some of his critics later maintained), but rather the scientific outlook itself, an outlook that an elite (the "classes") introduced into the mores in the modern democratic period. This "matter-of-factness" (as Sumner's former student Veblen termed it) allowed the social scientist, by examining the mores historically, to determine which had proved conducive to societal survival. The mores, that is, contained a self-correcting element.

Science thus provided an escape from the dreary logic of might-makes-right, anathema to a middle class threatened by socialism on the one hand and plutocracy on the other. The key was the difference between a *posterior* and an *anterior* view of things. In the posterior view, "nothing but might has ever made right, and ... nothing but might makes right now." In the anterior view, the case was different. "If we are about to take some action and are debating the right of it, the might that can be brought to support the view of it has nothing to do with the right of it." Science, when applied to the study of history (the sociologists' laboratory), could provide this anterior view—could, that is, demonstrate the superiority of one set of values over others, specifically the "virtue policy" over the "success policy."

Science was both relative and absolute, Sumner continued, restating a lifelong distinction between science as speculation and science as method. As "ism," science was subject to "fashion" as much as other human endeavors were. Even "evolutionism," although "now accepted as a final fact," might well turn out to be "only a fashion." On the other hand, science, defined as apprehension of facts-as-they-are, was not relative or ephemeral. It was the scientific outlook in this narrow sense that was gradually entering the mores of the "classes."

Working to these conclusions, Sumner attempted finally to come to grips with Darwin early in the new century, two decades after the furor he created in the eighties. His guide was his disciple Albert G. Keller, himself then immersed in the *Origin of Species* (1859) and *The Descent of Man* (1871) for a course on human evolution. While the younger man lectured, various questions took shape in Sumner's mind. Did the mores evolve? Could they be arranged "in a logical scale of advance" to support a theory of progress? Were they subject to natural selection? Could they be analyzed statistically? In a series of unpublished essays, his answer in each case was no. In the end, Sumner's eleventh-hour brush with Darwinian evolution merely confirmed his lifelong Baconianism, now almost caricatured in his celebration of "facts." "The Scientific Attitude of Mind," he told a meeting of Sigma Xi in 1905, produced a "knowledge of reality" that was neither a philosophy nor a mere consensus of trained observers. His "thirst" for this reality amounted to a passion.

But did the incorporation of the scientific outlook within the mores provide a basis for conscious social policy directed by a scientific elite? Sumner sometimes seemed to imply as much "The historical classes have . . . selected purposes, and have increased ways of fulfilling them." Whether for good or ill, they introduced "variation" that produced change. In a most un-Sumnerian statement, he saw the goal of the "science of society" to be the development of "an art of societal administration" that was "intelligent, effective, and scientific." In the manuscript version of one of his final essays, he insisted that the "masses" acknowledge "the authority of the specialist and expert."

In a more fundamental sense, however, his narrowly Baconian definition of the mores as "facts" distanced his proposals from those of progressives (such as fellow sociologist Lester Ward), who called for "sociocracy" and "creative intelligence." Although the mores were not "natural laws" in the older sense, as "facts" they were just as inexorable in operation. In their ubiquitous inevitability, they ruled out most social engineering almost as surely as did the "laws of physics" to which Sumner had appealed in the 1880s—but only almost. Although *Folkways* resounded with warnings against precipitous reform, Sumner only intended to insist that proposed changes conform to the mores. Although the mores of the "classes" (including the scientific outlook) were historically less basic than those of the "masses," this latest "variation" promised a better, if fragile, future.

There was, of course, a trick in Sumner's hard-nosed empiricism. The mores, insofar as they embraced beliefs as well as behavior, were not "facts" in quite the same sense as tables and chairs are. As one critic later asked: "Who ever saw a tradition?" Rather, the notion of the mores represented a new way of *conceptualizing* social reality. The term was no less an imaginative construct than "Gemeinschaft" or "primary group." Mores were "facts," not literally, but by analogy: They had the "authority of facts."

If old fashioned in one sense, Sumner's Baconian view of science disposed him to see something that escaped many reform-minded contemporaries. That is that social institutions and customs, although initially instrumental, assume a coercive character that transcends utility. Coercive here means that they are as difficult to deny as the "facts" of the natural world—a view similar to the one being developed by the French sociologist Émile Durkheim. As Sumner explained toward the end of his life, like natural "facts," the mores are "very difficult to discuss" and may be judged only in the light of history, and then only "within narrow limits." This coercive power did not rule out prudent change; but it explained why, as he put it earlier in one of his more quotable lines, "it is the greatest folly . . . to sit down with a slate and pencil to plan out a new social world."

## Prophet and Legacy

During his final decade, Sumner's professional and personal woes did not abate. The election of Arthur T. Hadley as Yale's president in 1899 brought concessions to the old antiscientific Yale College tradition and a new emphasis on publication over teaching, both disturbing to Sum-

ner. Keller later confided that Sumner's feelings toward Hadley were "deep and powerful and profane." Although Sumner gradually recovered from his nervous exhaustion, continuing debility forced him to abandon his "Science of Society" project. A stroke in late 1907 crippled his right arm for several months. One bright spot came two years later with his election as president of the recently founded American Sociological Society (A.S.S.). However, this honor finally proved to be his undoing when he suffered a final stroke after dragging himself to New York through a snowstorm to deliver the presidential address at the annual meeting in December. After lingering for several months, he died on April 10, 1910.

Increasingly during these final years, Sumner assumed the mantle of prophet in jeremiads worthy of the American Puritans. Already evident in his warnings against imperialism and war and in the posthumously published "Bequests of the Nineteenth Century to the Twentieth" (1900), this prophetic tone suffused the final portions of *Folkways*, where he excoriated plutocracy and socialism alike. Preaching a "cult of success," plutocracy brought a "deep depreciation of all social interests," he wrote, while the socialists' demand for "equality" posed an equal threat to national survival.

In "Bequests," Sumner also returned to the issue of "tradition" and "progress" and the related problems of cultural relativism, first developing the distinction between the thinking of the "masses" and "the classes" that reappeared in *Folkways*. Current clamor for "rights" and "power to the people" rested on a "popularity theory of truth, wisdom and right." To this he then opposed the "expert theory." " 'Authority' is out of date, but everyone must know that competent authority (on everything but political and social questions) is what we have to live by," he continued. But should an exception be made here? Although Sumner muffled his answer in a series of rhetorical questions, he made it clear that he had little sympathy for the "man-on-the-curbstone" who "resents expert advice." In the process, he also revealed his own frustrations. "The doctrine seems to be that if a man who was once humble and ignorant uses all the means mortals have to find out something, the result is that he knows less than his humble and ignorant comrades who never made any such attempt."

In "Mores of the Present and Future" (1909), this pessimism shaded into cynicism and near-despair. The eighteenth century "bequeathed to the nineteenth a great mass of abstract notions about rights and about the ultimate notions of political philosophy," he wrote, many of which

were later enshrined in laws and constitutions. "Rights, justice, liberty, and equality are the watchwords instead of church, faith, heaven, and hell." These slogans, and the mores associated with them, were possible only because humanity was currently in an "exceptional period" during which "global underpopulation" and "increasing control of natural forces" temporarily eased the "struggle for existence" against nature. Echoing the historian Frederick Jackson Turner, but on a worldwide scale, he warned that the inevitable return of "overpopulation and harder conditions" threatened an end to democracy. "The groups and parties will form and war will occur between them. Great dogmas will be put forth at all stages of these movements and appropriate watchwords will never be wanting."

Although the terms "folkways," "mores," "in-group," and "out-group" soon made their way into the literature, *Folkways* was initially less than a success in the limited arena where professional reputations are measured. The early reviewers faulted equally its methodology and its political implications. As one Chicago sociologist remarked: Ethnological data "seem at times to overweigh the book by their sheer bulk and multiplicity." Although at least one reviewer saw an affinity between Sumner's mores and Durkheim's "social facts," he made the point only to damn both as "objectivists." When a later generation became interested in the notion that social usages had the coercive power of "facts," it turned to the *Rules of Sociological Method* (1895), not to *Folkways*.

As the social sciences became increasingly specialized, Sumner seemed to represent an older, more amateurish age. Albion Small of Chicago later confessed that he never thought of Sumner as a sociologist until, quite to his surprise, Sumner was elected president of the A.S.S. To others, his writings seemed closer to anthropology or philosophical history, and his apparent lack of "methodology" compounded the problem. "The Method—if it can be called a method," commented the urban sociologist Robert Park, consisted essentially of collecting facts that Sumner barely analyzed.

Others faulted *Folkways* for its assumptions as much as for its methodology. The sociologist Edward Ross suggested that, although postulating possible differences between perceptions of right and good by the masses vs. those by the elite, Sumner failed to explore those differences, leaving open the possibility that the "mores are never right" because they are necessarily adaptations to past conditions. Although this charge erroneously equated Sumner with the most extreme of cultural relativists, its very existence suggested that his resolution of the problem was less than successful.

Problems in Sumner's formulation explain some of this criticism and even neglect, but intellectual merit was only part of the story. Another was Yale itself. Since the university still considered undergraduate education as important as graduate or professional training, Sumner left behind no "school" or even disciples, except for the all-too-faithful Keller, whose curmudgeon demeanor and rigid adherence to "Sumnerology" proved to be a barrier to cross-fertilization with theories at Chicago, Columbia, and elsewhere. Sumner himself trained only six doctoral students: Kate Halliday Claghorn (1896); James E. Cutler (1903); Henry Pratt Fairchild (1909); Arthur James Todd (1911); Frederick E. Lumley (1912); and Charles W. Coulter (1914). All occupied positions at academic institutions of the second rank, and at least four were primarily concerned with social work. Although Fairchild published *General Sociology* (1934), he was better known for *The Melting Pot Mistake* (1926) and polemical pieces supporting eugenics, birth control, and immigration restriction. Lumley's *The Means of Social Control* (1925) was closest to the *Folkways* tradition, but owed equally as much to the widely used *Introduction to the Science of Sociology* (1921), by Robert E. Park and Ernest W. Burgess, and to the work of Edward A. Ross and, in any case, made no claim to originality.

The fact that the best-known of Sumner's students and disciples repudiated his politics further diluted any legacy he might have claimed. An avowed socialist and vigorous critic of big business, Fairchild proposed governmental action on a scale that would have made Sumner wince, a factor that probably contributed to his dismissal at Yale in 1918 ("His continuance here would seriously hamper a development laid down by Sumner, followed by me, and approved by the faculty," Keller wrote to a friend). During his tenure at Minnesota, Arthur J. Todd also offended local conservatives, while Lumley, in *The Means of Social Control*, offered instruction to any who "find it necessary or desirable to take a hand in the work of control." Among the most prominent of non-Yale disciples, Luther Bernard of Chicago (Ph.D. 1911) drew on *Folkways* for a dissertation advocating an "objective standard for social control." However, Bernard's maverick behavior within the profession and his espousal of a curious brand of populist authoritarianism did little to foster any recognizable "Sumner tradition."

In the interwar years, Sumner's work was also caught in a political crossfire between proponents and opponents of the progressive-New Deal tradition. Carrying their earlier battles beyond the grave, socialist Upton Sinclair launched a scurrilous attack in *The Goose Step* (1923), labeling Sumner a "prime minister of . . . plutocratic education" who

took "ghoulish delight" in "glorifying commercialism." In *Man's Rough Road* (1932), Keller retaliated with an anti-New Deal rendition of *The Science of Society* (1927), his ponderous four-volume revision of Sumner's unpublished *magnum opus*. Responding in kind, liberals and socialists of various stripes launched the campaign that made Sumner a symbol of every imaginable excess of nineteenth-century capitalism. Although Keller was not without blame (since, in addition to his own propagandizing, his renditions of his mentor's work often distorted the original, notably in his insistence that the mores developed by a process of "social selection"), he was frankly appalled. "Some persons hopelessly allergic to 'isms' and 'ismics' have been ushered into the wrong pew," he wrote in a 1944 review of Richard Hofstadter's portrait of Sumner's "social Darwinism." But the label stuck.

In the post-World War II era, economists joined the attack, now supported by the work of John Maynard Keynes and his disciples. These critics argued that Sumner's insistence that any government intervention would weaken the joint struggle for existence was premised on the dubious assumption of full employment and an ignorance of the importance of consumer demand in mature industrial societies. Static and short-run, Sumner's analysis showed little understanding of the workings of impure or imperfect competition, which allows less than optimum allocation of resources under *laissez-faire*.

Meanwhile Sumner left a sociological legacy of sorts in a growing interest in behavioristic and "objectivist" approaches as case studies, statistical analyses, urban ecology, and other empirical work supplanted the armchair theorizing (as it was now labeled) of prewar sociology. As Robert Park put it, "The effect of his researches was to lay a foundation for more realistic, more objective, and more systematic studies in the field of human nature and society than had existed up to that time." In doctoral theses, a younger generation of objectivists seconded the point, among them William F. Ogburn of Chicago and F. Stuart Chapin of Minnesota, both leaders in efforts to make sociology more behavioristic in the interwar years. For these younger sociologists and their followers, social activities, previously studied for their contributions to human happiness and social well-being, became the impersonal data of science.

This objectivist legacy was no less ironic than portraits of Sumner's social Darwinism. For him, a "scientific attitude" offered an absolute standard to judge "errors" in the mores. In contrast, Ogburn and his disciples translated objectivity into a creed of the service intellectual, more interested in the *how* than the *why* of social policy. At the same

time, as agents of the emerging welfare state, they fostered a social engineering often longer on unintended consequences than positive results. College students compounded the irony by turning to *Folkways* for support of a now-fashionable cultural relativism that viewed no traditions or institutions to be better than others. Both interpretations would have made Sumner shudder. A moralist to the end, he prescribed in the act of describing. In treating mores as fact, he pictured an objective reality against which all plans for social reconstruction must be judged. Objectivity, in a word, did not mean ethical neutrality, social engineering, or unthinking relativism.

In portraits of Sumner's "social Darwinism," irony joined outright distortion. For one thing, most such accounts vastly exaggerated his influence. Far from being the Gilded Age's most influential theorist, Sumner watched as most in his generation, wherever positioned on the political spectrum, largely ignored his message, regardless of whether his message was a call for discipline and self-denial, a denunciation of luxury and the excesses of consumerism, or specific proposals for free trade and a government free of the influence of special interests. Just as Herbert Spencer finally felt that it was "Spencer against all of England," Sumner might easily have concluded that his alleged "influence" existed primarily in the minds of those whose own interests require ogres.

Charges of "social Darwinism" also caricature the substance of Sumner's thought. Although he defended private property and individual enterprise, he did not celebrate a struggle for existence or believe that Darwinism (or any other -ism) justified the dog-eat-dog struggle of modern America. Monumental struggles lay in the future, he warned in one of his last essays, but he abhorred the prospect. If he ever successfully resolved the issues of tradition and progress or morality and science, the creative tension between them enabled him to see the complexity of society and the intractability of custom and tradition more clearly than his more sanguine contemporaries. The naturalism of his later thought expressed a growing pessimism over human willingness (although not ability) to use social science responsibly to reshape the mores.

More than a century and a half since Sumner's birth, the successes and accomplishments of American capitalism and form of government stand in spectacular contrast to the collapse of the state socialism he so vigorously opposed. Yet it is as a critic of American society rather than an apologist for it that he most commands our attention. As contending factions continue to clamor in the political marketplace, "watchwords," as he predicted, are not wanting: From "deregulation," "balanced budget," and "standards" on the one side, to "tax fairness," "social justice," and "diversity" on the other. As the first two translate into political scandal and skyrocketing deficits, plutocracy again appears to threaten the republic. At the other extreme, "tax fairness" cloaks an age-old impulse to "soak the rich," while the relativism implicit in calls for "diversity" seems to some critics to herald a "closing of the American mind."

Although Sumner offers limited guidance on the specifics of current policy, his bold address of underlying issues provides a model of the hard-headed analysis too often missing in these debates—one major reason for renewed interest in his work during the past two decades (see bibliography). As the historian Bruce Curtis has put it, it was Sumner's virtue "to peer into mysteries where there were no eternal verities" and to celebrate the "moral absolutes of honesty, work, responsibility, and moral courage." To contemporary philosophers of science, his naively inductive view of science may appear hopelessly old-fashioned, just as developments in the economic and political realm have outrun some (if not all) of his specific proposals. Yet behind his defense of the "scientific attitude" and his polemics lay a regard for the truth and a disdain of sham and hypocrisy that are ever in short supply. For this reason alone, he deserves another hearing.

Robert C. Bannister

Robert C. Bannister is Scheuer Professor of History, Swarthmore College

# Editor's Note

In choosing among Sumner's voluminous writings, I followed several guidelines. Selections are grouped with reference to the various professional and social roles Sumner assumed during his career, from Episcopal clergyman to sociologist, thus roughly integrating the thematic and the chronological. When deciding between comparable essays, I chose those in which Sumner presented arguments in general terms, rather than those encumbered by examples or disagreements with other writers. Previously unpublished works are transcribed from the Sumner Papers at Yale. Where they occur, misspellings are silently corrected. Essays previously collected are reprinted as they appear in *War and Other Essays* (1911), *Earth Hunger and Other Essays* (1913), *The Challenge of Facts and Other Essays* (1914), and *The Forgotten Man and Other Essays*, ed. Albert G. Keller; and *Essays of William Graham Sumner* (2 vols., 1934), ed. Albert G. Keller and Maurice R. Davie. All were published by the Yale University Press. Sumner's footnotes are eliminated, except for several explanatory notes in previously unpublished pieces. With the exception of the excerpts from *Folkways* (Boston: Ginn and Company, 1906), all pieces are published in their entirety. Material in brackets is mine unless otherwise noted.

I want to thank Yale University for granting me access to the Sumner Papers and for permission to reprint previously unpublished manuscripts and the Yale University Press for permission to include "Laissez-Faire." I also wish to thank Judith A. Schiff and her staff at the Sterling Library at Yale for assistance in photocopying materials from the Sumner Papers.

Of the inevitable omissions, three deserve special comment. One is the absence of *What Social Classes Owe to Each Other* (New York: Harper and Brothers, 1883), one of Sumner's best-known works. Rather than present excerpts, I have chosen the full text of "The Forgotten Man," a synthesis of two chapters prepared for a lecture in which Sumner presents his argument more succinctly than in the book version. Also omitted are examples of Sumner's historical work, which includes biographies of Andrew Jackson, Alexander Hamilton, and Robert Morris and *The Financier and Finances of the American Revolution* (2 vols., New York: Dodd, Mead, and Co., 1891). Evidence of the importance of historical analysis in his thinking can be seen, however, in such pieces as "Republican Government" and "Presidential Elections and Civil Service Reform." Finally, Sumner's work on currency reform and the tariff, including *A History of American Currency* (New York: Henry Holt, 1874) and *Lectures on the History of Protection* (1877), are also omitted, although these issues surface in essays on other topics.

My own understanding of Sumner's career is indebted to the many scholars who have collected and interpreted his writings. In addition to the six volumes edited by Albert G. Keller, alone and in concert with Maurice Davie, later collections of his work include *The Conquest of the United States by Spain and Other Essays*, ed. Murray Polner (Chicago: Regnery Press, n.d.); and *Social Darwinism: Selected Essays of William Graham Sumner*, ed. Stow Persons (Englewood Cliffs, N.J.: Prentice-Hall, 1963). Among those scholars who have contributed to a reassessment of Sumner in recent years, I am especially indebted to Donald Bellomy, who generously shared with me the manuscript of his thoughtful, marvelously detailed dissertation, "The Moulding of an Iconoclast: William Graham Sumner, 1840–1885" (Harvard, 1980) and an unpublished essay, "Relativism and Modernism in Sumner's *Folkways*." The introduction and notes draw heavily upon these works for information, interpretation, and sequence of examples. I also wish to thank Ross Paulsen of Augustana College for allowing me to see portions of his forthcoming study of Sumner's early sermons. Portions of the introduction are adapted from my earlier treatment of Sumner in *Social Darwinism* (2d ed., 1989), chapter 5, and *Sociology and Scientism*, chapters 6, 7. For discussion of these and other sources see the bibliographical essay.

For my original interest in Sumner, I owe a special debt to the late Ralph Henry Gabriel (1890–1987), who first introduced me to Sumner and to intellectual history as a Yale undergraduate more than three decades ago.

# Bibliographical Essay

The major published sources on Sumner's life and career are biographies by Harris E. Starr, *William Graham Sumner* (New York: Henry Holt, 1925) and Bruce Curtis, *William Graham Sumner* (Boston: Twayne, 1981). Donald C. Bellomy, "The Moulding of an Iconoclast: William Graham Sumner, 1840–1885," unpublished Ph.D. diss., Harvard University, 1980, a work of meticulous scholarship, contributes immeasurably to an understanding of the first half of his career. Biographical information also can be found in testimonials by former students, and works written or edited by Sumner's two successors at Yale: Albert G. Keller, *Reminiscences (Mainly Personal) of William Graham Sumner* (New Haven, Conn.: Yale University Press, 1933), and Maurice R. Davie, ed. *Sumner Today* (New Haven, Conn.: Yale University Press, 1940).

A number of studies provide additional perspective on Sumner's first three decades. In "Victorians Abed: William Graham Sumner on the Family, Women, and Sex," *American Studies,* (1977), 101–122, Bruce Curtis opens the rich subject of Sumner's relation with his wife and attitudes toward sex and gender roles. For the clerical years, Merwin A. Sheketoff, "William Graham Sumner: Social Christian 1869–1872," unpublished Ph.D. diss., Harvard University, 1961, argues that Sumner anticipated "social Gospel" themes in later Protestantism. In *Scholarly Means to Evangelical Ends* (Baltimore, Md.: Johns Hopkins University Press, 1986), Louise L. Stevenson relates Sumner to an older tradition of "New Haven scholars," including Noah Porter. Among the more interesting reminiscences of Sumner as teacher and colleague are J. Pease Norton, "Talks with a Great Teacher," *World's Work* 20 (1910), 13290–13292; an anonymous tribute to "A Great Teacher," *Nation* 90 (1910), 394; and a symposium in the *Yale Review* 19 (1910), 1–12. Sumner's disagreement with Noah Porter is treated most fully in John D. and Barbara S. Heyl, "The Sumner-Porter Controversy at Yale," *Sociological Inquiry* 46 (1976), 41–49.

The portrait of Sumner's "social Darwinism," although rooted in controversies during his lifetime, received its most influential expression in Richard Hofstadter, *Social Darwinism in American Thought* (Philadelphia: 1944, rev. ed. Boston: Beacon Press, 1956). Albert Keller's immediate dissent appeared in "What Did Darwin Really Say?" *Saturday*

*Review of Literature* 28 (1945), 8. Alternative, if not always more favorable, assessments to Hofstadter's appeared during the 1940s through the 1960s in Ralph Henry Gabriel, *The Course of American Democratic Thought* (New York: Ronald Press, 1940; rev. ed. 1956); in Robert G. McCloskey, *American Conservatism in the Age of Enterprise* (Cambridge, Mass.: Harvard, 1951), chapters 2–3; in Robert B. Notestein's two articles based on his 1954 doctoral thesis at Wisconsin, "The Moral Rigorism of William Graham Sumner," *Journal of the History of Ideas* 16 (1955), 389–400, and "William Graham Sumner: An Essay in the Sociology of Knowledge," *American Journal of Economics and Sociology* 18 (1959), 397–413; in Stow Persons, *American Minds: A History of Ideas* (New York: Henry Holt, 1958); and in Donald K. Pickens, "William Graham Sumner: Moralist as Social Scientist," *Social Science* 43 (1968), 202–209.

Subsequent challenges to the Hofstadter thesis may be traced in Robert C. Bannister, "William Graham Sumner's 'Social Darwinism' Reconsidered," *History of Political Economy* 5 (1973), 89–109, reprinted with slight change as chapter 5 of *Social Darwinism: Science and Myth* (Philadelphia: Temple University Press, 1979, 2d ed. with new introduction 1989); and in Norman E. Smith, "William Graham Sumner as an Anti-Social Darwinist," *Pacific Sociological Review* 22 (1979), 332–347. Attesting to the strength of the Hofstadter thesis, Robert Garson and Richard Maidmont, in "Social Darwinism and the Liberal Tradition: The Case of William Graham Sumner," *South Atlantic Quarterly* 80 (1981), 61–76, write as if the controversy never existed. For a comprehensive overview of the entire issue, see Donald C. Bellomy, "Social Darwinism Revisited, *Perspectives in American History,* n.s., 1 (1984), 1–129.

Evolution aside, Sumner's economic and political views are also the subject of Dominick T. Armentano, *The Political Economy of William Graham Sumner* (Ann Arbor, Mich.: University Microfilms, 1966). Donald K. Pickens, "Westward Expansion and the End of American Exceptionalism: Sumner, Turner and Webb," *Western Historical Quarterly* 12 (1981), 409–418, relates Sumner's thinking to the frontier hypothesis. In "Sinclair and Sumner," *Mid-America* 60 (1978), 185–190, and "William Graham Sumner 'On the Concentration of Wealth'," *Journal of American History* 55 (1969), 823–832, Bruce Curtis describes Sumner's confrontation with a leading socialist, and a possible change of heart concerning control of the trusts shortly before his death.

For evidence of the ways partisan political battles shaped Sumner's reputation in the decades after his death, contrast Upton Sinclair, *The*

*Goose Step* (Pasadena, Ca.: the author, 1923) and Charles A. Beard, "The Idea of Let Us Alone," *Virginia Quarterly Review* 15 (1930), 500, with Albert G. Keller, "Discoverer of the Forgotten Man," *American Mercury* 27 (1932), 257–270. During the 1950s, conservative defenses included John Chamberlain, "Prophet of Utopia," *Plain Talk* (1950), 42–44; and his "William Graham Sumner and the Old Republic," *Modern Age* 4 (1959–60), 52–62; Mortimer Smith, "William Graham Sumner: the Forgotten Man," *American Mercury* 71 (1950), 358–359; and William L. Burton, "The Conservatism of William Graham Sumner," *Modern Age* 4 (1959–60), 45–51.

On Sumner's later career and the writing of *Folkways*, see Robert C. Bannister, *Sociology and Scientism: The American Quest for Objectivity 1880–1940* (Chapel Hill, N.C.: University of North Carolina Press, 1987), relating him to the emergence of "objectivism" in American sociology. Bruce Curtis, "William Graham Sumner and the Problem of Progress," *New England Quarterly* 51 (1978), 348–369, considers Sumner's embrace of a cyclical view of history during his final decade. For a start at untangling the complex relation between Sumner and his protégé Albert G. Keller, see Maurice R. Davie, "The Sociology of Albert G. Keller," *Sociology and Social Research* 41 (1957), 407–411; and Roscoe Hinkle and Norman E. Smith, "Sumner versus Keller and the Social Evolutionism of Early American Sociology," *Sociological Inquiry* 49 (1979), 41–48.

Among the countless references to Sumner's work by later sociologists, his changing reputation within the discipline can be reconstructed from Charles Horton Cooley, "Sumner and Methodology," *Sociology and Social Research* 12 (1928), 85–86; Robert E. Park, "The Sociological Methods of William Graham Sumner," in *Methods in Social Science,* ed. Stuart A. Rice (Chicago: University of Chicago Press, 1931) and his "William Graham Sumner's Conception of Society," *Chinese Social and Political Science Review* 17 (1933), 430–443; Luther L. Bernard, "The Social Science Theories of William Graham Sumner," *Social Forces* 19 (1940), 153–175; Donald W. Calhoun, "American Masters of Contemporary Sociology," *Social Forces* 24 (1945), 15–32. In *Class and American Sociology* (New York: Schocken Books, 1940), the sociologist Charles H. Page provides a useful account of Sumner's treatment of social class.

Detailed assessments of *Folkways* itself include Edwin M. Lemert, "The Folkways and Social Control," *American Sociological Review* 7 (1942), 394–399; and Harry V. Ball, et al., "Law and Social Change:

Sumner Reconsidered," *American Journal of Sociology* 67 (1962), 532–540. Donald K. Pickens, "Scottish Common Sense Philosophy and *Folkways*," *Journal of Thought* 22 (1987), 39–43, places *Folkways* in the "common sense" tradition. In "Liberalism, Unintended Orders, and Evolutionism," *Political Studies* 36 (1988), 251–272, Ellen Frankel Paul relates Sumner to F. A. Hayek and others, arguing against grounding liberalism in evolutionism. Two extended treatments of Sumner in the context of American sociology are Don A. Martindale, *The Nature and Types of Sociological Theory* (London: Routledge and Kegan Paul, 1961) and Roscoe C. Hinkle, *Founding Theory of American Sociology 1881–1915* (Boston: Routledge and Kegan Paul, 1980).

# ON LIBERTY,
# SOCIETY,
# AND POLITICS

# I

## Preacher

# Individualism

The Church of the Redeemer, Morristown, New Jersey, was founded in 1853 in opposition to St. Peter's, the town's Episcopalian High Church. It drew its congregation mostly from older New York families, but also had a sprinkling of commuting professionals. Sumner was assured that its members were "people of standing and refinement." During his first spring, his Lenten sermons included a trio on "Rationalism," "Individualism," and "Materialism." Speaking a month before his marriage to Jeannie Elliott, he argued in "Individualism" that the family was the primary source of education. "Individualism," March 11, 1871, sermon at The Church of the Redeemer, Morristown, New Jersey, MS. Sumner Papers, Yale, New Haven, Connecticut; not previously published.

"Am I my brother's keeper?"
Genesis 4.9

I spoke here a few weeks ago about rationalism. The subject is so vast and the philosophy ramifies so widely through the received doctrines and the approved institutions of our modern society that it is impossible to do it justice in one or a few discourses. In my remarks upon it, on the former occasion, I dealt chiefly with its philosophical aspects, and I discussed it as one of the philosophies which learned thinkers debate about. If I should leave the subject here some of you might not recognize in this philosophy anything whose practical operation you had ever noticed, any doctrine which you had ever heard anyone profess or seen anybody practice. I desire, therefore, before quitting this subject to speak of it in some of its practical manifestations.

Rationalism is a creed or a philosophy, but every set of ideas which men adopt produces its own appropriate fruit in their life and conversation. Rationalism, in its practical operation produces what we call *individualism*. We shall see how this is, if we simply recall what we observed in regard to the philosophy of rationalism. The rationalist is one who tears off from himself the restraints of tradition and custom and asserts his absolute independence. He endeavors to make his mind a blank; he makes a clean slate, so to speak, and begins all over again. He says: I will make myself as if I knew nothing, had learned nothing, had been taught nothing. I will begin to learn now, and I will meet every

5

fact, every law, every doctrine, with denial and opposition, and will not admit one of them into my mind, will not believe one of them until I am forced to do so by a demonstration! Hence the rationalist is destructive, he destroys all the faiths, customs, and institutions which we have received from the past. He is revolutionary; he does not ask how far an existing institution is faulty, or an existing belief erroneous, and then try to correct it, but, if he can detect a fault in it, he destroys it entirely on the spot. Half the time he destroys it carelessly and with a sneer, simply because it is old. The feeling of veneration for age and affection for what is old he regards as a foolish and pernicious piece of sentimentality. He is moreover suspicious and distrustful, and he falls into the perils which environ suspicion. In the first place he deprives himself of much which he might enjoy, if we were trustful and believing, and in the second place he is after all continually putting his trust in what does not deserve it. It is very remarkable to notice how this class of men will sometimes stake their judgment on a mere subordinate detail, and overlook the main point on which the judgment of a matter hinges. If a notion is presented to one of these men, which is new and startling, it will captivate him although it may be shallow and fallacious. If it is old and has tradition in its favor he will meet it with suspicion and draw his weapons against it. If it appeals to the conscience or the higher reason, and is not demonstrable to the understanding then he will dismiss it with scorn. But the things which are demonstrable to the human understanding are few in number, and the creed of the rationalist is narrow and meagre accordingly, I mean not only his religious, but also his social, moral, political, and educational creed. He becomes habituated only to narrow special pleading, to doubt, suspicion, denial, fear of being deceived, perversity, and obstinacy. This tendency first becomes bigoted, and then fanatical, just as regularly and necessarily as the contrary false tendency to dogmatism becomes first bigoted and then fanatical, and we come to those strange and abnormal developments, dogmatizing rationalism, and fanatical infidelity. Thus rationalism is factious, and perverse, and contrary; it is faultfinding and satirical; it is cold and unsympathetic; it holds aloof and raises objections; it opposes to the end and only submits then with a murmuring protest; it is mocking and contemptuous; it is continually asking "What is the use?" or "What is all this worth?" It is negative and obstructive; it measures everything by its own standards and destroys all which is either too small or too large for those standards. It is destructive and revolutionary. It is not constructive or creative. It makes no discoveries and no advances. It only stands on the negative and waits to test and find fault with what others discover or propose.

Now if we notice the feature which is permanently in all these different phases of rationalism, we shall find that it is this: that the individual is isolated and encouraged to selfish independence. Under this philosophy, the individual is emancipated from his responsibility to God, for, as we saw, the rationalist reduces God to a figment of the fancy. He is emancipated from his responsibility to the past or to history, for there is nothing which rationalism hates as heartily as it does tradition. He is emancipated from his obligations to society, or at least those obligations are reduced to the very minimum. The rationalist stands on the defensive against the restraints which the laws of society, or of the state impose upon him, and demands that they be as few in number as possible, and he always reserves a right to appeal from the law to his own judgment. He is emancipated from responsibility to himself even, in the ordinary acceptance of the code of honor, for he does not admit a code which is partly traditional and partly conventional. He is isolated as an individual over against the rest of society. The interests which occupy him are exclusively those which centre in his own person. He is in some sense hostile to all the rest of society. This rationalism takes its votaries out from under all the ordinary obligations of men and sets them up, each one in full and complete independence, a law unto himself, responsible to no one, and qualified to find out all truth, to establish all institutions, to attain all wisdom, alone and unaided. He is isolated from and independent of both the generation which preceded him and the men who surround him. Thus it is that rationalism, in its practical manifestations, is individualism. It teaches men to say: "Every one for himself," and so regard life as a great scramble, in which each one must use strength and cunning to get and to keep as much as he can. No one is to give quarter, none is to ask it. To every question which would call me to account for neglect of another or for harm done to him, to every obligation which is asserted to bind men together in mutual interest and responsibility, they answer with the question of Cain: "Am I my brother's keeper?"

Now let us observe this individualism in some of its commonest forms.

Observe first of all the effects of individualism on *character*. When a man has emancipated himself from all the obligations to God, to history, to society, to the state, to the code of honor, and has taken up an attitude, such as I have described, in which he says, I will submit to no restraints upon my liberty to pursue my own will and pleasure except such as I cannot resist, then he has lost and abandoned his character. Morally he is no better than a brute beast, and society has to protect itself against him as against a wild beast. If he desires a piece of property which belongs to his neighbor, what hinders him from taking it? Nothing but the law and the police force which executes it. If some chance advertence offers him an opportunity to overreach, or defraud, or take advantage of his neighbors, what hinders him from doing it? Nothing whatever, and if he can evade the technicality of the law while taking advantage of circumstances, he will do so without hesitation, and rather regard it as a piece of good luck. The habit of considering only the interests of self, and of regarding one's own interests as hostile to those of the rest of society, bases character upon selfishness, and poisons it at its very fountain. The question which arises is not: What ought I to do? but; What can I do for my own interest, without coming in contact with the law? When that point is reached a man can no longer be regarded as a fit member of a community of intelligent men, he has fallen to the level of the brutes who must be taught to control their appetites by fear of the rod.

The most unfortunate effects of individualism, however, are those which are produced on *social relations*, for individualism is of course destructive to society. It disintegrates it until it is no longer a society but a collection of hostile individuals. The foundation of human society is laid on trust, faith, confidence, generosity, cordiality, good faith and charity. Individualism involves suspicion, jealousy, envy, malice, selfishness. Society is only possible where the independence of the individual is curtailed somewhat for the sake of union and organization. As soon as the independence of the individual is asserted against society there is discord, dissension, and anarchy. Society is based upon the idea of *duty*, that is upon the idea that each individual is under obligation to forgo something of his own rights, or interests, or pleasure for the common good. Individualism lays all the stress upon *rights*; it teaches each individual to claim all the rights which he possesses over against other men, and to demand that they be paid in full. Society depends on mutual concessions; individualism inculcates the spirit which demands all its own and concedes nothing. Individualism destroys public spirit. Men come to look upon the public as material to be used for selfish and private aggrandizement. The idea of honor in serving the commonwealth is thrown into the limbo of worn out sentiments. The only object in taking office under the commonwealth is, not to serve the public, but to get additional facilities for prosecuting one's own ends.

The same spirit also appears in the form of many mercantile specu-lations, in the combinations both of capital and labor to control the market, which is only another expression for preying upon the public. The aim is not to fill one's place in regular and well ordered society and to earn a competence or it may be wealth by so doing, but a selfish plan is formed to extort money by artificial scarcities on behalf of a few who have united for the purpose. This is not only wrong in morals, and unsound in philosophy, but it is also unwise in policy. It is built upon the false philosophy of individualism, whereby God has so constituted men for society that their permanent interests depend on their mutual helpfulness, not their mutual hostility. A community in which the pol-icy of robbery should be adopted, whether it is highway robbery or plunder by speculation would soon come to poverty.

[Sumner wrote here "Omit."]

Individualism also teaches the individual to make his own happiness the aim of life. Each one is to follow the notions which, he thinks, will give him happiness, or, if he finds himself compressed or discommoded in his circumstances he is taught to break through the circumstances and secure happiness by change. Hence the widespread idea that the law of life is to struggle out of one situation into another in the pursuit of happiness. But in every new set of circumstances which is thus cre-ated a number of persons are forced to stake their happiness, such is the mutual interdependence of man in society, in spite of themselves, that it is impossible for one who considers himself unhappy under this set of circumstances to make a change without involving the happiness of all the others. This idea of chasing happiness, and hoping always to catch it, if we can only accomplish this or that, is the greatest folly, but we incur obligations, in spite of ourselves, in any position in which we are, and cannot change from it without breaking ties which are of greater or less importance to somebody else. This fact ought, in itself, to teach us how false and absurd is the notion which individualism teaches that we have only to change so long and so often as we are dissatisfied. We ought not to do so. We ought to consider the interests of others, or yield to them whenever they are important. In other words, we ought to live by duties, that is by our obligations to God and man; and not by rights alone, that is not by the claims which we may make on others. All rights and duties are reciprocal, and by the side of a right upon which we are ready to insist we shall always find a duty to modify it.

[Sumner wrote here "Begin."]

Furthermore this individualism which inculcates only personal in-dependence and lays all the stress on rights and not on duties threatens the gravest dangers to society by undermining and destroying the family. Some of the matters which are now clamoring for the public attention depend entirely upon the question *what is the unit of society*? Is human society made up of a number of families or of a number of individuals? It is evident that men, women, and children, do not enter into civil society each as a separate individual, but they are primarily related to each other as husband and wife, parents and children, in a family unit. Hence it is that the popular theories which are endeavoring to base the social fabric on individualism and to make the state deal with every individual in it as an independent person, free from any ties of sentiment to any other person are continually coming in contact with the theory of the family. It has always been the strength and beauty of the family that its members were firm and even irrational in their loyalty and attachment to each other, but the new theories enter into and break up this unit by teaching the members to cultivate an independence of each other, and it may be, an hostility to each other. I do not desire to enlarge upon this point because it is connected with sensational and popular questions which have no place here, but no discussion of this subject would be complete which should ignore a movement by which individualism threatens society in its most sacred and vital interest—that is, in the family.

[That feature in modern society which is more pure, most valuable, and most beneficent is that it is based upon the family. The public, civil, or political, or social, constitution does not invade the family. It does not break up the family unit, but is based upon it. It is assumed by society that men will form families and that the duty of educating children will be better performed in the family circle than elsewhere. Compare for a moment this plan of educating with a plan of educating them together in a public institution and who will not jealously sustain the truth and wisdom of this policy which has become traditional in our modern society? But now individualism threatens to break up the family unit, to destroy its contribution, and to set its members over against one another with separate and individual interests, and perhaps even to array them against one another in that selfishness and suspicion which, as I have said, is the spirit which this rationalizing individualism fosters and teaches.][1] The revolution in our social order which is involved in this movement surpasses our conception, but it is only one respect in which rationalism is leading us back to paganism.

---

[1]Sumner often used brackets to indicate portions of sermons he planned to omit if he was pressed for time.

The same philosophy also produces some peculiar fruits in the matter of political opinion. We have seen that the individual, whether he has taken pains to inform himself properly on the matter or not, is made judge and arbitrator in all things affecting his own rights, duties, and happiness. In strict consonance with this, we find that he is also supposed to possess some secret organ which is infallible in regard to all political wisdom. He discards history which is really the chief guide and teacher in politics. He rejects the testimony of experience, and the sober reflexions of trained men. He who has thought out his own God, shall not only think out his own State, or his own form of government? So this class of men are ready at any moment to overturn a state, not doubting but they can build a better one tomorrow. Revolution is, in fact, their grand means of curing ills in the body politic. This again is in thorough consonance with their philosophical ideas. As they trample a doctrine or faith underfoot because it is not good enough for them to understand it, so they do not hesitate to destroy the physical works of the past. Constitutions are in fact worth no more than a schoolboy's compositions until they have acquired the sacredness of age and generations have experienced the beneficial effects of their provisions, but there is a class of men who would make a new constitution and stake the fate of the nation upon some new notion of theirs every year. They are loud in their declamation about "reform," but their reform consists in destroying a great and beneficent custom or institution entirely on account of some slight individual evil connected with it.

This philosophy also has its effects upon education. It demands that only the "useful" sciences shall be taught. The useful sciences (according to its definition) are those by which men may win wealth from the stores of nature. All other sciences are regarded as waste of time. The sciences which are approved are those which will train the individual for the scramble into which he is to go, and will enable him to bring out a large share of the spoil. Those which are despised are those which would teach him to know himself, or mankind, or the deeds and thoughts of the past, or the God who surrounds and supports him. The sciences which are approved are those which enable men to get more; those which are despised are those which enable them to be more.

I cannot enlarge upon these points. They are necessary here in order to show how widely this philosophy taints all our practical interests. You are familiar with all these things which I have mentioned. You have seen these movements in progress; you have heard these doctrines advocated; your attention has been called to the tendencies which I have mentioned. You will therefore appreciate better the effects of the same philosophy in religion which I now proceed to notice.

It seems to be believed that it is not necessary for men to take the same steps to learn religious truth which they would take in order to learn scientific truth. A man who would simply confess ignorance of astronomy will stop and think a moment and give a decided reply as to his faith in a religious doctrine. It seems to be believed by many that we are provided at the outset in life with some special organ which reveals religious truth to us. Thus every man becomes his own guide and master in these matters; and, as I have said, invents his own creed and his own God. His great fear is lest he may believe too much and he forces [?] down the traditional creeds of the Church as far as possible. Especially, however, this habit of thought fastens upon sacraments, rites, ceremonies, and symbols. No doubt false dogmatism overestimates these things and produces disgust and revolt; no doubt also many persons attempt to counteract individualism and independence by asserting Church authority, and thus provoke a double reaction. But false rationalism approaches sacraments and ceremonies with the question: "What is the use?" and if this is not promptly answered its axe falls. It is asked: what good can a little water or a little bread do? What is the use of a ceremony or a symbol? and when the specific and, I may say, physical advantage of these things cannot be at once stated, then rationalism says: Do away with them! We will do nothing and say nothing unless we can at once specify the exact use and value of the performance or the words. All beyond that is sentiment and poetry and romance; we will have none of it. What kind of a hard and loveless world would this be, if any such ideas should really be put in practice? Politeness and courtesy and affection and friendship would be among the first of the "useless" things to be banished from the world. The son would estimate his filial affection at exactly as much as he expected to gain from his father. A man would not take the pains to give a polite salutation to his neighbor, because it would be a mere ceremony. He would refuse to give his hand to his friend because it is only a symbolical act, and of course the important thing is that the "heart should be right." If any such fashions should prevail do we not all feel sure that there would be a severe deterioration in manners and in all the feelings and sentiments which bind men together and serve to soften and ennoble life? We should soon return to the conviction that we must cultivate and preserve the forms and usages and ceremonies which, while they express and serve as an outward sign of our faiths and our feelings, also maintain them in distinct and active life. If we are careless about the sign we shall not long be tenacious of the thing signified, and if a man's "heart is right" we may be very sure that he will seek an early and satisfactory means of giving expression to its feelings. Many things are wise and expedient and even necessary whose "use" we cannot specify in the terms of value which are current in a mercantile age.

There is one thing of public interest which serves to illustrate many different details of this subject which we have been considering. It may be objected that the things which have been mentioned consist, in great part, in gloomy forebodings of possible consequences. Let us turn then to one instance in which this rationalizing and individualizing tendency has already been pushed to its true results. By studying its results in this case we may see what they will be in others.

All the arguments which may be made against any ceremony, as such, apply to the marriage ceremony. The logical rationalists long ago made this application. We already know the consequences. We hear continual complaints of the laxity in this respect which is growing in the community, and the better portion of the people have surrounded the marriage ceremony with greater formality and greater solemnity than was common twenty years ago as a means of restoring something of the sacredness which marriage has lost in the popular feeling.

But this is not the only respect in which the marriage relation has been influenced by popular rationalism. No doubt cases of hardship may arise under a stringent marriage law with no provision for divorce, but we have, in this matter, a good instance of the method of procedure of our rationalizing reformers. They have cured these cases of hardship by legal provisions which undermine the marriage relation, and the consequences are so grievous and so notorious as to be a public scandal. It is a good instance of the revolutionary and destructive method of "reform." Then to this folly and wickedness has been added the doctrine of the pursuit of happiness (to which I have referred), and anyone who is not "happy" in existing relations has been encouraged to seek happiness, though the step should involve the happiness of a number of other persons who are interested in existing relations.

I must now bring the consideration of this entire subject to a close. You see how wide is its scope, and you see that it is not a philosophical question simply, but that it is intensely practical, and is interwoven with the most absorbing questions of the day. There are many different schools of rationalists and if I were attempting to do more than give a summary view of this subject it would be necessary to distinguish them.

One school consists of a class of philosophers. It is represented by some German writers whose works of fiction have been translated and have been widely read in this country during the last few years. I referred to them in my former discourse. They certainly are men of high tone, and great learning, and deep thought, but they would lead the world back to the old pagan philosophy. If they should have their way they would feed abstractions to a little academy of philosophers and look down in contempt on the mass of men as philosophy always has done. If the abstractions which they teach have any value at all, then, as I said in my last discourse, it is as easy to believe in the doctrines of the Christian faith as in these caricatures of them. If there is any external, absolute, and universal essence of being which I ought to know and revere, I, an intelligent being, then that essence or being must be intelligent, and I prefer to call it God, rather than the "all." If there is a revelation of God by which He has come into the physical world and into time, it may indeed be nearly akin to thought, but I prefer to call it and to believe in it as the incarnate Word known in history as Jesus Christ. If there is a spirit or pervading power in all the physical world and in humanity with which I ought to come into communion, then I prefer to recognize in it the Holy Spirit of God, which, according to the scriptures, is present and active in nature and in man. Nature is only the hem of the robe of God, and since men have learned a faith which raises them up to look up to his face, let us not go back to the days of darkness and ignorance. So much for the philosophical rationalists. Their creed is no simpler; it is far more abstract. It makes just as much of an appeal to faith, and if we must believe, the old creed is best. Then too every philosophy or religion creates its own forms of human society. Our present society is what Christianity has moulded out of the material of the ancient world— Asiatic imagination, Greek philosophy, Roman energy. Jewish tenacity and ritual dogmatism contributed each its share. The elements have never yet been fused into a simple compound. These rationalists represent the Greek Element—fine and acute in thought, cold and critical and subtle in analysis, and sharp and incisive in logic. What man is there who is trained to thought and reasoning who does not feel a bond of sympathy with this school of thought. But when we look at the society which this philosophy created we see nothing there to tempt us to try to reproduce it. We may have much in our society which needs to be corrected but the old pagan civilization of Greece is not the model toward which we should strive.

In their way also, the popular rationalists, as we have seen today, are building up again a pagan society. They are stripping off from our civilization all which is Christian, or even religious, and making the interests of the individual his law, and his whim or pleasure his only guide. In opposition to the true law of human society according to which society is bound together by a thousand cords of relationship, affection, friendship, sympathy, and charity, this philosophy separates it into isolated individuals with independent or even opposed interests, and arrays them against one another as foes, or, at least, as rivals. It is the spirit which animated the answer of Cain elevated into the philosophy of human life: "Am I my brother's keeper?"

# Tradition and Progress

Rooted in the Oxford movement of the 1840s, High Church Episcopalianism sought salvation through an authoritative, institutional church and through the reintroduction of rituals abandoned early in the English reformation. Mounting an evangelical counterrevolution, its Low Church opponents sponsored revivals paralleling those within Congregationalism and Presbyterianism. During the 1850s, a Broad Church middle ground found expression in the writings of several prominent English clergymen and was soon favored by communicants who feared alliance with either Rome or other Protestant Evangelicals. Identifying traditionalism with a narrow and obstructive sectarianism, Sumner defended the Broad Church cause. "Tradition and Progress," January 14, 1872, sermon at the Church of the Redeemer, Morristown, New Jersey, MS. Sumner Papers, Yale, New Haven, Connecticut; not previously published.

"Why do ye also transgress the commandment
of God by your tradition?"
Matthew 15.3

Continuing the line of subjects on which I have already spoken two or three times, I take up this morning the subject of tradition, and I must bring it into relation with progress.

Conservatism and radicalism are two opposite limits between which men waver in the conduct of political, social, and ecclesiastical matters. Conservatism rests upon the past. It is hostile to change and fearful of it. It prefers to hold things as they are. It is unambitious. It does not look to the future, or plan for it. It does not form hopes or ideals. It rests content with such comforts and advantages as it possesses, and rests satisfied under such disadvantages as it is forced to endure. Every generation inherits from its predecessor a stock of institutions, ideas, doctrines, and tastes. These form what we call traditions, and it is the spirit of conservatism to cling to these traditions, to regard them as the sum of all wisdom, to make them the standard of all truth and rights, and to regard any deviation from them as folly and sin. Old things acquire a kind of sanctity. A tradition which has centuries of faith and usage in its favor seems to be elevated above human criticism. We are not allowed to examine it. We may not ask whether, after all, it may not be false, or

16

whether, in the process of time it may not have come to be misunderstood, or whether it may not have lost its value and applicability through the change of circumstances. Conservatism frowns down all such questions as presumptuous. It answers them by an avalanche of honored names of saints and sages who have held and believed these things, or have been content with these institutions, and crushes the presumptuous inquiry under the question whether he would be wiser, or better, or greater than they. It stands always with its face to the past, and, if it must advance, it advances backwards.

But the slightest experience and observation of life shows us that there is no such thing possible on earth as absolute rest. Everything is changing and moving. Nor is it possible for human thought to stand still, or for ideas to reach any culmination beyond which there is no advance. The most rigid conservative, or the most determined worshipper of tradition, finds, after years have elapsed, that his idea, his tastes, his feelings in regard to certain matters have undergone a change, though it may be an unconscious one. The theory of the conservative is, therefore, a false and impossible one on its very face. But it suffers also from a more potent enemy than its error and impossibility. Every one who looks back a few years can detect proofs enough that the fathers had not exhausted all wisdom. The principles of reform, improvement, and advance, have not, at least all, been illusory. Energy, ambition, and hope, have won principles which no one can dispute, but these principles have been won in battle with conservatism, which has therefore seemed to be only obstructive and harmful. Furthermore the very great men whom the conservatives and traditionalists worship won their position in human history by being innovators. No man has ever become great on earth by simply reiterating what men had said before him, or clinging doggedly to what he had learned from the past. The men who achieve greatness and are remembered throughout generations as benefactors or leaders of the human race are those who lead the way to new and hitherto unknown heights of thought, knowledge, or piety, and those who today are their true successors are not those who sit at their feet in mute admiration, but those who take up and carry on the work which they did.

All these facts serve to undermine the rigid conservative and traditional position, and to render it manifestly false and contemptible. But they do more than this; they also start a new tendency, and that is the tendency to spurn all tradition, all inherited faith and wisdom. We find that we gain by abandoning one of the ideas which our fathers solemnly believed, and by taking up a new one, and so we say let us abandon *all* their ideas, and get a new one in the place of each, and no doubt we shall profit by it in every case. Here we have the false inference which lies at the root of all false theories of progress. All those theories assail old things simply because they are old. Some old things are bad and ought to be corrected or destroyed not because they are old but because they are bad. But radicalism misses the distinction. It behaves as if antiquity were the cause or the sure sign of evil and it rages wildly against all antiquity and tradition. If anything exists, the radical spirit would destroy it, as a stumbling block in the way of progress. Radicalism hangs upon hope, not on memory. It chases ideals, and is indifferent to facts. It does not take the pains to examine the existing and inherited order of things, and so it does not understand its own point of departure. It aims only at vague ideals, and so does not know its own objective point, or purpose. It is like sailing out onto the broad ocean without chart or compass, with no definite port in view, and no means of returning to the haven in case of disaster. It may course grandly over the great ocean but it makes no fruitful voyage and it leaves no path behind.

Such then are the opposing extremes: a barren conservatism which clings only to tradition and stagnates in idle worship of the past and a wild and headlong progress which promises nothing but confusion and disaster. It needs no argument to show that either extreme is false and wrong, and yet these two extremes divide mankind. The sober and wise union of prudence with energy, of reflexion with hope, of experience with ideals, this is rare beyond calculation, and yet it is the only wise and true thing, and the one at which we must continually aim.

Now I have been at considerable pains to vindicate the authority of history. In this age and in this country the great danger is from a senseless and thoughtless progress. Against such a tendency it is necessary to maintain the true authority of history, but when I maintain that I do not by any means join hands with the blind devotees of tradition. I must therefore show explicitly what traditionalism is, as applied to religious matters and wherein it is false.

The text is only one of the passages in the gospels where our Lord places himself in opposition to the traditionalism of the Jews. It is evident therefore that there is a *kind* of traditionalism of which he disapproved. We have to see what kind that is, and to take care lest we fall into the same.

During the three or four centuries before the advent of our Lord, the course of the religious history of the Jews was, in brief, this. They no longer possessed a strong and living revelation of God. By that I do not mean that an external revelation had at one time existed amongst them which was now lost, but I mean that they no longer had any prophets or preachers of original and creative power. They were driven to study and make use of the records of the original and creative work which had once been done amongst them by Moses and the great prophets. The prophets, that is the original and spontaneous teachers, gave way to the priests, who only perform over and over again the routine of ritual, the scribe, who copies and perpetuates the written record of great deeds once done and grand truth once taught, and the rabbi who interprets, and explains, and comments on the recorded revelation. As for the priest and scribe, it is clear that they cannot be fountains of any new life. Their labors are mechanical and restricted to a simple routine. The priest has only to do over again what has been done for centuries. He performs at the altar functions which require no thought or intelligence, only a mechanical routine. Fidelity to the prescribed modes and methods is all that he can aim at. It is his highest virtue. The scribe's work is limited to copying with scrupulous exactness just what he finds handed down to him from former generations as the precise text of the sacred books. The Jewish scribes were not allowed even to correct a palpable error which had crept in. Thus to say: "It is written" became the sum and end of all thought or discussion. These two parties were, therefore, from the nature of the case devotees of tradition. They would never inculcate religious principle, or teach religious truth, or take any free, original, and active steps for the moral and spiritual good of the nation. But it may be thought that the rabbis, the interpreters and teachers of the law, occupied this office and performed this function of promoting the spiritual and moral life of the nation. However such was not the case. The spirit which had taken possession of the nation was that of a stiff, anxious, and fanatical orthodoxy. The nation was determined to know and practice, not what was true and right, but, just what Moses had taught. The distinction is of the utmost importance, and involves, as we shall see in a moment, the fundamental principle of all traditionalism. It followed that the work of the rabbis was not to take the Scriptures as a means of arriving at true and living principles, but to perpetuate all manner of quaint and curious traditions which were only remotely connected with the Scriptures. A Jew who would be faithfully religious sought to fulfill the Law of Moses in every detail, but Moses had not given directions as to all the details of life. Hence the rabbis sought to carry out and develop the commands which he had left and apply them to every minute incident and duty of life. The consequence was a

grotesque mass of ordinances, rules, traditions, fables, perverted interpretations, all fossilized and handed down in an inflexible tradition.
The Scripture itself was practically unknown, and instead of it these
traditions controlled all the thought and life of the nation. In the passage
from which the text is taken the care about washings, and gestures, and
purifications, is bitterly denounced, and one instance is especially mentioned in which tradition had entirely set aside the spirit of the law. If
an ungrateful son should refuse any longer to support his aged parent,
he might declare that he would pay into the temple, as an offering, a
sum which he considered equivalent to his obligation to them and he
was held acquitted from any further responsibility for their support. So
completely had the willful narrowing of the mind and heart to the limits
of a fixed tradition overthrown the law and the natural conscience.

If now we look at this instance of traditionalism we see what terrible
perversion of mind and conscience it may produce and we also see what
is its fundamental principle and its central error. Whenever men cease
to try to go back to the original fountain of truth, whenever they cease
to subject everything which they inherit from the past to the scrutiny of
reason and conscience, whenever they cease to examine the credentials
of the various authorities which claim to rule them, whenever, on the
contrary, they turn to one form of truth, or to the truth as it has appeared
to one man or one set of men at some time in the past, then they fall into
traditionalism. When they cease to say: "Let me know the truth," and
say instead: "Let me know what Moses said," or "Let me know what my
Church says," then they fall into traditionalism, and there is no error in
doctrine, or perversion in conscience, or blindness of spirit which is
impossible for them. Moses was indeed a great teacher. He unquestionably uttered the very oracles of God to the children of Israel in his day
and generation. But Isaiah, Jeremiah, and Ezekiel were likewise men of
God. They did not simply act as interpreters, or expounders, or teachers
of Moses. They nowhere inculcate obedience to Moses and faithful performance of his ordinances. What they insist on is that men shall do the
will of God, and obey His Laws, and when they talk of this law they do
not mean the things written in the Pentateuch but they mean the grand
and incomprehensible reality of God's spirit and will and purpose in
the world, and of this the Pentateuch presents only a single and imperfect picture of one single phase. David and Elijah and Isaiah penetrated
the veil and saw this reality face to face just as much as Moses did. They
taught just as originally as he, and they did not hesitate to teach differently from him where they saw good reason, as Ezekiel certainly does

do in the 16th and 18th chapters. In their day, therefore, you see that there was an original and direct approach to the spirit of truth. Moses was revered with justice, but he had not yet been elevated to that position where his name put an end to all thought and reflexion and conscience. In the later time, which I have been describing, that state of things had come about. In place of free and generous love to God, there was only tenacity and obstinacy in clinging doggedly to what Moses had said, or to what it was supposed that Moses had said, without even care to be sure that, if he had ever said it, he had meant it as it was understood. Instead of free, hearty, and honest conviction, there was only dogged prejudice. Instead of faith there was only bigotry and fanaticism. And this was no irregular or unnatural consequence. It was the regular and legitimate result of the traditionalism which had taken control of the nation, and the instance is valuable because it shows us this law which is also taught us by multitudes of other examples of men and nations: viz. that if we give up the love of God and the love of truth in and for themselves and if we sit down content and determined to follow only second hand truth and swear in the words of a human teacher or sect we shall fall into spiritual blindness and moral death. But traditionalism is the habit or principle of fidelity to one form of truth which some man or body of men have fixed upon at some period in the past.

Now let us see under what forms this principle presents itself amongst us.

Traditionalism appears in all sectarianism. We are born of parents who adhere to one or another religious body. Our starting point is therefore fixed for us by tradition. We become attracted to the body in which we were born and educated—all that is very natural and no fault can be found with it. But this religious body is marked by certain peculiarities as distinguished from other bodies. These have become graven upon it by tradition. If we follow them up to their source we find that they were fixed originally by the taste, whim, judgment, or opinion of Luther, or Calvin, or Wesley or the English reformers. We have the same Bible, the same gospel, the same X [Christ], the same sacraments, but the things which give us our external distinctions are the traditions of men which have been added to the truth. Now if we would only put these out of account, and all return to first principles once more and submit all the matters in question to a full and candid examination we should be astonished to find how petty and contemptible are our differences compared with our points of accord. If a dozen men should each claim the right to set the sun by their watches, they would certainly quarrel. No two of them would agree as to its correct position, but if they could all be persuaded to see that the watch of each one must be adjusted to the sun, they would soon come to harmony. But our traditionalism comes in to form a great barrier against any such sensible proceeding. We insist on educating our children in separate schools so that our sectarian traditions and no other may be brought to bear upon them. We prefer to make university education impossible in the country rather than give up the colleges which represent every sect and fragment of a sect in the land. We educate the religious teachers of our people in separate seminaries each one poor, weak, struggling, and naturally narrow and mean in its conception of Christianity, as if we had a High Church Bible, a Low Church Bible, a Presbyterian Bible, a Methodist Bible, a Baptist Bible, and so on to the end of the list. The present tendency, at least among ourselves, is to intensify and sharpen still more the distinctive features of the ecclesiastical body. There are many among us who limit their effort to a barren conservative exertion to keep all things as they have been or are supposed to have been for centuries. This is called churchmanship, but I beg you to notice that it is not churchmanship, it is mere Episcopalianism. We are reduced to an ism among isms. We are a sect among sects. We have no broader policy, no more healthful and vigorous spirit, no greater hope, no nobler ideal to offer than any of our rivals. It is reiterated again and again that we are a Church, that we possess some advantages of plan or theory over those whom we call the sects, but if we simply insist upon all the traditions of the English reformation in all their integrity, if we will admit no flexibility in their application, and if we propose to our fellow Christians no broader, deeper, or truer theory and ideal of the Church than they already possess then we are only an Episcopal sect, we are no *Church*, we have no idea of what is meant by a Church and the churchmanship on which we pride ourselves is nothing but Episcopalianism, that is, stubborn and fanatical fidelity to the traditions of the body in which we are enrolled. For consider what true churchmanship is and how it differs from sectarianism. Sectarianism is the spirit which maintains that on all points men must think thus and so if they would be right. Therefore those who hold just this set of opinions and who can fit exactly into the fixed scheme go off and form a body by themselves. They seek to make converts to the sect, but hold a rigid line of demarcation which shuts out all who do not submit to its restrictions as aliens. They do not care to embrace the others in any manner or to any degree. They do not take responsibility for mankind as a whole, for a nation as a whole, but only for a certain religious clique as such. Churchmanship, as I understand it, is the contrary spirit. It maintains that in, through, and under all these parties and divisions there is a true Church of Jesus Christ on earth, which is an historic and organic growth; that all good proceeds from God's Holy Spirit whether its source be recognized or not; that this Church is robbed of its power and efficiency in the world by the divisions and rivalries and traditions of men, and that the grand aim of those who hold to the true gospel spirit must be to bring this conception of the Church out of its obscurity, to relieve it of its traditional limitations, and enforce it upon the mind and consciences of men.

It is permitted us to love our own traditions and to cherish them. Loyalty to the Church is as laudable a virtue as patriotism or loyalty to our country but the traditionalist in the Church is like the citizen who adopts that shallow and contemptible motto: "our country, right or wrong." Any such principle or habit of mind is wrong. It secures popular applause for its thoroughness. A man becomes popular with any party if he makes parade of extreme and reckless devotion to its principles and interests, but we have here a high and solemn duty to God and right and truth. Popularity and applause are pleasant but we are not permitted to take them into account here. What we serve is the kingdom of heaven and the cause of the gospel, and we may not measure this by the traditions of any religious body, we must make it the standard by which those traditions are to be measured. Keep this ever in mind. Let your supreme interest always be given to what is right and true, to the will and law of God in the purest and best conception you can form of it by Scripture, reason, and conscience. Let no thing interfere between you and it lest you also fall under the terrible condemnation which our Lord addressed to the Pharisees: "Ye have made the commandments of God of none effect by your tradition." Be candid and open and ready to learn. Be sure that what we believe can only gain by the fullest examination, if it is indeed sound and true. Keep a warm and genuine interest for all which concerns the kingdom of heaven, and assist in it when you can. Have a true and firm ideal of the Christian Church and be not led astray from it by any inferior theory. Do not oppose to movements of reform and progress simply stubborn conservatism and reckless adherence to tradition, but know well that movement is necessary to life, and that when we cease to grow we shall die. The only domain of faith is the future and under traditionalism there is no true faith. Faith, as the traditionalists use the word, means only the obedient repetition of what we have been taught to say, it does not refer to any true spiritual assent. Also, be

not deceived as to the true authority of the great men who have lived in
the past. If a great man could really fetter the world and forbid it ever
to think any more than he had thought, or know any more than he had
known, or have a purer and more correct faith than he had had, then
great men would be only great curses. But no man who has ever been
truly great would say or think that the world had nothing more to do
after him than to learn his words and follow his steps. If we could call
up the great sages and saints of the past and could put to them the
questions: shall we limit ourselves to perpetuating the tradition of your
teachings? we greatly misapprehend the spirit which has animated all
the truly great among the sons of men, or the answer would come back
as with one voice: not so! We fell upon the steps of the throne, make
stepping stones of us to mount higher than we!

Neither be led astray by that specious doctrine of progress which
seems to worship movement, and which exhausts itself in a feverish
hunger for change. When we move let us move slowly and soberly. The
traditions of centuries have a true *moral* authority. No wise man will
disregard it. They form for us at any rate the point of departure from
which we must start in all our efforts for the benefit of mankind. We
must begin with the world as we find it, that is, as it is handed down to
us from the past. This gives us our starting point. We must also think
well what we aim at and rather wait for the movements which naturally
develop themselves in the life of the race than proceed to invent an ideal
world and try to realize it by rash innovations. You may know that if a
man endeavors to cross a trackless prairie keeping his eyes fixed on his
feet, he will make a very devious path and that it is entirely uncertain
wither he will go. If he wishes to cross it on a straight and certain path,
he must look up, must observe the bearings of such landmarks as there
are, and must correct the little errors of each step in the succeeding one
that he may thus arrive at the point which he has chosen. Much of our
modern progress is like the path of the man who keeps his eyes fixed
on his feet. It has cut loose from the past. It does not start on any given
lines. It has not any trained foresight to choose the point at which it
would arrive. It starts at hazard and proceeds only step by step and it is
uncertain whither it will go. On the other hand, the illustration may
serve to show what is the true use of tradition as distinguished from
traditionalism. Our progress should be like that of the man who looks
up and around with a free observation and a firm intelligence. It should
proceed from the past, not throwing away, but rather retaining and preserving with care the inheritance of truth which has come down to us.

It should make use of this inherited wisdom to choose its objects of gain and pursuit, to discriminate between truth and falsehood, the wise policy and the foolish. It should thus guard itself against the repetition of old errors, and against the delusions of worn out falsehoods. It should correct its own errors step by step by means of the landmarks which it sees about it. Such a progress would be real and true, for it would be a natural and normal growth. I know of no one who thinks that the Kingdom of God has ever yet been realized on earth, and I know of no one who does not believe that that kingdom is the object of the hope, and the faith, and the thirst of mankind. It would seem to be clear therefore that those who worship tradition will be found with their backs to the dawn when it shall break; and that those only, whatever their mistakes, who stand with their faces to the future will meet and enjoy its coming.

# Solidarity of the Human Race

Sumner first encountered the idea of human solidarity in 1869 in a sermon by Charles Loyson (1827–1912), known as Père Hyacinthe, a liberal French Catholic priest who won favor among American Protestants for his opposition to Pope Pius IX. Discussing why God chose the victims of a recent Peruvian earthquake to punish humanity for its sins, Père Hyacinthe argued that the question was irrelevant since, in the modern world, everyone is responsible for the sins of others. Although Sumner initially found the idea "strange & untenable," he was converted after hearing the same priest lecture in America during the following winter. Sumner adopted the idea in a sermon in 1871.

This 1873 version, a revision of the sermon using the same title, revealed important shifts in the tone and substance of Sumner's thought as he moved from pulpit to classroom. Secular in tone, it stressed the material along with the spiritual dimensions of human solidarity. While continuing to stress the need for charity in the face of suffering, it also placed new emphasis on enlightened self-interest. "Solidarity of the Human Race," January 11, 1873, lecture delivered at the Sheffield Scientific School, MS. Sumner Papers, Yale, New Haven, Connecticut; not previously published.

I think it appropriate to this occasion and these circumstances to bring before you a subject which is perhaps too scientific for a sermon, and too broad and fundamental in its character to find a place in the class-room discussion of any special science, while its moral and religious aspects are of the highest importance. It is one of those few doctrines in which the highest science and the best theology are already in substantial accord. It is one of those broad generalizations of which it is difficult to say whether they are the final results or the first postulates of all human thought, a generalization so wide that to establish it thoroughly would require volumes rather than a single discourse, and faith in it issues, and must issue I believe, from wide acquaintance with science and philosophy and reflection on their results, rather than from a special induction. It is not as yet popular and familiar, but it commands the faith of the best thinkers in all departments. It follows from these facts that I can only attempt to sketch it in the rudest outline, and in a suggestive manner, and leave you to perceive for yourselves, as you advance in your studies, those facts, laws, and analogies which go to confirm it.

The doctrine in question is the solidarity of the human race. It will be necessary for me in the first place to define what it is.

The word solidarity is much more familiarly used by the French than by us, and it has here peculiar power and propriety. It is of course metaphorical and it is by analyzing the metaphor that we discern its meaning. We are familiar with various forms of relation and combination in the physical world. There is organic combination and inorganic combination. Solidarity, differing from solidity, includes the idea of harmonious relation of parts which is represented in organic combinations. Inorganic bodies may be combined mechanically or naturally. They may have relations to each other like the parts of a machine, or artificial combinations like the materials of a house, or a mechanical union like a bundle of sticks. In none of these combinations is there solidity, and neither of them furnishes the basis of the metaphorical term solidarity. Solidity is a property of some body which is necessarily regarded as a unit, be it large or small. It is properly predicated only of the combination of particles in that unit. If the unit is broken the fragments may be solid but, generally speaking, no recombination can restore the former unit. Now the metaphor before us is based on this physical property, and we are more concerned with the familiar than with the technical properties of solid bodies. Any movement of one part of a solid body implies a movement, equal and corresponding, of all other parts of the same body. The effect of a blow on any one part is transmitted with diminishing intensity to all the parts. Heat and cold are transmitted from part to part, and all such effects are ultimately equalized throughout the whole mass. Here is the kernel of the metaphor before us. Our term solidarity is applied to things which are made up of parts, but it implies that their combination is complete and harmonious, that effects exerted upon a part ultimately pervade the whole though with diminishing intensity, and are ultimately equalized throughout the whole, that motion in one part implies an equal movement in the same direction of the whole. You see then what is meant by the solidarity of the human race. It is meant to affirm that all mankind form a unit, and especially to affirm that the combination in question is close and perfect, so that whatever affects a part, affects the whole, that a movement of a part involves a movement of the whole, that a change in state or condition of a part is ultimately equalized throughout the whole. It is affirmed that all the men on this globe form a unit under bonds from which they cannot escape. They are shut out from the inhabitants, if there be any, of any other planet, but, as amongst themselves, they are shut up to a common lot and a common destiny. Whatever affects one man affects the whole human race. There is no gap or break in the lines on which influences are transmitted throughout our race any more than there is a break or gap in the ocean by which movements of a part are hindered from transmission and equalization throughout the mass.

This doctrine is not altogether new. It is found, in germ at least, in St. Augustine, and from time to time, thinkers of every age have expanded their conception of the conditions of progress and culture and of the power of members of the human race to influence each other until they have boldly grasped the idea that the factors in human progress were the whole of mankind, but such assertions have fallen still born, and are only suggested in various attempts to construct Utopias. In these later times, however, the theological ideas of charity and of the brotherhood of man have received new form and scope; science has accustomed us to throw down artificial and traditional barriers and to base our combinations on principles and natural laws. And art has brought the various members of the human family into such close and actual contact that the truth of the doctrine before us is made manifest to our experience. Indeed the last of these means has outstripped the others. Our arts have diminished the distance between us and foreign nations faster than our religion has taught us the true interpretation of St. Paul's theory of Christianity, and faster than our science has taught us to trust universal doctrines, and it is time that we should, if possible cast off our prejudices, dispel the darkness which covers us while we endeavor to reconcile traditional habits of thought with new relations, and that we should secure freedom and light by grasping the broad principle which underlies all human progress, and therefore constitutes its first and most essential condition.

The doctrine in question will become more apparent in its meaning, and perhaps also in its truth, if we proceed to illustrate it. Your minds may follow it to a certain point with ease. You may see that civilized nations have a close interdependence. I doubt not that you are free from that vulgar error which leads us to look on with indifference at the affairs of other nations. You know that the great American war of ten years ago affected not only those human beings who lived upon a certain portion of the earth's surface. You know that it had effects which knew no boundaries of state or national sovereignty. It entered the homes of European operatives, it diverted the course of some of the most important branches of international traffic, it altered the industries of India and South America, it affected the movements of population during a whole series of years, and it has permanently influenced the distribution of capital. These effects lie upon the surface, but when we come down to those which are never recorded in history and which the imagination must follow we know that our war bore heavily upon the weal or woe of millions in all quarters of the globe who never owned a slave. Human slavery had become an institution in the world. It was a wrong to which certain men had committed themselves and before their error and folly could be cured, thousands upon thousands of their fellow men who were ignorant and innocent of their crime must suffer. All this you no doubt see very readily. Neither, then, will it require long argument to convince you that a European war must have great influence upon our interests, or that the movements of European politics must influence our affairs. Such influence appears in the effect on prices, and on emigration, on the movements of capital and on the relations of business. These are the material effects and they are the ones which are most apparent, but every event in history of this character bears fruit in the dissemination of ideas. Democracy gained a wonderful stride when the system of the United States proved equal to the strain of a great civil war. Feudalism suffered a terrible blow when Austria was defeated at Sadowa. Cesarism was buried under the ruins of Sedan. The relations of commerce and trade cannot be hemmed within national boundaries. The inferences from historical facts may be drawn by observers in all countries. The lessons of experience and the results of political experiments are open to mankind.

Furthermore, you will probably see at once that no nation abandons an old error and develops a new sound principle without thereby contributing to the welfare of all its neighbors. There is a mean and narrow doctrine that nations profit by each other's misfortunes. It is a doctrine fit only for thieves quarreling over their booty, but it has, unfortunately, found advocates in high places. The present head of the French nation opposed the unity of Italy in '59 and the union of Germany in '66 on the grounds of this policy. It was thought to be profound statesmanship for France to keep Italy and Germany weak. But to a more enlightened view it needs no detailed argument to prove that the world was better off when Italy began to contribute rather than to waste, or when Austria finally abandoned its intricate and expensive system of repression and sought prosperity in peace and reconciliation under constitutional order, or when Germany ceased to be a political laughing stock and took its place among the nations. The fruits of the new prosperity, the material products, the scientific discoveries, the literary and artistic creations, the inventions, which are brought forth by nations thus regenerated are contributed to the common stock. They become the possession of the race. They could not be kept and preserved within the political boundaries in which they arose even if that should be attempted, and nations find that the prosperity of their neighbors overflows upon them, and that when they weaken their neighbors they rob themselves.

I have touched already on the influence of ideas generated in one nation upon another. This point deserves more careful attention. As an illustration look at the effect of French literature and of the French drama upon the civilized world, during the Second Empire. When a French opera bouffe is presented at Cairo and San Francisco, and French novels are read with avidity at Constantinople and New York certainly there are unifying forces at work tending to bring about uniformity of sentiment and feeling between different nations and races, compared with which the barriers of nationality are only like bulrushes in a stream. Fashions in dress, habits of thought, tone of sentiment, popular jests and epigrams, manners of life, these are the things which carry the one touch of nature which makes the whole world kin. They pass from language to language, from zone to zone, from empire to republic. No custom house bars their entrance; no passport system arrests them at the frontier. And by a slow but steady infusion they raise the tone of mankind to their level or lower it to their baseness. German diligence, thought, and science, French wit, grace, elegance, and frivolity, English traditionalism and practical tact, American energy, haste, and scorn of painstaking all go to form the man of this generation and he is the product of their effect upon him according to their measure.

Yet you may say that though the chief civilized nations are thus closely dependent upon each other, yet between them and the uncivilized there is a great gulf. In the first place it is to be observed that there is an imperceptible gradation between civilized and uncivilized nations. There is no sharp dividing line between them. Still it is true that the form in which different nations affect progress in culture does differ widely. Some lead it or contribute to it weightily, some follow it without contributing to it or hindering it, some are a drag upon it. The Chinese have severed themselves from the rest of the human race to the utmost of their ability, and they are still striving to ward off the influences from without while profiting to a certain extent by commercial relations. The unnatural struggle produces continual discord and confusion, and while they are unable to stem the tide of influence which outside civilization exerts upon them, they appear in the catalogue of nations among the resisting forces. The course of the world's commerce, especially of the movements of the precious metals, has long been controlled by the steadfast refusal of the Chinese to adopt the forms and modes of life which prevail among the most civilized nations of the world.

The whole interior of the Asiatic continent, once the seat of rich empires, is now closed to civilization by fanaticism and violence. Africa is buried in barbarism, and lost to the best interests of the race. The little we can learn of that continent, is wrested from ignorance guarded by violence, by the self-sacrificing labors of a few. Most of South America is the seat of perennial anarchy. Our researches into the antiquities of our religion are blocked by the fanatic ignorance of the Arabs, and their mischievous quarrels make the Euphrates valley, the old course of Oriental trade, impassable for commerce. In Russia civilization is barred by a despotism which is descended by a true succession from Babylon and Byzantium. In Southern Europe culture beats against the stubborn resistance of superstition. In Spain long habits of repression and factious division seem like to stifle hopes of a new era. In France the necessity of facing political problems was long deferred and we have seen the storm fall at last with the pent up violence due to long years of fallacious peace. Now progress there is fettered by the old bonds of centralization which it is striving to burst. In Germany new hopes and purposes find that they must fight their way against petty interests and vested privileges, and local jealousies. In England progress is in a grapple with prescription, and caste privilege, and dogmatic tradition, while with us our true progress is endangered to the utmost by political corruption and financial crime. Thus this cursory view of the state of the world as regards culture shows us that the so-called uncivilized nations are only those in which the progress of the human race is barred by simpler and wider forms of ignorance, superstition, dogmatism and fanaticism, than those which appear in so-called civilized nations, but these are everywhere the wall against which our human growth breaks itself in its efforts to advance. The resisting force is the same everywhere. And we must take cognizance of it in its full extent. Culture can never drop certain nations as barbarous and devote its whole effort to those which at present seem most worthy of it, no more than religion can consent that any shall be permanently dropped from their claim upon it. The human race is the only definition we can give to the objects of culture, and so long as any lag behind there will be reflex hindrances coming from them to stem the tide of progress. It is becoming more and more apparent that the world will never advance steadily and permanently until it advances as a whole. We talk of the progressive nations, but we deceive ourselves if we think that one or a few nations can go on freely and leave others behind. There is a strange law here which is not yet sufficiently traced out in its operations, according to which nations cannot advance independently. They must wait until their development has made itself felt in the education of others before they can take new steps. There may be a front and a rear to the army of progress, but disaster follows if they become separated.

I say this law is not yet wrought out as fully as we might desire and this is not an opportunity for attempting it. I give you only one illustration. At the commencement of the Christian era there was a high civilization in the basin of the Mediterranean while beyond its outskirts was barbarism. There were scarcely any relations between the two. In the second and third centuries of our era the barbarians burst in upon the civilization and reduced it to ruins. The two halves of the human race had become separated by a great gulf. One half had advanced without a care, or a thought that it needed to care, for the other. And instead of growing into relations which should be homogeneous if not equal, they found themselves in hostility, and all the culture which had been gained was sacrificed. The task of progress had to begin anew.

Whether hordes of barbarians can ever again pour over Europe from Asia may indeed be doubted. In these days of trade and literature and science the influence of uncivilized nations will come back upon us through these channels. The stream of progress widens. Nations hithertofore unnoticed become factors in it and they must be educated to take their part.

However, this does not exhaust my meaning in the proposition I have stated, that the nations of the world must advance steadily and equally in culture if their advance is to be real and permanent. There are some other operations of the law which govern this fact which are more occult, and their results more strange.

I am aware that the assertion which I am about to make may seem more bold and less well-founded than any which have preceded, but I ask your candid attention to it.

We often speak of *free* nations and we often hear it asserted that the United States is the freest nation in the world. Freedom or liberty is a negative term. It presupposes some restraint. Progress for the last three hundred years has consisted in breaking restraints or, as we express it positively, in advancing liberty. Now I venture the assertion that in the three leading nations of the present time, the amount of liberty is equal.

Liberty varies in form, or attaches to different things in each, but in amount it is substantially equal. In each long struggles have been made to acquire liberty and acquisitions have been made by each, but it has attached to different things, or taken different directions, but the acquisitions have on the whole been equal. It is a startling observation and one not easily to be explained, but it seems to depend upon this law of the moral order that, on account of the subtile and hidden influences which are continually acting and reacting upon the culture-nations, their degree of progress shall be substantially the same, however different its forms.

Look for a moment at the facts. In Germany liberty attaches to thought and science. These are more free from dogmatical or traditional restraint there than anywhere else on earth. The scientific method is more perfectly understood and more rigidly applied there than elsewhere and it meets with few or no barriers from Church or State. At the same time political and social circumstances in Germany, when judged by English or American standards, are by no means free. In England, on the contrary, we observe civil liberty in its highest development but a caste system in the social order which is rigid to the last degree. Science also suffers in that country from the restraints of dogma and tradition, and education suffers from caste, from traditionalism, and from dogmatism all combined. In the United States we have highly developed liberty in the social order and the most completely democratic forms in civil affairs. It is true that political liberty, in its real sense, is greatly impaired by the manipulation to which these forms are subject, but personal liberty at least is wide and secure. As if in revenge for all this mercantile exchanges are loaded with restrictions, and one must seek in the middle ages, if he can find even there, parallels for the injurious and irrational restraints which are imposed on this branch of human interest in America. Moreover, in estimating the sum of liberty enjoyed by us as compared with other nations, we must not fail to notice the theological and political restraints which from time to time more or less hamper our education.

Thus it will be seen that liberty attaches in each of these countries to a particular subject, and to a different one in each. I by no means claim to prove now that it is equal in all, but I throw out the question as one of great interest and worthy of grave consideration whether it is not true that no nation as yet has understood and grasped the meaning of liberty so thoroughly as to apply it fearlessly over the whole domain of human interest. It is as if the task had been too great for their attention and as if, while winning liberty in one department they had been forced to sacrifice it in others, or as if the grade of social education attained in the foremost nations had only sufficed from the development of a certain degree of liberty. They had the choice of the field in which to win it, but not the power to enlarge its measure. This, you will remember, is in support of the still wider proposition that the nations are bound together by occult social influences which force the whole race to advance as a whole.

The illustrations which I have given have all been calculated to break down the habit of measuring in our minds the extent of social influences by the frontiers of the nation in which they arise. Very slight reflexion serves to show us that such boundaries are for the most part traditional and arbitrary. They have no existence for the spread of ideas or for the subtler forces by which men are really most powerfully educated. It is time that we broke away from the habit of judging by national, local, partisan or personal prejudices. We must break down these barriers to sound judgment and throw the decision of all questions and the estimated merits of all institutions upon natural principles and universal laws. It is the office of science in its true sense, not merely as natural science, but as the methodical operation of the human reason in the investigation of truth, to train men to this habit of mind in which they close their ears to all national, sectional, and personal rivalry, and regard universal principles only in the formation of judgments.

Let me then, in conclusion, call your attention to the manner in which disregarding race divisions and national divisions, influences spread amongst mankind and to the extent of their ramifications. Trade is one of the most powerful of the means by which social influences are transmitted, and it ensures their effect upon the minds of men by appealing to motives which are material and low but are therefore all the more universal. Trade stretches lines of intercourse between persons and communities at the ends of the earth. Its lines cross in every direction and bind the human race together in the most complex relations. A convulsion at one point is felt throughout the whole fabric. A contribution at one point spreads throughout the whole. It may become so divided as to be lost, but it is there nevertheless and is a real addition to the whole or to any of the parts. Anything which is withdrawn at one point must be lost by all in imperceptible quotas perhaps, but nevertheless as a reality. For instance. If millions of value perish in a conflagration we know from recent experience how wide is the influence. It comes home to everyone in one form or another. It is felt beyond the ocean, and he would be a bold man who should dare to say where on earth it could not possibly be felt. In like manner a war or a pestilence or a famine becomes the affair not only of those immediately interested but of all mankind. Or, to take an example on the other side. Let a new science, or a new machine, or a new art be produced on earth and in time the advantage which accrues is shared by all. Upon the lines of intercourse established by trade the literature, the learning, the sciences, the arts, the inventions of the old nations are carried to the new. The latter do not have to go over all the road of investigation and experiment. They receive and enjoy the results, and, unless the ideas thus transmitted are met by ignorance, and prejudice, they serve to bind the nations together and to secure steadiness and harmony in the culture of the race.

The doctrine before us, however, has bearing also upon individual policy and individual duty. It follows from the same principle that the acts of an individual cannot be restrained in their effects to himself, or to any group immediately about him. You do a good action and its fruits follow on in a series which you cannot follow or compute. They are reaped by those whom you do not know or have never seen. Or an evil action draws a train of consequences reaching on forever. As the action is good or evil so will its consequences be eternally. Good never produces evil nor evil good. A falsehood spoken now becomes a contribution to human sin and human woe. It comes back to you again and again in strange echoes, in distorted proportions, in ghastly colors, with a whole train of weird offspring, bad passions, bitter memories, and endless strife and confusion. If you could follow it what might you not find in its train? Broken friendships, blighted hopes, and perhaps a series of crimes. You may be sure that you will find no good thing. On the other hand you speak out the truth and though it seems to be neglected or despised you may trust it to go on and grow. In one mind it leaves a doubt, in another a hope, in another a wish, and at last a faith. It will grow and propagate and it will never bring forth anything evil. It may go from land to land or from pole to pole, but it will bring blessing wherever it goes. It is a contribution to human welfare. In the vast mass of such acts of which each human life is made up we have to see an infinite number of such influences which are continually arising, spreading, and falling again in places which we can never foresee, just as the moisture which arises from our locality in imperceptible particles is wafted away to fall again in places which we never know.

The sum of human good is the sum of all these acts of production, thought, and love. The sum of human ill is the sum of all our acts of neglect, folly, willfulness, and passion. They bind us together for time, and it may be for eternity, for the misery which falls upon my brother is the fruit of my sin, and the woe that I endure is the fruit of his. The misery of mankind is the correlative to the sin of mankind. Today the calamity is mine, tomorrow it is yours, and if we bow together in sorrow and penitence as our religion teaches us we only do what our reason also commands. When we exert ourselves to reclaim the erring, or rescue the fallen, we only try to pluck up one of the causes which sooner or later will produce a harvest of misery to mankind of which we shall have to bear our share. When we educate a neglected child we only avert a calamity which would otherwise fall on some men, perhaps upon ourselves. When we send the means of civilization to new countries, we only endeavor to plant good seed lest we should have to reap the evil crop which would otherwise grow there. It is this actual and inevitable bond uniting all mankind that science finds the grounds for teaching which has long enjoyed the authority of religion that man is his brother's keeper, that there is not a wrong anywhere which is not our business, nor a good anywhere in which we may not rejoice, nor ignorance anywhere which we ought not to help to dispel, nor an error anywhere against which it is not our duty to fight. Thus the doctrine of the solidarity of the human race throws a new light upon many of the vexed social questions of our time. It shows us the true form of self-interest, the mighty motive upon which modern society is more and more thoroughly established. Each man serves himself best in serving the whole. It shows us the *rationale* of philanthropy in all its forms, and rescues that duty from the control of irregular and unclear sentimentalism. It shows us the ground of missionary enterprise, and although it may alter materially some of the principles on which missions have been conducted hitherto and may reveal some of their mistakes, yet it goes far to justify the earnest, if not always wise, zeal of those who have labored for them. It shows us also the amount of truth involved in socialistic systems, and the true doctrine for which communists have been blindly groping, as well as the faults of that individualism to which the doctrine of self-interest, when not rationally interpreted, continually tends. Finally, it offers a better solution than any other theory I know of, of some of the mysteries of Divine Providence, especially in the relation of sin to misery. Why do the good suffer? Why do the wicked prosper? It is because we men are partners in sin and partners in suffering. The sin in the mass entails the suffering in the mass, and its distribution is not personal. It is by this law that men are bound together and that they acquire the closest and most vital interest in each others' wisdom, enlightenment, purity and diligence.

# II

## Educational Reformer

# The "Ways and Means" for Our Colleges

Written in early June 1870, this article was doubtless part of Sumner's campaign to win a chair at Yale, where his authorship was an open secret. However, editorial delay at the *Nation* foiled this aim. By the time the article appeared, Sumner was already installed in his new pulpit at Morristown, New Jersey. The article nonetheless voiced sentiments that allied him with the Young Yale movement. First published anonymously in the *Nation* 11 (September 8, 1870), 152–154; not previously reprinted.

The matter of university reform has been widely discussed in its various phases during the last few years. Those who are intimately acquainted with the affairs and workings of our colleges, and upon whom devolves the task of putting the suggestions in practical operation, know that the whole discussion hinges upon two questions: How much can we accomplish with the material which the schools supply? and, How much can we accomplish with the pecuniary means at our disposal? On the first of these questions it is not here proposed to say anything. We turn our attention to the second one. The colleges are now doing as much as they can do with the pecuniary means which they possess, and the question of doing more and better is a question of money.

The fact is well known to those who are acquainted with the affairs of Yale College, for example, that it is pecuniarily in the most straitened circumstances; in other words, that its pecuniary resources are strained to the utmost by the work which it is trying to accomplish. The demands upon its funds are continually increasing. The appliances of education are being continually improved and multiplied. The machinery of education has been improved as much within fifty years as the machinery of locomotion. The improved machinery, however, is expensive. A great deal of the fault which is found with the college resolves itself into this, that it is trying to turn out modern, highly-finished work with antiquated and clumsy machinery. People are dissatisfied with it just as they would be with a railroad run upon strap rail, with springless and cushionless cars, and rickety locomotives. The state of things can be improved only by the investment of capital, and the question is, how to raise the capital? It is a simple mercantile problem, neither more nor less, and as such it ought to be discussed.

It is worth while to see distinctly, by two or three examples, that we are right in asserting that the grounds for dissatisfaction are due to pecuniary weakness. The college is now using recitation-rooms which are as inconvenient and as ill-adapted for the uses to which they are put as if they had been built for stables. While our best modern school-houses are furnished with convenient rooms, fitted up expressly and ingeniously to serve the purposes of recitation, and provided with all the most finished appliances for the work of instruction, the rooms, furniture, maps, blackboards, etc., which are in use in college are those of thirty or forty years ago. The authorities of the college know this as well as the critics, graduate and undergraduate, who urge it upon their attention. They would be glad enough to make the proper alterations and improvements, but where is the money to come from? "The college," in the ordinary use of terms, is the faculty, or, at most, the corporation, but no one expects the individuals who compose these bodies to pay the bills, and if any one did, we shall see before we get through that there is the best reason in the world why this expectation should be disappointed.

The library stands among the most important of the instrumentalities of education. A good library belongs to the definition of a college or university. An institution which cannot buy the new books which are being continually produced in every department of science, is doomed to become a fossil. Weakness in this particular does not strike the popular mind, in its judgment of a college, so distinctly as weakness in many others, but there is no defect more fatal, or more important in the view of those who hold a high theory of what a college ought to be and do. The purchase of books, however, involves money resources, and we are thrown back again upon the same vulgar necessity.

The "tutorial system," as it is called, although it is very far from being a system, is one of the most vulnerable points of the institution. It is one of the things upon which adverse criticism fastens most frequently, and with the most pungency. It certainly is an antiquated and rickety machine for the work of education. The time when a college instructor fulfilled his duty if he looked on the book and saw that the young men repeated from memory what was written in it, has gone by. We now have a few men, at least, who hold another theory of the work of their office. The instructors who are now demanded are men of thought, research, and genius who can make books, or even dispense with them, and teach directly, personally, from an independent and original knowledge of the subject. Only such men can inspire enthusiasm and awaken interest.

They are as rare as the men of excellent qualifications for any other branch of work, but we need to find them and see that they are secured for their proper calling. A book is a dead thing. We have to make it answer because we cannot all come into personal relations with the scholar who wrote it and acquire the knowledge he has to impart with the added force and the added charm of his spoken words. A book which is crammed and recited to a man who hears it as a routine duty only is worse than dead, it is *killing*. Now, it is impossible, in the nature of things, that a young man who has only been out of college for a year or two, and has perhaps spent those years in some foreign pursuit, should come to the task of teaching, at a month's notice perhaps, with either the knowledge of human nature, or the power to enforce discipline, or the scientific culture, or the plain matter-of-fact information in regard to the subject, which the position requires. Still less is it to be expected that any large number of the persons so chosen shall turn out to have talents for this kind of work. This much is bad enough, but it is not the whole story. The schools address the best of the young graduates and try to secure them as teachers. They offer salaries to men only one or two years out of college which are sometimes twice as large as the tutors receive. When, at the end of three years, the college elects tutors, it finds that the most desirable men are either engaged in other pursuits, or are employed as teachers at such salaries that to take a tutorship would involve a heavy pecuniary sacrifice. Once the college could make its own terms. It could take only graduates of three years' standing, and could insist that they should stay for at least two years. Now it has to take men of two or even one year's standing, and they will not bind themselves to stay more than a year. What does this mean? Simply this: that the college offers remuneration which is below the market price for the article it wants. All things considered—the amount of labor, the "position," the opportunities for other work, the amount of compensation, etc.—the place is not attractive to the men who are desired. There may have been formerly a class of men who had the requisite talents and attainments, and who were willing to devote them gratuitously, or almost gratuitously, to the work of preparing the young men of the country to win fame and wealth in the learned professions. If such a class ever existed, it is now extinct. The laws of supply and demand, of the relation between price and quality, rule here as everywhere else. If you will not pay the market price of the article you want, you must take the inferior article which your money will buy. Professors or potatoes, the law is universal. If, therefore, this country does not want the higher education, let us ascertain that fact, and then it will make little difference whether the colleges are bad or good, and we can stop talking about them. If college and university education of a high character is wanted, let us make up our minds that we have got to *pay* for it the money which it is worth.

There is no such thing yet at Yale as an academical *career*. There is no course marked out for a man who feels called to this work, and desires to pursue it. To a young man who has the talents and industry which make him a candidate for a position of this kind, the *chance* of a tutorship at $900, and the still remoter chance of a professorship at $2,600 at the vanishing point in the vista of life, are not attractive. The impulsion of natural tastes is strong, but the chances are very slight, the individual has no means of working towards the end he desires to attain, he must "wait to be asked," and, when he foresees the unsentimental and pitiless regularity with which butchers' and bakers' bills will be presented, and also the size of them, he can hardly be considered mercenary if he turns away from his "calling." Most men, under these circumstances, vacillate between the pulpit and the professor's chair. The pulpit is a career, and one which offers, to men who have the choice between the two, superior pecuniary inducements. Many men, therefore, go into the pulpit, engage in parish work, cultivate the homiletical faculties, and form the habits of clergymen, and then are elected professors, and have to form new habits, cultivate other faculties, and train themselves to other pursuits than those into which their lives have already hardened. But we cannot have scholarships, fellowships, tutorships, and professorships, graduated into a career, gathering up all the proper talent and fitting it for this work, without money.

It is clear, then, that the question of college reform in some of the points in regard to which it is most pressingly urged, is a question of ways and means. It is *money*, or the want of it, which is the root of all the evil. It is also clear that the ordinary laws of trade and mercantile modes of thought have invaded a domain hitherto controlled, in great part at least, by sentimental considerations. Nobody expects that this sort of work will ever be attractive on account of its pecuniary return, or that any one will ever acquire wealth by it, but it is hard in these days and in this country to get men to choose poverty if they can escape it, and the position of a college professor nowadays is one of positive poverty. It is impossible for a man to live in any community without incurring money-debts, and if his labor, his contribution to the work of society, does not secure him such a money-return that he can discharge those debts, he cannot long maintain his self-respect or the respect of his fellow-men. This is a mercantile, not to say a mercenary, view of the subject, but the man who ignores it, although he may be very sentimental and self-sacrificing, must expect to face the question whether he is *honest* before he dies.

If, then, the great practical question as to the reform, and increased efficiency, of our colleges is one of ways and means, the question arises: What can we do about it? There are three plans worth noticing.

The first is the plan of *state appropriations*. This is substantially the plan of the German universities. It avoids the dangers which are inherent in wealthy endowments, and provides year by year for the current expenses. It assumes, however, that the state takes an enlightened pride and interest in its institutions of learning, that it appreciates their needs and provides for them liberally, and that it will continue to do so with regularity. The dangers of it, under our political system, are that the state will *not* take interest in the higher education, but will suffer it to languish, its interest being limited to popular education; that it will not provide regular and consistent control for the university on account of the continual changes in the *personnel* of the government; that the jealousies of different sectarian institutions will wreck the plan; and that the influence of political parties will control the appointments of the professors and the working of the institution. These dangers are so serious and so probable that this plan finds few supporters. The second plan is that of *endowments*. This is the plan now in operation, and it is unquestionably necessary at least to provide buildings and apparatus— the fixed capital of the institution. But endowments are essentially a mediaeval notion. The time has gone by when men believed that they would save their souls by diverting their property from their heirs to the foundations of a college. That faith was once universal in Western Europe. The English colleges owe their wealth to it. Since it lost its hold upon the minds of men, the fashion of endowing public charitable institutions has declined. It was already dead when the oldest American colleges were founded. The men who founded them did so from pure interest in the cause of education, but though they acted from another *motive*, they preserved the same *form* as the benefactors of the English colleges. We are still at work on the same system. We go begging the wealth of the country to act with equal liberality, and from the same motive, as the first founders of the colleges. In fact, however, it has not responded so as to keep pace with the growth of the country, the increased demands upon the institutions, and the increased expensiveness of the process of education. It is high time for us to look about us for another resource. We can find this resource only by observing the conditions of the case as enumerated above, and by adopting the forms which are familiar to existing society. We find that the wants of the college can be expressed in the crassest and most vulgar terms of the dialect of trade, and that they can be satisfied only by adopting business processes.

The third plan, therefore, is the *business* plan. This admits of two subdivisions. In the first place, when we get tired of waiting for the rich man's thousands, we can begin to take the poor man's dollars. We have examples enough before us of success in business which has been won by seeing that there was more money to be made out of the pennies of the million than out of the dollars of the upper ten thousand. No graduate of the college has ever paid in full what it cost the college to educate him. A part of the expense was borne by the funds given by former benefactors of the institution. A great many can never pay the debt. Very few can, in their turn, become munificent benefactors. There is a very large number, however, between these two, who can, and would cheerfully, give according to their ability, in order that the college might hold the same relative position to future generations which it held to their own. The sense of gratitude, the sense of responsibility, the enlightened interest in the cause of education, which are felt by these men, constitute a resource which has never yet been tried, but which would yield richly. They stand by as idle spectators while the college is applying to a few wealthy individuals. Their share in its labor now consists in simply rejoicing in its good luck when it succeeds. A *popular* effort, which should seize upon the indebtedness of these men to the institution and their interest in it, and make it yield money, would be a step in the right direction. We are familiar with popular efforts of this kind for other causes. It is time that we applied it here. If every graduate who could afford it should give the college ten dollars, and others should give more in proportion, we should enter on a plan whose financial soundness is unquestionable. We should be paying a debt which we all owe. We should be applying principles which are thoroughly in sympathy with the ideas of this popular and democratic age, and we should reach results which we never can attain by waiting for the tardy generosity of a few men of extraordinary wealth.

In the second place, the business plan requires that the men who enjoy the benefits of the institution should pay for them in money all that they cost in money. At present, we are going on the principle that education is a thing which ought to be given away, or, at least, partially given. We proceed on the theory that it is desirable that every man should have a college education, and so we *give* it to as many as possible as a free gift. Whether this plan encourages many to acquire the higher education upon whom it is not worth while to expend the labor and money, is a question we may here pass over. Many men who could not pay for an education, if it were sold as its full money cost, make the best use of it as things now are. If the price of tuition were to be raised so far as fully to remunerate the college for its outlay on each student, especially on the supposition that the college should secure the best talent for this work and pay for it, and should provide the most approved appliances, it would, no doubt, become a serious burden. Many are now compelled to secure remissions. This number would be increased. But why make the pride or the impecuniosity of some fix the rate of payment for all? Why should not those who can pay pay fully? The normal principle of the institution should be to ask those who enjoy its benefits to pay for them. When men come who want the benefits and cannot pay for them, express provision should be made for them by the beneficence of individuals. Why interfere with the business methods of the institution, for sentimental reasons, to accomplish sentimental ends? Business should be the rule, and sentiment the exception; not sentiment the rule, and the consequent financial and business weakness a constant source of complaint. In the financial statement of the college, the income from room-rents, tuition, etc., should stand over against the running expenses, and present a balance on the right side. If, then, any persons step in and make the payments for those who are unable to pay themselves, so much the better. It is the best form which their benevolence can take, and it is earnestly to be hoped that there may be so much generosity of this kind that no proper and deserving person need ever lose the benefit of the institution. The discussion of theories of university education must, of course, go on, and the theories must be tested by practice. With those matters of pure theory we have not here been concerned. There is, however, a great deal of loose and aimless criticism of the present state of things which has no practical value. Our aim has been to see where the root of the difficulty is, and how to deal with it. Our prejudices may keep us for a long time from following the plan here sketched out, but it is the only sound solution of the question of ways and means.

# What Our Boys Are Reading

During his student days Sumner found an emotional outlet in writing numerous short stories, including an action-adventure account of "Fernando the Chieftain of Northern Corsica" and a vaguely Irvingesque tale of "The Phantom Locomotive." As an adult, he enjoyed reading a good novel, his tastes running to the realists George Eliot and Thomas Hardy, rather than the moralistic Charles Dickens or "immoral" Alexandre Dumas, *fils.* "To write and read novels is perhaps the most royal road to teaching and learning which has ever been devised," he wrote in 1881. But he was disgusted by the vulgar, sensationalistic elements in boy's literature of the Gilded Age, a charge he leveled at the entire genre in this essay. Originally published in *Scribner's Monthly* 15 (1877–78), 681–685; reprinted as the introduction to *Books and Reading for the Young* by J. H. Smart (New York: Scribner's, 1880), and in *Earth Hunger,* ed. Albert Galloway Keller, pp. 367–377.

Few gentlemen who have occasion to visit news offices can have failed to notice the periodical literature for boys, which has been growing up during the last few years. The increase in the number of these papers and magazines, and the appearance from time to time of new ones which, to judge by the pictures, are always worse than the old, seem to indicate that they find a wide market. Moreover, they appear not only among the idle and vicious boys in great cities, but also among schoolboys whose parents are careful about the influences brought to bear on their children. No student of social phenomena can pass with neglect facts of this kind—so practical and so important in their possible effects on society.

These periodicals contain stories, songs, mock speeches, and negro minstrel dialogues—and nothing else. The literary material is either intensely stupid, or spiced to the highest degree with sensation. The stories are about hunting, Indian warfare, California desperado life, pirates, wild sea adventure, highwaymen, crimes and horrible accidents, horrors (tortures and snake stories), gamblers, practical jokes, the life of vagabond boys, and the wild behavior of dissipated youths in great cities. This catalogue is exhaustive—there are no other stories. The dialogue is short, sharp, and continuous. It is broken by the minimum of description and by no preaching. It is almost entirely in slang of the most exaggerated kind, and of every variety—that of the sea, of California, and of the Bowery; of negroes, "Dutchmen," Yankees, Chinese, and Indians, to say nothing of that score of the most irregular and questionable occupations ever followed by men. When the stories even nominally treat the school-life they say nothing of *school*-life. There is simply a succession of practical jokes, mischief, outrages, heroic but impossible feats, fighting and horrors, but nothing about the business of school, any more than if the house in which the boys live were a summer boarding-house. The sensational incidents in these stories are introduced by force, apparently for the mere purpose of producing a highly spiced mixture.

One type of hero who figures largely in these stories is the vagabond boy in the streets of a great city, in the Rocky Mountains, or at sea. Sometimes he has some cleverness in singing, dancing, or ventriloquism, or negro acting, and he gains a precarious living while roving about. This vagabond life of adventure is represented as interesting and enticing, and when the hero rises from vagabond life to flash life, that is represented as success. Respectable home life, on the other hand, is not depicted at all and is only referred to as stupid and below the ambition of a clever youth. Industry and economy in some regular pursuit, or in study, are never mentioned at all. Generosity does not consist in even luxurious expenditure, but in wasting money. The type seems to be that of the gambler, one day "flush," and wasteful, another day ruined and in misery.

There is another type of boy who sometimes furnishes the hero of a story, but who also figures more or less in all of them. That is the imp of mischief—the sort of boy who is an intolerable nuisance to the neighborhood. The stories are told from the standpoint of the boy, so that he seems to be a fine fellow, and all the world, which is against him, is unjust and overbearing. His father, the immediate representative of society, executes its judgments with the rod, which again is an insult to the high-spirited youth and produces on his side either open war or a dignified retreat to some distant region.

These stories are not markedly profane, and they are not obscene. They are indescribably vulgar. They represent boys as engaging all the time in the rowdy types of drinking. The heroes are either swaggering, vulgar swells of the rowdy style, or they are in the vagabond mass below the rowdy swell. They are continually associating with criminals, gamblers, and low people who live by their wits. The theater of the stories is always disreputable. The proceedings and methods of persons of the criminal and disreputable classes who appear in the stories, are all described in detail, so that the boy reader obtains a theoretical and literary acquaintance with methods of fraud and crime. Sometimes drunkenness is represented in its disgrace and misery but generally drinking is represented as jolly and entertaining, and there is no suggestion that boys who act as the boys in these stories do ever have to pay any penalty for it in after life. The persons who are held up to admiration are the heroes and heroines of bar rooms, concert saloons, variety theaters, and negro minstrel troupes.

A few illustrations may serve to bring out some of the foregoing statements. One of the school stories before us has a "local color" which is purely English, although the names are Americanized. The mixture is ridiculous in the extreme. The hero is the son of a "country gentleman" of Ohio, and comes to school with an old drunkard, "ex-butler" of the Ohio country gentleman, whom he allows to join him at the Grand Central Depot. This scandalous old rascal is kept in the story apparently because an old drunkard is either a good instrument or a good victim for practical jokes. The hero goes to dine with a gentleman whose place, near the school, is called the "Priory." While waiting for dinner he goes out for a stroll in the "Park." He rescues a girl from drowning, sends back to school for another suit of clothes, goes out again and takes a ride on a bison, is thrown off, strikes, in falling, a professor, who is fortunately fat enough to break his fall, goes to the "snake house" with the professor, is fascinated by the rattlesnake which gets loose, seizes the reptile and throws it away after it has bitten through the professor's trousers—all before dinner. All the teachers, of course, are sneaks and blackguards. In this same story, one of the assistant teachers (usher, he is called) gets drunk and insults the principal, whereupon the latter, while he directs some of the boys to work a garden pump, holds the nozzle and throws water on the assistant, who lies helplessly drunk on the grass—all of which is enforced by a picture. There is not a decent good boy in the story; there is not even the old type of sneaking good boy. The sneaks and bullies are all despicable in the extreme. The heroes are continually devising mischief which is mean and cruel, but which is here represented as smart and funny. They all have a daredevil character, and brave the principal's rod as one of the smallest dangers of life. There is a great deal of the traditional English brutality in exaggerated forms. The nearest approach to anything respectable is that *after* another boy has been whipped for mischief done by the hero, the latter tells an accomplice that they ought to have confessed, whereat the friend replies with the crushing rejoiner that then there would only have been three flogged instead of one.

A character very common in these stories is the city youth, son of a rich father who does not give his son as much pocket-money as the latter considers suitable. This constitutes stinginess on the father's part, although it might be considered pardonable, seeing that these young men drink champagne every day, treat the crowd generally when they drink, and play billiards for one hundred dollars a game. The father, in this class of stories, is represented as secretly vicious and hypocritically pious. In the specimen of this class before us the young man is "discovered" in the police court as a prisoner, whence he is remanded to the Tombs. He has been arrested for collaring a big policeman, to prevent him from overtaking a girl charged with pocket-picking. He interfered because he judged from the girl's face that she was innocent, and it is suggested, for future development in the story, that she was running away from insult and that the cry of "stop thief" was to get help from the police and others to seize her. The hero, who is in prison under an assumed name, now sends for his father's clerk and demands one thousand dollars, saying that otherwise he will declare his real name and disgrace the family. He gets the money. He then sends for a notorious Tombs lawyer, to whom he gives five hundred dollars, and with this sum his release is easily procured. He then starts with his cousin to initiate the latter into life in New York. They go to a thieves' college, where they see a young fellow graduated—his part consists of taking things from pockets of a hanging figure, to the garments of which bells are attached, without causing the bells to ring. Of this a full-page illustration is given. The two young men then go up to the Bowery to a beer saloon, where the hero sustains his character by his vulgar familiarity with the girl waiters. Next they hear a row in a side street; they find a crowd collected watching a woman who hangs from a third-story window, while her drunken husband beats and cuts her hands to make her fall. The hero solves this situation by drawing his revolver and shooting the man. As he and his companion withdraw unobserved, the former wards off the compliments of the latter by saying modestly that he could not bear to stand there and see such a crowd looking on and not knowing what to do, so he just did the proper thing. Next day the hero, meeting the thieves' college graduate in the corridor of the Fifth Avenue Hotel, agrees to receive and hold for him any booty he may seize in the bar room, which he does. At night he and his friend go to a disreputable masked ball, where the hero recognizes his father in disguise amongst the dancers. Securing a place in the same set, during a pause in the dance he snatches the mask from his own face and his father's at the same moment. This edifying incident is enforced by a full-page illustration. A friend suggests the question: what demon of truthfulness makes the artist put such brutal and vulgar faces on the men? In this class of stories, fathers and sons are represented as natural enemies, and the true position for the son is that of suspicion and armed peace.

Here, again, is a story of a boy who is left in charge of a country grocery store. To amuse his leisure he takes a lump of butter from the stock and greases the platform in front of the store. Several village characters, among them an old maid, the parson, and the squire, come to perform on this arena for the amusement of the youth and one or two of his friends. While the squire is trying to get up or get off the platform, the owner of the grocery returns and he and the squire have a fight on the grass-plot over the question whether the grocer greased his own platform or not. Next comes Nemesis in the shape of the boy's father. The conversation between the two, and the denouement, may be worth quoting. In the soliloquy at the end there seems to be a reminiscence of Fisk.

"James," said he, "you are breaking my heart with your incorrigible conduct."

"Is dat a chowder-gag?" calmly inquired Jimmy.

"Slang—slang, always slang!" groaned his father. "James, will you never reform?"

"Don't wanter; I'm good enough now."

"Think of what you might be, a pattern boy, a—"

"Brass-bound angel, silver-plated cherub, little tin missionary on rollers," put in Jimmy, apparently in confidence to a fly on the ceiling.

"Actually sassing his protector," the deacon said. "Oh, James, you wicked son of Belial."

"Pop's name is Dennis, and he was a short-haired Cincinnati ham," indignantly corrected Jimmy. "I don't know anybody named Belial."

The deacon made a horrified mouth.

"Will you never hearken in quietude and meekness of spirit to words of reproval and advice?" said he.

"Darned sight ruther listen to funny stories," muttered Jimmy.

"You are hopeless," sighed the deacon, "and I shall have to chastise you."

"Dat means a week's soreness," Jimmy reflected; then he changed his tune. "Let me off this time, dad, and I'll be the best boy you ever saw after dis. Stay in nights, stop chewing tobacco, clean my teeth every morning, and welt the life out of anybody dat won't say their prayers regular and go to church every day in the week."

The deacon nodded his head the wrong way.

"You can't play that on the old man again," he said; "it's lost its varnish, it's played out. Step up, my son."

Unwillingly Jimmy stepped up.

In a moment he was stepping up more than ever, for the deacon was pelting him all over with a stout switch, which felt the reverse of agreeable.

But finally he was released and crawled dolefully up to bed.

There are things nicer than going to bed at four o'clock on a bright, breezy, fall day, and Jimmy knew so.

"This here is getting awful stale," he meditated, rolling and tossing in his cot, "and you can smother me with fish-cakes if I stand it. I'm going to run away, and come back to dis old one-hoss town when I'm a man, in a gold-band wagon with silver wheels and six Maltese mules a-drawing it. Probably the old man will be in the poorhouse then, swallerin' shadow soup with an iron spoon, and it will make him cranky to think dat he didn't used ter let me have my own way and boss things. Yes, by golly, I'll give him the sublime skip."

The songs and dialogues are almost all utterly stupid. The dialogues depend for any interest they have on the most vapid kind of negro minstrel buffoonery. The songs, without having any distinct character, seem often to be calculated to win applause from tramps and rioters. The verse, of all before us, which has the most point to it, is the following. What the point is requires no elucidation:

> Boss Tweed is a man most talked about now,
> His departure last winter caused a great row;
> Of course we all knew it was not a square game,
> But show me the man who would not do the same.
>
> When Sweeney, Genet, and Dick Connolly took flight,
> He stood here alone and made a good fight;
> He did wrong, but when poor men were greatly in need,
> The first to assist them was William M. Tweed.

From the specimens which we have examined we may generalize the following in regard to the views of life which these stories inculcate and the code of morals and manners which they teach.

The first thing which a boy ought to acquire is physical strength for fighting purposes. The feats of strength performed by these youngsters in combat with men and animals is ridiculous in the extreme. In regard to details the supposed code of English brutality prevails, especially in the stories which have English local color, but it is always mixed with the code of the revolver, and in many of the stories the latter is taught in its fullness. These youngsters generally carry revolvers and use them at their good discretion; every youth who aspires to manliness ought to get and carry a revolver.

A boy ought to cheat the penurious father who does not give him as much money as he finds necessary, and ought to compel him to pay. A good way to force him to pay liberally, and at the same time to stop criticizing his son's habits, is to find out his own vices (he always has some) and then to levy blackmail on him. Every boy who does not want to be "green" and "soft," ought to "see the elephant." All fine manly young fellows are familiar with the actors and singers at variety theaters and the girl waiters at concert saloons. As to drinking, the bar room code is taught. The boys stop in at bar rooms all along the street, swallow drinks standing or leaning with rowdy grace on the bar, treat and are treated, and consider it insulting to refuse or to be refused. The good fellows meet every one on a footing of equality—above all in a bar room.

Quiet home life is stupid and unmanly; boys brought up in it never know the world or life. They have to work hard and to bow down to false doctrines which parsons and teachers in league with parents have invented against boys. To become a true man, a boy must break with respectability and join the vagabonds and the swell mob. No fine young fellow who knows life need mind the law, still less the police—the latter are all stupid louts. If a boy's father is rich and has money, he can easily find smart lawyers (advertisement gratis) who can get the boy out of prison and will dine with him at Delmonico's afterward. The sympathies of a manly young fellow are with criminals against the law, and he conceals crime when he can. Whatever good or ill happens to a young man he should always be gay—the only ills in question are physical pain or lack of money and these should be borne with gaiety and indifference, but should not alter the philosophy of life.

As to the rod, it is not so easy to generalize. Teachers and parents in these stories act faithfully up to Solomon's precept. When a father flogs his son, the true doctrine seems to be that the son should run away and seek a life of adventure. When he does this he has no difficulty in finding friends, or in living by his wits, so that he makes money and comes back rich and glorious, to find his father in the poorhouse.

These periodicals seem to be intended for boys from twelve to sixteen years of age, although they often treat of older persons. Probably many boys outgrow them and come to see the folly and falsehood of them. It is impossible, however, that so much corruption should be afloat and not exert some influence. We say nothing of the great harm which is done to boys of that age, by the nervous excitement of reading harrowing and sensational stories, because the literature before us only participates in that harm with other literature of far higher pretensions. But what we have said suffices to show that these papers poison boys' minds with views of life which are so base and false as to destroy all manliness and all chances of true success. How far they are read by boys of good home influences we are, of course, unable to say. They certainly are within the reach of all; they can be easily obtained, and easily concealed, and it is a question for parents and teachers how far this is done. Persons under those responsibilities ought certainly to know what the character of this literature is.

# Our Colleges before the Country

In the battle over admissions requirements and electives, Charles Francis Adams, Jr., in the summer of 1883 termed Harvard's requirement in Greek "A College Fetich." Soliciting replies, the *Princeton Review* turned to Sumner and George P. Fisher, his Yale colleague and close friend. In his contribution, Sumner criticized the classical curriculum, while also making the case for limiting electives. Originally published in the *Princeton Review* n.s., 13 (March 1884), 127–140; reprinted in *War*, ed. Albert Galloway Keller, pp. 355–373.

There is no subject which is to-day so submerged in cant and humbug as education. Both primary and secondary education are suffering from this cause, but in different ways. Primary education is afflicted by the cant and humbug of progress and innovation, and secondary education is afflicted by the cant and humbug of conservatism and toryism. The former affliction is less grievous than the latter, because it pertains to life—may proceed from an excess of vitality; the latter pertains to death and leads down to it.

It is not my present intention to discuss primary education, but it belongs to my subject to notice one fact in the relation of secondary to primary education. There is a notion prevalent in college circles that the colleges have an important public duty to perform in marking out the line of study for the preparatory schools, and in keeping them up to their duty. It seems to me that this is a mischievous notion. The high-schools and academies of the country are doing their duty far better than the colleges are doing theirs. The teachers in the schools have as high a standard of duty as the teachers in the colleges, and the former have more care and zeal to devise and adopt good methods than the latter. Methods of instruction are yet employed in colleges which have long been discarded in the schools, and, if either has anything to learn from the other, it is the colleges which need instruction from the schools. The colleges, by their requirements, do exercise a certain control over the curriculum of the schools. It is an open question whether this control is generally beneficial to the education of the young men of the country. If the colleges have prescribed courses of study, and if the schools have to follow a prescribed course of study leading up to it, then a few gentlemen with strong prejudices and limited experience of life obtain power to set up a canon of what things may be taught and learned in the country. That such a power has been possessed and used, that it still remains to a great extent unbroken, and that it is purely mischievous, I take to be facts beyond contradiction. In no civilized country is mandarinism in education so strong as in the United States. Its stronghold is in the colleges, and they use such control as they possess to establish it in the schools. One great gain of the reform which is not needed in the colleges would be that they would confine themselves to their own functions and leave the academies and high-schools to follow their own legitimate development.

I ought not to speak as if there had been no improvement in American colleges within a generation. It is well known that, both by founding new institutions and reforming old ones, great improvements have been made. A great college has a life of its own. It grows by its own vital powers and pushes on even the most timid or reactionary of its *personnel*. Probably bigotry and stupidity could kill it in time. One knows of ancient seats of learning which have met that fate. But it does not come all at once. Still, I believe that if the question whether the college course had been valuable, had been raised in a class of graduates twenty or fifty years ago, more would have said that they looked back upon it as a grand advantage than would say so now.

It is affirmed, and from such evidence as has come to my knowledge I believe it to be true, that the youth of the country do not care for a university education as the youth of former generations did. They consider that a high-school education is education enough. They do not look upon the colleges as offering anything of high and specific value which it is worth four years' time and a large expenditure of capital to get. Of course there has always been a large class of people who despised a culture which they never understood. The present temper of the youth and their parents is, as I understand it, a very different thing. They look upon the colleges as the gate of admission to a caste of people who are technically "educated" and "cultivated," who have a kind of free-masonry of culture amongst themselves, but who are not educated or cultivated, if we take those words in any liberal and rational sense, any better than large masses of people who are not college graduates, and so not members of the gild of the learned. Facts are indisputable that free and generous familiarity with the best thought and knowledge of the time, as well as intellectual power, activity, and elasticity, are displayed by men who have never visited a university, but have devoted time judiciously to intellectual pursuits. Therefore a notion has found place that college training only confers artificial accomplishments which serve to mark the members of the learned caste. Once it was thought that the only learning fit for a gentleman was heraldry, and that his only accomplishments should be those of arms, music, and gallantry. A flunkey once said that a certain woman could not be a lady: she played the piano so well that she must have been educated for a governess. In the old gilds a man could only become a master by producing a very costly and useless masterpiece. A belle in Siam lets her finger-nails grow inches long, so that she cannot even dress herself, and everyone who sees her knows that she is helpless and elegant. All these instances, heterogeneous as they are, have elements in common with each other and with the traditional work of our colleges. They present the notion that what is useful is vulgar, that useless accomplishments define a closed rank of superior persons, and that entrance into that rank should be made difficult. However, we live in a day and a country where these notions have only a feeble footing. Our people are likely to turn away with a smile and go on to things which are of use and importance, and no elegance of rhetoric and poetry, devising subtle and far-fetched explanations of the real utility of classical accomplishments, will avail to hold them. So I take to be the significance of the fact that the youth do not appreciate a college education or feel an eager desire for it as their fathers did. I have heard it argued that it is a great misfortune that the boys should be contented with a high-school education and should not care to go to college; also that something should be done to persuade them to seek a college education. I do not so argue. A college or school ought to stand on its own footing as a blessing to anybody who can get its advantages, and its advantages ought to be so obvious and specific that they should advertise themselves. If a college does not offer such advantages that anyone who can may gladly seize them, then the young men may better not enter it. If special inducements are necessary to persuade men to go to college, then the condemnation of the college is pronounced. It has no reason to exist.

It is no doubt true that a classical education once gave a man a positive and measurable advantage in the career which he might choose in life. At a time when the sciences which teach us to know the world in which we live were still in their infancy; when the studies by which the mind is trained to high, strict, and fearless thinking were as yet undeveloped; when history was still only a record of curious and entertaining incidents in war and diplomacy; when modern civil institutions were yet in many respects below the standard of the ancients, and still on the same military basis; when no notion of law had yet found footing in the conception of society—at such a time no doubt study of classical types and models was valuable; ideas were obtained from an old treasure-house which could not have been obtained from the experience of actual life; literary culture was the only possible discipline; grammar stood first as a training in thought and expression; formal logic was a practical tool; perhaps even introspective metaphysics was not entirely a scholastic and dialectic exercise. In those times a young man who possessed a classical education, with a few touches of metaphysics and theology to finish it off, was put on a true superiority to his uneducated contemporaries as regarded his stock of ideas, his powers of expression, his horizon of knowledge, and the general liberality of his attitude towards life. He felt this his whole life long. It made him earnestly grateful to the institution which had educated him. Every young man who grew up saw distinctly the superior advantages which a college man possessed, and, if he felt at all fit for it, was eager to win the same advantage. There certainly never has been, in the United States, any appreciation of the rose-water arguments about "culture" which are now put forward in defense of classical training. We, when we were boys, sought classical training because it was *the* training which then put the key of life in our hands, and because we saw positive and specific advantages which we could obtain by it.

At the present time all is altered, and the changes which have come about have made necessary a great change in the character of our colleges, in their courses of study, and in their whole attitude towards the public. I do not say that they need to come into direct and close relations with the life of the nation to-day: I say that they must take heed to themselves lest they fall out of that intimate relation to the life of the nation in which they once stood, and out of which they have no importance or value at all. A college which is a refuge for mere academicians, threshing over the straw of a dead learning, is no better than a monastery. Men who believe that they can meet the great interests of mankind which to-day demand satisfaction, by a complacent reference to what satisfied them when they were young, are simply building for themselves a fool's paradise.

It must be said here that college officers are, for many reasons, unfit for college management. They are exposed to all the pitfalls of every pedagogue. They have to guard themselves against the vices of dogmatism, pedantry, hatred of contradiction, conceit, and love of authority. They, of course, come each to love his own pursuit beyond anything else on earth. Each thinks that a man who is ignorant of *his* specialty is a barbarian. As a man goes on in life under this discipline he becomes more self-satisfied and egotistical. He has little contact with active life; gets few knocks; is rarely forced into a fight or into a problem of diplomacy; gets to hate care or interruption, and loves routine. Men of this type, of course, are timid, and even those traits which are most admirable in the teacher becomes vices in the executive officer. Such men are always over-fond of *a priori* reasoning and fall helpless the moment they have to face a practical undertaking. They have the whole philosophy of heaven and earth reduced, measured out, and done up in powders, to be prescribed at need. They know just what ought to be studied, in what amount and succession of doses. That is to say, they are prepared to do any amount of mischief at a juncture when the broadest statesmanship is needed to guide the development of a great institution. Certainly the notion that any body of men can now regulate the studies of youth by what was good for themselves twenty, forty, or sixty years ago is one which is calculated to ruin any institution which they control. It is always a hard test of the stuff men are made of when they are asked to admit that a subject of which they have had control would profit by being taken out of their control and intrusted to liberty.

On the other hand, the system of heterogeneous and nondescript electives, jumbled together without coordination of any kind, and offered to the choice of lazy youth, can never command the confidence of sober teachers. A university ought to teach everything which anybody wants to know. Such is the old idea of a university—a universe of letters. It ought to give complete liberty in the choice of a *line* or *department* of study, but it ought to prescribe rigidly what studies must be pursued in the chosen department by anyone who wants its degree. A Yale diploma ought not to mean that a man knows everything, for that would be absurd; nor that he knows "something about the general principles" of all those things which "every educated man ought to know," for this is a formula for superficiality and false pretence. It ought to mean that he has acquired knowledge in some one line of study, sufficient to entitle him to be enrolled amongst the graduates of the institution, and the college ought to define strictly the kind and quantity of attainment which it considers sufficient, in that line or department, to earn its degree.

Now, however, the advocates of the old classical culture, ignoring or ignorant of all the change which has come over human knowledge and philosophy within fifty years, come forward to affirm that that culture still is the best possible training for our young men and the proper basis for the work of our colleges. How do they know it? How can anybody say that one thing or another is just what is needed for education? Can we not break down this false and stupid notion that it is the duty of a university, not to teach whatever anyone wants to know, but to prescribe to everybody what he ought to want to know? Some years ago, at a school meeting in one of our cities, a gentleman made an argument against the classics. A distinguished clergyman asked him across the room whether he had ever studied the classics. He replied that he had not. "I thought not," replied the clergyman, as he sat down. He was thought to have won a great victory, but he had not. His opponent should have asked him whether he had ever studied anything else. Where is the man who has studied beyond the range of the classical culture who retains his reverence for that culture as superior to all other for the basis of education? No doubt a man of classical training often looks back with pleasure and gratitude to his own education and feels that it has been of value to him; but when he draws an inference, either that no other course of discipline would have been worth more to himself, or that no other discipline can be generally more useful as a basis of education, he forms a judgment on a comparison one branch of which is to him unknown.

I am not in the same position on this question as that held by certain other writers of the day. I may say that I profited fairly by a classical education. I believe that I am in a position to form a judgment as to how much is truth and how much is humbug in the rhapsodies about the classics to which we are treated. The historical sciences and language will always have great value for certain classes of scholars. Clergymen will always need the ancient languages as a part of their professional training. Teachers in certain departments will always need them. No professor of modern languages could be considered equipped for his work if he were unacquainted with Greek and Latin. Philologists and special students in the science of language contribute in a high degree and in an indispensable manner to the stock of our knowledge. Literary men and some kinds of journalists, classes who are sure in the future to seek a more special and detailed training than they have enjoyed in the past, will find utility in classical study. All these classes need, not less Greek and Latin than hitherto, but more. One evil result of trying to force the classics on everybody is that those for whom the classics have value cannot get as much of them as they need. Of modern languages, two at least are to-day indispensable to an educated man. As nations come nearer to each other, and as their literatures grow richer and richer, the need of being able to step over the barrier of language becomes greater. It is easy for anyone who watches the course of things to see how, from one decade to another, the necessity of learning the modern languages makes itself more distinctly felt. Those languages were formerly accomplishments. Now they are necessities for anyone who intends to pursue literary or scientific work, or even practical work in many departments. Hence language will always enter into the scope of education, especially in its elementary stages. Latin has especial utility and advantage. If one wanted to learn three or four modern languages, it might pay him to learn Latin first, and Latin will always have value for an introduction to the ancient classical world. Greek is a rich and valuable accomplishment to any man of literary or philological tastes, or to an orator or public debater, or to anyone who needs the art of interpretation. I know of no study which will in general develop gifts of expression, or chasten literary style, like the study of Greek. That language more than any other teaches the delicate power of turns in the phrase, of the collocation of words, of emphasis, of subtle shading in synonyms and adjectives. Then, too, surely no student of politics and political economy can pass over the subject-matter of Aristotle, or Demosthenes and the orators, nor the life and polity of the Greek State.

When, however, all this is admitted in regard to the uses of a classical training, what does it prove in regard to the claims of the classics to be made the basis of all higher education or the toll which everyone must pay before he can be admitted to the gild of the learned? Nothing at all. I have known splendid Greek scholars who could not construct a clear and intelligible argument of six sentences. They always become entangled in subtleties of phrase and super-refinement of words. I have known other great Greek scholars who wrote an English which was so dull that scarcely anyone could read it. On the other hand, there are men whose names are household words wherever the English language is spoken because they can say what they mean in clear, direct, and limpid English, although they have never had any classical culture at all. I have known whole classes to graduate at our colleges who have never read a line of Aristotle, and who had not a single correct notion about the life and polity of the Greeks. Men graduate now all the time who know nothing of Greek history and polity but the fragments which they pick out of the notes on the authors which they read. It is grotesque to talk about the recondite charms and graces of classical culture when one knows what it amounts to for all but here and there one. It is a rare thing for a man to graduate who has read Grote or Curtius, although he has studied Greek for five or six years. Anyone who reads no Greek and never goes to college, but reads Grote or Curtius, knows far more of Greek life, polity, and culture than any but the most exceptional college graduate. I do not believe that this was formerly true. It appears that faithful students in former times used such means as then existed for becoming familiar with classical life and history far more diligently than is now customary. Classical studies, having sunk to a perfunctory character, now stand in the way of faithful study of anything.

I go further, and if the classics are still proposed as the stem of a liberal education, to be imposed upon every student who seeks a university training, I argue that classical culture has distinct and mischievous limitations. The same may no doubt be said of any other special culture, and whenever any other culture is put forward as possessing some exclusive or paramount value, it will be put in order to show that fact. I do not doubt that I gained great profit from a classical training. Part of the profit I was conscious of. I think it very likely that I won other profit of which I was unconscious. I know that it cost me years of discipline to overcome the limitations of the classical training and to emancipate my mind from the limited range of processes in which it had been trained. For the last ten years I have taught political economy to young men of twenty-one years or thereabouts who had been prepared for me by training in a curriculum based on classics. They have acquired certain facilities. They have a facility in "recitation" which is not always produced by familiarity with the subject. The art of recitation is an art all by itself. Very often it is all a man has won from his college training. Sometimes it consists in beating out a little very thin, so as to make it go a great way; sometimes it consists in "going on one's general information," and profiting to the utmost by any hint in the question; sometimes it consists in talking rapidly about something else than the question. Some men never can come to a point, but soar in lofty circles around and over the point, showing that they have seen it from a distance; others present rags and tags of ideas and phrases, showing that they have read the text and that here and there a word has stuck in the memory without sequence or relation. The habit of reading classics with a "pony" for years has produced these results. Many of these men must be regarded with pity because their mental powers have been miseducated for years, and when they try to acquire something, to make it their own, to turn it into a concise and correct statement and utter it again, they cannot do it. They have only acquired some tricks of speech and memory.

The case of men who have studied honestly, but who have been educated almost exclusively on grammar, is different. No doubt they have
gained a great deal, but I find that they hardly ever know what a "law"
is in the scientific sense of the word. They think that it is like a rule in
grammar, and they are quite prepared to find it followed by a list of
exceptions. They very often lack vigor and force in thinking. They either
accept authority too submissively, if the notion which is presented does
not clash with any notions they had received before, or if they argue,
they do so on points of dialectical ingenuity. They do not join issue
closely and directly, and things do not fall into order and range in their
minds. They seem to be quite contented to take things and hold them
in a jumble. It is rare to find one who has scholarship enough to look
up a historical or biographical reference. It is generally assumed by them
that if "no lesson has been given out" they have nothing to do. One of
the most peculiar notions is that a "lecture" has no such importance as
a "recitation"; that to cut the former is of no consequence, but that to
cut the latter is serious. In short, the habits and traditions in which men
have been trained when they reach senior year in college are such that
they are yet boys in responsibility, and, although they are very manly
and independent in many respects, they are dependent and unmanly in
their methods of study, in their conceptions of duty, in their scholarship,
and in their code of conduct in all that effects the institution. It has been
claimed for the classics that they give guidance for conduct. This is, to
me, the most amazing claim of all, for, in my experience and observation,
the most marked fact about classical culture is that it gives no guidance
in conduct at all.

In contrast with what I have stated, it is most important to notice that,
in every class, men distinguish themselves in political economy who
have been very poor scholars in the classics and have lost whatever
mental drill a classical training might have given.

I shall be asked whether I attribute the facts which I have mentioned
about the mental habits of students to the study of classics. Evidently
many of them are attributable to a system of school discipline continued
until a too advanced age, and to a puerile system of discipline. Others
are due to a text-book and recitation-with-marks system which breeds
into a man unscholarly ideas and methods. But I affirm from my own
experience and observation that the most serious of the mental faults
and bad intellectual habits which I have described are caused by a training which is essentially literary, grammatical, and metaphysical. No
doubt it is true that a large fraction of the men will shirk work; that they

are slovenly in all their mental habits; that they will be as idle as they dare; that they seize gladly upon a chance to blame somebody else or "the system" for their own shortcomings. These facts, however, belong only to the imperfection of all things earthly. They are true; but if they are put forward as an excuse for routine and neglect on the part of the university authorities, then those authorities simply lower themselves to the level of the bad students. A rigid discipline in prescribed tasks, with especial care for the dull scholars, is in place for youth up to a certain age, but in any good system of education the point must be judiciously chosen at which this system shall yield to a system of individual responsibility. The point at which this change should be made is certainly some years before the point at which young men become men by the laws of their country. That more responsibility would bring out more character is beyond question. The present method of prolonging tutelage and inculcating character by big doses of "moral science" is certainly a failure. I maintain that it is an impertinence for any authority whatever to withhold from young men twenty years of age anything which they desire to learn, or to impose upon them anything whatever which the authority is question thinks they ought to know.

The tendency of classical studies is to exhalt authority, and to inculcate reverence for what is written rather than for what is true. Men educated on classics are apt to be caught by the literary form, if it is attractive. They are fond of paradoxes, and will entertain two contradictory ideas, if only each come in a striking literary dress. They think that they prove something when they quote somebody who has once said it. If anyone wants to keep out "new ideas," he does well to cling to classical studies. They are the greatest barrier to new ideas and the chief bulwark of modern obscurantism. The new sciences have produced in their votaries an unquenchable thirst and affection for what is true in fact, word, character, and motive. They have taught us to appreciate and weigh evidence and to deal honestly with it. Here a strong contrast with classical training has been developed, not because classical training led men to be false, but because the scientific love of truth is something new and intense. Men of classical training rarely develop the power to go through from the beginning to end of a course of reasoning on a straight line. They go on until they see that they are coming out at a result which they do not like. Then they make a bend and aim for a result which they do like, not regarding the broken continuity, or smoothing it over as carefully as possible. Classical training, in the world of to-day, gives a man a limited horizon. There is far more beyond it than within it. He is taught to believe that he has sounded the depths of human knowledge when he knows nothing about its range or amount. If anyone wants to find prime specimens of the Philistinism which Matthew Arnold hates, he should seek them among the votaries of the culture which Matthew Arnold loves. The popular acuteness long ago perceived this, and the vile doctrines of anti-culture have sprung up and grown just in proportion as culture has come to have an artificial and technical definition, as something foreign to living interests.

An American college ought to be the seat of all the learning which would be of value to an American man in the American life of to-day. It ought to offer that training which would draw out and discipline the mental powers which are to-day useful. It ought to offer to its pupils an opportunity of becoming acquainted with all which is, or is coming to be, in the great world of thought, and it ought to offer such opportunities that those who profited by them faithfully would be highly trained men, drilled and disciplined for any of the tasks of life. If a college were such a place as this, its usefulness would be recognized at once. Every young man in the country would desire, if possible, to enjoy its advantages, because he would feel that, if he could get a college education, he would be as it were lifted upon a higher plane for all work of his subsequent life, no matter what career he might choose. His ambition would have won a new footing. In the competition of life he would have won new skill and new weapons. No college can possibly take any such place if it "clings to the classics." In face of the facts it is ludicrous to talk about maintaining the old classical culture. We might as well talk of wearing armor or studying alchemy. During the last fifty years all the old sciences have been reconstructed and a score of new ones have been born. Shall a man be educated now at our highest seats of learning and not become acquainted with these facts and doctrines which are revolutionizing the world of knowledge? Shall he only be allowed a bit here and a fragment there, or spend his best years in pursuits which end in themselves? In every journal or conversation, and in many sermons, topics are treated which belong to the substance of modern thinking. Shall the colleges ignore these topics, or only refer to them in order to preach them down?

History does not any longer mean what it meant twenty years ago. As a disciplinary pursuit it has changed entirely from any exercise of memory to an analysis and investigation of relations and sequences. Constitutional history has grown into a great branch of study of the highest importance to the student of law, political science, jurisprudence, and sociology. It has totally altered the point of view and mode of conceiving of those subjects since the days when the study of them began with the classical authors. The years spent on Greek grammar and literature would be priceless to the whole mass of our youth if they could be spent on this study. Sociology is still in its infancy. Only its most elementary notions are, as yet, available for purposes of education. It is sure to grow into a great science, and one of the first in rank as regards utility to the human race. It is plain that progress in other directions is producing problems in society which we cannot meet because our social science is not proportionately advanced. Biology is a science which is still young and new, but, with its affiliated sciences, it holds the key to a number of our most important problems and to a new philosophy destined to supersede the rubbish of the schools. Physics in all its subdivisions, dynamics, anthropology, archaeology, and a host of other sciences, with new developments in mathematics, offer just the stimulus which is proper and necessary to draw out youthful energies and to awaken youthful enthusiasm. The studies which I have mentioned and others are ready at our hand to-day to give our young men intellectual training and high scholarship and to carry them on to heights of enjoyment and useful activity of which they have no conception. In the mean time they are studying Latin and Greek, and the college authorities are boasting that they cling to the old curriculum and to classical culture.

Our colleges cannot maintain themselves in any such position before the country. They must have the best possible learning, and they must impart it freely. They cannot do this if they "run themselves" or live on their reputation. There is nothing else which now calls for such high statesmanship as the guidance of our old colleges into the new duties and functions which they ought to fulfill. It is a task which calls for great sagacity and good judgment, but above all, for constant study and care. There is here one remarkable consideration by way of encouragement. A great university can be subjected to experiments without any harm at all. It is a great mistake to think that an experiment, if it fails, will leave permanent evils behind. It will not do so. Every academic year stands by itself. Every year it is possible to begin anew, adopting a new plan or recurring to an old one, and no harm at all is done. No one proposes to do away with the study of the classics. For those who desire to pursue that study we desire far fuller opportunities than now exist. The assault is aimed entirely at the pre-eminent and privileged position which is claimed for the classics. We desire that the universities should offer equal chances for a liberal education on the basis of any of the other great lines of study. If it should prove, upon experiment, that men educated in other sciences could not hold their own in life in competition with the classically educated, there would undoubtedly be a revival of classical study and a return to it by those who are seeking an education.

# Discipline

In this talk to students sometime in the 1880s, Sumner joined a debate begun by Matthew Arnold's *Culture and Anarchy* (1869), a book that outraged many Americans with its charge that the New World lacked the "sweetness and light" of Old World culture. Rejecting Arnold's ideal as a goal for education, Sumner also eschewed a narrow utilitarianism that stressed only technical competence. Updated essay (ca. 1880–89), reprinted from *Forgotten Man*, ed. Albert Galloway Keller, pp. 423–438.

It occurs very frequently to a person connected as a teacher with a great seat of learning to meet persons who, having completed a course of study and having spent a few years in active life, are led to make certain reflections upon their academical career. There is a great uniformity in the comments which are thus made, so far as I have heard them, and they enforce upon me certain convictions. I observe that an academical life is led in a community which is to a certain extent closed, isolated, and peculiar. It has a code of its own as well for work as for morals. It forms a peculiar standpoint, and life, as viewed from it, takes on peculiar forms and peculiar colors. It is scarcely necessary to add that the views of life thus obtained are distorted and incorrect.

I should not expect much success if I should undertake to correct those views by description in words. It is only in life itself, that is, by experience, that men correct their errors. They insist on making experience for themselves. They delude themselves with hopes that they are peculiar in their persons and characters, or that their circumstances are peculiar, and so that in some way or other they can perpetrate the old faults and yet escape the old penalties. It is only when life is spent that these delusions are dispelled and then the power and the opportunity to put the acquired wisdom to practice is gone by. Thus the old continually warn and preach and the young continually disregard and suffer.

Although I could not expect better fortune than others if I should thus preach, yet there are some things which, as I have often been led to think, young men in your situation might be brought to understand with great practical advantage, and which, if you did understand them, and act upon them, would save you from the deepest self-reproach and regret which I so often hear older men express; and the present occasion seems a better one than I can otherwise obtain, for presenting those things. I allude to some wider explanations of the meaning and purpose of academical pursuits. I do not mean theories of education about which people dispute, but I mean the purposes which any true education has in view, and the responsibilities it brings with it. It surely is not advisable that men of your age should pursue your education as a mere matter of routine, learning prescribed lessons, performing enforced tasks, resisting, unintelligent, and uninterested. Such an experience on your part would not constitute any true education. It would not involve any development of capability in you. It could only render you dull, fond of shirking, slovenly in your work, and superficial in your attainments. Unless I am greatly mistaken, some counteraction to such a low and unworthy conception of academical life may be secured by showing its relation to real life, and attaching things pursued here to practical and enduring benefits. I have known men to get those benefits without knowing it; and I believe that you would get them better if you got them intelligently, and that you would appreciate them better if you got them consciously.

In the first place, it will be profitable to look at one or two notions in regard to the purpose of education which do not seem to be sound. One is that it is the purpose of education to give special technical skill or dexterity and to fit a man to get a living. We may admit at once that the object of study is to get useful knowledge. It was, indeed, the error of some old systems of academical pursuits that they gave only a special dexterity and that too in such a direction as the making of Greek and Latin verses, which is a mere accomplishment and not a very good one at that. It must be ranged with dancing and fencing; it is not as high as drawing, painting, or music. There is, moreover, a domain in which special technical training is proper. It is the domain of the industrial school, for giving a certain theoretical knowledge of persons who will be engaged for life in the mechanic arts. With this limitation, however, we have at once given to us the bounds which preclude this notion from covering the true conception of an academic career. It does not simply provide technical training for a higher class of arts which require longer preparation. You know that this conception is widely held through our American community, and that it is laid down with great dogmatic servity by persons who sometimes, unfortunately, are in a position to turn their opinions into law. It is one of the great obstacles against which all efforts for higher education amongst us have to contend.

I pass on, however, to another opinion just now much more fashionable and held by people who are, at any rate, much more elegant than the supporters of the view just mentioned, that is, the opinion that what we expect from education is "culture." Culture is a word which offers us an illustration of the degeneracy of language. If I may define culture, I have no objection to admitting that it is the purpose of education to produce it; but since the word came into fashion, it has been stolen by the dilettanti and made to stand for their own favorite forms and amounts of attainments. Mr. Arnold, the great apostle, if not the discoverer, of culture, tried to analyze it and he found it to consist of sweetness and light. To my mind, that is like saying that coffee is milk and sugar. The stuff of culture is all left out of it. So, in the practice of those who accept this notion, culture comes to represent only an external smoothness and roundness of outline without regard to intrinsic qualities.

We have got so far now as to begin to distinguish different kinds of culture. There is chromo culture, of which we heard much a little while ago, and there is bouffe culture, which is only just invented. If I were in the way of it, I should like to add another class, which might be called sapolio culture, because it consists in putting a high polish on plated ware. There seems great danger lest this kind may come to be the sort aimed at by those who regard culture as the end of education.

A truer idea of culture is that which regards it as equivalent to training, or the result of training, which brings into intelligent activity all the best powers of mind and body. Such a culture is not to be attained by writing essays about it, or by forming ever so clear a literary statement or mental conception of what it is. It is not to be won by wishing for it, or aping the external manifestations of it. We men can get it only by industrious and close application of the powers we want to develop. We are not sure of getting it by reading any number of books. It requires continual application of literary acquisitions to practice and it requires a continual correction of mental conceptions by observation of things as they are. For the sake of distinguishing sharply between the true idea of culture and the false, I have thought it better to call the true culture discipline, a word which perhaps brings out its essential character somewhat better.

Here let me call your attention to one very broad generalization on human life which men continually lose sight of, and of which culture is an illustration. The great and heroic things which strike our imagination are never attainable by direct efforts. This is true of wisdom, glory, fame, virtue, culture, public good, or any other of the great ends which men seek to attain. We cannot reach any of these things by direct effort. They come as the refined result, in a secondary and remote way, of thousands of acts which have another and closer end in view. If a man aims at wisdom directly, he will be very sure to make an affectation of it. He will attain only to a ridiculous profundity in commonplaces. Wisdom is the result of great knowledge, experience, and observation, after they have all been sifted and refined down into sober caution, trained judgment, skill in adjusting means to ends.

In like manner, one who aims at glory or fame directly will win only that wretched caricature which we call notoriety. Glory and fame, so far as they are desirable things, are remote results which come of themselves at the end of long and repeated and able exertions.

The same holds true of the public good or the "cause," or whatever else we ought to call that end which fires the zeal of philanthropists and martyrs. When this is pursued directly as an immediate good, there arise extravagances, fanaticisms, and aberrations of all kinds. Strong actions and reactions take place in social life, but not orderly growth and gain. The first impression no doubt is that of noble zeal and self-sacrifice, but this is not the sort of work by which society gains. The progress of society is nothing but the slow and far remote result of steady, laborious, painstaking growth of individuals. The man who makes the most of himself and does his best in his sphere is doing far more for the public good than the philanthropist who runs about with a scheme which would set the world straight if only everybody would adopt it.

This view cuts down a great deal of the heroism which fills such a large part of our poetry, but it brings us, I think, several very encouraging reflections. The first is that one does not need to be a hero to be of some importance in the world. Heroes are gone by. We want now a good supply of efficient workaday men, to stand each in his place and do good work. The second reflection to which we are led is that we do not need to be straining our eyes continually to the horizon to see where we are coming out, or, in other words, we do not need to trouble ourselves with grand theories and purposes. The determination to do just what lies next before us is enough. The great results will all come of themselves and take care of themselves. We may spare ourselves all grand emotions and heroics, because the more simply and directly we take the business of life, the better will be the result. The third inference which seems to be worth mentioning is that we come to understand the value of trifles.

All that I have said here about wisdom, fame, glory, "public good," as ends to be aimed at, holds good also of culture. It becomes a sham and affectation when we make it an immediate end, and comes in its true form only as a remote and refined result of long labor and discipline.

Before I speak of it, however, in its direct relation to education, let me introduce one other observation on the doctrine I have stated that we cannot aim at the great results directly. That is this: the motive to all immediate efforts is either self-interest or the desire to gratify one's tastes and natural tendencies. I say that all the grand results which make up what we call social progress are the results of millions of efforts on the part of millions of people, and that the motive to each effort in the heart of the man who made it was the gratification of a need or a tendency of his nature. I know that some may consider this a selfish doctrine, eliminating all self-sacrifice and martyr or missionary spirit, but to me it is a pleasure to observe that we are not at war with ourselves, and that the intelligent pursuit of our best good as individuals is the surest means to the good of society. Moreover, do you imagine that if you set out to make the most of yourself in any position in which you are placed, that you will have no chance for self-sacrifice, and no opportunity of martyrdom offered you? Do you think that a man who employs thoroughly all the means he possesses to make his one unit of humanity as perfect as possible, can do so without at every moment giving and receiving with the other units about him? Do you think that he can go on far without finding himself stopped by the question whether his comrades are going in the same direction or not? Will he not certainly find himself forced to stand against a tide which is flowing in the other direction? It will certainly be so. The real martyrs have always been the men who were forced to go one way while the rest of the community in which they lived were going another, and they were swept down by the tide. I promise you that if you pursue what is good for yourself, you need not take care for the good of society; I warn you that if you pursue what is good, you will find yourself limited by the stupidity, ignorance, and folly of the society in which you live; and I promise you also that if you hold on your way through the crowd or try to make them go with you, you will have ample experience of self-sacrifice and as much martyrdom as you care for.

Now, if I have not led you too deep into social philosophy, let us turn again to culture. We find that culture comes from thought, study, observation, literary and scientific activity, and we find that men practice these for gain, for professional success, for immediate pleasure, or to gratify their tastes. The great motive of interest provides the energy and this culture is but a secondary result. It is a significant fact to observe that when the motive of interest is removed, culture becomes flaccid and falls into dilletantism.

I think that we have gained a standpoint now from which we can study undergraduate life and make observations on it which have even scientific value. During an undergraduate career, the motive of interest in each successive step is wanting. There is no immediate object of pleasure or gain in the lesson to be learned next. Only exceptionally is it true that the learning of the lesson will gratify a taste or fill a desire. The university honors are only artificial means of arousing the same great motive, which is in the social body what gratification is in physics. The penalties which are here to be dreaded are but imitations of life's penalties. I think that many who have undertaken to give advice and rebuke and warning to young men in a state of pupilage have failed because they have not fully analyzed or correctly grasped this fact, that the academical world is a little community by itself in which the great natural forces which bind older men to sobriety and wisdom act only imperfectly. Life is far less interesting when the successive steps are taken under compulsion or for a good which is remote and only known by hearsay, than it is when every step is taken for an immediate profit. I doubt very much whether the hope of culture or self-sacrificing zeal for the public good would make older men toil in lawyer's offices and counting-houses, unless there were such immediate rewards as wealth and professional success. In real life it is true that men must do very many things which are disagreeable and which they do not want to do, but there too the disagreeable things are made easier to bear. The troubles of academical life seem to be arbitrary troubles, inflicted by device of foolish or malicious men. Troubles of that kind always rouse men to anger and rankle in their hearts. But there is no railing against those ills of life which are inherent in the constitution of things. A man who rails at those is laughed at. So the man just emancipated from academical life finds himself freed from conventional rules but subjected to penalties for idleness and extravagance and folly infinitely heavier than any he has been accustomed to, and inflicted without warning or mercy or respite. On the other hand, he finds that life presents opportunities and attractions for him to work, where work has a zest about it which comes from contact with living things. His academical weapons and armor are stiff and awkward at first and he may very probably come to despise them, but longer experience will show that his education, if it was good, gave him rather the power to use any weapons than special skill in the use of particular ones. Special technical skill always tends to routine. Although it is an advantage in itself, it may under circumstances become a limitation. The only true conception of a "liberal" education is that it gives a broad discipline to the whole man, which uses routine without being conquered by it and can change its direction and application when occasion requires.

This brings me then to speak of the real scope and advantage of a disciplinary education. A man who has enjoyed such an education has simply had his natural powers developed and reduced to rule, and he has gained for himself an intelligent control of them. Before an academical audience it is not necessary for me to stop to clear away the popular notions about untutored powers and self-made men. It is enough to say that the "self-made" man is, by the definition, the first bungling essay of a bad workman. An undeveloped human mind is simply a bundle of possibilities. It may come to much or little. If it is highly trained by years of patient exercise, judiciously imposed, it becomes capable of strict and methodical action. It may be turned to any one of a hundred tasks which offer themselves to us men here on earth. It may have gained this discipline in one particular science or another, and it may have special technical acquaintance with one more than another. Such will almost surely be the case, but there is not a more mistaken, one-sided, and mischievous controversy than that about *the* science which should be made the basis of education. Every science has, for disciplinary purposes, its advantages and its limitations. The man who is trained on chemistry will become a strict analyst and will break up heterogeneous compounds of all kinds, but he will be likely also to rest content with this destructive work and to leave the positive work of construction or synthesis to others. The man who is trained on history will be quick to discern continuity of force or law under different phases, but he will be content with broad phases and heterogeneous combinations such as history offers, and will not be a strict analyst. The man who is trained on mathematics will have great power of grasping purely conceptional relations, or abstract ideas, which are, however, most sharply defined; but he will be likely to fasten upon a subordinate factor in some other kind of problem, especially if that factor admits of more complete abstraction than any of the others. The man who is trained on the science of language approaches the continuity and development of history with a guiding thread in his hand, and his comparisons, furnishing stepping-stones now on the right and now on the left, lead him on in a course where induction and deduction go so close together that they can hardly be separated; but the study of language again always threatens to degenerate into a cram of grammatical niceties and a fastidiousness about expression, under which the contents are forgotten. Now, in individual affairs, family, social, and political affairs, all these powers of mind find occasion for exercise. They are needed in business, in professions, in technical pursuits; and the man best fitted for the demands of life would be the man whose powers of mind of all these diverse orders and kinds had all been harmoniously developed. How shallow then is the idea that education is meant to give or can give a mass of monopolized information, and how important it is that the student should understand what he may expect and what he may not expect from his education. As your education goes on, you ought to gain in your power of observation. Natural incidents, political occurrences, social events, ought to present to you new illustrations of general principles with which your studies have made you familiar. You ought to gain in power to analyze and compare, so that all the fallacies which consist in presenting things as like, which are not like, should not be able to befog your reason. You ought to become able to recognize and test a generalization, and to distinguish between true generalizations and dogmas on the one hand, or commonplaces on another, or whimsical speculations on another. You ought to know when you are dealing with a true law which you may follow to the uttermost; when you have only a general truth; when you have an hypothetical theory; when you have a possible conjecture; and when you have only an ingenious assumption. These are most important distinctions on either side. Some people are affected by a notion, fashionable just now, that it belongs to culture never to go too far. Mr. Brook, in "Middlemarch," you remember, is a type of that culture. He believed in things up to a certain point and was always afraid of going too far. We have a good many aspirants after culture nowadays whose capital consists in a superficial literary tradition and the same kind of terror of going too far. They would put a saving clause in the multiplication table, and make reservations in the rule of three. On the other hand, we have those who can never express anything to which they are inclined to assent without gushing. A simple opinion must be set forth in a torrent fit to enforce a great scientific truth. One is just as much a sign of an imperfect training as the other, and you meet with both, as my description shows, in persons who pride themselves on their culture. I will not deny that they are cultivated; I only say that they are not well disciplined, that is, not well educated.

Your education, if it is disciplinary, ought also to teach you the value of clear thinking, that is, of exact definitions, clear propositions, well-considered opinions. What a flood of loose rhetoric, distorted fact, and unclear thinking is poured out upon us whenever a different question falls into popular discussion! You cannot find that people who assume to take part in the discussion have a clear definition in their minds of even what they conceive the main terms in the discussion to mean. They do not seem able to make a proposition which will bear handling so as to see what it is, and whether it is true or not. They cannot analyze even such facts as they have collected, and hence cannot draw inferences which are sound. It needs but little discussion of any great political or social question to show instances of this, and to show the immense importance of having in the community men of trained and disciplined intellects, who can think with some clearness and resist plain confusion of terms and thought. For instance, I saw the other day a long argument on an important public topic which turned upon the assertion and belief on the part of the writer that a mathematical ratio and a subjective opinion were things of the same nature and value. Perhaps, when he was at school, his father thought there was no use in studying algebra and geometry. It would not make so much difference if he would not now meddle with things for which he did not prepare himself, but it is this kind of person who is the pest of every science, traversing it with his whims and speculations; and perhaps I feel the more strongly the importance of this point because the political, economic, and social sciences suffer from the want of high discipline more than any others.

I ought not to pass without mention here the mischief which is done in every science by its undisciplined advocates who, while admitted to its inner circle, distract its progress and throw it into confusion by neglect of strict principles, by incorrect analyses or classifications, or by flinching in the face of fallacies. They render the ranks unsteady and delay the march, and the reason is because they have never had rigorous discipline either before or since they enlisted.

If your education is disciplinary, it ought also to teach you how to organize. I add this point especially because I esteem it important and it is rarely noticed. It is really a high grade of discipline which enables men to organize voluntarily. If men begin to study and think, they move away from tradition and authority. The first effect is to break up and dissolve their inherited and traditional opinions as to religion, politics, and society. This is a necessary process of transition from formal and traditional dogma to intelligent conviction. It applies to all the notions of religion, as has often been noticed, but it applies none the less to politics and to one's notions of life. The commonplaces of patriotism, the watchwords of parties and tradition, the glib and well-worn phrases and terms have to be analyzed again, and under the process much of their dignity and sanctity evaporates. So too one's views of life, of the meaning of social phenomena, and of the general rules for men to pursue with each other, undergo a recasting. Now during this process, men diverge and break up. They do not agree. They differ by less and more, and also by the various recombinations of the factors which they make. Pride, vanity, and self-seeking come in to increase this divergence, it being regarded as a sign of independence of thought.

It is not too much to say that so long as this divergence exists, it is a sign of a low and imperfect development of science. If pride and vanity intermingle, they show that discipline has not yet done its perfect work. It is only on a higher stage of culture or discipline that self is so overborne in zeal for the scientific good that opinions converge and organization becomes possible. But you are well aware that without organization we men can accomplish very little. It is not the freedom of the barbarian who would rather live alone than undergo the inevitable coercion of the neighborhood of others that we want. We want only free and voluntary coordination, but it belongs to discipline itself to teach us that we must have coordination in order to attain to any high form of good.

I have now tried to show you the scope, advantages, and needs of a disciplinary education. I have one remark more to make in this connection. A man with a well-disciplined mind possesses a tool which he can use for any purpose which he needs to serve. I do not consider it an important question by the study of what sciences he shall get this discipline, for, if he gets it, the acquisition of information in any new department of learning will be easy for him, and he will be strong, alert, and well equipped for any exigency of life.

Before quitting the subject, I desire to point out its relation to one other matter, that is, to morals, or manners. It is a common opinion that the higher man attains, the freer he becomes. A moment's reflection will show that this is not true—but rather quite the contrary. The rowdy has far less restraints to consider than the gentleman. "Noblesse oblige" was perverted in its application, perhaps, before the Revolution, but it contains a sound principle and a great truth. The higher you go in social attainments, the greater will be the restraints upon you. The gait, the voice, the manner, the rough independence, of one order of men is unbecoming in another. Education above all brings this responsibility. Discipline in manners and morals does not belong to the specific matter of education, but follows of itself on true education. The educated man must work by himself without any overseer over him. He finds his compulsion in himself and it holds him to his task longer and closer than any external compulsion.

This responsibility to self we call honor, and it is one of the highest fruits of discipline when discipline, having wrought through intellect, has reached character. Honor falls under the rule which I mentioned early in this lecture. You cannot reach it because you want it. You cannot reach it by direct effort. It cannot be taught to you as a literary theory. True honor can only grow in men by the long practice of conduct which is good and noble under motives which are pure. We laugh at the artificial honor of the Middle Ages and despise that of the dueling code, but let us not throw away the kernel with the shell. Honor is a tribunal within one's self whose code is simply the best truth one knows. There are no advocates, no witnesses, and no technicalities. To feel one's self condemned by that tribunal is to feel at discord with one's self and to sustain a wound which rankles longer and stings more deeply than any wound in the body. It is the highest achievement of educational discipline to produce this sense of honor in minds of young men, which gives them a guide in the midst of temptation and at a time when all codes and standards seem to be matter of opinion. I have said some things about lack of discipline in thought and discussion, but that is nothing compared with the lack of discipline in conduct which you see in a man who has never known what honor is, whose whole moral constitution is so formless and flabby that it can perform none of its functions, and who is continually seeking some special plea, or sophistry, or deceptive device for paying homage to the right while he does wrong. Education ought to act against all this and in favor of a high code of honor, not simply the education of schools and academies, but that together with the education of home and family. Our great educational institutions ought to have an atmosphere of their own and impose traditions of their own, for the power which controls in the academic community is not the voice of authority but the voice of academic public opinion. That might root out falsehood and violence and meanness of every kind, which no penalties of those in authority could ever reach; and I submit that such a public opinion would be becoming in a body of young men of good home advantages and the best educational opportunities the country affords. Call it high training, or culture, or discipline, or high breeding, or what you will, it is only the sense of what we owe to ourselves, and it is greater and greater according to our opportunities.

# III

---

# Polemicist

---

# Republican Government

Delivered soon after Sumner's return from investigating the Hayes-Tilden election in Louisiana, this speech reflected his disillusionment with the democratic process in Gilded Age America when contrasted with the "republican" principles that inspired the nation's founders. Sumner's estimation of the Reconstruction governments had never been high. Carpetbaggers, he once wrote, were "sneaks—the meanest set of men to whose hands the fortunes of the state could possibly be committed," a judgment that may have included his carpetbagging brother Joseph. The reference to "proletariat" also registered his concern over a growing army of transients who wandered from door to door in New Haven begging food from frightened residents. Speech at McCormick Hall, Chicago, as reported in *Chicago Tribune*, January 1, 1877, and reprinted in *Challenge of Facts*, ed. Albert Galloway Keller, pp. 223–240.

The best definition of a republican form of government I know of is one given by Hamilton. It is government in which power is conferred by a temporary and defeasible tenure. Every state must have and exert authority; the state gathers together and enforces in concrete form the will of the governing body as to what ought to be done. I may leave aside here those cases in which the governing body is an autocrat or an oligarchy or an aristocracy, because these forms of the state are dead or dying, and take into account only the states in which the people rule and in which, therefore, the governing body is so wide as to embrace at least all who contribute to the active duties and burdens of the state. You observe that, even in the widest democracies, their body is not commensurate with the population. The "people," for political purposes, does not include women, or minors, or felons, or idiots, even though it may include tramps and paupers. The word "people," therefore, when we talk of the people ruling, must be understood to refer to such persons as the state itself has seen fit to endow with political privileges. The true rule which every state which is to be sound and enduring must set for itself in deciding to whom political functions may be entrusted, is that political rights and political duties, political burdens and political privileges, political power and political responsibility must go together and, as far as may be, in equal measure. The great danger of all wide democracies comes from the violation of this rule. The chief doctrine of democracy is equality, that is, equality of rights without respect to duties, and its theory of power is that the majority has the power without responsibility. If, then, it so happens that the rights and the powers fall to a numerical majority, while the duties and burdens are borne by a minority, we have an unstable political equilibrium, and dishonesty must follow.

In a state, however, in which the limits of co-ordinate rights and duties are observed in determining who shall be the people to rule, whether the limit includes a greater or smaller number of the inhabitants, we see the modern state which is capable of self-government and realizes self-government. Those who pay taxes, do jury duty, militia duty, police duty on the sheriff's posse, or are otherwise liable to bear the burdens of carrying out what the nation may attempt, are those who may claim of right to have a voice in determining what it shall attempt. They therefore make the national will, and out of the nation they form a state. The nation is an organism like a man; the state is like the man clothed and in armor, with tools and weapons in his hand. When, therefore, the will of the state is formed, the state must act with authority in the line of its determination and must control absolutely the powers at its disposal.

Right here, however, we pass over from the abstract to the concrete, from plain and easy reasoning on principles to practical contact with human nature. Power and authority in exercise must be in the hands of individuals. When wielded by boards and committees we find that they are divided and dispersed, and especially we find that, when divided, they escape responsibility. Thence arises irresponsible power, the worst abomination known to the modern constitutional or jural state. The most important practical questions are, therefore: Who shall be endowed with the authority of the state? How shall he be designated? How shall the authority be conferred? How shall the organs of authority be held to responsibility?

In constitutional monarchies these questions are answered by reducing the monarch to an emblem of stability, unity, and permanence, and surrounding him with ministers appointed by him, but under conditions which make them organs of the public will and which hold them to continual responsibility for all the acts of the state. The end is accomplished by indirect means which, nevertheless, secure the result with satisfactory certainty. In republics the organs of authority are designated by the express selection of the people; the people directly signify whom they choose to have as their organs or agents; they express their confidence distinctly either by word of mouth or by other convenient process; they show their will as to the policy of the state by choosing between advocates of different policies submitted to their selection. They do this either by the spoken word or the lifted hand, or by the ballot; they decide by majority vote or by such other combination as they may themselves think wisest; they confer authority for such time as they may determine; and they prescribe methods of responsibility such as they think adapted to the end. These general prescriptions and limitations they lay down beforehand in the organic law of the state.

It follows that elections are the central and essential institution of republics, and that the cardinal feature in a republican form of government is the elective system. We may therefore expand Hamilton's definition as follows: A republican government is a form of self-government in which the authority of the state is conferred for limited terms upon officers designated by election.

I beg leave here to emphasize the distinction between a democracy and a republic because the people of the United States, living in a democratic republic, almost universally confuse the two elements of their system. Each, however, must stand or fall by itself. Louis Napoleon gave the French democracy, under his own despotism; France is now called a republic although MacMahon was never voted for on a popular vote. If the principle of equality is what we aim at we can probably get it— we can all be equally slaves together. If we want majority rule, we can have it—the majority can pass a *plebiscite* conferring permanent power on a despot. A republic is quite another thing. It is a form of self-government, and its first aim is not equality but civil liberty. It keeps the people active in public functions and public duties; it requires their activity at stated periods when the power of the state has to be re-conferred on new agents. It breaks the continuity of power to guard against its abuse, and it abhors as much the irresponsible power of the many as of the one. It surrounds the individual with safeguards by its permanent constitutional provisions, and by no means leaves the individual or the state a prey to the determination of a numerical majority. In our system the guarantees to liberty and the practical machinery of self-government all come from the constitutional republic; the dangers chiefly from democracy. Democracy teaches dogmas of absolute and sweeping application, while, in truth, there are no absolute doctrines in politics. Its spirit is fierce, intolerant, and despotic. It frets and chafes at constitutional restraints which seem to balk the people of its will and it threatens all institutions, precedents, and traditions which, for the moment, stand in the way. When the future historian comes to criticise our time, he will probably say that it was marked by a great tendency toward democratic equality. He will perhaps have to mention more than one nation which, in chasing this chimaera, lost liberty.

If now a republican form of government be such as I have described it, we must observe first of all that it makes some very important assumptions. It assumes, or takes for granted, a high state of intelligence, political sense, and public virtue on the part of the nation which employs this form of self-government. It is impossible to exaggerate the necessity that these assumptions should be calmly observed and soberly taken to heart. Look at the facts. A people who live under a republican form of government take back into their own hands, from time to time, the whole power of the state; every election brings with it the chances of a peaceful revolution, but one which may involve a shock to the state itself in a sudden and violent change of policy. The citizen, in casting his vote, joins one phalanx which is coming into collision with another inside the state. The people divide themselves to struggle for the power of the state. The occasion is one which seems fitted to arouse the deadliest passions—those which are especially threatening to civil order.

The opinion of the people is almost always informal and indefinite. A small group, therefore, who know what they want and how they propose to accomplish it, are able by energetic action to lead the whole body. Hence the danger which arises for us, in this country, from incorporated or combined interests; it is and always has been our greatest danger. An organized interest forms a compact body, with strong wishes and motives, ready to spend money, time, and labor; it has to deal with a large mass, but it is a mass of people who are ill-informed, unorganized, and more or less indifferent. There is no wonder that victory remains with the interests. Government by interests produces no statesmen, but only attorneys. Then again we see the value of organization in a democratic republic. Organization gives interest, motive, and purpose; hence the preliminaries of all elections consist in public parades, meetings, and excitement, which win few voters. They rather consolidate party ranks, but they stimulate interest; they awaken the whole mass to a participation which will not otherwise be obtained. So far, then, it is evident that the republican system, especially in a democratic republic, demands on the part of the citizen extraordinary independence, power to resist false appeals and fallacies, sound and original judgment, farsighted patriotism, and patient reflection.

We may, however, go farther than this. The assumption which underlies the republican system is that the voter has his mind made up, or is capable of making up his mind, as to all great questions of public policy;

but this is plainly impossible unless he is well informed as to some great principles of political science, knows something of history and of experiments made elsewhere, and also understands the great principles of civil liberty. It is assumed that he will act independently of party if party clashes with patriotism. He is assumed to be looking at the public good with independent power to discern it and to act for it. Thus it follows, in general, that the citizen of a republic is animated by patriotism, that he is intelligent enough to see what patriotism demands, that he can throw off prejudice and passion and the mysterious influence of the public opinion of the social group to which he belongs, that he has education enough to form an opinion on questions of public policy, that he has courage enough to stand by his opinion in the face of contumely and misrepresentation and local or class unpopularity, that he will exercise his political power conscientiously and faithfully in spite of social and pecuniary allurements against his opinion, and that he is intelligent enough to guard himself against fraud. Finally it is assumed that the citizen will sacrifice time, interest, and attention, in no slight degree, to his public duty. In short, it comes to this: the franchise is a prerogative act; it is the act of a sovereign; it is performed without any responsibility whatever except responsibility to one's judgment and one's own conscience. And furthermore, although we are fond of boasting that every citizen is a sovereign, let us not forget that if every one is a sovereign every one is also a subject. The citizen must know how to obey before he is fit to command, and the only man who is fit to help govern the community is the man who can govern himself.

With these assumptions and requirements of republican self-government before us, you are ready to ask: "Where are there any men who fulfill the requirements?" If we apply the standards vigorously no men satisfy them; it is only a question of less or more, for the assumptions of republic self-government are superhuman. They demand more of human nature than it can yet give, even in the purest and most enlightened communities which yet exist. Hence republican self-government does not produce anything like its pure, theoretical results. The requirements, however, must be satisfied up to a reasonable limit or republican self-government is impossible. No statesman would propose to apply the republican system to Russia or Turkey to-day; our American Indians could not be turned into civilized states under republican forms; the South American republics present us standing examples of states in which the conditions of republican government are not sufficiently well fulfilled for the system to be practicable. In our own experience faults and imperfections present themselves which continually arouse our fears, and the present condition of some of our southern states raises the inquiry, with terrible force and pertinency, whether the assumptions of republican self-government are sufficiently realized there for the system to succeed. I may add, in passing, that the current discussion of questions pending in those states is marked by a constant confusion between democracy and the republican form of government.

I go on, however, to discuss the theory of elections, since this is the essential feature of the republic. Recent events have forced us to re-examine the whole plan and idea of elections, although the institution is one in familiarity with which we have all grown up. When an election is held in a town meeting by *viva voce* vote, or by a show of hands, the process is simple and direct. When the town grows to such a size that the body of voters cannot be brought within the sound of one voice, the physical difficulties become so great that this method is no longer available. It becomes necessary to adopt some system or method, aside from those previously employed, by which the question can be put and the vote taken. We are so familiar with the ballot as hardly to appreciate the fact that it is a distinct invention to accomplish a purpose and meet a new necessity. Right here, however, lies the birth of the political "machine"; for in the next step it is found that organization and previous concert are necessary. With this comes the necessity for nomination, and it is then found that the center of gravity of the system lies rather in the nomination than in the election. The nomination takes the form of a previous and informal election; it offers an opportunity for the majority to exert controlling power. The machinery is multiplied at every step, and with every increase of machinery comes new opportunity for manipulation and new demand for work. The election is to be popular throughout the state, but, for the purpose of nominating, the constituency is broken up into districts which send nominating delegates. Thus this subdivision enables labor to be concentrated upon small bodies in which chicanery, bargaining, and improper influence can be brought to bear. By ward-primaries, caucuses, nominating committees, pledged delegations, and so on, the ultimate power is concentrated in the hands of a few who, by concerted action, are able to control the result. At the same time the body of voters, finding political labor increased and political duty made more burdensome, abandon this entire department of political effort, while the few who persist in it have the continual consciousness of being duped. Upon the larger constituency of voters it is impossible to act, save by public methods, by public writing and speaking, which, although they often deal with base and unworthy motives, are nevertheless generally bound in decency to handle proper arguments. With every increase of machinery come new technicalities, new and arbitrary notions of regularity, fresh means of coercing the better judgment of delegates, and new opportunities for private and unworthy influences to operate. I do not hesitate to say that the path of political reform lies directly in the line of more independent and simple methods of nomination.

To return, however, to the election proper, the theory is that the body of voters shall cast ballots with the name of one or the other candidate. The votes are to be secret in the interest of independence; they are to be impersonal or anonymous, no man's vote being distinguishable from that of any other man after it is cast; they are to be equal, that is, every voter is to cast but one. The law can provide guarantees for all these limitations. Can the law go any further? Having endowed certain persons with certain qualifications to cast ballots, under the assumption that they are fit and qualified to discharge the duty, can it go any further? I think not. I do not see how the law can even confer upon the voter a power to do his duty, if he does not possess that power. If the people think that a man who cannot read his ballot is not fit to cast it, they can by the law of the state exclude all persons who cannot read from the franchise; but if they do not judge that such a qualification is essential, while in fact it is, they cannot possibly eliminate from the ballot-boxes the error or mischief which has come into them by the votes of illiterate or incompetent persons. They can provide for universal education and in time they can thus eliminate this element of harm, but that cannot operate for the time being. Again, if the state by its laws has given a share in political power to men who cannot form an opinion, or can be cheated, or can be frightened out of an opinion, or can be induced to use their power, not as they think best, but as others wish, then the ballot-boxes will not contain a true expression of the will of the voters, or it will be a corrupt and so, probably, a mischievous and ruinous will; but I do not see how a law can possibly be framed to correct that wrong, and make foolish men give a wise judgment or corrupt men give an honest judgment which shall redound to the public welfare. There is no alchemy in the ballot-box. It transmutes no base metal into gold. It gives out just what was put in, and all the impersonality and other safeguards may obscure but they never alter this fact. If the things which the elective system assumes to be true are not true, then the results which are expected will not follow; you will not get any more honor, honesty,

ligence, wisdom, or patriotism out of the ballot-box than the body of
voters possess, and there may not be enough for self-government. You
have to understand that you will certainly meet with fraud, corruption,
ignorance, selfishness, and all the other vices of human nature, here as
well as elsewhere. These vices will work toward their own ends and
against the ends of honest citizens; they will have to be fought against
and it will take the earnest endeavor of honest citizens to overcome
them. The man who will never give time and attention to public duty,
who always votes with his party, who wants to find a ballot already
printed for him, so that he can cast it in a moment or two on his way to
business on election day, has no right to complain of bad government.
The greatest test of the republican form of government is the kind of
men whom it puts in office as a matter of fact, and in any republic the
indolence of the public and its disposition to trust to machinery will
steadily detract from so much virtue, honesty, wisdom, and patriotism
as there may be in the community.

Here I say again, I do not see how the law can help in the matter. All
the machinery of nominating conventions and primaries lies outside of
the law. It is supported only by public acquiescence and it is the strongest tyranny among us. The fact is that everything connected with an
election is political, not legal; that is to say, it is the domain of discretion,
judgment, sovereign action. It is a participation in government; it presupposes the power and the will to act rightly and wisely for the ends
of government. Where that power and will exist the ends of government
will be served; where they do not exist those ends will not be served—
and it is plain that no one can create them. Law prescribes only methods
of action; action itself comes from human thought, feeling, and will, and
government is action. The autocrat of Russia governs Russia; suppose
that he were corrupt or perverse, or ignorant, or otherwise incompetent,
and it must follow that the purposes of government would be lost in
Russia—no law could give the autocrat of Russia a better mind or heart
for his duties. Just so if the sovereign people in any state taken as a
whole have not the mind or heart to govern themselves, no law can give
them these. We can never surround an incompetent voter by any legal
restraint, or protection, or stimulus, or guarantee, which shall enable
him to exercise his prerogative, if he is not able to do so as an antecedent
matter of fact. His motives lie in his own mind, beyond the reach of all
human laws and institutions; the conflicting arguments, prejudices, passions, fears, and hopes which move him meet in an arena where we
cannot follow them. If a body of voters in the commonwealth, so large
as to control it, are below the grade of intelligence and independence

which are necessary to make the election process practicable, then you cannot apply the republican form of government there; it is a hopeless task to take any such community, and by any ingenious device of legal machinery try to make the republican form of government work there so as to produce good government.

It follows, then, that the law can only mark out the precautions necessary to be observed to secure the true expression of the people's will, provided there be a people present who are capable of forming a will and expressing it by this method. The domain of these precautions is in the period anterior to the election—the law must define beforehand who are people fit, on general principles, to share in the government of the state. It will necessarily define these persons by classes and will leave out some who are fit if examined rationally and individually, and it will include many others who are unfit if examined in the same way. It must aim at a practical working system; it must then provide by registration or other appropriate means for finding out who among the population come within the defined qualifications; it must then surround the actual act of voting with such safeguards as seem necessary to secure to each voter a single impersonal vote. When the votes are cast, however, and the polls are closed, the public will is expressed as well as it is possible to have it expressed by an election in that community at that time. It might have been possible to get an expression of the will of that community in some other way, and perhaps in some better way, but that would not have been a republican form of government. The republican way to find out what the people want is to hold an election. If anybody proposes an improved method it may be worth while to consider it as a matter of political speculation, for every one knows by ample observation and experience that the process of elections is open to serious imperfections; it is liable to many abuses, and scarcely ever does an election take place anywhere in which there is not more or less abuse practiced. We know that it is really an imperfect makeshift and practical expedient for accomplishing the end in view. It only accomplishes it better than any other plan yet devised, but if any one can propose a better plan we are ready to give it attention. One thing, however, we never can allow to be consistent with a republican form of government, and that is, that we should hold an election and then correct the result as thus reached by some other result, reached in some other way by guess, estimate, magic, census, clairvoyance, or revelation.

If we pursue the republican system, we must accept the fact that we have in the boxes an arithmetical product which represents the will of the people, expressed as accurately as our precautions have been able to secure. If there was a qualified voter who had no opinion, or was afraid to express it, we have not got his will there, but we have got all that the republican system could get. To secure the truth, now, as to what the will of the people is, we have before us a simple process of counting the ballots. The truth will be presented as an arithmetical fact; it will not be open to any doubt or guess, but will be as positive as anything on earth. Simple as this matter of counting mere units may appear, we all know that the greatest dangers of the election system lie in this very process. The question of who shall count has become quite as important as who shall vote. The whole republican plan or system runs its greatest risk in the manipulation of the ballots after they are cast, and the question of its practicability comes down to this: Can we secure simple fidelity to the arithmetical facts in the count? This we certainly cannot do unless it is understood that absolute fidelity to the facts is the highest and only function of all officers and persons who are allowed to handle the ballots after they are cast. Every man who has grown up in familiarity with the election process knows that when we abandon the count of the votes as cast we go off into arbitrary manipulations and decisions for which we have no guarantee whatever, and that the political power of the state, if we allow any such manipulation, is transferred from those who vote to those who manipulate. If it is charged that frauds have been perpetrated in the election, that is to say that any of the laws which limit and define the exercise of the elective franchise have been broken, such charges raise questions of fact. If the charges are proved true, each charge affects the result by a given arithmetical quantity, and these effects can be added or subtracted as the case may be. Here we are dealing with facts, not opinions; we have solid ground under our feet. We do not work backward from the results, we work forward from the evidence; and so long as we use tribunals which seek only facts and remain steadfast to the truth as proved, the republican system suffers no shock. If, however, legislative committees or any other tribunals decide, in cases of contested elections, not by the truth but by party interest, we are face to face with the greatest treason against republican institutions which can possibly exist.

I believe that the American people love republican institutions. I have no doubt whatever that if we keep our records clean in regard to what republican institutions are, so that we recognize and repel the first inroads upon them, we can adapt our institutions to any exigencies that may arise. I think that the country has, to a certain extent, outgrown some of its institutions in their present form. I believe it has given its faith to some false and pernicious doctrines about equality and the rights of man. I believe that the astonishing social and economic developments of the last few years, together with some of the heavy problems which are legacies of the war, have thrown upon us difficulties whose magnitude we hardly yet appreciate and which we cannot cope with unless we set to work at them with greater energy and sobriety than we have yet employed. Some of these things involve or threaten the republic in its essence. We can deal with them all under its forms and methods if we have the political sense which the system requires. Here, however, lies the difficulty. Political institutions do not admit of sharp definition or rigid application; they need broad comprehension, gentle and conciliatory application; they require the highest statesmanship in public men. Self-government could not be established by all the political machinery which the wit of man could invent; on the contrary, the more machinery we have the greater is the danger to self-government. Civil liberty could not be defined by constitutions and treatises which might fill libraries; civil liberty cannot even be guaranteed by constitutions— I doubt if it can be stated in propositions at all. Yet civil liberty is the great end for which modern states exist. It is the careful adjustment by which the rights of individuals and the state are reconciled with one another to allow the greatest possible development of all and of each in harmony and peace. It is the triumph of the effort to substitute right for might, and the repression of law for the wild struggles of barbarism. Civil liberty, as now known, is not a logical or rational deduction at all; it is the result of centuries of experience which have cost the human race an untold expenditure of blood and labor. As the result we have a series of institutions, traditions, and positive restraints upon the governing power. These things, however, would not in themselves suffice. We have also large communities which have inherited the love of civil liberty and the experience of it—communities which have imperceptibly imbibed the conception of civil liberty from family life and from the whole social and political life of the nation. Civil liberty has thus become a popular instinct. Let us guard well these prejudices and these instincts, for we may be well assured that in them lies the only real guarantee of civil liberty. Whenever they become so blunted that an infringement of one of the old traditions of civil liberty is viewed with neglect and indifference then we must take the alarm for civil liberty. It seems to me a physical impossibility that we should have a Caesar here until after we have run through a long course of degeneration. That is not our danger, and while we look for it in that direction we overlook it

on the side from which it may come. There are numberless ways beside
the usurpation of a dictator in which civil liberty may be lost; there are
numberless forms of degeneration for a constitutional republic besides
monarchy and despotism. We can keep the names and forms of republican self-government long after their power to secure civil liberty is
lost. The degeneration may go on so slowly that only after a generation
or two will the people realize that the old tradition is lost and that the
fresh, spontaneous power of the people, which we call political sense,
is dead. Such is the danger which continually menaces the republic,
and the only safeguard against it is the jealous instinct of the people,
which is quick to take the alarm and which will not, at any time or under
any excuse, allow even a slight or temporary infringement upon civil
liberty. Such infringements when made are always made under specious
pretexts. Kings who set aside civil liberty always do it for "higher reasons of state"; in a republic likewise you will find, especially at great
public crises, that men and parties are promptly ready to take the same
course and assume the role of "saviors of society," for the sake of something which they easily persuade themselves to be a transcendent public
interest. The constitutional republic, however, does not call upon men
to play the hero; it only calls upon them to do other duty under the laws
and the constitution, in any position in which they may be placed, and
no more.

# Presidential Elections
# and Civil-Service Reform

An independent Republican, and later a Mugwump who bolted from Republican James G. Blaine to vote for the Democrat Grover Cleveland in 1884, Sumner shared the patrician view that the spoils system was at the root of many of the nation's political problems. At the request of the Civil Service Reform Association, he preached this gospel in various parts of the country. In this essay, he stated the historical case for this reform during the "lame duck" interval between the presidencies of Rutherford B. Hayes and James A. Garfield, an election he sat out. Whereas Sumner opposed many laws as beyond the scope of proper legislative authority, he later supported the Pendleton Civil Service Reform Act of 1883, convinced that, unlike the later Interstate Commerce Act of 1887, it established a commission merely to oversee the administration of executive business. Originally published in the *Princeton Review*, n.s., 7 (January 1881), 129–148; reprinted in Sumner, *Collected Essays in Political and Social Science* (New York: Henry Holt, 1885), pp. 140–159.

We have very little light, from history or tradition, upon the conception formed by our constitution-makers of the executive office which they created. It has been asserted, with great show of reason, that they did not know what they were making. The best suggestion we have in regard to their intention is in the assertion that they made the office to fit General Washington. Washington found that a great number of questions of detail arose in the office, in regard to which he was able to mould it according to his judgment of what was expedient. He established certain precedents. Jefferson rather ostentatiously overthrew many of the precedents which had been established, and others have followed his example, both in overthrowing precedents and introducing innovations. There has, therefore, been no steady tradition moulding the office, as there was no close definition to control it from the outset.

It seems, however, that the theory of the presidential office in the minds of the constitution-makers was substantially as follows: They took the view of the English constitution which was held by the Whigs during the first half of the last century. They assumed that the chief executive might have, and ought to have, certain prerogatives. If he were a king, he might be incompetent to exercise these prerogatives, or might abuse them. If he were an elected officer of a republic, he would, of course, be selected for his competency, and he would only hold power for a limited period, and by a defeasible tenure, so that abuse would be guarded against. Here there were two points of detail—the chief executive could only be named by an election, and he must hold office only for a limited period. In regard to the election, it is obvious that the constitution-makers never intended to provide for a grand democratic mass vote, in the nature of a *plebiscite*. They feared intrigue if the election were committed to Congress, and they thought that a great mass vote (if they ever conceived of such a thing) would be unwieldy and unsuitable. The election was to be by States, by an assembly of notables in some respects analogous to Congress, yet guarded against intrigue by the provision that they were to meet only in their separate States. Viewed upon the surface, this might seem to be a very ingenious and satisfactory system. In fact, we know that the history of this device has only illustrated the futility of all such devices. The device has only served to offer the material on which the social, political, and economic forces at work in our society—what we might call the genius of the nation—has wrought itself to accomplish its own ends. We have no unwritten laws. We do not rely on tradition, precedent, and prescription; but some "unwritten laws" have been developed over and around this electoral machinery, for the purpose of wresting it into a thoroughly democratic shape, which are the most inexorable laws of our political order. The political and social sanctions of those laws are so strong and sure that no one will break them.

As to the period of the presidential office, the constitution-makers were hedged in between the difficulty of putting an end to a bad administration within its term, on the one side, and the disadvantage of frequent elections, on the other. In providing for a four years' term, with re-eligibility, they seemed to have hit upon a wise and moderate solution of the problem.

In experience it has been necessary once to amend and reconstruct the machinery of presidential elections, and there has scarcely been a time when some amendment has not been pending in Congress which proposed to do away with the electoral college, to blot out the States as organs in the election, to shorten or lengthen the term, or to do away with re-eligibility, to say nothing of the propositions to entirely alter the character of the office. These propositions (except the last class) have been serious, and have received attention as something more than the vagaries of political speculators or the whims of discontented persons. We know that there has been enough in our experience of the working of the plan to call for modification and improvement, if only public opinion could crystallize into the conviction that certain specific modifications are called for. I am not concerned in the present paper to express my opinion of the propositions which have been made; but it is worth while, in passing, to remember that, according to all experience, it is better for political institutions to be simple and direct, and that, however one might disapprove of the theory of selecting the chief executive by a great mass vote, if we are to have that arrangement in fact and effect, it is better to have it openly and plainly than covertly and by indirection.

In fact, then, the intention of the constitution-makers has gone for very little in the historical development of the presidency. The office has been moulded by the tastes and faiths of the people, and it interests us now to note what has been made of it. The most interesting and important question which can be raised in regard to the theory of this high office, as it has existed in history, is whether the President is the head of the nation or the head of the party. Many Presidents have shown a desire to construe the office in the former sense. Any man who reaches the presidential chair, no matter by what means, and no matter what may be the calibre of the man, is sure to feel a noble desire to make a record for statesmanlike success of a high order. His position is historical. He is sure of a place of some sort in the annals of the nation. He would be a strange man who did not care to make this place an honorable one. The position has about it also elements of grandeur, romance, and sentiment which cannot fail of effect on most men. If a man has any good stuff in him, such an office must appear to him a great chance and a great responsibility, and it must inspire a desire to be worthy. All this expands the conception of the office beyond that of a party leader, even of a prime minister. I think we all hold a conception of the office, according to which it is more, altho we cannot tell how much more, than the leadership of a party. The minority party are not out of the nation. They are not without rights and interests which are under the national protection, and in regard to which the President is the organ and representative of the nation. There are also often public functions which involve no party questions, in regard to which unanimity is essential to propriety, and where the party leader cannot act with the proper effect because he brings party amities and hostilities with him in spite of

himself. In England it is often necessary in such cases for the prime
minister to confer with the leader of the opposition. We have no analogous arrangement. In social matters the same difficulty presents itself.
Something of social leadership seems to belong to the presidential office.
The ornamental or dignity element is reduced to its lowest terms, but
something of it remains. This element, however, belongs to the civil
head of the nation, not to a party leader. These points are of small importance compared with a wide and statesmanlike view of policy, which
would seem to belong to the presidential office, if the President is anything more than a party leader. We can understand the position of a
constitutional king who holds aloof from parties, or uses an independent
position to moderate excesses, and we can understand the position of a
prime minister who leads a party and enforces a policy; but an American
President, if he tries to be more than the prime minister and less than
the king—if he tries to moderate, soothe, and arbitrate instead of leading
the fighting—assumes a most ambiguous and difficult duty. Many presidents have tried it. No President has ever succeeded in it. Some have
fallen between two stools; others have been condemned as traitors to
their party, and have passed into history under unjust and contemptuous
condemnation; others, after a short trial, have surrendered to party control. Washington had the best opportunity of trying the "head-of-the-
nation" theory. He was, in a certain sense, bound to try it, and he did
so; but he was a conspicuous example of falling between two lines of
policy and failing of both. A President who has no party must try to
carry on the government without a party, and that is plainly impossible.

At this writing, an administration is drawing to a close which no doubt
enjoys, in the opinion of the great mass of the people, the judgment of
being a clean, respectable, and satisfactory administration. If it had not
been so, what points of attack it would have offered to an opposition
outraged by its defective title! Yet this administration is hated and despised by the politicians. It is, therefore, weak. It has an air of Philistine
goodness and imbecility. It will enjoy no honor or credit in history. It
resembles that of John Quincy Adams in many respects, and is inferior
to it in some respects, but it will probably rest under much the same
unjust misapprehension and contempt. In fact, Mr. Hayes' administration could not have carried us through any period of political struggle.
It probably benefited by having to deal with an opposition Congress.

All the tendency has been to make the President the leader of a party,
or perhaps, more strictly, the standard-bearer of a party who goes where
the leaders direct him. If he does this, he has a peaceful, smooth, and

prosperous path. He finds also a consistent position, which he and others can understand. He puts himself in a position which has a moral basis in the character and relation of political institutions.

So soon as we have reached this point, we see what a presidential election is, and how the whole of our political life centres around these periodical conflicts. Ambition, love of power, civil emolument, and greed of gain have been the great moving forces in politics under all forms of government. It is a childish hope to expect that "republics" are to be free of greed and vanity. They only have their own forms of greed and vanity to deal with. Political power and civil emolument, under our republican system, depend either on elections or on patronage, and if elected officers exercise the patronage the two are combined. The patronage becomes the force which moves the political machinery, of which elections are the central and most important part. Patronage is power to him who wields it, and emolument to him who receives it. The action and reaction are therefore equal, and the circuit is complete. The scattered forces concentrate in the election on an effort to elevate a certain candidate to power. On that candidate's power are centered all the hopes of all his supporters. From him, again, streams out to them the gratifications of greed and vanity which consolidate their ranks for the continually recurring struggle.

The presidency is the centre of party organization and the crown of party effort, because it is the greatest organ in the vast political organism of the country. State and city politics are interwoven with it. The federal officers manipulate the local politics in order to prepare strength for the presidential election, success in which will perpetuate the same corps of federal officers. The patronage therefore reaches behind the Congressmen also, and they must either control it or be controlled by it. It becomes the power by which the President urges a policy on Congress, or a power by which the Senate coerces the President. It becomes the bond between the executive and the legislature, whom the Constitution very mistakenly endeavored to sunder and to put into an affected attitude of indifference and independence towards each other.

What follows from this is that the presidential elections are conflicts renewed every four years to see which of two sets shall have possession of the organism described. The system of electing the chief executive of the nation every four years, and the abuse of the civil service to stimulate political work and to reward political work, are interdependent, and are inextricably interwoven with each other. As far as I can judge from conversation with experienced politicians, it is because they know that, in fact and practice, what is called the abuse of the civil-service is just as essential to the system of elections as steam is to the locomotive, that they cannot understand what the civil-service reformers are talking about. I am so far in accord with the politicians that I do not see how the civil service is to be reformed so long as the chief executive office is put up to be struggled for every four years. It is a very significant fact, as pointing to a true connection in nature and adaptedness between the system of party republican government and party abuse of the civil service, that the French are being led by the logic of their new institutions to methods of party proscription in their civil service.

I have said that the presidency is not bound about by any firm traditions. It is crude and unformed in many respects. The century which has elapsed has not sufficed to establish any firm grooves for it. Hence it is anomalous in many of its details, and it includes inconsistent principles and relations. The firm developments which have been forced upon it have lain in the direction of its partisan value and efficiency. In regard to that, a steady sequence through all administrations of all parties may be traced. In no respect has the steady partisan development been more remarkable than in the presidential elections. In primitive agricultural societies, such as existed here a century ago, it was not difficult to hold these elections. Each State was to vote by and for itself, on different days, in different ways, giving its voice for the executive head of the confederation in such way as it saw fit. There was not then facility of transportation or communication. Life was simple and dull. The mild excitement of a presidential election was pleasant and beneficial. The excitement was not to be compared with that of such an election held simultaneously by ten million voters, with such facilities of communication that the whole nation is wrought up to a common pulsation. The case is far different now, both as regards the excitement and as regards the community which has to endure it. We are now a great nation, with complex and varied interests. The presidential election throws an artificial and injurious excitement athwart all the industrial and other permanent interests of the country. This must be more and more the case as time goes on, and as our society is bound together by the finer fibres which only grow as a nation gets older and more settled. Everything about a presidential election tends to stimulate excitement, to cloud reason, to breed delusions, and to betray good sense. It is held on one day only, and the same day throughout the country. It is concentrated on the election of one of two men—not of a Congress. It is foreseen for a definite period, and prepared for by regular means.

It is, therefore, a great disturbance to the country, and it comes about every four years whether there is any real political crisis or not. No doubt the "outs" are fully ready after four years to try again whether they cannot get in, but peaceful and industrious citizens need have little interest in this effort if there is no important question of administration to be put to the decision of the nation.

The mere fact of the campaign and election is a hindrance and injury to business. A business scare is sure to be the accompaniment of every presidential election hereafter. It has a basis of truth in the facts already stated, and it is such a valuable piece of capital to the "ins," who can always trace it to fear of a change, that it is sure not to be neglected. We must, of course, get ourselves governed, and we must do it by the methods of self-government; but the question by which all political institutions must be tested is, whether they attain the result with the least possible expense, annoyance, and loss. Is there not an unnecessary expense, annoyance, and loss, for the end accomplished, in holding a presidential election every four years? How shall we be better off in April, 1881, for getting Mr. Hayes out of the presidency and Mr. Garfield into it? We had Mr. Hayes, and were going on satisfactorily. There was no agitating question before us. Agitation was settling down. Every one was contented except the office-seekers. What was gained by the expense, annoyance, excitement, etc., of 1880?

There is now noticeable, I think, in the public mind, a growing terror of presidential elections. Before the late election it was said, on both sides, that a candidate was wanted who would take the office if he was elected to it. Here was a new conception of the presidential office on the part of those who made this remark, and here was also a menace to the peace of the country in the contingency (which was contemplated in the remark) of a disputed election. With the easy optimism which characterizes our politics, this remark and all its significance have been forgotten; but there are other instances. In one of the best speeches made during the campaign, it was argued, in conclusion, that voters in New York should vote for Garfield because, if New York gave its vote to him, he would be elected without possibility of dispute; whereas, if it voted for Hancock, there might be room for a disputed election. A great newspaper also said, a few days after the election, and no doubt with truth, that the people were greatly relieved to be free from the danger of a contested election. What view of the election was involved in this argument and this remark? Certainly the election was not regarded as the free and untrammelled selection of a chief magistrate, nor as a smooth and harmless means of carrying on the government. It was regarded as a peril. The controlling motives in regard to it were to reduce it or avoid it, and to get out of it as easily as possible.

That there is this feeling of peril, since 1876, is indisputable. As New York voted for Garfield, there was no dispute in 1880. If New York had voted for Hancock, he would have had just the requisite number of votes, leaving out California. His vote must, however, have included Nevada, a frontier, doubtful State, and we must have hung upon the slow returns from California for enough margin to establish the election. What controversy and chicane might we not have seen renewed? The blunder in Indiana by which the Republicans lost a vote also shows on what contingencies a close election might turn. It is to be noted that whenever a contested election occurs, it will not turn upon the vote of an old State, where methods are sure, communication rapid and open, evidence plentiful, etc.; but on some frontier State, where returns come in slowly, methods are loose, and technical questions, on which there are two good sides, are plentiful. The fourth presidential election ever held issued in a contested election. Fortunately the seat of government had just been removed to Washington. If it had still been in Philadelphia, the mob of that city would probably have settled the question. In 1876 we escaped by a *coup d'état* from another contest. It is living in a fool's paradise for a free self-governing people to go on from one election to another, congratulating themselves that they have escaped the peril again this time, but taking no steps to avert a political calamity of which we have had two warnings, and which is the greatest that can happen to us. Why is it anything but a question of time when we shall have another contested election?

Any one who will look back at the history of our presidential elections will see by what steady strides the art of electing Presidents has been perfected. Each new election has seen more comprehensive and more pertinacious generalship. Every part in the machinery of the campaign has a history. The conventions, the committees, the platforms, the campaign fund, the stump-speaking, the campaign literature, the campaign songs and singing, the torch-light processions, the semi-military clubs, the banners, and the mud-machines, have each a history of its own. Each organ or engine of campaign work has been developed by itself; and as each in higher perfection co-operates with all the rest in each succeeding campaign, and as each is employed on either side, the expenditure of energy is greater at every election, and the struggle is made more and more intense. Every one of these organs of the campaign bears upon the purpose of perfecting organization, stimulating interest, and concentrating force upon the party victory; that is, upon elevating to power him from whom, if in power, bounty may be expected by the party in question. No institutions have been invented whose purpose is to make sure of getting a competent statesman into the presidency, or to secure a direct and simple verdict by the voters upon the administration, or to draw out public opinion on any measure. The institutions which had that purpose have perished, or have been distorted to suit the other purpose. In short, the life-principle in the presidential election is the desire for power and emolument, and this controlling force has crushed everything else or absorbed everything else. The most serious questions and the most important measures are treated only as means to the great end. Here we have the reason why elections fail of the educating influence which is alleged in their defence. It is open to every one's observation that documents, speeches, and arguments have little effect. Tradition is strong in their favor, but the political managers begrudge the cost of them. Drill and spectacular effect nowadays play a far more important part in the election. The education the election exerts is education in the art of elections, in the tactics of party management, in shrewd and cynical dealing with the weaknesses of human nature, and not in the principles of self-government or the knowledge of public questions. I allege in proof of this the fact that the principles of self-government and the tactics of party warfare are continually confused with each other in the press and on the stump. Party platforms represent the sacrifice of public questions to party interest. In theory, they are statements of party dogmas and convictions. In practice, they have become proverbs for empty phrases and Janus-faced propositions. A model platform is one in which two contradictory propositions are combined in the same sentence, or a non-proposition is so stated that each man may read there just what will suit his own notions.

The student of political institutions knows that they never go backward. He must look in the future for advance along the lines marked out by the past. The Chicago convention of 1880 was certainly a very refined and highly developed specimen of the national nominating convention. The history of that convention is most instructive, but it is now almost forgotten. As soon as the candidates were named, the convention dissolved, and was as speedily forgotten as the broken shell from which the fowl has emerged. It is a mistake, however, to forget it too soon. The congratulations that "the machine was smashed," with which some of us welcomed the members of the convention home, were too hasty. The triumvirate of "bosses" failed there because, altho their scheme was carefully and skilfully prepared, they had not secured the national committee. The defeat which was inflicted on them was one of those costly victories which educate the enemy, point out his errors, and enable him to ensure victory the next time. The next triumvirate of bosses will have the national committee.

The developments in the use of money from campaign to campaign are a subject deserving treatment by itself, if any one who could command the necessary information would at the same time study the matter. There are three different matters embraced under this head:

1. The increasing need for money drives the party in power to political assessments. From the politician's stand-point, these assessments are logical and proper. The office-holders should contribute to support the party which put them in place and will keep them there. The election, in this point of view, is the occasion of a periodical tax, or toll, or fine, levied on the office-holder. We have here a specific abuse of the civil service, one which is indefensible, easily defined and reached, and therefore a good object upon which to exercise the initial measures of reform. The fire and movement of the campaign, however, are sure to overthrow this reform. The fears of the office-holder coincide with the interests and desires of the party managers to break over such feeble resistance as the reform has been able to accumulate.

2. The use of money for elaborate campaign artifices and machinery reaches sums which no one seems able to guess at. I have not been able to form any conjecture about it which is worth anything. It is certain only that it amounts to millions, and that it is almost a pure waste of capital. One phenomenon which has become very familiar in some of the States has not yet appeared on the federal arena: that is, the man of wealth and political ambition who is ready to spend a large sum to win the presidency. I think that if any one will estimate the cost of paying all the expenses of all the delegates to a nominating convention, he will be astonished at the smallness of the sum.

3. The illegitimate use of money in the presidential election is something which is known to everybody, but which we agree to ignore and to pass over with certain conventional phrases. It is difficult, of course, to get at facts or to justify general assertions. A correspondent of the *Nation* of November 18th seems to have been quite close to the facts, and to have been very much shocked by them. In view of what we all know, and what any two of us in private conversation will agree upon, it is rather amusing to read the newspaper comments on bribery in other

countries. There have recently been some great scandals of this sort in England, which have furnished the text for thanksgivings that we are not as other men are. It is forgotten that these scandals are brought to light by a public investigation whose object is to reach and correct the abuse. Such an investigation amongst us would be considered very "impractical."

Presidential elections are chargeable with many of the worst errors and mishaps in our history. I have already alluded to the contested election of 1800, which put the newly formed Union to a very severe strain. If there had been no presidential election in 1812, there would have been no second war with England. The tariffs of 1816, 1824, 1828, and 1832 resulted from the bidding of the two parties, in the election years, for the support of the protectionists. The protectionists tricked both parties, and voted for either as they chose, because both voted for protection. In this way the protective policy was fastened on the country in spite of the interest of the nation, and the early set of the people to freedom in trade as well as to every other kind of freedom. The election of 1836 caused the distribution of the surplus revenue in that year. Neither party dared resist a mischievous measure which seemed to contain elements of popularity. Presidential intrigues cost us the war with Mexico, the repeal of the Missouri Compromise, the Kansas-Nebraska Act, and the civil war in Kansas. Presidential intrigues wrought up the sectional misunderstanding until "Yankees" and "Southerners" formed legendary and fabulous notions of each other. It was on account of the importance of the Southern vote to all presidential aspirants that the Southern "arrogance" and the Northern "truckling" were developed. The politicians found their account in stimulating sectional pride and animosity until a presidential election became the occasion of the civil war. Presidential intrigues in Johnson's administration frustrated the most peaceful and promising efforts at reconstruction, and brought about the carpet-bag era with tyranny on one side and Kuklux outrages on the other. In 1876 we had a very narrow escape from another civil war. The fact that we put up the office of highest power and dignity every four years to be contended for in an election contest has been the controlling fact in our political history. The question how and by whom to get that office filled has been constantly present, and it has superseded all other questions. Time and labor have been exhausted in the constantly renewed necessity for getting the office filled, and we have not been able to profit by its functions for any length of time before the toil and annoyance of choosing a new man to fill it have recommenced. The

time of Congress has always been largely taken up with President-mak-
ing, especially in the last session before the election. Between the bick-
erings over the last election and preparations for the next one, sometimes
almost the whole four years have slipped away. Matters of urgent importance must be postponed until after the election. Measures of doubtful expediency must be pushed through to make capital for the election.
Measures which were right and expedient might not be brought forward
lest they should be troublesome in the election. These delays, make-
shifts, and concessions, however, have all passed into the life of the
nation and become part of its history. Every such political incident—
the thing done or the thing undone—combines with others, produces
consequences, affects public opinion, forms a precedent, strengthens or
weakens a tradition, and influences the habits of thought of the people.
No political incident stands alone. No incident can be brought about
temporarily and then set aside. It remains in its consequences and effects, whatever may be done to revoke it. Witness the educational effect
of the early tariff laws; the present feeling and prejudice of the people
about a national bank; the long struggle which was necessary before
"distribution" schemes were finally brought to rest; the secondary effects of violating the compromise tariff; the real effect of the Dred Scott
decision, regarded as a political maneuver; and the effects of the legal-
tender law, passed to meet a temporary necessity. The principle of continuity and propagation has applied fully to all the presidential intrigues
which have played so large a part in our history. It is difficult to conceive
how different our history would have been if we had had some way of
filling the chief executive place without periodical elections.

Presidential elections must also be charged with corrupting the public
men of the country. Presidential ambition has been the bane of our public men. Very few of the first-rate ones have escaped the infection of this
ambition, and, within the last forty years, it has rioted amongst the third,
fifth, and tenth rate ones. As one of the last said some time ago, when
he was rallied upon his " chances": "I do not see why the lightning may
not strike me as well as any other man." Presidential ambition has forced
those who were afflicted by it to do what they would not do, and leave
undone what they would do, if they took counsel only of reason and
conscience. One after another of them has belittled himself before the
nation by his inability to conceal disappointment and chagrin. The eagerness for this honor, on the part of public men, can easily be understood; but it has been a moral disease amongst our statesmen. To offset

this evil, we have the proud boast that any American may be President. Do we not pay too dearly for this bit of claptrap? How many of us want to be President? How many of us would surrender our reversion in the office if we could only be sure that no American could become President unless he were fit and competent?

Presidential elections corrupt local politics. State and city politics enjoy favorable chances in the "off-years," as they have come to be designated. The federal office-holder then sometimes relaxes his interference. On the approach of a presidential election, however, everything else has to bend to the organization and labor of the campaign. It is not simply because all persons who are in any degree "in politics" find their interest all absorbed, so that they cannot attend, with free minds, to anything else, but the selection of local officers suffers directly. Local offices are used as makeweights or bonuses with which to win strength in the great contest, and the momentum of the presidential election carries into many subordinate and local offices party candidates who would at another time have failed because they could not have drawn out the party vote.

Presidential elections act upon timid reforms and newly planted improvements as a storm acts on sprouting plants. The election of 1880 has destroyed all that had been accomplished of civil-service reform during Mr. Hayes' administration. It is said that Mr. Hayes has done very little. In fact, when we consider the nature and difficulty of the task, he has done a great deal. He has not been supported as he deserved in what he has done. Those who believed in the reform and desired it were bound to understand the difficulty of it, to welcome little beginnings towards it, to take what they could get and nurse it carefully in hopes of more, to appreciate the President's efforts, and to support and encourage him. They have, on the contrary, taken the position of spectators and critics. The beginnings of reform seemed to me hopeful. They were such as might grow if they had time, peace, and toleration. The recurrence of the election has crushed them out. The employés have been assessed, the office-holders have managed the campaign, the rules have been broken over, and we are back again at the beginning, only worse off than before, because the reform has become ridiculous. Now, in politics, when a thing becomes ridiculous before it is widely or fairly understood, it suffers great harm.

The case here stated in regard to civil-service reform illustrates a general tendency. When the election period comes around again, there is a tendency to fall back into the old ruts. Serious issues are excluded so far as possible, since, of course, the parties can be held together more easily, and the election can be managed with less trouble, if old issues are maintained and old methods retained. The considerations which would have great weight in time of peace, and in the undisturbed flow of affairs, seem to be of inferior importance, and one is ready to sacrifice them when an exciting campaign has wrought one up to the point of believing that the main thing "now" is to elect our man. The way free trade was treated by its republican friends during the last campaign was a conspicuous illustration of this. The election acts, therefore, as a blight upon struggling reforms, and as a hindrance to important political measures.

So far, now, I have noticed the difficulties, dangers, and evils incident to the election of the chief executive by a popular vote in periods of only four years. The abuses of the civil service and the obstacles to reform in it seem to be in close and organic connection with this system of providing for the filling of the chief executive office. If the civil service should be reformed as the "reformers" want to see it reformed, presidential elections, and indeed local elections also, would cease to be what they are now. Note what proportion of the voters will take the trouble to vote on a constitutional amendment which may be of the very first importance. If the personal element were reduced, as it would be reduced by the contemplated reform, elections would lose their heat, agitation, noise, and expense, and would be far more sober, rational, and fruitful. On the other hand, if the elections should be made less frequent, the civil service would be reformed to a great extent, simply as a consequence. The workers and office-seekers would either lose or forget their trade, and they could not hold out through a long period of delay and hope. Which of the two branches of the evil, the too frequent elections or the abuse of the civil service, may be the best point of attack is yet to be considered. It is evident that for new States out of Europe the republican form of government is to prevail in the future. A monarchy is for us, for a hundred reasons, out of the question. The republican form of government is, however, yet new, crude, and unformed. This is especially true of our own government. For instance, the present session of Congress opens with a hot party fight on a question about the respective functions of Congress and the Vice-President in counting the electoral votes. Centuries perhaps must elapse before precedent, habit, and experience shall have made our system smooth and easy, and shall have so defined its separate organs, and their spheres of activity, that they may act upon each other without friction. We are fettered, as yet, by the traditions of monarchy and by youthful deference to foreign models. We lack the independent energy to deal with our own problems according to the genius of our institutions.

Republican, or presidential, government is weak in two respects. It lacks stability and it lacks elasticity. The continuity of national life is more or less broken at every change of administration, and it is distinctly broken by every change of party. The unity and continuity of the nation need to be not only represented, but sustained and defended against the conception that the majority or the major party are the nation. The more democratic the institutions are, the greater is the need of just this guarantee against an abuse of democracy. Political changes should be brought about by political institutions just when the occasion for them arises, and at no other time. This is what is meant by elasticity or flexibility. When officers are elected for a set period, elections must recur whether there is any political crisis or not, whether there is any real occasion to appeal to the country or not. The perfection of republican institutions will call for improvements or new devices to introduce greater stability with greater flexibility. As we have seen above, any gain in this direction will be a gain also in civil-service reform.

Most students of statecraft turn from our institutions to English institutions for guidance in the way of modification. English institutions have the smooth, steady, frictionless action which is in strongest contrast with our harsh and grinding system. The executive has two organs—the ornamental or dignity organ, which supports the unity and continuity of the nation, and the working organ, which carries on self-government under party organization. The latter organ is designated by the play of institutions upon each other which amounts to a kind of natural selection. The man is elected by nobody, but he is set in evidence by the action of parliamentary and official life during a long period. Every one knows who it ought to be, perhaps even to the sole possible individual, or, at most, within a possibility of two or three. One of these it must be. It can be no one else. This is very beautiful and very captivating, as it is managed in England by men whose social and political training combine to make them moderate and careful to observe "the limits." It does not work well, however, in the English colonies. They are far too frequently in the throes of a cabinet crisis. They have governors appointed from England to carry the dignity part of the executive,

an officer for whom we could find no parallel. I have never been able to
see how we could graft any part of the English system on ours without
entirely giving up ours and adopting theirs.

The French experience with a republican form of government is full
of instruction. They have had three Presidents, who have each adopted
a different theory of the presidential office in regard to the point I have
discussed above; viz., whether the President is to be like a Constitutional
King or like a Prime Minister. M. Thiers construed his office as if he had
been a minister. He attended the legislature and defended his own policy. MacMahon was elected for a definite term of seven years. He did
not attend the legislature. He had a parliamentary ministry. Nevertheless
he had opinions of his own, and he tried to bring them to bear on the
administration of affairs. The consequence was that he was obliged to
resign, in spite of his set term of office, before it had expired. M. Grèvy
seems to have assumed the neutral role of a constitutional sovereign
who reigns but does not govern. He enjoys peace, but is scarcely mentioned in the administration. This series of experiments only confirms
political theory and also our American experience. A prime minister is
a functionary whose moral basis is consistent, harmonious, and well
rounded. A constitutional king is another functionary who has a true
moral basis in facts and nature. The former is a party leader. He conducts
self-government by party. The latter's first duty is to be out of and above
party. A *tertium quid*, something between these two and partaking of
both, is an impossibility. It has no true moral relations, and it will grav-
itate either towards a constitutional monarch, as the French presidency
has done, or towards a party leader and working ruler, as the American
presidency has done.

The legislatures of modern times are the real depositaries of the power
and will of the State. The centre of gravity of our system tends all the
time to settle more firmly in the House of Representatives. Such a tendency is revolutionary as regards the existing constitution; that is, it
tends to entirely reconstruct it. It is an interesting subject for speculation
whether our House of Representatives would not gain dignity and be
cured of many of its worst faults if it had the power it is always reaching
after, and had also the responsibility which must go with the power.
That it will win more and more power by virtue of the very fact that it
has the most and strongest independent elements of strength in its popular constituency and its power over money, seems most probable.
When it really has power, will it submit to the opposition of the executive to a thing on which it has resolutely determined? I think not. All

precedent and analogy shows that it will not. How long it may take for the development which has been indicated to work itself out I do not pretend to foresee. It seemed to me that the collision of the Democratic House with the Republican Senate, and then with the Republican President, and the use of "riders" on the appropriation bill, were premonitions of a struggle in which, in the end, the House, if it had a strong majority and a good support in public opinion on the point in question, was sure to win. If, then, this change should be brought about, the presidency would become more of an ornamental office; its power would be lessened; the chiefs of departments would become a true cabinet; the President might, without any reason to the contrary, be elected for a much longer term; it would no longer make any difference if he had no qualities not possessed by respectable mediocrity, and the functions of the political worker would lose importance. This proposition might equally well be stated in another form: We can lengthen the term of the presidential office if we strip it of the most important powers which it now possesses to control legislation, and we can then solve the problem of civil-service reform.

To sum up: We have found that the corruption of the civil service is an historical product of the forces at work in American political life, under the conditions set by American political institutions. It is not an artificial product. No one brought it about. It was in no program. It is a growth. Its origin and its law are to be sought in facts of human nature, and of the political order, together with historical conditions. It follows that no artificial remedies will correct the abuses of the civil service unless they are such as reach to the remolding of political institutions. The elective system as employed by us, especially the system by which the President is elected, is the institution most in question. It follows also that the prejudice of those who do not want any change either of spirit or form in political institutions, and who regard civil-service reform as something foreign and hostile to their favorite political dogmas and methods, is well founded. It follows, finally, that the dogmas referred to are false and the methods are mischievous, and that the corrections here and the reform of the civil service must go hand in hand.

# The Argument against Protective Taxes

The passage of the Morrill Tariff in 1861 inaugurated five decades of protectionist legislation, reaching a high in the Dingley Tariff of 1897. Throughout his career, Sumner's energies were directed toward this one issue more than any other. In his classroom, he won converts to free trade, as annual polls of graduating seniors revealed margins of four to one in favor. Newspapers printing his *Lectures on the History of Protection* (1877) included the *New York Times* and the *World*. Among his chief foes were Matthew and Henry Carey, the father and son economists of Philadelphia who supported protectionism. Two years after the publication of this article, Sumner's criticism of the tariff on thread and of the Willimantic Woolen Company in *Social Classes* caused a major uproar at Yale and throughout the Northeast. Originally published in the *Princeton Review*, n.s., 7 (January 1881), 241; reprinted in Sumner, *Collected Essays in Political and Social Science* (New York: Henry Holt, 1885), pp. 58–76.

The most absurd assertion which can be put into language is that a thing (e.g., free trade) is true in theory but is false in practice. For, if free trade is not true in practice, something else, viz., restricted trade, is alleged to be true and beneficial in practice. It will therefore be a matter of scientific investigation to find out how restriction acts, what forces it brings into action, what are the laws of those forces, what are the conditions of successful restriction, etc. etc.—in short, to find out the theory and philosophy of restriction. The theory thus found will be "true" because deduced from observation and ratified by experience. But it was conceded, at the outset, that free trade is true in theory. Hence it would follow, if free trade is true in theory but not in practice, that two opposite and contradictory propositions about the same subject-matter could both be true at the same time. This is the height of absurdity. Any one, therefore, who makes this assertion is either guilty of very loose thinking, or else he seeks an escape, at all hazards, from rational conclusions against which he can no longer contend.

There remain two possible positions which a protectionist may assume:

1. He may boldly declare that there is a science of wealth based on restriction; that he can discover the principles of it and reduce them to

a theory; that trade between countries is a mischievous thing, at least if it runs on parallels of latitude; that isolation and antagonism of nations is the law of nature upon which wealth and civilization depend; that there is therefore no universal science of wealth, but only a national science of wealth, and that this science, in its final analysis, is only a generalization from certain empirical maxims of economic policy. This is the position of the dogmatic or philosophical protectionists, who seek to give a certain abstract and philosophical cast to their speculations. It is the position of the List-Carey school, whose "unscientific science and unhistorical history" (as Roscher called it) seems to impose with such weight on some people. It is a view of the matter which is especially cultivated now by the learned protectionists of Germany, and which issues in some of the most remarkable curiosities of economic literature which have ever been produced either by the learned or the unlearned.

2. The other ground which the protectionist may take is that protection does not increase wealth, but is, for some reason or other, expedient.

In taking up again now the effort to put into simple, brief, and comprehensive form the argument against protection, I will separate these two modes of defending protection and take them in order. It is obvious that the two positions are inconsistent with each other, and every one who is familiar with the history of this controversy knows that its fruitlessness has been due, in a large measure, to the ambiguities, false definitions, and confusion which have prevailed in it. It has been a constant phenomenon in the discussion that the expediency of protection, in spite of the harm done by it, has been argued, and then the general utility of protection has been assumed as resulting from the argument. I do not know of any disputant on the protectionist side who does not move from one to the other of these positions, as his convenience or the pressure of the argument may force him, or who does not confuse them with each other.

It will be noted also that my point of attack is *protection* under any form or in any degree, and not import duties or taxes on consumption. This distinction can perhaps best be brought out by examining one of the peculiar and whimsical notions which avail to keep people from actually examining the matter in issue, viz., the notion of "revenue tariff with incidental protection." The people who believe that this jingle of words has any meaning in it must believe that the same man in supplying his needs does it at the same time in two ways, by importing and by buying at home too. If A wants a ton of iron and imports it, he pays duties on it which go to the public treasury. Not a cent for this transaction goes to the American producer of iron. This is why the American producer is so often heard to cry out in horror at the amount imported. If B wants a ton of iron and buys it at home, he pays the protective taxes to the home producer, and not a cent goes in revenue to the public treasury for that transaction. What incidental relation exists between these two transactions? They are independent and exclusive of each other. If we discard the empty formula of "revenue with incidental protection," we find that we are simply face to face with the problem of free trade *vs.* protection, or revenue *vs.* protection, as in the first place. Nothing has been done by this formula towards solving either of those problems. A only wanted one ton and took one way of getting it. B only wanted one ton and took another way of getting it. The question why either of them chose the course he did choose, and what the effects were on the interests of either of them, and on the welfare of the country, of the tax laws in question, remains still all before us. What is clear is only that protection and revenue are exclusive of each other. They do not overlap each other at all. The line between them is sharp and precise, and we can discuss the wisdom of protection entirely aside from the wisdom of raising revenue from customs duties. The latter question shall not therefore now be taken into account, and we confine our attention only to the former.

In this connection we may also dispose of another of the glib commonplaces by which people get rid of the trouble of thinking about the tariff controversy: that we have a large debt and therefore must have a high (protective) tariff. It is evident, since protection and revenue exclude each other, that not one cent which is paid in a protective tax goes into the public treasury or helps to pay either the principal or the interest of the debt, while, on the other hand, every cent paid in protective taxes lessens the power of the citizen to pay revenue taxes for the discharge of the public burdens. Hence the fact that we have heavy public burdens is just the reason why we cannot afford to squander our means in paying taxes to our neighbors for carrying on (as they themselves allege) unproductive industries. The especial iniquity of the present tariff, in a political point of view, is that it was laid under the cover of war taxes, taking advantage of the popular ignorance of the relation between protection and revenue, and of the popular willingness to submit to taxation for the purpose of the war. To argue that we want protective taxes because we have a large debt to pay is like arguing that a man ought to squander his income in benevolence because his means are just now being strained by an expensive lawsuit.

Having disposed of these notions which interfere with the approach to the real merits of the question, we may consider first whether protection can increase the wealth of the country.

## I

The problem of economic science is presented in the ratio between the efforts which men have to exert to supply their material needs and the amount and excellence of the food, clothing, lodging, furniture, fuel, etc., which they obtain. Political economy investigates the laws which govern this ratio so as to find out how we may determine the ratio as much as possible in our favor. Throwing aside all technicalities, the case is to find out how, for a given exertion and sacrifice, to get the maximum of material good. I maintain against any system of restriction whatsoever that it renders that ratio less favorable to men than it would be under freedom, taking the arts and sciences, the land and the population, as they are in the country where restriction is applied. Instead of increasing wealth, it is mathematically demonstrable that it lessens wealth, makes it harder to get a living and lowers the comfort of the population, and that it does this by taking away one man's earnings to give them to another. I mean to say that a man must work harder and longer to get a given amount of product under protection than under free trade, and I mean to say that this state of things is due to the statute law, which steps in and takes away part of his product and gives it to another man. The issue is purposely stated here without the use of any of the technical terms of political economy, because the simpler and homelier the language is the more correctly does it state the question, both in its economic and its political aspects, both in its scientific and in its popular significance, free from all admixture of either sentimental or pedantic rubbish. The economic question about the tariff is: Does it enable the population of the country to command greater material good for a given effort? The political question about protection is: Does the statute enacted by the legislature alter the distribution of property so that one man enjoys another man's earnings? Has the state a law in operation which enables one citizen to collect taxes of another? The scientific question about protection is: Does it lessen the ratio of effort and sacrifice to comfort and enjoyment? The popular question about protection is: Does it prevent me from supporting myself and family, by my labor, as well as I could do if there were no protective taxes?

The philosophical protectionists at once reply that this is not the question, or at least not the whole of it. To them political economy is not an independent science. They are not willing to consider the question of wealth aside from other things. They want to embrace in the view what they call moral, political, social, aesthetical, and sentimental considerations. Their instinct is perfectly correct when they oppose those operations of analysis and classification which would introduce clearness and precision into the discussion. The part of social science which has the most positive and mathematical character is the one against which they cannot stand. They write no books on political economy, but always on social science, in order to keep clear mixed with the unclear, the physical with the metaphysical, the positive with the arbitrary. They are eagerly followed by all the popular orators and writers on economic questions, and generally by those metaphysicians and students of other sciences who take part in sociological discussions, and almost always prove themselves the most reckless dogmatizers when they do so. The attraction of the *a priori* method, and of abstract and general propositions for ill-trained men, is well known, and, generally, in proportion as one is untrained in a particular science (whatever may be his status in others) will be his readiness to fly to *a priori* methods and to dogmas which are conveniently vague, loose, and broad, when he engages in the discussion of questions appertaining to the science in which he has not been trained.

Mr. Carey, for instance, filled his books with vague diatribes about "association." He thought to have found a great principle under this name. He wanted to break off all the natural ties and bonds of mankind in order to piece the parts together again on a plan of his own. He accordingly wrote big books on "social science," and he never reached the first conception of the forces which may truly be called social, or the laws by which they act. He and his school, in this country and in Germany, have never learned to see the great bonds of human society which are developed by intercourse and communication, which hold the nations to a mutual giving and taking as they grow in civilization, which are stronger in proportion as they are natural, informal, impersonal, spontaneous, and in comparison with which all artificial co-operation is ridiculously insignificant. For our present purpose, however, the thing to note is that social speculations and sociological investigations have nothing whatever to do with the tariff for protection. They only obscure and confuse the tariff question. If we should classify them we should find that they are either broader generalizations which flow necessarily from sound economic principles, and so can be left to take care of themselves while the economic investigations are going on; or else they are sociological doctrines which are parallel with sound economic doctrines, but which are most successfully pursued in special investigations; or else (which is by far the largest class) they are sentimental whims, popular notions, and metaphysical dogmas, which are not true, or at best are only half true, but which cannot be refuted without allowing the discussion to fritter itself away in innumerable side issues. We have to understand that an economic investigation may be carried on just as independently as a chemical or physical or biological investigation. The economist does not need to be on the lookout all the time to correct his results by reference to some outside considerations, or to the dogmas of jejune and rickety systems of metaphysical speculation. On the contrary, he should regard the introduction of extraneous elements, no matter under what high-sounding names, of moral, political, and social, as sure signs of impending confusion and fallacy, and he should especially repel any attempt to measure and criticise his results by the facile generalizations of *a priori* speculation. So much being here briefly set out, we may devote ourselves to the question of protection as a question of wealth and political economy only, as above described.

Let us take the case of a new country. It is claimed that a new country needs protection in order to get a start. Mill seemed to make some concession to this case. I have heard a man who was not a protectionist and who was a professional economist say that he thought a new colony might get into a situation in which it might need a lift to move it on in the way of growth. I will take up this latter view of the matter for discussion because it is the case which, if disproved, will *a fortiori* carry all the other forms of this claim with it.

I pass over the practical difficulty involved in the question who is to decide when the juncture supposed has come about, and who is to prescribe or give the lift; I pass over the unscientific and incorrect conception of economic forces involved in the hypothesis that a nation can get into any such position, and also in the notion of a "lift" to be given to a nation, in order that I may come to the real test of the remedy proposed, if the case could arise, and if the remedy were practically available. It is evident that a protective tariff cannot render any foreign capital or labor available to help the nation which lays the tariff. If a nation lays import duties for revenue some part of them may fall on the foreigner, but if it lays such duties for protection it keeps foreign goods out. If, then, the foreigner stays at home and is forced to keep his goods at home, the protecting country cannot make use of him or his goods in any way whatever to suit its ends or avert its misfortunes. Whatever effect the protective taxes exert must be exerted in the protecting country, on its own labor and capital. Any favor or encouragement which the protective system exerts on one group of its population must be won by an equivalent oppression exerted on some other group. To suppose the contrary is to deny the most obvious application of the conservation of energy to economic forces. If the legislation did not simply transfer capital it would have to make capital out of nothing. Now the transfer is not simply an equal redistribution; there is loss and waste in the case of any tax whatsoever. There is especial loss and waste in the case of a protective tax. We cannot collect taxes and redistribute them without loss; much less can we produce forced monopolies and distorted industrial relations without loss. It follows then that if a nation could come into some temporary industrial compression or arrested growth, a protective tariff not only would not help it out, but would contribute to still further limit its powers of self-development and to restrain its recuperative energies.

We have then reduced the issue which we are discussing to such terms that, after analyzing the phenomena, we are able to test the protectionist theory by universal canons of science, and we have a mathematical demonstration that protection is a delusion, which, like bimetallism, fiat money, socialism, and utopianism, is an attempt to make something out of nothing, or to create energy by law.

Here we shall be met, however, by the people who insist on believing that a better organization of labor, or greater activity of labor, or some other advantage which is real altho not specific, more than offsets the injury, or that the injured ones participate again in some vague gain. It is very singular that the people who believe in these notions are so slow to understand the fact that whatever lessens the wealth of a community, in the widest generalization or deduction only lessens its wealth! and cannot possibly increase it, and that the result is either to lessen the wealth *per capita,* or, if some do not become poorer, then others must be rendered still more poor. The protective tariff must act on people who without it would distribute their industry according to the chances of the greatest profit. The tariff is needed, by the protectionist hypothesis, in order to counteract the distribution which is thus brought about. But the tariff itself can appeal to no motive save that of desire for profit. It does so by providing that a certain industry shall, under protection, pay higher profits than it could under freedom, and it expects that this inducement will operate to make labor and capital seek this industry. If then desire for profit was not a sufficient and wise guide under freedom, what makes it such under protection? The notion that the legislature has a wisdom greater than that of the people, and can point out the industries they ought to pursue, has often been refuted; but the protective theory really assumes more than that. It assumes that the law can enlighten the desire for profit, and make it a more trustworthy guide than it would be under freedom. In truth there is nothing at all wanted in the cases to which protection is applied but capital, which the law can never produce. The efficiency of the tariff is that it does get this capital—from other people. The rest is all phrases intended to occupy attention while the thimblerig is going on. If this is not so, let some protectionist analyze the operation of his system, and show by reference to undisputed economic principles where and how it exerts any effect on production to increase it. Customs sometimes grow up under the efforts of men to bring about arrangements which will be convenient for industry and commerce. The law can often follow these customs, recognize them, and give them positive form. Institutions grow out of needs, and to meet purposes, to which institutions the law can give form and sanction. I know of nothing more than this which the law can do for industry.

What has been proved now of a new country holds true all the more of an old one. The only difference is that a new country may endure protection while an old one cannot. A new country which produces, as all new countries do, food and raw materials may create parasite industries to live on the exuberant productions of its natural industries, and on the special advantage in exchange which a new country has when it exchanges food and raw materials for finished products. An old country cannot exclude food and raw materials. In a new country the burden of the tariff system falls on the superfluity of the people—superfluity not in respect to what they would like to have, but in comparison with what people in old countries have. In an old country there are large classes persons who are at best on the verge of poverty, and who are forced to labor hard and for long hours to win subsistence. Taxes on food and raw materials would crush these classes down to misery. Germany is trying it with a tariff which is quite insignificant compared with ours. What I have proved, therefore, with regard to the effect of a protective tariff in a new country holds a fortiori in an old country, and is true universally. A restricted trade lowers the physical well-being of the population, and, with that, all chance of intellectual and moral well-being, below what it would be under free trade, with the same conditions of labor, capital, and land.

## II

I go on then to consider the other protectionist position: that protection is not a means of wealth, but is temporarily expedient.

Under this head the controversy has rambled over the whole field of economic speculation, embracing also all history and all statistics, and here also the vague sentimental and metaphysical considerations have had the greater scope, as this is the more popular branch of the controversy. I propose to notice only two or three of the arguments for the expediency of the protective tariff, and those I must take more by way of illustration.

During the recent political campaign the chief argument which was used was that the tariff made wages high. I have before me a circular which was widely distributed in which wage-receivers were told that free trade would either force employers to close their shops or to reduce their wages to foreign rates. In Germany the argument is that English workers get higher wages, which proves that they are better workmen, and that the Germans need protection against them. In America the argument is that the Englishmen do not get as good wages as the Americans, and that therefore the Americans need protection. The advantage of an empirical argument is that it goes as well one end foremost as the other. Suppose the Germans should argue like the Americans. They would then have to argue that free trade would *raise* their wages to the English rate, as the Americans argue that free trade would lower *their* wages to the English rate. Suppose the Americans should borrow the German argument. They would then have to argue that, as the Americans get higher wages, it proves that they are better workmen that the English, and need no protection against them, and *a fortiori* none against the workmen of the Continent.

There is one entirely American element in this argument, however. That is the claim or assumption that the high comfort of the American laborers is due to the tariff. One orator during the last campaign, who spoke with the authority of high official position, spoke with contempt and impatience of the low plane on which this tariff question is discussed, as if it were a mere question of dollars and cents, when in fact it is a question of status of the population and of the well-being of the wages classes.

We must distinguish here two propositions about wages which are constantly confused with each other, and which the protectionists find it very useful to confuse, altho they are inconsistent with each other, and both are false.

It is argued (1) that we want protection because wages are high, and (2) that we want protection in order to make wages high. To the legislature the high wages are represented as caused by some independent forces, and as a fact in the condition of the country which constitutes a reason for protection. To the workman it is argued that, the politicians and the employers having considered the matter and agreed that the American workingman ought to be well fed, clothed, etc., they have decided that he must have high wages, and that the tariff is the way to get them for him. This picture of the employers neglecting their business to lobby for a rise in the wages of their own men would be entertaining if it were not really so successful in deceiving those to whom it is addressed. The two branches of this argument about wages demand separate consideration.

1. Sociology is such a new science, and is as yet so little understood, that it is not strange if its doctrines have not yet spread very far through the community, but a superficial acquaintance with it would prevent any one from believing that politicians and statesmen can plan what sort of a people it would please them to have, or what degree of comfort they consider appropriate for the working classes. Nevertheless we have hundreds of politicians and orators who always start from a conception of this sort. It is evident, however, that the people of the United States must get their living out of the soil of the United States. We have an immense amount of land of the best quality, navigable rivers, great forests, mines of metal and coal, and we have to get out what we can with the labor and capital at our disposal. Whatever we get out will be distributed amongst us according to our shares in the production. As the natural stores are very rich and easy to get at, and as the laborers are few, it follows that the average product per laborer is greater than can be obtained in old countries, where the soil is more or less exhausted, and where the population is so dense as to make the competition of life very hard. This latter state of things affords us the second term of comparison by which we measure our status. Taken absolutely, there is plenty of room for improvement in our situation, and in the status of whole classes of our population.

We have, then, a perfectly obvious and sufficient explanation of the status of our people in natural facts. The statesmen have never planned this or done anything to help it. They have only marred it more or less. What we are is the result of our inherited traits and traditions, and of our physical surroundings. What there is about us which is good or bad, strong or weak, is alike to be attributed to these causes. High wages,

therefore, or, more properly speaking, high average comfort, with little
pauperism or misery, are incidents of our situation as early comers on
a new continent. Yet there are people who tell us that they, in their
wisdom, have made us well off by taxing us, and that we should not be
so well off any more if we should get rid of the taxes, and they persuade
the people who pay nearly all the taxes on consumption—namely, the
artisans and laborers—that they could not get their living on this continent if they did not pay taxes. That is like telling a laborer who opens
his dinner-pail that he would have more dinner if he would throw away
a slice of bread.

This continent, however, is not so exclusively favored that it is likely
to draw to itself all the population of the globe. Other continents have
their advantages, and the one which has the best advantages for food
and raw materials cannot in the nature of things have those advantages
which come from a dense population and a high development of the
arts and sciences. No one will be willing to turn away from the industries
for which the country offers the best advantages to take up those in
which other countries have the best advantages, unless the difference
can be made up to him in some way. Hence manufacturing industry here
has always had to contend with the profits possible in agricultural pursuits. Wages—so far as any wages class has ever yet been developed
here—must be high enough to give the same scale of comfort as can be
won in using land. The high wages and general high average of comfort
are, therefore, plainly the same thing, and both proceed together out of
the actual physical circumstances of the people.

What, then, can the tariff do about wages? It can only increase the
wages in mechanical pursuits by deducting from the gains of agriculture.
As we said above, it can win nothing for some without an equivalent or
greater deduction from others. It no doubt draws upon each mechanical
industry to make it help support all the others, and so it weakens them
all; but whatever strength and help it brings to them as a group it must
take from other groups. If, then, we are candidly seeking for the true
effects of the restrictive system on the national welfare, and on the welfare of special classes, we must note that this operation cannot increase
the national welfare, and we must look to see on whom it is that the
corresponding loss falls. It is plain that it is upon the agricultural industries of the country, and accordingly a special bundle of fallacies has
been devised for deceiving the agriculturists into the belief that they are
gainers by it. It is evident, however, that every reduction in agricultural
profits makes it easier for the employer to compete with the land for

labor. The rising wages and the falling profits of agriculture meet each other at a point below what the profits of agriculture would be under freedom. If there were no tariff, the wages of the wages class must go up to the full measure of the agricultural profits under freedom. Hence the tariff lowers wages. It never has had and never can have any other effect. The employer in a protected industry pays no more than market rates for wages, and he could not possibly pay any less. The notion that he could lower wages to some foreign level in the midst of the country where labor could win higher rewards is of course absurd.

We see, then, that the argument that the tariff makes wages high is entirely without foundation. It has lowered wages. We see that the notion of having a tariff in order to secure to our people what they have as their birthright, and what the tariff only diminishes, viz., a comparatively better and easier existence than the people of older countries, is an imposture. It has very great popular effect because the popular notion is generally that we owe all our prosperity to ourselves and to what we call "our institutions," when in truth we owe everything that we are to historical antecedents and physical conditions.

Having stripped off this humbug from the issue, as stated by the protectionists, we may come back to the scornful complaint that we are discussing the question on a low level. We were told that we ought to debate it as a great question of status of the population, etc., and we have found that this was all rhetoric and fustian except the effect of the tariff to lower the status of the population. It follows, then, that we were right to debate it as a question of dollars and cents only. There is nothing else in it. A wants protection; that is, he wants B's money. B does not want to let him have it. A talks sentiment and metaphysics finely, and, after all, all there is in it is that he wants B's money. A does not otherwise show much interest in sentiment and patriotism and metaphysical goods generally. He never goes to Washington to lobby for education, or scientific research, or geographical exploration, or for any philanthropic scheme, unless there is a chance in it for him to get B's money. He is then moved to scorn at B's sordid love of money, and he goes to hear a lecture on "materialism" to gratify his wounded feelings because B will not give up his money. The matter is all stated from A's standpoint. We see him all the time. For him to want B's money is patriotic. It is "developing our resources." It is noble. For B to want to keep the same money is mean. I insist upon the matter being stated in the most crass and vulgar way, just because that is all there is of it when the humbug is all eliminated. The student of history then recognizes a very old

friend. The robber-barons, Robin Hood, Dick Turpin, and others have
had the same opinion of the nobility of wanting other people's money,
and of the meanness of the "trader" or laborer who did not want to lose
his earnings.

2. Let us next look at the other doctrine, that we need a protective
tariff because wages are high; or the equivalent doctrine, that we cannot
compete. The people of the United States can compete with anybody in
getting wealth. The high wages are a proof of it; but they cannot compete
with everybody else in every form of industry. They have only a limited
number of laborers and a limited amount of capital. The same man
cannot be doing two things at once. The same capital cannot be employed in two uses. Hence it will be wise and necessary to choose the
most profitable of all the profitable employments which are possible. It
will follow that we cannot afford to compete in any industry which will
not pay here as well as those which have special advantages here. If we
cannot compete, it is because we cannot afford to compete. We are too
well off. We cannot compete with "foreign paupers," just because we
are not paupers. "Pauper," of course, is one of those silly and invidious
terms which have been introduced into this discussion in the interest
of falsehood and folly. Paupers and princes live in idleness supported
by taxation. No one can compete with them. Seriously, then, we cannot
compete with men who are fiercely competing with each other for low
wages in a dense population because we are not fiercely competing with
each other. We have abundant chances. The protectionists are not content, however, to use our advantages and avoid competition, which is
what every sensible man does in private life. According to them we
must go to seek competition. It will be told in history that a public bureau
of our government spent part of the capital of the nation in seeking
competition with Chinamen in making tea, at the very moment when
the same government was trying to devise means to prevent Chinese
competition in this country, where it could do no harm. As we shall
seek competition with less favorably situated people only at a constant
loss as compared with the gains we might win in our own favored industries, those who are carrying on the self-supporting industries must
pay taxes to make up the loss, and the wealth of the country must
undergo a constant waste. If a blacksmith should say that he could not
compete with the shoemaker at making shoes, and therefore that he
ought to be paid twice as much as the shoemaker for making shoes, his
sanity would be doubted, but that is just the argument that we need a
tariff because wages are high. It is because wages are high that we do

not need one, and it is because we cannot compete in certain industries that we ought not to try. Some people think it is derogatory to us not to do everything for ourselves; and as they always seem glad to hear that we are exporting more and more, they seem to be desirous that we should make things for all the rest of the world too. What, then, I ask, is the rest of the world to do for us? If we take all the industries, how will they pay us for what we do for them? Competition is the force which under freedom indicates to us what we can do for ourselves and them, and what we can let them do for us to our final maximum advantage. To shut off competition and go into the industries which the ignorant empiricism of Congress or the caprice of individuals may select, is like unhinging the compass and steering the ship by chance.

3. There is no argument for the expediency of the tariff to be found in the matter of wages in any of its aspects, but it is sometimes claimed that it is expedient to force certain industries into existence. This is called "developing our industries." We are good-natured enough to call them "our" industries, perhaps because we all pay taxes to support them, not because we own stock in them or participate in the profits. There is a very strong popular notion that it is a good thing for A, B, and C that there should be certain mills, factories, etc., up and down the country—a notion which has no support in fact at all, unless A, B, and C are owners of land near the factories, etc. If an individual were shown statistics of men employed, wages, capital, plant, output, etc., of a certain establishment, and were asked to invest in it, he would no doubt inquire, after all, whether the establishment made profits, since unfortunately not every big chimney does so; but when we are making speeches or writing essays about tariff, this last question is entirely ignored, and big figures and exclamation-points take the place of the only question which is important. If an industry does not pay, it is an industrial abomination. It is wasting and destroying. The larger it is the more mischief it does. The protected manufacturer is forced to allege, when he asks for protection, that his business would not pay without it. He proposes to waste capital. If he should waste his own wealth he would not go on long. He therefore asks the legislature to give him power to lay taxes on his fellow-citizens, to collect from them the capital which he intends to waste, and good wages for himself while he is carrying on that business besides. This is what is called "developing our industries," and the operation of the law is such that the waste and destruction can go on indefinitely. Either an industry can pay under freedom, in which case it does not need protection, or else it would not pay under freedom,

in which case it is wasting the wealth of the nation as long as it goes on.
It follows that the protective tariff is not a temporary expedient, and it
is mathematically impossible that it should ever issue in an independent
and productive industry. Other forces may come into play in time, viz.,
those which would at that time have called the industry in question into
existence, and these forces may render the industry independent, but
the tariff can never produce any such result.

4. Some have believed that the tariff system brought capital into the
country, and two or three instances of foreign manufacturers who have
established branches here have been pointed to as triumphant proofs of
it. I know of no statistics either of the amount of capital so imported or
the amount which the tariff has caused to be exported; but I should
judge from such information as I have that one just about equalled the
other. What is far more important, however, is that if the tariff were
taken off any one of a great number of important articles, the people
could save more capital in a month out of their diminished cost of living
than all the capital which has been brought in here in twenty years on
account of the tariff. A similar observation applies to the argument for
deferring the reform of the tariff, that it would destroy capital now invested. No one proposes or desires any reckless action which would
disregard vested interests of any kind, altho I do not see what difference
it would make with what any one would really *do*, whether he had
warning that the tariff would be repealed in five years or in five days,
but that is a question for a statesman, and not for an economist. The
economist may point out that, if any capital were destroyed, the savings
of the people from a diminished cost of living would constitute an enormous fund for replacing that capital and offsetting that loss, so that, as
far as the mere loss of capital is concerned, there would be no argument
for delay.

5. I proceed to a brief but very cogent argument why a protective tariff
is not expedient. Protection works all the time against improvement. In
April, 1838, New York City indulged in great rejoicings over the arrival
of the first steamships from Europe. In April, 1842, at an "Industrial
Convention" held in New York City, the opening of steam navigation on
the ocean was alleged as one of the chief arguments for protection. We
are taxed to open our rivers and harbors, and the result is cheaper goods.
That is the benefit which we anticipated and were working for, thinking
that it would be a gain. As soon as it is realized, however, comes a clamor
from home-producers of those kinds of goods which have been cheap-
ened. "What! Do you mean to say that it is a good thing for the country

to have people get the things which we make at a low price? This will never do;" and so a tax-barrier is set up across the rivers and harbors to imitate the former barrier of sand and rock, and make things as dear and as hard to get as before. If protection is expedient, then this argument is sound, and we need more protection the more our communication with foreign nations is facilitated. Steamships, ocean cables, and cheap newspapers are all the time neutralizing the existing protection, and more taxes are necessary to give the same protection. If protection is sound, then those who rejoice over improvements in communication and transportation and support protection are guilty of absurd folly. If improvements, inventions, and discoveries are real benefits to mankind, then protection is inexpedient as well as philosophically absurd.

Commerce is plainly entering on a new stage. Common-sense makes its way very slowly into the minds of men when it has to rely on its own merits, but the course of progress in industry and commerce is such that self-interest often becomes hand-maid to common-sense, and then common-sense gets a chance. We have seen five or six new industries grow up in this country within a few years. They are all "land" industries; that is, they belong to the natural advantages of the country. They are in their infancy, but they are already great, and what they are to become no one can guess. They depend on a foreign market, and they have been made possible by cheap and quick ocean transit. Within a year a fleet of new steamers promises new growth in the same direction. The internal transportation of the country, especially in the West and South-west, will support the same growth. The effect is to cause great changes in the distribution of labor, great absorptions of capital in new orders of investments, and the creation of immense new interests. It would be over-bold to predict specific results, but this much is clear: the competition of American agriculture will drive English labor and capital more exclusively into manufacturing and commerce. The complementary effect must be exerted here, and the profits of land industries will draw off labor and capital from manufactures and commerce. In other words, the international division of labor will be rendered more perfect, and the consequence must be greater wealth for all. But if the tariff still remains as a barrier to imports, *i.e.*, return cargoes, the exchanges must rule low to the detriment of all the exporting interests, and if specie is imported prices must advance. But the exports cannot rise, since they are forced to seek a foreign market. They will therefore be low, while everything else inside the country is high. This is, of course, the operation of the tariff now all the time, and it is the mode in which the tariff oppresses the land industries; but the whole course of the development which I am anticipating will be to make this oppression harder and sharper, while the tariff will all the time need to be raised higher and higher if it is to be of any avail at all. How long will the system stand such a double strain? If there is any industry which really depends upon the tariff, it cannot too soon begin to learn to do without it.

# The Philosophy of Strikes

Although Sumner bitterly denounced the railway strikers in 1877, his position had softened by the time the telegraphers struck in 1883. No longer condemning all unions, he also rejected the cooperative movement's position that employers and employees shared a common interest. Rather, he now judged strikes to be a legitimate part of the industrial process precisely because the two groups were locked in a process partly cooperative but necessarily antagonistic. His comments on "progress" were aimed at Henry George. Originally published in *Harper's Weekly* 27 (September 15, 1883), 586–587; reprinted in *Forgotten Man*, ed. Albert Galloway Keller, pp. 239–246.

The progress in material comfort which has been made during the last hundred years has not produced content. Quite the contrary: the men of to-day are not nearly so contented with life on earth as their ancestors were. This observation is easily explainable by familiar facts in human nature. If satisfaction does not reach to the pitch of satiety, it does not produce content, but discontent; it is therefore a stimulus to more effort, and is essential to growth. If, however, we confine our study of the observation which we have made to its sociological aspects, we perceive that all which we call "progress" is limited by the counter-movements which it creates, and we also see the true meaning of the phenomena which have led some to the crude and silly absurdity that progress makes us worse off. Progress certainly does not make people happier, unless their mental and moral growth corresponds to the greater command of material comfort which they win. All that we call progress is a simple enlargement of chances, and the question of personal happiness is a question of how the chances will be used. It follows that if men do not grow in their knowledge of life and in their intelligent judgment of the rules of right living as rapidly as they gain control over physical resources, they will not win happiness at all. They will simply accumulate chances which they do not know how to use.

The observation which has just been made about individual happiness has also a public or social aspect which is important. It is essential that the political institutions, the social code, and the accepted notions which constitute public opinion should develop in equal measure with the increase of power over nature. The penalty of failure to maintain due proportion between the popular philosophy of life and the increase of material comfort will be social convulsions, which will arrest civilization and will subject the human race to such a reaction toward barbarism as that which followed the fall of the Roman Empire. It is easy to see that at the present moment our popular philosophy of life is all in confusion. The old codes are breaking down; new ones are not yet made; and even amongst people of standing, to whom we must look to establish the body of public opinion, we hear the most contradictory and heterogeneous doctrines about life and society.

The growth of the United States has done a great deal to break up the traditional codes and creeds which had been adopted in Europe. The civilized world being divided into two parts, one old and densely populated and the other new and thinly populated, social phenomena have been produced which, although completely covered by the same laws of social force, have appeared to be contradictory. The effect has been to disturb and break up the faith of philosophers and students in the laws, and to engender numberless fallacies amongst those who are not careful students. The popular judgment especially has been disordered and misled. The new country has offered such chances as no generation of men has ever had before. It has not, however, enabled any man to live without work, or to keep capital without thrift and prudence; it has not enabled a man to "rise in the world" from a position of ignorance and poverty, and at the same time to marry early, spend freely, and bring up a large family of children.

The men of this generation, therefore, without distinction of class, and with only individual exceptions, suffer from the discontent of an appetite excited by a taste of luxury, but held far below satiety. The power to appreciate a remote future good, in comparison with a present one, is a distinguishing mark of highly civilized men, but if it is not combined with powers of persevering industry and self-denial, it degenerates into mere day-dreaming and the diseases of an overheated imagination. If any number of persons are of this character, we have morbid discontent and romantic ambition as social traits. Our literature, especially our fiction, bears witness to the existence of classes who are corrupted by these diseases of character. We find classes of persons who are whining and fault-finding, and who use the organs of public discussion and deliberation in order to put forth childish complaints and impossible demands, while they philosophize about life like the *Arabian Nights*. Of course this whole tone of thought and mode of behavior is as far as possible from the sturdy manliness which meets the problems of life and wins victories as much by what it endures as by what it conquers.

Our American life, by its ease, exerts another demoralizing effect on a great many of us. Hundreds of our young people grow up without any real discipline; life is made easy for them, and their tastes and wishes are consulted too much; they grow to maturity with the notion that they ought to find the world only pleasant and easy. Every one knows this type of young person, who wants to find an occupation which he would "like," and who discusses the drawbacks of difficulty or disagreeableness in anything which offers. The point here referred to is, of course, entirely different from another and still more lamentable fact, that is, the terrible inefficiency and incapability of a great many of the people who are complaining and begging. If any one wants a copyist, he will be more saddened than annoyed by the overwhelming applications for the position. The advertisements which are to be found in the newspapers of widest circulation, offering a genteel occupation to be carried on at home, not requiring any previous training, by which two or three dollars a day may be earned, are a proof of the existence of a class to which they appeal. How many thousand people in the United States want just that kind of employment! What a beautiful world this would be if there were any such employment!

Then, again, our social ambition is often silly and mischievous. Our young people despise the occupations which involve physical effort or dirt, and they struggle "up" (as we have agreed to call it) into all the nondescript and irregular employments which are clean and genteel. Our orators and poets talk about the "dignity of labor," and neither they nor we believe in it. Leisure, not labor, is dignified. Nearly all of us, however, have to sacrifice our dignity, and labor, and it would be to the purpose if, instead of declamation about dignity, we should learn to respect, in ourselves and each other, work which is good of its kind, no matter what the kind is. To spoil a good shoemaker in order to make a bad parson is surely not going "up"; and a man who digs well is by all sound criteria superior to the man who writes ill. Everybody who talks to American schoolboys thinks that he does them and his country service if he reminds them that each one of them has a chance to be President of the United States, and our literature is all the time stimulating the same kind of senseless social ambition, instead of inculcating the code and the standards which should be adopted by orderly, sober, and useful citizens.

The consequences of the observations which have now been grouped together are familiar to us all. Population tends from the country to the city. Mechanical and technical occupations are abandoned, and those occupations which are easy and genteel are overcrowded. Of course the persons in question must be allowed to take their own choice, and seek their own happiness in their own way, but it is inevitable that thousands of them should be disappointed and suffer. If the young men abandon farms and trades to become clerks and bookkeepers, the consequence will be that the remuneration of the crowded occupations will fall, and that of the neglected occupations will rise; if the young women refuse to do housework, and go into shops, stores, telegraph offices and schools, the wages of the crowded occupations will fall, while those of domestic servants advance. If women in seeking occupation try to gain admission to some business like telegraphing, in competition with men, they will bid under the men. Similar effects would be produced if a leisure class in an old country should be compelled by some social convulsion to support themselves. They would run down the compensation for labor in the few occupations which they could enter.

Now the question is raised whether there is any remedy for the low wages of the crowded occupations, and the question answers itself: there is no remedy except not to continue the causes of the evil. To strike, that is, to say that the workers will not work in their chosen line, yet that they will not leave it for some other line, is simply suicide. Neither can any amount of declamation, nor even of law-making, force a man who owns a business to submit the control of it to a man who does not own it. The telegraphers have an occupation which requires training and skill, but it is one which is very attractive in many respects to those who seek manual occupation; it is also an occupation which is very suitable, at least in many of its branches, for women. The occupation is therefore capable of a limited monopoly. The demand that women should be paid equally with men is, on the face of it, just, but its real effect would be to keep women out of the business. It was often said during the telegraphers' strike that the demand of the strikers was just, because their wages were less than those of artisans. The argument has no force at all. The only question was whether the current wages for telegraphing were sufficient to bring out an adequate supply of telegraphers. If the growing boys prefer to be artisans, the wages of telegraphers will rise. If, even at present rates, boys and girls continue to prefer telegraphing to handicraft or housework, the wages of telegraphers will fall. Could, then, a strike advance at a blow the wages of all who are now telegraphers? There was only one reason to hope so, and that was that the monopoly of the trade might prove stringent enough and the public inconvenience great enough to force a concession—which would, however, have been speedily lost again by an increased supply of telegraphers.

Now let us ask what the state of the case would be if it was really possible for the telegraphers to make a successful strike. They have a very close monopoly; six years ago they nearly arrested the transportation of the country for a fortnight; but they were unable to effect their object. More recently the freight-handlers struck against the competition of a new influx of foreign unskilled laborers, and in vain. The printers might make a combination, and try to force an advance in wages by arresting the publication of all the newspapers on a given day, but there are so many persons who could set type, in case of need, that such an attempt would be quite hopeless. In any branch of ordinary handicraft there would be no possibility of creating a working monopoly or of producing a great public calamity by a strike. If we go on to other occupations we see that bookkeepers, clerks, and salesmen could not as a body combine and strike; much less could teachers do so; still less could household servants do so. Finally, farmers and other independent workers could not do it at all. In short, a striker is a man who says: "I mean to get my living by doing this thing and no other thing as my share of the social effort, and I do not mean to do this thing except on such and such terms." He therefore proposes to make a contract with his fellow-men and to dictate the terms of it. Any man who can do this must be in a very exceptional situation; he must have a monopoly of the service in question, and it must be one of which his fellow-men have great need. If, then, the telegraphers could have succeeded in advancing their wages fifteen per cent simply because they had agreed to ask for the advance, they must have been far better off than any of the rest of their fellow-men.

Our fathers taught us the old maxim: Cut your coat according to your cloth; but the popular discussions of social questions seem to be leading up to a new maxim: Demand your cloth according to your coat. The fathers thought that a man in this world must do the best he could with the means he had, and that good training and education consisted in developing skill, sagacity, and thrift to use resources economically; the new doctrine seems to be that if a man has been born into this world he should make up his mind what he needs here, formulate his demands, and present them to "society" or to the "state." He wants congenial and easy occupation, and good pay for it. He does not want to be hampered by any limitations such as come from a world in which wool grows, but not coats; in which iron ore is found, but not weapons and tools; in which the ground will produce wheat, but only after hard labor and self-denial; in which we cannot eat our cake and keep it; in which two and two make only four. He wants to be guaranteed a "market," so as not to suffer from "overproduction." In private life and in personal relations we already estimate this way of looking at things at its true value, but as soon as we are called upon to deal with a general question, or a phenomenon of industry in which a number of persons are interested, we adopt an entirely conventional and unsound mode of discussion. The sound gospel of industry, prudence, painstaking, and thrift is, of course, unpopular; we all long to be emancipated from worry, anxiety, disappointment, and the whole train of cares which fall upon us as we work our way through the world. Can we really gain anything in that struggle by organizing for a battle with each other? This is the practical question. Is there any ground whatever for believing that we shall come to anything, by pursuing this line of effort, which will be of any benefit to anybody? If a man is dissatisfied with his position, let him strive to better it in one way or another by such chances as he can find or make, and let him inculcate in his children good habits and sound notions, so that they may live wisely and not expose themselves to hardship by error or folly; but every experiment only makes it more clear that for men to band together in order to carry on an industrial war, instead of being a remedy for disappointment in the ratio of satisfaction to effort, is only a way of courting new calamity.

# The Family Monopoly

Although Sumner celebrated the monogamous family, he was acutely aware of the gap between ideal and reality. In his marriage to Jeannie Elliott, he seemed to have found everything that his earlier family life lacked. Their first two years together were "among the happiest" of his life. However, the death of their firstborn at four months in July 1872 heralded a series of mishaps that blighted their life together. Although Jeannie gave birth successfully to two sons during the next decade, by 1880 her mental health had deteriorated for reasons unspecified. During 1882, she spent a full year in lodgings in Atlantic City recovering from nervous prostration, and she was later known for her "invalidism." The derelictions of Sumner's brother Joe now included charges of pilfering funds from the New Orleans Freedman's Bureau. His half-brother Henry embezzled money due to a sister, leaving Sumner to invite her and her daughter into his New Haven household. A passing reference in this essay to the difference between an unattached fifty year-old man and a married one "overwhelmed by anxiety" told much of the story of his own life in these years. Originally published in the *Independent*, May 10, 1888; reprinted in *Earth Hunger*, ed. Albert Galloway Keller, pp. 254–258.

In the current discussions about property, rights, and social relations, it is very rare to see any appreciation manifested of the connection between the family and property. Yet this connection lies at the root of the whole matter. The grandest and most powerful monopoly in the world is the family, in its monogamic form; we have sects which have perceived this and made it an object of their agitation. They are not large, and, for obvious reasons, they are regarded with suspicion and abhorrence by respectable people; but it is undeniable that when they inveigh against monogamic marriage as monopoly, and against the monogamic family as the hotbed of selfishness, they have facts to support their position which are as true and as much to the point as any of the current denunciations of monopoly and selfishness in reference to capital and the industrial system.

I beg the reader to note carefully the form and limits of the statement which I have just made. The parallel which I affirm is not rhetorical, it is in the essence of the facts; when I say that one set of assertions are as well grounded as the other, the force and point of the assertion lie in the "just as much as." Both are correct as to the facts in a certain measure and way; both are fallacious as they are ordinarily asserted and employed. It is not easy to deal with the matter from the side of the family within the proper restrictions, but the necessity of a better popular understanding of the general subject is so great that I am compelled to try it.

Speaking from the standpoint of social science, I hold monogamy to be the greatest step in the history of civilization. This opinion is, it is true, treated by some sociologists with ridicule; I, however, make bold to hold it and to believe that the present generation is not more false to its interests in any other respect than in its inadequate and distorted conception of what the monogamic family yet needs in the way of perfection and sanctity. I use the last term also with distinct intention, meaning thereby that religion has no higher function, in modern society, than to maintain all its institutional effect on marriage and the family.

The specific influence of the family is exerted on women and on children. The monogamic wife is the only wife who shares the life of her husband. Some other kinds of wives are greater than their husbands, and some are lower; the monogamic wife alone can have an independent and co-ordinate sphere, on an equal footing with her husband, yet different from his sphere. The children of a monogamic marriage alone have that home life, that atmosphere of affection and care, which produces the best human beings. They alone get true education; for it does not come from books and schools, it comes from tireless watching, patient training, persistent restraint and encouragement, at the fire-side and at all moments of life, weaving a tissue of unconscious habit into the fiber of the life of the future men and women.

This is, undoubtedly, an ideal, but it is not an ideal which floats in the air as a poetic vision alone. It is realized often enough and sufficiently in our observation for us to know that it can be, and is.

Monogamic marriage, however, is a great monopoly. It is grand and noble for those who get into it, but like other monopolies, it wins an advantage for those who are included at the cost of depression to those who are excluded; and millions, of course, in trying to attain to the heights of a monogamic marriage, fail. If they fall, they fall far lower than they would be under lower forms of marriage. The children of a monogamic family have a far better chance than those of any other form of the family, provided the monogamic family realizes approximately its own theory; but it is not impossible that the children reared in a Turkish harem may have a happier fate than the children of a monogamic household in which the parents quarrel or are divorced.

The monogamic family evidently owes its strength and value, then, to the fact that it constitutes a close and solid unit with greater internal cohesion than any other form of the family, and more complete severance externally from every other unit. Its exclusiveness is of its essence; it exerts an intenser educating power on its members on account of its distinctness and comparative isolation. Accordingly any form of communal life, any higher development of social relations, as in hotel life in this country, or in the case of fashionable life, where the attention of the parents is occupied outside of the family, causes the family life, the domestic influences, and the family education to suffer.

The people who, just now, are captivated by any "altruistic" notion cannot decide whether the family is to be included in the sphere of the selfish or the altruistic. Their quandary has its good causes in the facts of the case. The selfish and the altruistic sentiments are inextricably interwoven, and their interlacings or common ground lie in the family sphere; but the family institution, the isolated family group, as a unit, sharply severed and highly and distinctly developed against all other family units, is, in fact, the hotbed of those sentiments which are denounced as selfish—above all such of them as are connected with social rank and property.

The facts are open to the observation of all. "He that hath wife and children hath given hostages to fortune." If you intensify his family affection, you will in the same degree absorb his energies in the determination to redeem those pledges. If, therefore, the growth of social institutions is in the direction of monogamy, if we thereby win a better position for women and a better education for children, we also intensify a man's feeling of cohesion with his own wife and his own children, aside from and against all the world; and his and their interests, while more absolutely identified with each other, are set in more complete indifference or more pronounced antagonism to those of other people than any other social arrangement. This consequence is inevitable and it plainly exists. The sentiments which are nowadays jumbled together under the head of "individualism," in accordance with the general confusion and looseness with which all these matters are treated, are, in fact, products of this family sentiment.

The selfishest man in the world will pour out his money like water on his children. A man who fights all the world with pitiless energy in the industrial conflict, will show himself benevolent to his family. It is for them that he fights. A man of fifty, alone in the world, might feel indifferent about the accumulation of wealth, or look with comparative indifference upon the danger of monetary loss, but a similar man, with a family dependent upon him, is eager to win wealth, or is overwhelmed by anxiety at the danger of loss. It is not for themselves that men in middle life work; it is for wives and children.

I, therefore, agree perfectly with the socialists as to the facts of the case. They have always recognized the fact that property and the family are inextricably interwoven with each other from their very roots in the remotest origin of civilization. The more logical they are the more fearlessly they follow out this fact, and attack the family in order to succeed in their attack on property. It is to be conceded to them, at least, that they can see facts and estimate their significance, while the sentimentalists and semi-socialists only muddle everything. The issue is a plain one, and one which admits of no compromise whatever: property and the family stand or fall together; we must either maintain them both with the individualists, or overthrow them both with the socialists.

The people who talk about rooting out monopoly will never succeed in their undertaking until they root out that family monopoly which alone gives significance to all the others. It may be that in some abstract sense the earth was given to all mankind. What I want is a piece of it with which to support my family. When I get it (which I must do by going on until I find unoccupied land, or by a peaceful contract with some one already holding a monopoly, unless I propose to kill a monopolist family in order to put mine in its place) I shall want it as a monopoly, that is, I shall want to be sure that my children, and not any other man's, will eat the crop. There will, therefore, be "private property in land" there and I shall have no need of the "state," unless the state means simply that my neighbors will join with me in a mutual assurance that we can each guarantee the existence of our families by the monopoly of our land.

# Democracy and Plutocracy

Although Sumner inveighed against the dangers of "plutocracy" from the early 1870s, his definition of the term gradually changed. Initially, he identified plutocracy with the crass materialism of the new rich. By the mid-1880s, he viewed it more narrowly to describe those who made money through political rather then economic means. Originally published in the *Independent*: "Democracy and Plutocracy" on November 15, 1888; "Definitions of Democracy and Plutocracy" on December 20, 1888; and "The Conflict of Plutocracy and Democracy" on January 10, 1889; reprinted in *Earth Hunger*, ed. Albert Galloway Keller, pp. 283–300.

## Democracy and Plutocracy

One of the most difficult things to learn in social science is that every action inside of the social organism is attended by a reaction, and that this reaction may be spread far through the organism, affecting organs and modifying functions which are, at the first view of the matter, apparently so remote that they could not be affected at all. It is a more simple statement of the same fact to say that everything in the social organism displaces everything else. Therefore, if we set to work to interfere in the operation of the organism, with our attention all absorbed in one set of phenomena, and regulate our policy with a view to those phenomena only, we are very sure to do mischief. The current speculations about social policy and social reform suffer very largely from this error.

The organization of a modern civilized society is intensely high; its parts are extremely complicated. Their relations with each other are close, and all the tendencies of our time are making them closer; and the closer they are, the more surely and immediately are interferences distributed through them. The bonds of connection between them are constantly becoming more delicate and subtle; and they are sublimated, as it were, so that they escape the observation of the senses. In a simple society, even though it be on the height of the best civilization, all the parts of the organization lie bare to view, and every one can see the relations of agriculturist, transporter, banker, merchant, professional man, debtor, creditor, employer, and employee, in their visible operation. In a highly organized society as, for instance, in a big city, those same relations have all become automatic and impersonal. They have escaped from control; they are regulated by assumptions and understandings that every one is to do so and so; that certain uniform and constant motives, aims, and desires will present themselves as long as human society endures; and that men will, therefore, continue to exert themselves in a certain manner for the satisfaction of their wants. This is what we mean by natural law, and by the field of a science of society. If any one will look over his dinner table the next time he sits down to dinner, he can see the proofs that thousands of producers, transporters, merchants, bankers, policemen, and mechanics, through the whole organization of society and all over the globe, have been at work for the last year or more to put that dinner within his reach, on the assumption that he, too, would do his work in the organization, whatever it is, and be prepared to pay for the dinner when it reaches him. All these thousands and millions of people, therefore, have co-operated with each other for the common good of all, without acquaintance or conventional agreement, and without any personal interest in each other, under the play of forces which lie in human nature and in the conditions of human existence on this earth.

Now, the organs of society do not impinge upon each other with hard and grating friction, like blocks of granite wedged together. If they did the case would be easier, for then we should have only a mechanical contact, and the relations would be of a simple order. Neither are the relations those of an orchestra, which produces harmony by voluntary co-operation under training, according to a predetermined scheme, yet subject to the laws of harmony in sound. Nor are the relations like those of an army, where the co-operation is arbitrary, and enforced by discipline, although controlled by expediency for the attainment of an end under set conditions. The organs are elastic and they are plastic. They suffer both temporary and permanent modifications in form and function by their interaction on each other, and by the arbitrary interferences to which they are subjected by legislation or artifice of any kind. Thus, for instance, it is impossible to say how taxes will diffuse themselves; they may force a change in the immediate organ on which they fall—transporters, merchants, bankers—or they may be transmitted more or less through the organization.

It is this elasticity and plasticity of the organs of society which give the social tinker his chance, and make him think that there are no laws of the social order, no science of society; no limits, in fact, to the possibilities of manipulation by "The State."

He is always operating on the limit of give and take between the organs; he regards all the displacement which he can accomplish as positively new creation; he does not notice at all, and probably is not trained to perceive, the reaction—the other side of the change; he does not understand that he must endure a change on one side for all the change which he affects on the other. Since it is so hard to learn that exchange means exchange, and therefore has two sides to it, a giving and a taking—since, I say it is so hard to learn this, and people talk even about buying and selling as if they were independent operations, a fallacy which is itself the outcome of a high organization with a money system—then it is not strange that it should be so hard to learn that all social change is change, has two sides to it—the cost and the gain, the price and the product, the sacrifice and the obtainment.

Hence we see one fallacy of nearly all the popular propositions of "reform": they would not be amiss, perhaps, if the change which they propose could be made and everything else remain the same.

In the proposition it is assumed that everything else is to remain the same. But it is inevitable that other things will not remain the same; they will all of them adjust themselves to the new elements which are introduced. If we make a change involving expense, taxes must be increased, and every taxed interest must undergo a change to fit it to the new conditions. I know of no reform by state agency which does not involve increased taxation.

Let us note another fact. In the advancing organization of society, the tendency is all the time to subdivide the functions, and each one is assumed by a different set of persons; thus the interests of living men and women become enlisted in all the play of the organs, and are at stake in all the legislative and other interferences. What I have called the elasticity and plasticity of the organs means in fact the rights, interest, happiness, and prosperity of the one set of human beings versus the same interests of another set of human beings. It is men who strive, and suffer, and plan, and fight, and steal, and kill, when the great impersonal and automatic forces push them up against each other, or push group against group. The tendency is all the time to go back from the industrial struggle to the military struggle. Every strike illustrates it. Better educated people, while talking about respect for the law, seize upon legislation as the modern mode of pursuing the military struggle under the forms of peace and order—that is to say, they turn from industrial competition and industrial effort to legislative compulsion, and to arbitrary advantages won and secured through the direction and the power of the state. When the strikers and Knights of Labor declare that they are going to reach after this power, they have simply determined to contend for the latest form of force by which to supersede the industrial struggle for existence by a struggle of craft and physical force. Yet there are those who tell us that this is really a supersession of the struggle for existence by intelligence and "ethical" forces, as if every page of the Congressional Record did not reveal the sordidness of the plans and motives by which it is all controlled.

Here comes in another fallacy in the philosophy of state interference. Let the reader note for himself with what *naïveté* the advocate of interference takes it for granted that he and his associates will have the administration of their legislative device in their own hands and will be sure of guiding it for their purposes only. They never appear to remember that the device, when once set up, will itself become the prize of a struggle; that it will serve one set of purposes as well as another, so that after all the only serious question is: who will get it? Here is another ground for a general and sweeping policy of non-interference. Although you may be in possession of the power of the state to-day, and it might suit you very well, either to triumph over your business rivals and competitors; or to bend to your will the social organ which stands next to you, and with which you have the most friction (as, for instance, shippers with transporters); or to see your pet reform (temperance, for instance) marching on, you would far better consent to forego your satisfaction, lest presently your rivals, or the railroads, or the liquor-sellers, should beat you in a political struggle; and then you must suffer wrong and in the end be forced to give up industrial and persuasive methods altogether and devote your whole energy to the political struggle, as that on which all the rest depends.

Of all that I have here said, the Interstate Commerce Law is the instance which stands out in point with the greatest distinctness. The shippers and transporters, the competing railroads, the people who can extort passes and those who do not want to give them, the people at way-stations and those at competing points, and other interests also which cluster about the transportation, which is the most important element in the opening up of this great and rich continent, all clash and struggle for shares in the wealth which the people of the United States produce. The contest has phases and vicissitudes of every description. The politicians, editors, economists, *littérateurs*, lawyers, labor agitators, and countless others who, in one way or another, have something to make out of it, join in the struggle, taking sides with the principal parties, or hovering around the strife for what may turn up in it. When once the fatal step is taken of invoking legislation, the contest is changed in its character and in its arena. That is all that is accomplished; from that time on the questions are: who will get this legislative power? Which interest or coalition of interests (such as passed the bill) will get this, the decisive position in the battle, under its control? Already, in some of the Western States, the next phase has developed itself. The majority interest, by numbers, seizes the power of the state and proceeds to realize its own interest against all others in the most ruthless fashion. That capital has means of defense is unquestionable; that it will defend itself is certain; that it cannot defend itself without resorting to all the vices of plutocracy seems inevitable. Thus the issue of democracy and plutocracy, numbers against capital, is made up. It is the issue which menaces modern society, and which is destined to dispel the dreams which have been cherished, that we were on the eve of a millennium. On the contrary, it will probably appear that the advance of civilization constantly brings new necessity for a still more elevated activity of reason and conscience, and does not tend at all to a condition of stability, in which the social and political problems of the race would reach a definitive solution.

## Definitions of Democracy and Plutocracy

All the words in -ocracy properly describe political forms according to the chief spring of political power in them: an autocracy is a political form in which the predominant force is the will of the monarch himself; an aristocracy is a form in which the predominant and controlling force is the will of a limited body, having the possession of the qualities which are most esteemed and envied in that society; a theocracy is a form in which the predominant force is some conception of God and his will, and, inasmuch as the will of God can come to men only through some finite channel, a theocracy easily passes into a hierocracy, in which the predominant force is possessed and wielded by a priesthood; a bureaucracy is a form in which the ultimate control of things political lies in the hands of a body of office-holders. In each case the name designates that organ which, upon ultimate analysis, is found to have the power to say what shall be and what shall not be.

A democracy, then, is a political form in which the ultimate power lies with the *demos*, the people. This mass, however, while unorganized, could not express its will or administer the affairs of the state; there has

never been any state organized on such a plan. The *demos*, for political
purposes, has always excluded women, minors, resident aliens, slaves,
paupers, felons, etc., according to the constitution in each case; the
"people," therefore, has always meant some defined section of the population, not the whole of it. Furthermore, in any modern state, even a
superficial study of the current phrases and accepted formulae will show
that the word "people" is used in a technical sense to mean, not even
the whole body of legal voters, but a limited number of them. A writer
who rages at the idea that there are any "classes" will, in the next paragraph, reiterate all the current formulae about the "people," and reveal
by the context that he means to distinguish the people as peasants,
artisans, and uneducated persons, from the rich, the educated, and the
banking, mercantile, and professional classes.

Yet the current dogmas about the rights and wisdom of the people
have no truth whatever, and no moral beauty, except when they are
affirmed of the whole population, without any exception whatever. The
dogmas in question are not really maxims or principles of actual political life and administration; they are sublime conceptions of the undeveloped power of growth and civilization in human society. As inspiring
ideals, as educational motives, as moral incentives, they have incalcu-
lable value; but then they are philosophical and academical generalities,
not every-day rules of action for specific exigencies. When they are once
dragged down into the mud of practical politics, and are cut to the
measure of party tactics, they are most pernicious falsehoods.

For instance, the notion that a human society, acting as a whole, bringing its reason and conscience to bear on its problems, traditions, and
institutions, constantly reviewing its inherited faiths, examining its experiments, profiting by its own blunders, reaching out after better judgment and correcting its prejudices, can, in the sweep of time, arrive at
the best conclusions as to what is socially true and wise and just, that
man can get on earth, is a grand conception, and it is true. If the doctrine
that the people ought to rule, and that the people know what is wise
and right means this, it is true and fruitful. It will be noticed, however,
that this doctrine implies that the people are to embrace every element
in the society, including all the women and children, for in no sense
could this grand consensus be true unless it was universal. It is of its
very essence that the whole voice should be in it; it is its catholicity
which constitutes its guarantee. If the feminine element is left out of it,
its guarantee is gone; it is one-sided and imperfect; it is no longer human
and social; it has sunk from the grade of a grand and inspiring conception

to that of the party cry of a dominant interest. Neither is it true if the children are left out of it, for it is only in the sweep of time, after long and patient revision, that the judgments have authority. It must therefore be the work of generations to make those judgments; it is only the undying society, in its continuity and undistinguished generations, which can make them, and if they are to be true, the fire and hope of youth are as essential components as the inertness and conservatism of age.

Now, however, turn this same dogma into a maxim that peasants and artisans are the "people," that they are the depositaries of social and political wisdom, as distinguished from the sages and philosophers. Tell the young man not to worry about learning, to sneer at culture, to spend his nights on the street and his Sundays reading dime novels and the *Police Gazette*, and, when election day comes, to throw his vote so as to make a political job for himself or his friend; tell him that this is what is meant by the doctrine that the people ought to rule, and that in doing all this he will be uttering the oracles of political wisdom—then the great doctrine has turned into one of the most grotesque and mischievous falsehoods ever imagined.

In practise, therefore, democracy means that all those who are once admitted to political power are equal and that the power lies with the numerical majority of these equal units. If then the political divisions form themselves class-wise, then the most numerous class becomes the *demos* and is the depositary of political power. For this reason if we establish a democracy and then set the classes and the masses against each other, it is the utmost treason against democracy, because it ingrafts upon it from the start the worst vices of social discord and social greed which have disgraced the older political forms.

A plutocracy is a political form in which the real controlling force is wealth. This is the thing which seems to me to be really new and really threatening; there have been states in which there have been large plutocratic elements, but none in which wealth seemed to have such absorbing and controlling power as it threatens us. The most recent history of the civilized states of Western Europe has shown constant and rapid advance of plutocracy. The popular doctrines of the last hundred years have spread the notion that everybody ought to enjoy comfort and luxury—that luxury is a sort of right. Therefore if anybody has luxury while others have it not, this is held to prove that men have not equally shared in the fruits of civilization, and that the state in which such a condition of things exists has failed to perform its function; the next thing to do is to get hold of the state and make it perform its function of guaranteeing comfort and physical well-being to all. In the mean time, with the increasing thirst for luxury and the habit of thinking of it as within the scope of every man's rights, the temptations of dishonest gain increase, and especially are all those forms of gain which come, not from defalcation and theft, but from the ingenious use of political opportunities, put under a special code by themselves. A man who is "on the make," to use a slang phrase produced from the very phenomena to which I refer, does not think of himself as dishonest, but only as a man of the world. He is only utilizing the chances which he can get or make to win gain from the conjuncture of political and social circumstances, without intentional crime such as the statute has forbidden. This runs all the way from the man who sells his vote to the statesman who abuses official power, and it produces a class of men who have their price.

The principle of plutocracy is that money buys whatever the owner of money wants, and the class just described are made to be its instruments. At the same time the entire industrial development of the modern world has been such as to connect industry with political power in the matter of joint-stock companies, corporations, franchises, concessions, public contracts, and so on, in new ways and in great magnitude. It is also to be noted that the impersonal and automatic methods of modern industry, and the fact that the actual superintendent is often a representative and quasi-trustee for others, has created the corporate conscience. An ambitious Roman used by buy and bribe his way through all the inferior magistracies up to the consulship, counting upon getting a province at last out of which he could extort enough to recoup himself, pay all his debts, and have a fortune besides. Modern plutocrats buy their way through elections and legislatures, in the confidence of being able to get powers which will recoup them for all the outlay and yield an ample surplus besides.

What I have said here about the venality of the humbler sets of people, and about the greed and arrogance of plutocrats, must not be taken to apply any further than it does apply, and the facts are to be taken only as one's knowledge will warrant. I am discussing forces and tendencies, and the magnitude attained as yet by those forces and tendencies ought not to be exaggerated. I regard plutocracy, however, as the most sordid and debasing form of political energy known to us. In its motive, its processes, its code, and its sanctions it is infinitely corrupting to all the institutions which ought to preserve and protect society. The time to recognize it for what it is, in its spirit and tendency, is when it is in its germ, not when it is full green.

Here, then, in order to analyze plutocracy further, we must make some important distinctions. Plutocracy ought to be carefully distinguished from "the power of capital." The effect of the uncritical denunciations of capital, and monopoly, and trust, of which we hear so much, is, as I shall try to show further on, to help forward plutocracy.

## The Conflict of Plutocracy and Democracy

Not every rich man is a plutocrat. In the classical nations it was held that the pursuits of commerce and industry were degrading to the free man; and as for commerce, it was believed that every merchant was necessarily a cheat, that he must practise tricks from the necessity of the case, and that a certain ever-active craftiness and petty deceit were the traits of character in which his occupation educated him. As for the handicrafts, it was argued that they distorted a man's body and absorbed his mind and time, so that he was broken in spirit, ignorant, and sordid. The same ideas as to commerce and, in part, as to handicrafts, prevailed through the Middle Ages.

The classical civilization was built upon human slave power. For that reason it exhausted itself—consumed itself. It reached a climax of organization and development, and then began to waste capital and use up its materials and processes. It is, however, clear that any high civilization must be produced and sustained by an adequate force. In the case just mentioned it was human nerve and muscle. Now, modern civilization is based on capital, that is, on tools and machines, which subjugate natural forces and make them do the drudgery. It is this fact which has emancipated slaves and serfs, set the mass of mankind free from the drudgery which distorts the body and wears out the mind, at the same time producing a high civilization and avoiding the wear and tear on men.

The "dignity of labor" and the "power of capital" are therefore both products of the same modern movement. They go together; it is the power of capital which has made labor cease to be servile; it is the power of capital which has set women free from the drudgery of the grain-mill and the spinning-room; it is the power of capital which has enabled modern men to carry on mining and quarrying without misery, although in the classical times those forms of labor were so crushing that only the worst criminals or the lower order of slaves were condemned to them. Every high civilization is unnatural, inasmuch as it is the product of art and effort. It is, therefore, unstable—ready to fall again to the original level, if the force and intelligence by which it is produced and maintained should fail. Our civilization is supported by capital and by modern science; it either of these fail—if we exhaust our capital, or if our science is not adequate to the tasks which fall upon it, our civilization will decline.

The dignity of capital is correlative with the dignity of labor. The capitalist has not simply fallen under the ban from which the laborer has escaped; the modern times have produced classes of men, masters of industry and accumulators of capital, who are among the most distinct and peculiar products of modern times. At what other epoch in history has any such class of men existed? There have, in earlier times, been great merchants, who have shown that the notion of a merchant as a man who cheats in weights and bets on differences, is a contemptible and ignorant calumny; the great masters of industry, however, are something entirely modern, and the vituperation of such a class as parasites, plunderers, speculators, and monopolists, is as ignorant and inexcusable as the older misconceptions of laborers which have gone out of fashion. A great capitalist is no more necessarily a plutocrat than a great general is a tyrant.

A plutocrat is a man who, having the possession of capital, and having the power of it at his disposal, uses it, not industrially, but politically; instead of employing laborers, he enlists lobbyists. Instead of applying capital to land, he operates upon the market by legislation, by artificial monopoly, by legislative privileges; he creates jobs, and erects combinations, which are half political and half industrial; he practises upon the industrial vices, makes an engine of venality, expends his ingenuity, not on processes of production, but on "knowledge of men," and on the tactics of the lobby. The modern industrial system gives him a magnificent field, one far more profitable, very often, than that of legitimate industry.

I submit, then, that it is of the utmost importance that we should recognize the truth about capital and capitalists, so as to reject the flood of nonsense and abuse which is afloat about both; that we should distinguish between the false and the true, the good and the bad, and should especially form a clear idea of the social political enemy as distinguished from everybody else. The recent history of every civilized state in the world shows the advance of plutocracy, and its injurious effects upon political institutions. The abuse and the vice, as usual, lie close beside the necessary and legitimate institution. Combinations of capital are indispensable, because we have purposes to accomplish which can be attained in no other way; monopolies exist in nature, and, however much modified by art, never cease to have their effect. Speculation is a legitimate function in the organization, and not an abuse or a public wrong. Trusts, although the name is a mistake, are evidently increasing in number all over the world, and are in great measure a result of the modern means of communication, which have made it possible for persons having a common interest, although scattered over the earth, if their number is not too great, to form combinations for the exploitation of a natural monopoly. What is gained by uncritical denunciation of these phenomena, or by indiscriminate confusion of definitions? The only effect of such procedure will be to nourish the abuses and destroy the utilities.

The first impulse is, when a social or industrial phenomenon presents itself, which is not considered good or pleasant, to say that we must pass a law against it. If plutocracy is an abuse of legislation and of political institutions, how can legislation do away with it? The trouble is that the political institutions are not strong enough to resist plutocracy; how then can they conquer plutocracy? Democracy especially dreads plutocracy, and with good reason.

There is no form of political power which is so ill-fitted to cope with plutocracy as democracy. Democracy has a whole set of institutions which are extra-legal, but are the most powerful elements in it; they are the party organization, the primary, the convention, etc. All this apparatus is well adapted to the purposes of plutocracy: it has to do with the formative stage of political activity; it is very largely operated in secret; it has a large but undefined field of legitimate, or quasi-legitimate, expenditure, for which there is no audit. As the operations of this apparatus are extra-legal they are irresponsible, yet they reach out to, and control, the public and civil functions. Even on the field of constitutional institutions, plutocracy always comes into the contest with a small body, a strong organization, a powerful motive, a definite purpose, and a strict discipline, while on the other side is a large and unorganized body, without discipline, with its ideas undefined, its interests illy understood, with an indefinite good intention.

If legislation is applied to the control of interests, especially when the latter are favored by the facts of the situation, the only effect is to impose on the interests more crafty and secret modes of action. Mr. Adams says that, since the Interstate Commerce Law was passed, the methods of railroad men have become more base and more secret than ever before.

The legislator, in further efforts to succeed in his undertaking, can only sacrifice more of the open and honest rights which are within his reach, just as the Russian Government, in trying to reach the discontented elements in its society, and crush them by severity, only puts honest people to unlimited inconvenience and loss, but does not catch the Nihilists. Under a democracy, when the last comes to the last, the contest between numbers and wealth is nothing but a contest between two sets of lawyers, one drawing Acts in behalf of the state, and the other devising means of defeating those Acts in behalf of their clients. The latter set is far better paid in consideration, in security, and in money.

I therefore maintain that this is a lamentable contest, in which all that we hold dear, speaking of public interests, is at stake, and that the wise policy in regard to it is to minimize to the utmost the relations of the state to industry. As long as there are such relations, every industrial interest is forced more or less to employ plutocratic methods. The corruption is greater, perhaps, on those who exercise them than on the objects of them. *Laissez-faire*, instead of being what it appears to be in most of the current discussions, cuts to the very bottom of the morals, the politics, and the political economy of the most important public questions of our time.

# The Concentration of Wealth: Its Economic Justification

In the late 1890s, a round of industrial mergers, capped by the formation of the United States Steel Corporation in 1901, sparked new interest in the trusts. Moving beyond his concern with "plutocracy," Sumner provided a detached analysis of the implications of the organizational revolution in business and society, including developments sociologists would soon consider under the rubric of "bureaucratization." Although uneasy with aspects of this change (universities, for example, paying more to administrators than to faculty), Sumner insisted that "natural selection" would lead to the breakup of inefficient combinations just as it had initially chosen the men who created them. The use of this phrase, probably the first and only time it appears in his writing, reflected an ambivalence toward an aspect of Darwin's theory upon which he had recently focused.

An unattributed manuscript of the same title in Sumner's papers raises the possibility that he may have changed his mind by 1909 to favor government-regulated competition along the lines of Woodrow Wilson's "New Freedom." However, its stilted, often awkward prose suggests that the author was probably not Sumner but a graduate student who, like others, took Sumner's premises to conclusions not shared by Sumner. Originally published in the *Independent* 54 (April–June, 1902); reprinted in *Challenge of Facts*, ed. Albert Galloway Keller, pp. 81–90.

The concentration of wealth I understand to include the aggregation of wealth into large masses and its concentration under the control of a few. In this sense the concentration of wealth is indispensable to the successful execution of the tasks which devolve upon society in our time. Every task of society requires the employment of capital, and involves an economic problem in the form of the most expedient application of material means to ends. Two features most prominently distinguish the present age from all which have preceded it: first, the great scale on which all societal undertakings must be carried out; and second, the transcendent importance of competent management, that is, of the personal element in direction and control.

I speak of "societal undertakings" because it is important to notice that the prevalent modes and forms are not confined to industrial undertakings, but are universal in all the institutions and devices which have for their purpose the satisfaction of any wants of society. A modern church is a congeries of institutions which seeks to nourish good things and repress evil ones; it has buildings, apparatus, a store of supplies, a staff of employees, and a treasury. A modern church (parish) will soon be as complex a system of institutions as a mediaeval monastery was. Contrast such an establishment with the corresponding one of fifty years ago. A university now needs an immense "concentration of wealth" for its outfit and work. It is as restricted in its work as the corresponding institution of fifty years ago was, although it may command twenty times as much capital and revenue. Furthermore, when we see that all these and other societal institutions pay far higher salaries to executive officers than to workers, we must recognize the fact that the element of personal executive ability is in command of the market, and that means that it is the element which decides success. To a correct understanding of our subject it is essential to recognize the concentration of wealth and control as a universal societal phenomenon, not merely as a matter of industrial power, or social sentiment, or political policy.

Stated in the concisest terms, the phenomenon is that of a more perfect integration of all societal functions. The concentration of power (wealth), more dominant control, intenser discipline, and stricter methods are but modes of securing more perfect integration. When we perceive this we see that the concentration of wealth is but one feature of a grand step in societal evolution.

Some may admit that the concentration of wealth is indispensable, but may desire to distinguish between joint-stock aggregations on the one side and individual fortunes on the other. This distinction is a product of the current social prejudice and is not valid. The predominance of the individual and personal element in control is seen in the tendency of all joint-stock enterprises to come under the control of very few persons. Every age is befooled by the notions which are in fashion in it. Our age is befooled by "democracy"; we hear arguments about the industrial organization which are deductions from democratic dogmas or which appeal to prejudice by using analogies drawn from democracy to affect sentiment about industrial relations. Industry may be republican; it never can be democratic, so long as men differ in productive power and in industrial virtue. In our time joint-stock companies, which are in form republican, are drifting over into oligarchies or monarchies because one or a few get greater efficiency of control and greater vigor of administration. They direct the enterprise in a way which produces more, or more economically. This is the purpose for which the organization exists and success in it outweighs everything else. We see the competent men refuse to join in the enterprise, unless they can control it, and we see the stockholders willingly put their property into the hands of those who are, as they think, competent to manage it successfully. The strongest and most effective organizations for industrial purposes which are formed nowadays are those of a few great capitalists, who have great personal confidence in each other and who can bring together adequate means for whatever they desire to do. Some such nucleus of individuals controls all the great joint-stock companies.

It is obvious that "concentration of wealth" can never be anything but a relative term. Between 1820 and 1830 Stephen Girard was a proverb for great wealth; to-day a man equally rich would not be noticed in New York for his wealth. In 1848 John Jacob Astor stood alone in point of wealth; to-day a great number surpass him. A fortune of $300,000 was then regarded as constituting wealth; it was taken as a minimum above which men were "rich." It is certain that before long some man will have a billion. It is impossible to criticize such a moving notion. The concentration of capital is also necessarily relative to the task to be performed; we wondered lately to see a corporation formed which had a capital of a billion. No one will wonder at such a corporation twenty-five years hence.

There seems to be a great readiness in the public mind to take alarm at these phenomena of growth—there might rather seem to be reason for public congratulation. We want to be provided with things abundantly and cheaply; that means that we want increased economic power. All these enterprises are efforts to satisfy that want, and they promise to do it. The public seems to turn especially to the politician to preserve it from the captain of industry; but when has anybody ever seen a politician who was a match for a captain of industry? One of the latest phenomena is a competition of the legislatures of several states for the profit of granting acts of incorporation; this competition consists, of course, in granting greater and greater powers and exacting less and less responsibility.

It is not my duty in this place to make a judicial statement of the good and ill of the facts I mention—I leave to others to suggest the limitations and safeguards which are required. It is enough to say here that of course all power is liable to abuse; if anybody is dreaming about a millennial state of society in which all energy will be free, yet fully controlled by paradisaic virtue, argument with him is vain. If we want results we must get control of adequate power, and we must learn to use it with safeguards. If we want to make tunnels, and to make them rapidly, we have to concentrate supplies of dynamite; danger results; we minimize it, but we never get rid of it. In late years our streets have been filled with power-driven cars and vehicles; the risk and danger of going on the streets has been very greatly increased; the danger is licensed by law, and it is inseparable from the satisfaction of our desire to move about rapidly. It is in this light that we should view the evils (if there are any) from the concentration of wealth. I do not say that "he who desires the end desires the means," because I do not believe that that dictum is true; but he who will not forego the end must be patient with the incidental ills which attend the means. It is ridiculous to attempt to reach the end while making war on the means. In matters of societal policy the problem always is to use the means and reach the end as well as possible under the conditions. It is proper to propose checks and safeguards, but an onslaught on the concentration of wealth is absurd and a recapitulation of its "dangers" is idle.

In fact, there is a true correlation between (a) the great productiveness of modern industry and the consequent rapid accumulation of capital from one period of production to another and (b) the larger and larger aggregations of capital which are required by modern industry from one period of production to another. We see that the movement is constantly accelerated, that its scope is all the time widening, and that the masses of material with which it deals are greater and greater. The dominant cause of all this is the application of steam and electricity to transportation, and the communication of intelligence—things which we boast about as great triumphs of the nineteenth century. They have made it possible to extend efficient control, from a given central point, over operations which may be carried on at a great number of widely separated points, and to keep up a close, direct, and intimate action and reaction between the central control and the distributed agents. That means that it has become possible for the organization to be extended in its scope and complexity, and at the same time intensified in its activity. Now whenever such a change in the societal organization becomes possible it also becomes *inevitable*, because there is economy in it. If we confine our attention to industrial undertakings (although states, churches, universities, and other associations and institutions are subject to the same force and sooner or later will have to obey it) we see that the highest degree of organization which is possible is the one that offers the maximum of profit; in it the economic advantage is greatest.

There is therefore a gravitation toward this degree of organization. To make an artificial opposition to this tendency from political or alleged moral, or religious, or other motives would be to have no longer any real rule of action; it would amount to submission to the control of warring motives without any real standards or tests.

It is a consequence of the principle just stated that at every point in the history of civilization it has always been necessary to concentrate capital in amounts large relatively to existing facts. In low civilization chiefs control what capital there is, and direct industry; they may be the full owners of all the wealth or only the representatives of a collective theory of ownership. The organization of industry was, at the time, the most efficient, and the tribes which had it prospered better than others. In the classical states with slavery and in the mediaeval states with serfdom, the great achievements which realized the utmost that the system was capable of were attained only where wealth was concentrated in productive enterprises in amounts, and under management, which were at the maximum of what the system and the possibilities of the time called for. If we could get rid of some of our notions about liberty and equality, and could lay aside this eighteenth century philosophy according to which human society is to be brought into a state of blessedness, we should get some insight into the might of the societal organization: what it does for us, and what it makes us do. Every day that passes brings us new phenomena of struggle and effort between parts of the societal organization. What do they all mean? They mean that all the individuals and groups are forced against each other in a ceaseless war of interests, by their selfish and mutual efforts to fulfill their career on earth within the conditions set for them by the state of the arts, the facts of the societal organization, and the current dogmas of world philosophy. As each must win his living, or his fortune, or keep his fortune, under these conditions, it is difficult to see what can be meant in the sphere of industrial or economic effort by a "free man." It is no wonder that we so often hear angry outcries about being "slaves" from persons who have had a little experience of the contrast between the current notions and the actual facts.

In fact, what we all need to do is to be taught by the facts in regard to the notions which we ought to adopt, instead of looking at the facts only in order to pass judgment on them and make up our minds how we will change them. If we are willing to be taught by the facts, then the phenomena of the concentration of wealth which we see about us will convince us that they are just what the situation calls for. They ought to be because they are, and because nothing else would serve the interests of society.

I am quite well aware that, in what I have said, I have not met the thoughts and feelings of people who are most troubled about the "concentration of wealth." I have tried to set forth the economic necessity for the concentration of wealth; and I maintain that this is the controlling consideration. Those who care most about the concentration of wealth are indifferent to this consideration; what strikes them most is the fact that there are some rich men. I will, therefore, try to show that this fact also is only another economic justification of the concentration of wealth.

I often see statements published, in which the objectors lay stress upon the great *inequalities* of fortune, and, having set forth the contrast between rich and poor, they rest their case. What law of nature, religion, ethics, or the state is violated by inequalities of fortune? The inequalities prove nothing. Others argue that great fortunes are won by privileges created by law and not by legitimate enterprise and ability. This statement is true, but it is entirely irrelevant; we have to discuss the concentration of wealth within the facts of the institutions, laws, usages, and customs which our ancestors have bequeathed to us and which we allow to stand. If it is proposed to change any of these parts of the societal order, that is a proper subject of discussion, but it is aside from the concentration of wealth. So long as tariffs, patents, etc., are part of the system in which we live, how can it be expected that people will not take advantage of them; what else are they for? As for franchises, a franchise is only an x until it has been developed. It never develops itself; it requires capital and skill to develop it. When the enterprise is in the full bloom of prosperity the objectors complain of it, as if the franchise, which never was anything but an empty place where something might be created, had been the completed enterprise. It is interesting to compare the exploitation of the telephone with that of the telegraph fifty years earlier. The latter was, in its day, a far more wonderful invention, but the time and labor required to render it generally available were far greater than what has been required for the telephone, and the fortunes which were won from the former were insignificant in comparison with those which have been won from the latter. Both the public and the promoters acted very differently in the two cases. In these later times promoters seize with avidity upon an enterprise which contains promise, and they push it with energy and ingenuity, while the public is receptive to "improvements"; hence the modern methods offer very great opportunities, and the rewards of those men who can "size up" a situation and develop its controlling elements with sagacity and good judgment, are very great. It is well that they are so, because these rewards stimulate to the utmost all the ambitious and able men, and they make it certain that great and useful inventions will not long remain unexploited as they did formerly. Here comes, then, a new reaction on the economic system; new energy is infused into it, with hope and confidence. We could not spare it and keep up the air of contentment and enthusiastic cheerfulness which characterizes our society. No man can acquire a million without helping a million men to increase their little fortunes all the way down through all the social grades. In some points of view it is an error that we fix our attention so much upon the very rich and overlook the prosperous mass, but the compensating advantage is that the great successes stimulate emulation the most powerfully.

What matters it then that some millionaires are idle, or silly, or vulgar; that their ideas are sometimes futile and their plans grotesque, when they turn aside from money-making? How do they differ in this from any other class? The millionaires are a product of natural selection, acting on the whole body of men to pick out those who can meet the requirement of certain work to be done. In this respect they are just like the great statesmen, or scientific men, or military men. It is because they are thus selected that wealth—both their own and that intrusted to them—aggregates under their hands. Let one of them make a mistake and see how quickly the concentration gives way to dispersion. They may fairly be regarded as the naturally selected agents of society for certain work. They get high wages and live in luxury, but the bargain is a good once for society. There is the intensest competition for their place and occupation. This assures us that all who are competent for this function will be employed in it, so that the cost of it will be reduced to the lowest terms; and furthermore that the competitors will study the proper conduct to be observed in their occupation. This will bring discipline and the correction of arrogance and masterfulness.

# IV

---

# Social Theorist

---

# Socialism

One of four manuscripts in Sumner's papers with this title, this essay was recaptioned "The Challenge of Facts" by Albert Keller and dated sometime in the 1880s. Internal evidence suggests that it was written in 1880, possibly as a lecture Sumner presented at the Harvard Finance Club in December. Keller's imprecise dating, along with the misdating as ca. 1900 of a similar use of the "fittest-unfittest" analogy in "The Predicament of Sociological Study," created the impression that Sumner used such language often, over two decades, rather than tentatively, mostly in unpublished talks of the early 1880s. From *Challenge of Facts*, ed. Albert Galloway Keller, pp. 17–52.

Socialism is no new thing. In one form or another it is to be found throughout all history. It arises from an observation of certain harsh facts in the lot of man on earth, the concrete expression of which is poverty and misery. These facts challenge us. It is folly to try to shut our eyes to them. We have first to notice what they are, and then to face them squarely.

Man is born under the necessity of sustaining the existence he has received by an onerous struggle against nature, both to win what is essential to his life and to ward off what is prejudicial to it. He is born under a burden and a necessity. Nature holds what is essential to him, but she offers nothing gratuitously. He may win for his use what she holds, if he can. Only the most meager and inadequate supply for human needs can be obtained directly from nature. There are trees which may be used for fuel and for dwellings, but labor is required to fit them for this use. There are ores in the ground, but labor is necessary to get out the metals and make tools or weapons. For any real satisfaction, labor is necessary to fit the products of nature for human use. In this struggle every individual is under the pressure of the necessities for food, clothing, shelter, fuel, and every individual brings with him more or less energy for the conflict necessary to supply his needs. The relation, therefore, between each man's needs and each man's energy, or "individualism," is the first fact of human life.

It is not without reason, however, that we speak of a "man" as the individual in question, for women (mothers) and children have special disabilities for the struggle with nature, and these disabilities grow greater and last longer as civilization advances. The perpetuation of the race in health and vigor, and its success as a whole in its struggle to expand and develop human life on earth, therefore, require that the head of the family shall, by his energy, be able to supply not only his own needs, but those of the organisms which are dependent upon him. The history of the human race shows a great variety of experiments in the relation of the sexes and in the organization of the family. These experiments have been controlled by economic circumstances, but, as man has gained more and more control over economic circumstances, monogamy and the family education of children have been more and more sharply developed. If there is one thing in regard to which the student of history and sociology can affirm with confidence that social institutions have made "progress" or grown "better," it is in this arrangement of marriage and the family. All experience proves that monogamy, pure and strict, is the sex relation which conduces most to the vigor and intelligence of the race, and that the family education of children is the institution by which the race as a whole advances most rapidly, from generation to generation, in the struggle with nature. Love of man and wife, as we understand it, is a modern sentiment. The devotion and sacrifice of parents for children is a sentiment which has been developed steadily and is now more intense and far more widely practiced throughout society than in earlier times. The relation is also coming to be regarded in a light quite different from that in which it was formerly viewed. It used to be believed that the parent had unlimited claims on the child and rights over him. In a truer view of the matter, we are coming to see that the rights are on the side of the child and the duties on the side of the parent. Existence is not a boon for which the child owes all subjection to the parent. It is a responsibility assumed by the parent towards the child without the child's consent, and the consequence of it is that the parent owes all possible devotion to the child to enable him to make his existence happy and successful.

The value and importance of the family sentiments, from a social point of view, cannot be exaggerated. They impose self-control and prudence in their most important social bearings, and tend more than any other forces to hold the individual up to the virtues which make the sound man and the valuable member of society. The race is bound, from generation to generation, in an unbroken chain of vice and penalty, virtue and reward. The sins of the fathers are visited upon the children, while, on the other hand, health, vigor, talent, genius, and skill are, so far as we can discover, the results of high physical vigor and wise early training. The popular language bears witness to the universal observation of these facts, although general social and political dogmas have come into fashion which contradict or ignore them. There is no other such punishment for a life of vice and self-indulgence as to see children grow up cursed with the penalties of it, and no such reward for self-denial and virtue as to see children born and grow up vigorous in mind and body. It is time that the true import of these observations for moral and educational purposes was developed, and it may well be questioned whether we do not go too far in our reticence in regard to all these matters when we leave it to romances and poems to do almost all the educational work that is done in the way of spreading ideas about them. The defense of marriage and the family, if their sociological value were better understood, would be not only instinctive but rational. The struggle for existence with which we have to deal must be understood, then, to be that of a man for himself, his wife, and his children.

The next great fact we have to notice in regard to the struggle of human life is that labor which is spent in a direct struggle with nature is severe in the extreme and is but slightly productive. To subjugate nature, man needs weapons and tools. These, however, cannot be won unless the food and clothing and other prime and direct necessities are supplied in such amount that they can be consumed while tools and weapons are being made, for the tools and weapons themselves satisfy no needs directly. A man who tills the ground with his fingers or with a pointed stick picked up without labor will get a small crop. To fashion even the rudest spade or hoe will cost time, during which the laborer must still eat and drink and wear, but the tool, when obtained, will multiply immensely the power to produce. Such products of labor, used to assist production, have a function so peculiar in the nature of things that we need to distinguish them. We call them capital. A lever is capital, and the advantage of lifting a weight with a lever over lifting it by direct exertion is only a feeble illustration of the power of capital in production. The origin of capital lies in the darkness before history, and it is probably impossible for us to imagine the slow and painful steps by which the race began the formation of it. Since then it has gone on rising to higher and higher powers by a ceaseless involution, if I may use a mathematical expression. Capital is labor raised to a higher power by being constantly multiplied into itself. Nature has been more and more subjugated by the human race through the power of capital, and every human being now living shares the improved status of the race to a degree which neither he nor any one else can measure, and for which he pays nothing.

Let us understand this point, because our subject will require future reference to it. It is the more short-sighted ignorance not to see that, in a civilized community, all the advantage of capital except a small fraction is gratuitously enjoyed by the community. For instance, suppose the case of a man utterly destitute of tools, who is trying to till the ground with a pointed stick. He could get something out of it. If now he should obtain a spade with which to till the ground, let us suppose, for illustration, that he could get twenty times as great a product. Could, then, the owner of a spade in a civilized state demand, as its price, from the man who had no spade, nineteen-twentieths of the product which could be produced by the use of it? Certainly not. The price of a spade is fixed by the supply and demand of products in the community. A spade is bought for a dollar and the gain from the use of it is an inheritance of knowledge, experience, and skill which every man who lives in a civilized state gets for nothing. What we pay for steam transportation is no trifle, but imagine, if you can, eastern Massachusetts cut off from steam connection with the rest of the world, turnpikes and sailing vessels remaining. The cost of food would rise so high that a quarter of the population would starve to death and another quarter would have to emigrate. To-day every man here gets an enormous advantage from the status of a society on a level of steam transportation, telegraph, and machinery, for which he pays nothing.

So far as I have yet spoken, we have before us the struggle of man with nature, but the social problems, strictly speaking, arise at the next step. Each man carries on the struggle to win his support for himself, but there are others by his side engaged in the same struggle. If the stores of nature were unlimited, or if the last unit of the supply she offers could be won as easily as the first, there would be no social problem. If a square mile of land could support an indefinite number of human beings, or if it cost only twice as much labor to get forty bushels of wheat from an acre as to get twenty, we should have no social problem. If a square mile of land could support millions, no one would ever emigrate and there would be no trade or commerce. If it cost only twice as much labor to get forty bushels as twenty, there would be no advance in the arts. The fact is far otherwise. So long as the population is low in proportion to the amount of land, on a given stage of the arts, life is easy and the competition of man with man is weak. When more persons are trying to live on a square mile than it can support, on the existing stage of the arts, life is hard and the competition of man with man is intense. In the former case, industry and prudence may be on a low grade; the penalties are not severe, or certain, or speedy. In the latter case, each individual needs to exert on his own behalf every force, original or acquired, which he can command. In the former case, the average condition will be one of comfort and the population will be all nearly on the average. In the latter case, the average condition will not be one of comfort, but the population will cover wide extremes of comfort and misery. Each will find his place according to his ability and his effort. The former society will be democratic; the latter will be aristocratic.

The constant tendency of population to outstrip the means of subsistence is the force which has distributed population over the world, and produced all advance in civilization. To this day the two means of escape for an overpopulated country are emigration and an advance in the arts. The former wins more land for the same people; the latter makes the same land support more persons. If, however, either of these means opens a chance for an increase of population, it is evident that the advantage so won may be speedily exhausted if the increase takes place. The social difficulty has only undergone a temporary amelioration, and when the conditions of pressure and competition are renewed, misery and poverty reappear. The victims of them are those who have inherited disease and depraved appetites, or have been brought up in vice and ignorance, or have themselves yielded to vice, extravagance, idleness, and imprudence. In the last analysis, therefore, we come back to vice, in its original and hereditary forms, as the correlative of misery and poverty.

The condition for the complete and regular action of the force of competition is liberty. Liberty means the security given to each man that, if he employs his energies to sustain the struggle on behalf of himself and those he cares for, he shall dispose of the product exclusively as he chooses. It is impossible to know whence any definition or criterion of justice can be derived, if it is not deduced from this view of things; or if it is not the definition of justice that each shall enjoy the fruit of his own labor and self-denial, and of injustice that the idle and the industrious, the self-indulgent and the self-denying, shall share equally in the product. Aside from the *a priori* speculations of philosophers who have tried to make equality an essential element in justice, the human race has recognized, from the earliest times, the above conception of justice as the true one, and has founded upon it the right of property. The right of property, with marriage and the family, gives the right of bequest.

Monogamic marriage, however, is the most exclusive of social institutions. It contains, as essential principles, preference, superiority, selection, devotion. It would not be at all what it is if it were not for these characteristic traits, and it always degenerates when these traits are not present. For instance, if a man should not have a distinct preference for the woman he married, and if he did not select her as superior to others, the marriage would be an imperfect one according to the standard of true monogamic marriage. The family under monogamy, also, is a closed group, having special interests and estimating privacy and reserve as valuable advantages for family development. We grant high prerogatives, in our society, to parents, although our observation teaches us that thousands of human beings are unfit to be parents or to be entrusted with the care of children. It follows, therefore, from the organization of marriage and the family, under monogamy, that great inequalities must exist in a society based on those institutions. The son of wise parents cannot start on a level with the son of foolish ones, and the man who has had no home discipline cannot be equal to the man who has had home discipline. If the contrary were true, we could rid ourselves at once of the wearing labor of inculcating sound morals and manners in our children.

Private property, also, which we have seen to be a feature of society organized in accordance with the natural conditions of the struggle for existence produces inequalities between men. The struggle for existence is aimed against nature. It is from her niggardly hand that we have to wrest the satisfactions for our needs, but our fellow-men are our competitors for the meager supply. Competition, therefore, is a law of nature. Nature is entirely neutral; she submits to him who most energetically and resolutely assails her. She grants her rewards to the fittest, therefore, without regard to other considerations of any kind. If, then, there be liberty, men get from her just in proportion to their works, and their having and enjoying are just in proportion to their being and their doing. Such is the system of nature. If we do not like it, and if we try to amend it, there is only one way in which we can do it. We can take from the better and give to the worse. We can deflect the penalties of those who have done ill and throw them on those who have done better. We can take the rewards from those who have done better and give them to those who have done worse. We shall thus lessen the inequalities. We shall favor the survival of the unfittest, and we shall accomplish this by destroying liberty. Let it be understood that we cannot go outside of this alternative: liberty, inequality, survival of the fittest; not-liberty, equality, survival of the unfittest. The former carries society forward and favors all its best members; the latter carries society downwards and favors all its worst members.

For three hundred years now men have been trying to understand and realize liberty. Liberty is not the right or chance to do what we choose; there is no such liberty as that on earth. No man can do as he chooses: the autocrat of Russia or the King of Dahomey has limits to his arbitrary will; the savage in the wilderness, whom some people think free, is the slave of routine, tradition, and superstitious fears; the civilized man must earn his living, or take care of his property, or concede his own will to the rights and claims of his parents, his wife, his children, and all the persons with whom he is connected by the ties and contracts of civilized life.

What we mean by liberty is civil liberty, or liberty under law; and this means the guarantees of law that a man shall not be interfered with while using his own powers for his own welfare. It is, therefore, a civil and political status; and that nation has the freest institutions in which the guarantees of peace for the laborer and security for the capitalist are the highest. Liberty, therefore, does not by any means do away with the struggle for existence. We might as well try to do away with the need of eating, for that would, in effect, be the same thing. What civil liberty does is to turn the competition of man with man from violence and brute force into an industrial competition under which men vie with one another for the acquisition of material goods by industry, energy, skill, frugality, prudence, temperance, and other industrial virtues. Under this changed order of things the inequalities are not done away with. Nature still grants her rewards of having and enjoying, according to our being and doing, but it is now the man of the highest training and not the man of the heaviest fist who gains the highest reward. It is impossible that the man with capital and the man without capital should be equal. To affirm that they are equal would be to say that a man who has no tool can get as much food out of the ground as the man who has a spade or a plough; or that the man who has no weapon can defend himself as well against hostile beasts or hostile men as the man who has a weapon. If that were so, none of us would work any more. We work and deny ourselves to get capital just because, other things being equal, the man who has it is superior, for attaining all the ends of life, to the man who has it not. Considering the eagerness with which we all seek capital and the estimate we put upon it, either in cherishing it if we have it, or envying others who have it while we have it not, it is very strange what platitudes pass current about it in our society so soon as we begin to generalize about it. If our young people really believed some of the teachings they hear, it would not be amiss to preach them a sermon once in a while to reassure them, setting forth that it is not wicked to be rich, nay even, that it is not wicked to be richer than your neighbor.

It follows from what we have observed that it is the utmost folly to denounce capital. To do so is to undermine civilization, for capital is the first requisite of every social gain, educational, ecclesiastical, political, aesthetic, or other.

It must also be noticed that the popular antithesis between persons and capital is very fallacious. Every law or institution which protects persons at the expense of capital makes it easier for persons to live and to increase the number of consumers of capital while lowering all the motives to prudence and frugality by which capital is created. Hence every such law or institution tends to produce a large population, sunk in misery. All poor laws and all eleemosynary institutions and expenditures have this tendency. On the contrary, all laws and institutions which give security to capital against the interests of other persons than its owners, restrict numbers while preserving the means of subsistence. Hence every such law or institution tends to produce a small society on a high stage of comfort and well-being. It follows that the antithesis commonly thought to exist between the protection of persons and the protection of property is in reality only an antithesis between numbers and quality.

I must stop to notice, in passing, one other fallacy which is rather scientific than popular. The notion is attributed to certain economists that economic forces are self-correcting. I do not know of any economists who hold this view, but what is intended probably is that many economists, of whom I venture to be one, hold that economic forces act compensatingly, and that whenever economic forces have so acted as to produce an unfavorable situation, other economic forces are brought into action which correct the evil and restore the equilibrium. For instance, in Ireland overpopulation and exclusive devotion to agriculture, both of which are plainly traceable to unwise statesmanship in the past, have produced a situation of distress. Steam navigation on the ocean has introduced the competition of cheaper land with Irish agriculture. The result is a social and industrial crisis. There are, however, millions of acres of fertile land on earth which are unoccupied and which are open to the Irish, and the economic forces are compelling the direct corrective of the old evils, in the way of emigration or recourse to urban occupations by unskilled labor. Any number of economic and legal nostrums have been proposed for this situation, all of which propose to leave the original causes untouched. We are told that economic causes do not correct themselves. That is true. We are told that when an economic situation becomes very grave it goes on from worse to worse and that there is no cycle through which it returns. That is not true, without further limitation. We are told that moral forces alone can elevate any such people again. But it is plain that a people which has sunk below the reach of the economic forces of self-interest has certainly sunk below the reach of moral forces, and that this objection is superficial and short-sighted. What is true is that economic forces always go before moral forces. Men feel self-interest long before they feel prudence, self-control, and temperance. They lose the moral forces long before they lose the economic forces. If they can be regenerated at all, it must be first by distress appealing to self-interest and forcing recourse to some expedient for relief. Emigration is certainly an economic force for the relief of Irish distress. It is a palliative only, when considered in itself, but the virtue of it is that it gives the non-emigrating population a chance to rise to a level on which the moral forces can act upon them. Now it is terribly true that only the better ones emigrate, and only the better ones among those who remain are capable of having their ambition and energy awakened, but for the rest the solution is famine and death, with a social regeneration through decay and the elimination of that part of the society which is not capable of being restored to health and life. As Mr. Huxley once said, the method of nature is not even a word and a blow, with the blow first. No explanation is vouchsafed. We are left to find out for ourselves why our ears are boxed. If we do not find out, and find out correctly, what the error is for which we are being punished, the blow is repeated and poverty, distress, disease, and death finally remove the incorrigible ones. It behooves us men to study these terrible illustrations of the penalties which follow on bad statesmanship, and of the sanctions by which social laws are enforced. The economic cycle does complete itself; it must do so, unless the social group is to sink in permanent barbarism. A law may be passed which shall force somebody to support the hopelessly degenerate members of a society, but such a law can only perpetuate the evil and entail it on future generations with new accumulations of distress.

The economic forces work with moral forces and are their handmaidens, but the economic forces are far more primitive, original, and universal. The glib generalities in which we sometimes hear people talk, as if you could set moral and economic forces separate from and in antithesis to each other, and discard the one to accept and work by the other, gravely misconstrue the realities of the social order.

We have now before us the facts of human life out of which the social problem springs. These facts are in many respects hard and stern. It is by strenuous exertion only that each one of us can sustain himself against the destructive forces and the ever recurring needs of life; and the higher the degree to which we seek to carry our development the greater is the proportionate cost of every step. For help in the struggle we can only look back to those in the previous generation who are responsible for our existence. In the competition of life the son of wise and prudent ancestors has immense advantages over the son of vicious and imprudent ones. The man who has capital possesses immeasurable advantages for the struggle of life over him who has none. The more we break down privileges of class, or industry, and establish liberty, the greater will be the inequalities and the more exclusively will the vicious bear the penalties. Poverty and misery will exist in society just so long as vice exists in human nature.

I now go on to notice some modes of trying to deal with this problem. There is a modern philosophy which has never been taught systematically, but which has won the faith of vast masses of people in the modern civilized world. For want of a better name it may be called the sentimental philosophy. It has colored all modern ideas and institutions in politics, religion, education, charity, and industry, and is widely taught in popular literature, novels, and poetry, and in the pulpit. The first proposition of this sentimental philosophy is that nothing is true which is disagreeable. If, therefore, any facts of observation show that life is grim or hard, the sentimental philosophy steps over such facts with a genial platitude, a consoling commonplace, or a gratifying dogma. The effect is to spread an easy optimism, under the influence of which people spare themselves labor and trouble, reflection and forethought, pains and caution—all of which are hard things, and to admit the necessity for which would be to admit that the world is not all made smooth and easy, for us to pass through it surrounded by love, music, and flowers.

Under this philosophy, "progress" has been represented as a steadily increasing and unmixed good; as if the good steadily encroached on the evil without involving any new and other forms of evil; and as if we could plan great steps in progress in our academies and lyceums, and then realize them by resolution. To minds trained to this way of looking at things, any evil which exists is a reproach. We have only to consider it, hold some discussions about it, pass resolutions, and have done with it. Every moment of delay is, therefore, a social crime. It is monstrous to say that misery and poverty are as constant as vice and evil passions of men! People suffer so under misery and poverty! Assuming, therefore, that we can solve all these problems and eradicate all these evils by expending our ingenuity upon them, of course we cannot hasten too soon to do it.

A social philosophy, consonant with this, has also been taught for a century. It could not fail to be popular, for it teaches that ignorance is as good as knowledge, vulgarity as good as refinement, shiftlessness as good as painstaking, shirking as good as faithful striving, poverty as good as wealth, filth as good as cleanliness—in short, that quality goes for nothing in the measurement of men, but only numbers. Culture, knowledge, refinement, skill, and taste cost labor, but we have been taught that they have only individual, not social value, and that socially they are rather drawbacks than otherwise. In public life we are taught to admire roughness, illiteracy, and rowdyism. The ignorant, idle, and shiftless have been taught that they are "the people," that the generalities inculcated at the same time about the dignity, wisdom, and virtue of "the people" are true of them, that they have nothing to learn to be wise, but that, as they stand, they possess a kind of infallibility, and that to their "opinion" the wise must bow. It is not cause for wonder if whole sections of these classes have begun to use the powers and wisdom attributed to them for their interests, as they construe them, and to trample on all the excellence which marks civilization as on obsolete superstition.

Another development of the same philosophy is the doctrine that men come into the world endowed with "natural rights," or as joint inheritors of the "rights of man," which have been "declared" times without number during the last century. The divine rights of man have succeeded to the obsolete divine right of kings. If it is true, then, that a man is born with rights, he comes into the world with claims on somebody besides his parents. Against whom does he hold such rights? There can be no rights against nature or against God. A man may curse his fate because he is born of an inferior race, or with an hereditary disease, or blind, or, as some members of the race seem to do, because they are born females; but they get no answer to their imprecations. But, now, if men have rights by birth, these rights must hold against their fellow-men and must mean that somebody else is to spend his energy to sustain the existence of the persons so born. What then becomes of the natural rights of the one whose energies are to be diverted from his own interests? If it be said that we should all help each other, that means simply that the race as a whole should advance and expand as much and as fast as it can in its career on earth; and the experience on which we are now acting has shown that we shall do this best under liberty and under the organization which we are now developing, by leaving each to exert his energies for his own success. The notion of natural rights is destitute of sense, but it is captivating, and it is the more available on account of its vagueness. It lends itself to the most vicious kind of social dogmatism, for if a man has natural rights, then the reasoning is clear up to the finished socialistic doctrine that a man has a natural right to whatever he needs, and that the measure of his claims is the wishes which he wants fulfilled. If, then, he has a need, who is bound to satisfy it for him? Who holds the obligation corresponding to his right? It must be the one who possesses what will satisfy that need, or else the state which can take the possession from those who have earned and saved it, and give it to him who needs it and who, by the hypothesis, has not earned and saved it.

It is with the next step, however, that we come to the complete and ruinous absurdity of this view. If a man may demand from those who have a share of what he needs and has not, may he demand the same also for his wife and for his children, and for how many children? The industrious and prudent man who takes the course of labor and self-denial to secure capital, finds that he must defer marriage, both in order to save and to devote his life to the education of fewer children. The man who can claim a share in another's product has no such restraint. The consequence would be that the industrious and prudent would labor and save, without families, to support the idle and improvident who would increase and multiply, until universal destitution forced a return to the principles of liberty and property; and the man who started with the notion that the world owed him a living would once more find, as he does now, that the world pays him its debt in state prison.

The most specious application of the dogma of rights is to labor. It is said that every man has a right to work. The world is full of work to be done. Those who are willing to work find that they have three days' work to do in every day that comes. Work is the necessity to which we are born. It is not a right, but an irksome necessity, and men escape it whenever they can get the fruits of labor without it. What they want is the fruits, or wages, not work. But wages are capital which some one has earned and saved. If he and the workman can agree on the terms on which he will part with his capital, there is no more to be said. If not, then the right must be set up in a new form. It is now not a right to work, nor even a right to wages, but a right to a certain rate of wages, and we have simply returned to the old doctrine of spoliation again. It is immaterial whether the demand for wages be addressed to an individual capitalist or to a civil body, for the latter can give no wages which it does not collect by taxes out of the capital of those who have labored and saved.

Another application is in the attempt to fix the hours of labor *per diem* by law. If a man is forbidden to labor over eight hours per day (and the law has no sense or utility for the purposes of those who want it until it takes this form), he is forbidden to exercise so much industry as he may be willing to expend in order to accumulate capital for the improvement of his circumstances.

A century ago there were very few wealthy men except owners of land. The extension of commerce, manufactures, and mining, the introduction of the factory system and machinery, the opening of new countries, and the great discoveries and inventions have created a new middle class, based on wealth, and developed out of the peasants, artisans, unskilled laborers, and small shop-keepers of a century ago. The consequence has been that the chance of acquiring capital and all which depends on capital has opened before classes which formerly passed their lives in a dull round of ignorance and drudgery. This chance has brought with it the same alternative which accompanies every other opportunity offered to mortals. Those who were wise and able to profit by the chance succeeded grandly; those who were negligent or unable to profit by it suffered proportionately. The result has been wide inequalities of wealth within the industrial classes. The net result, however, for all, has been the cheapening of luxuries and a vast extension of physical enjoyment. The appetite for enjoyment has been awakened and nourished in classes which formerly never missed what they never thought of, and it has produced eagerness for material good, discontent, and impatient ambition. This is the reverse side of that eager uprising of the industrial classes which is such a great force in modern life. The chance is opened to advance, by industry, prudence, economy, and emigration, to the possession of capital; but the way is long and tedious. The impatience for enjoyment and the thirst for luxury which we have mentioned are the greatest foes to the accumulation of capital; and there is a still darker side to the picture when we come to notice that those who yield to the impatience to enjoy, but who see others outstrip them, are led to malice and envy. Mobs arise which manifest the most savage and senseless disposition to burn and destroy what they cannot enjoy. We have already had evidence, in more than one country, that such a wild disposition exists and needs only opportunity to burst into activity.

The origin of socialism, which is the extreme development of the sentimental philosophy, lies in the undisputed facts which I described at the outset. The socialist regards this misery as the fault of society. He thinks that we can organize society as we like and that an organization can be devised in which poverty and misery shall disappear. He goes further even than this. He assumes that men have artificially organized society as it now exists. Hence if anything is disagreeable or hard in the present state of society it follows, on that view, that the task of organizing society has been imperfectly and badly performed, and that it needs to be done over again. These are the assumptions with which the socialist starts, and many socialists seem also to believe that if they can destroy belief in an Almighty God who is supposed to have made the world such as it is, they will then have overthrown the belief that there is a fixed order in human nature and human life which man can scarcely alter at all, and, if at all, only infinitesimally.

The truth is that the social order is fixed by laws of nature precisely analogous to those of the physical order. The most that man can do is by ignorance and self-conceit to mar the operation of social laws. The evils of society are to a great extent the result of the dogmatism and self-interest of statesmen, philosophers, and ecclesiastics who in past time have done just what the socialists now want to do. Instead of studying the natural laws of the social order, they assumed that they could organize society as they chose, they made up their minds what kind of a society they wanted to make, and they planned their little measures for the ends they had resolved upon. It will take centuries of scientific study of the facts of nature to eliminate from human society the mischievous institutions and traditions which the said statesmen, philosophers, and ecclesiastics have introduced into it. Let us not, however, even then delude ourselves with any impossible hopes. The hardships of life would not be eliminated if the laws of nature acted directly and without interference. The task of right living forever changes its form, but let us not imagine that the task will ever reach a final solution or that any race of men on this earth can ever be emancipated from the necessity of industry, prudence, continence, and temperance if they are to pass their lives prosperously. If you believe the contrary you must suppose that some men can come to exist who shall know nothing of old age, disease, and death.

The socialist enterprise of reorganizing society in order to change what is harsh and sad in it at present is therefore as impossible, from the outset, as a plan for changing the physical order. I read the other day a story in which a man dreamt that somebody had invented an application of electricity for eradicating certain facts from the memory. Just think of it! What an emancipation to the human race, if a man could so emancipate himself from all those incidents in his past life which he regrets! Let there no longer be such a thing as remorse or vain regret! It would be half as good as finding a fountain of eternal youth. Or invent us a world in which two and two could make five. Two two-dollar notes could then pay five dollars of debts. They say that political economy is a dismal science and that its doctrines are dark and cruel. I think the hardest fact in human life is that two and two cannot make five; but in sociology while people will agree that two and two cannot make five, yet they think that it might somehow be possible by adjusting two and two to one another in some way or other to make two and two equal to four and one-tenth.

I have shown how some men emerge from barbarism only by the use of capital and why it is that, as soon as they begin to use capital, if there is liberty, there will be inequality. The socialist looking at these facts says that it is capital which produces the inequality. It is the inequality of men in what they get out of life which shocks the socialist. He finds enough to criticize in the products of past dogmatism and bad statesmanship to which I have alluded, and the program of reforms to be accomplished and abuses to be rectified which the socialists have set up have often been admirable. It is their analysis of the situation which is at fault. Their diagnosis of the social disease is founded on sectarian assumptions, not on the scientific study of the structure and functions of the social body. In attacking capital they are simply attacking the foundations of civilization, and every socialistic scheme which has ever been proposed, so far as it has lessened the motives to saving or the security of capital, is anti-social and anti-civilizing.

Rousseau, who is the great father of the modern socialism, laid accusation for the inequalities existing amongst men upon wheat and iron. What he meant was that wheat is a symbol of agriculture, and when men took to agriculture and wheat diet they broke up their old tribal relations, which were partly communistic, and developed individualism and private property. At the same time agriculture called for tools and machines, of which iron is a symbol; but these tools and machines are capital. Agriculture, individualism, tools, capital were, according to Rousseau's ideas, the causes of inequality. He was, in a certain way, correct, as we have already seen by our own analysis of the facts of the social order. When human society reached the agricultural stage machinery became necessary. Capital was far more important than on the hunting or pastoral stage, and the inequalities of men were developed with great rapidity, so that we have a Humboldt, a Newton, or a Shakespeare at one end of the scale and a Digger Indian at the other. The Humboldt or Newton is one of the highest products produced by the constant selection and advance of the best part of the human race, viz., those who have seized every chance of advancing; and the Digger Indian is a specimen of that part of the race which withdrew from the competition clear back at the beginning and has consequently never made any advance beyond the first superiority of man to beasts. Rousseau, following the logic of his own explanation of the facts, offered distinctly as the cure for inequality a return to the hunting stage of life as practiced by the American Indians. In this he was plainly and distinctly right. If you want equality you must not look forward for it on the path of advancing civilization. You may go back to the mode of life of the American Indian, and, although you will not then reach equality, you will escape those glaring inequalities of wealth and poverty by coming down to a comparative equality, that is, to a status in which all are equally miserable. Even this, however, you cannot do without submitting to other conditions which are far more appalling than any sad facts in the existing order of society. The population of Massachusetts is about two hundred to the square mile; on the hunting stage Massachusetts could not probably support, at the utmost, five to the square mile; hence to get back to the hunting stage would cost the reduction of the population to two and a half where there are now one hundred. In Rousseau's day people did not even know that this question of the power of land to support population was to be taken into account.

Socialists find it necessary to alter the definition of capital in order to maintain their attacks upon it. Karl Marx, for instance, regards capital as an accumulation of the differences which a merchant makes between his buying price and his selling price. It is, according to him, an accumulation of the differences which the employer gains between what he pays to the employees for making the thing and what he obtains for it from the consumer. In this view of the matter the capitalist employer is a pure parasite, who has fastened on the wage-receiving employee without need or reason and is levying toll on industry. All socialistic writers follow, in different degrees, this conception of capital. If it is true, why do not I levy on some workers somewhere and steal this difference in the product of their labor? Is it because I am more honest or magnanimous than those who are capitalist-employers? I should not trust myself to resist the chance if I had it. Or again, let us ask why, if this conception of the origin of capital is correct, the workmen submit to a pure and unnecessary imposition. If this notion were true, co-operation in production would not need any effort to bring it about; it would take an army to keep it down. The reason why it is not possible for the first comer to start out as an employer of labor is that capital is a prerequisite to all industry. So soon as men pass beyond the state of life in which they live, like beasts, on the spontaneous fruits of the earth, capital must precede every productive enterprise. It would lead me too far away from my present subject to elaborate this statement as it deserves and perhaps as it needs, but I may say that there is no sound political economy and especially no correct conception of wages which is not based on a complete recognition of the character of capital as necessarily going before every industrial operation. The reason why co-operation in production is exceedingly difficult, and indeed is not possible except in the highest and rarest conditions of education and culture amongst artisans, is that workmen cannot undertake an enterprise without capital, and that capital always means the fruits of prudence and self-denial already accomplished. The capitalist's profits, therefore, are only the reward for the contribution he has made to a joint enterprise which could not go on without him, and his share is as legitimate as that of the hand-worker.

The socialist assails particularly the institution of bequest or hereditary property, by which some men come into life with special protection and advantage. The right of bequest rests on no other grounds than those of expediency. The love of children is the strongest motive to frugality and to the accumulation of capital. The state guarantees the power of bequest only because it thereby encourages the accumulation of capital on which the welfare of society depends. It is true enough that inherited capital often proves a curse. Wealth is like health, physical strength, education, or anything else which enhances the power of the individual; it is only a chance; its moral character depends entirely upon the use which is made of it. Any force which, when well used, is capable of elevating a man, will, if abused, debase him in the same proportion. This is true of education, which is often and incorrectly vaunted as a positive and purely beneficent instrumentality. An education ill used makes a man only a more mischievous scoundrel, just as an education well used makes him a more efficient, good citizen and producer. So it is with wealth; it is a means to all the higher developments of intellectual and moral culture. A man of inherited wealth can gain in youth all the advantages which are essential to high culture, and which a man who must first earn the capital cannot attain until he is almost past the time of life for profiting by them. If one should believe the newspapers, one would be driven to a philosophy something like this: it is extremely praiseworthy for a man born in poverty to accumulate a fortune; the reason why he wants to secure a fortune is that he wants to secure the position of his children and start them with better advantages than he enjoyed himself; this is a noble desire on his part, but he really ought to doubt and hesitate about so doing because the chances are that he would do far better for his children to leave them poor. The children who inherit his wealth are put under suspicion by it; it creates a presumption against them in all the activities of citizenship.

Now it is no doubt true that the struggle to win a fortune gives strength of character and a practical judgment and efficiency which a man who inherits wealth rarely gets, but hereditary wealth transmitted from generation to generation is the strongest instrument by which we keep up a steadily advancing civilization. In the absence of laws of entail and perpetuity it is inevitable that capital should speedily slip from the hold of the man who is not fit to possess it, back into the great stream of capital, and so find its way into the hands of those who can use it for the benefit of society.

The love of children is an instinct which, as I have said before, grows stronger with advancing civilization. All attacks on capital have, up to this time, been shipwrecked on this instinct. Consequently the most rigorous and logical socialists have always been led sooner or later to attack the family. For, if bequest should be abolished, parents would give their property to their children in their own life-time; and so it becomes a logical necessity to substitute some sort of communistic or socialistic life for family life, and to educate children in masses without the tie of parentage. Every socialistic theory which has been pursued energetically has led out to this consequence. I will not follow up this topic, but it is plain to see that the only equality which could be reached on this course would be that men should be all equal to each other when they were all equal to swine.

Socialists are filled with the enthusiasm of equality. Every scheme of theirs for securing equality has destroyed liberty. The student of political philosophy has the antagonism of equality and liberty constantly forced upon him. Equality of possession or of rights and equality before the law are diametrically opposed to each other. The object of equality before the law is to make the state entirely neutral. The state, under that theory, takes no cognizance of persons. It surrounds all, without distinctions, with the same conditions and guarantees. If it educates one, it educates all—black, white, red, or yellow; Jew or Gentile; native or alien. If it taxes one, it taxes all, by the same system and under the same conditions. If it exempts one from police regulations in home, church, and occupation, it exempts all. From this statement it is at once evident that pure equality before the law is impossible. Some occupations must be subjected to police regulation. Not all can be made subject to militia duty even for the same limited period. The exceptions and special cases furnish the chance for abuse. Equality before the law, however, is one of the cardinal principles of civil liberty, because it leaves each man to run the race of life for himself as best he can. The state stands neutral but benevolent. It does not undertake to aid some and handicap others at the outset in order to offset hereditary advantages and disadvantages, or to make them start equally. Such a notion would belong to the false and spurious theory of equality which is socialistic. If the state should attempt this it would make itself the servant of envy. I am entitled to make the most I can of myself without hindrance from anybody, but I am not entitled to any guarantee that I shall make as much of myself as somebody else makes of himself.

The modern thirst for equality of rights is explained by its historical origin. The mediaeval notion of rights was that rights were special privileges, exemptions, franchises, and powers given to individuals by the king; hence each man had just so many as he and his ancestors had been able to buy or beg by force or favor, and if a man had obtained no grants he had no rights. Hence no two persons were equal in rights and the mass of the population had none. The theory of natural rights and of equal rights was a revolt against the mediaeval theory. It was asserted that men did not have to wait for a king to grant them rights; they have them by nature, or in the nature of things, because they are men and members of civil society. If rights come from nature, it is inferred that they fall like air and light on all equally. It was an immense step in advance for the human race when this new doctrine was promulgated. Its own limitations and errors need not now be pointed out. Its significance is plain, and its limits are to some extent defined when we note its historical origin.

I have already shown that where these guarantees exist and where there is liberty, the results cannot be equal, but with all liberty there must go responsibility. If I take my own way I must take my own consequences; if it proves that I have made a mistake, I cannot be allowed to throw the consequences on my neighbor. If my neighbor is a free man and resents interference from me he must not call on me to bear the consequences of his mistakes. Hence it is plain that liberty, equality before the law, responsibility, individualism, monogamy, and private property all hold together as consistent parts of the same structure of society, and that an assault on one part must sooner or later involve an assault on all the others.

To all this must be added the political element in socialism. The acquisition of some capital—the amount is of very subordinate importance—is the first and simplest proof that an individual possesses the industrial and civil virtues which make a good citizen and a useful member of society. Political power, a century ago, was associated more or less, even in the United States, with the possession of land. It has been gradually extended until the suffrage is to all intents and purposes universal in North and South America, in Australia, and in all Europe except Russia and Turkey. On this system political control belongs to the numerical majority, limited only by institutions. It may be doubted, if the terms are taken strictly and correctly, whether the non-capitalists outnumber the capitalists in any civilized country, but in many cities where capital is most collected they certainly do. The powers of government have been abused for ages by the classes who possessed them to enable kings, courtiers, nobles, politicians, demagogues, and their friends to live in exemption from labor and self-denial, that is, from the universal lot of man. It is only a continuation of the same abuse if the new possessors of power attempt to employ it to secure for themselves the selfish advantages which all possessors of power have taken. Such a course would, however, overthrow all that we think has been won in the way of making government an organ of justice, peace, order, and security, without respect of persons; and if those gains are not to be lost they will have to be defended, before this century closes, against popular majorities, especially in cities, just as they had to be won in a struggle with kings and nobles in the centuries past.

The newest socialism is, in its method, political. The essential feature of its latest phases is the attempt to use the power of the state to realize its plans and to secure its objects. These objects are to do away with poverty and misery, and there are no socialistic schemes yet proposed, of any sort, which do not, upon analysis, turn out to be projects for curing poverty and misery by making those who have share with those who have not. Whether they are paper-money schemes, tariff schemes, subsidy schemes, internal improvement schemes, or usury laws, they all have this in common with the most vulgar of the communistic projects, and the errors of this sort in the past which have been committed in the interest of the capitalist class now furnish precedents, illustration, and encouragement for the new category of demands. The latest socialism divides into two phases: one which aims at centralization and despotism—believing that political form more available for its purposes; the other, the anarchical, which prefers to split up the state into townships, or "communes," to the same end. The latter furnishes the true etymology and meaning of "communism" in its present use, but all socialism, in its second stage, merges into a division of property according to the old sense of communism.

It is impossible to notice socialism as it presents itself at the present moment without pointing out the immense mischief which has been done by sentimental economists and social philosophers who have thought it their professional duty, not to investigate and teach the truth, but to dabble in philanthropy. It is in Germany that this development has been most marked, and as a consequence of it the judgment and sense of the whole people in regard to political and social questions have been corrupted. It is remarkable that the country whose learned men have wrought so much for every other science, especially by virtue of their scientific method and rigorous critical processes, should have furnished a body of social philosophers without method, discipline, or severity of scholarship, who have led the nation in pursuit of whims and dreams and impossible desires. Amongst us there has been less of it, for our people still possess enough sterling sense to reject sentimental rubbish in its grosser forms, but we have had and still have abundance of the more subtle forms of socialistic doctrine, and these open the way to the others. We may already see the two developments forming a congenial alliance. We have also our writers and teachers who seem to think that "the weak" and "the poor" are terms of exact definition; that government exists, in some especial sense, for the sake of the classes so designated; and that the same classes (whoever they are) have some especial claim on the interest and attention of the economist and social philosopher. It may be believed that, in the opinion of these persons, the training of men is the only branch of human effort in which the labor and care should be spent, not on the best specimens but on the poorest.

It is a matter of course that a reactionary party should arise to declare that universal suffrage, popular education, machinery, free trade, and all the other innovations of the last hundred years are all a mistake. If any one ever believed that these innovations were so many clear strides towards the millennium, that they involve no evils or abuses of their own, that they tend to emancipate mankind from the need for prudence, caution, forethought, vigilance—in short, from the eternal struggle against evil—it is not strange that he should be disappointed. If any one ever believed that some "form of government" could be found which would run itself and turn out the pure results of abstract peace, justice, and righteousness without any trouble to anybody, he may well be dissatisfied. To talk of turning back, however, is only to enhance still further the confusion and danger of our position. The world cannot go back. Its destiny is to go forward and to meet the new problems which are continually arising. Under our so-called progress evil only alters its forms, and we must esteem it a grand advance if we can believe that, on the whole, and over a wide view of human affairs, good has gained a hair's breadth over evil in a century. Popular institutions have their own abuses and dangers just as much as monarchical or aristocratic institutions. We are only just finding out what they are. All the institutions which we have inherited were invented to guard liberty against the encroachments of a powerful monarch or aristocracy, when these classes possessed land and the possession of land was the greatest social power. Institutions must now be devised to guard civil liberty against popular majorities, and this necessity arises first in regard to the protection of property, the first and greatest function of government and element in civil liberty. There is no escape from any dangers involved in this or any other social struggle save in going forward and working out the development. It will cost a struggle and will demand the highest wisdom of this and the next generation. It is very probable that some nations— those, namely, which come up to this problem with the least preparation, with the least intelligent comprehension of the problem, and under the most inefficient leadership—will suffer a severe check in their development and prosperity; it is very probable that in some nations the development may lead through revolution and bloodshed; it is very probable that in some nations the consequence may be a reaction towards arbitrary power. In every view we take of it, it is clear that the general abolition of slavery has only cleared the way for a new social problem of far wider scope and far greater difficulty. It seems to me, in fact, that this must always be the case. The conquest of one difficulty will only open the way to another; the solution of one problem will only bring man face to face with another. Man wins by the fight, not by the victory, and therefore the possibilities of growth are unlimited, for the fight has no end.

The progress which men have made in developing the possibilities of human existence has never been made by jumps and strides. It has never resulted from the schemes of philosophers and reformers. It has never been guided through a set program by the wisdom of any sages, statesmen, or philanthropists. The progress which has been made has been won in minute stages by men who had a definite task before them, and who have dealt with it in detail, as it presented itself, without referring to general principles or attempting to bring it into logical relations to an *a priori* system. In most cases the agents are unknown and cannot be found. New and better arrangements have grown up imperceptibly by the natural effort of all to make the best of actual circumstances. In this way, no doubt, the new problems arising in our modern society must be solved or must solve themselves. The chief safeguard and hope of such a development is in the sound instincts and strong sense of the people, which, although it may not reason closely, can reject instinctively. If there are laws—and there certainly are such—which permit the acquisition of property without industry, by cunning, force, gambling, swindling, favoritism, or corruption, such laws transfer property from those who have earned it to those who have not. Such laws contain the radical vice of socialism. They demand correction and offer an open field for reform because reform would lie in the direction of greater purity and security of the right of property. Whatever assails that right, or goes in the direction of making it still more uncertain whether the industrious man can dispose of the fruits of his industry for his own interests exclusively, tends directly towards violence, bloodshed, poverty, and misery. If any large section of modern society should rise against the rest for the purpose of attempting any such spoliation, either by violence or through the forms of law, it would destroy civilization as it was destroyed by the irruption of the barbarians into the Roman Empire.

The sound student of sociology can hold out to mankind, as individuals or as a race, only one hope of better and happier living. That hope lies in an enhancement of the industrial virtues and of the moral forces which thence arise. Industry, self-denial, and temperance are the laws of prosperity for men and states; without them advance in the arts and in wealth means only corruption and decay through luxury and vice. With them progress in the arts and increasing wealth are the prime

conditions of an advancing civilization which is sound enough to endure. The power of the human race to-day over the conditions of prosperous and happy living are sufficient to banish poverty and misery if
it were not for folly and vice. The earth does not begin to be populated
up to its power to support population on the present stage of the arts; if
the United States were as densely populated as the British Islands, we
should have 1,000,000,000 people here. If, therefore, men were willing
to set to work with energy and courage to subdue the outlying parts of
the earth, all might live in plenty and prosperity. But if they insist on
remaining in the slums of great cities or on the borders of an old society,
and on a comparatively exhausted soil, there is no device of economist
or statesman which can prevent them from falling victims to poverty
and misery or from succumbing in the competition of life to those who
have greater command of capital. The socialist or philanthropist who
nourishes them in their situation and saves them from the distress of it
is only cultivating the distress which he pretends to cure.

# Sociology

In this essay, Sumner made one of several early attempts to define a science of society. Other attempts included a speech at the dinner for Herbert Spencer in New York in November 1882, published in Edward J. Youmans, ed. *Herbert Spencer on the Americans* (New York: D. Appleton & Co., 1883), 35–40; and a manuscript of a talk given at the Nineteenth Century Club in New York in March 1882, originally titled "Sociology" but reprinted (silently abridged and wrongly dated ca. 1900) by Albert Keller as "The Predicament of Sociological Study," *Challenge of Facts*, 415–425. Although the latter drew an attack on "The Selfish Sciences" from the editors of the *New York Times*, March 9, 1883, these pieces suggest how tentative and uncertain Sumner's grasp of the new discipline was at this time. Originally published in the *Princeton Review*, n.s. 8 (November 1881), 303–323; reprinted in *War*, ed. Albert Galloway Keller, pp. 167–192.

Each of the sciences which, by giving to man greater knowledge of the laws of nature, has enabled him to cope more intelligently with the ills of life, has had to fight for its independence of metaphysics. We have still lectures on metaphysical biology in some of our colleges and in some of our public courses, but biology has substantially won its independence. Anthropology is more likely to give laws to metaphysics than to accept laws from that authority. Sociology, however, the latest of this series of sciences, is rather entering upon the struggle than emerging from it. Sociology threatens to withdraw an immense range of subjects of the first importance from the dominion of *a priori* speculation and arbitrary dogmatism, and the struggle will be severe in proportion to the dignity and importance of the subject. The struggle, however, is best carried forward indirectly, by simply defining the scope of sociology and by vindicating its position amongst the sciences, while leaving its relations to the other sciences and other pursuits of men to adjust themselves according to the facts. I know of nothing more amusing in these days than to see an old-fashioned metaphysician applying his tests to the results of scientific investigation, and screaming with rage because men of scientific training do not care whether the results satisfy those tests or not.

Sociology is the science of life in society. It investigates the forces which come into action wherever a human society exists. It studies the structure and functions of the organs of human society, and its aim is to find out the laws in subordination to which human society takes its various forms and social institutions grow and change. Its practical utility consists in deriving the rules of right social living from the facts and laws which prevail by nature in the constitution and functions of society. It must, without doubt, come into collision with all other theories of right living which are founded on authority, tradition, arbitrary invention, or poetic imagination.

Sociology is perhaps the most complicated of all the sciences, yet there is no domain of human interest the details of which are treated ordinarily with greater facility. Various religions have various theories of social living, which they offer as authoritative and final. It has never, so far as I know, been asserted by anybody that a man of religious faith, in any religion, could not study sociology or recognize the existence of any such science; but it is incontestably plain that a man who accepts the dogmas about social living which are imposed by the authority of any religion must regard the subject of right social living as settled and closed, and he cannot enter on any investigation the first groundwork of which would be doubt of the authority which he recognizes as final. Hence social problems and social phenomena present no difficulty to him who has only to cite an authority or obey a prescription.

Then again the novelists set forth "views" about social matters. To write and read novels is perhaps the most royal road to teaching and learning which has ever been devised. The proceeding of the novelists is kaleidoscopic. They turn the same old bits of colored glass over and over again into new combinations. There is no limit, no sequence, no bond of consistency. The romance-writing social philosopher always proves his case, just as a man always wins who plays chess with himself.

Then again the utopians and socialists make easy work of the complicated phenomena with which sociology has to deal. These persons, vexed with the intricacies of social problems and revolting against the facts of the social order, take upon themselves the task of inventing a new and better world. They brush away all which troubles us men and create a world free from annoying limitations and conditions—in their imagination. In ancient times, and now in half-civilized countries, these persons have been founders of religions. Something of that type always lingers around them still and among us, and is to be seen amongst the reformers and philanthropists, who never contribute much to the improvement of society in any actual detail, but find a key principle for making the world anew and regenerating society. I have even seen faint signs of the same mysticism in social matters in some of the green-backers who have "thought-out" in bed, as they relate, a scheme of wealth by paper money, as Mohammed would have received a surah or Joe Smith a revelation about polygamy. Still there are limits to this resemblance, because in our nineteenth century American life a sense of humor, even if defective, answers some of the purposes of common sense.

Then again all the whimsical people who have hobbies of one sort or another come forward with projects which are the result of a strong impression, an individual misfortune, or an unregulated benevolent desire, and which are therefore the product of a facile emotion, not of a laborious investigation. Then again the *dilettanti* make light work of social questions. Everyone, by the fact of living in society, gathers some observations of social phenomena. The belief grows up, as it was expressed some time ago by a professor of mathematics, that everybody knows about the topics of sociology. Those topics have a broad and generous character. They lend themselves easily to generalizations. There are as yet no sharp tests formulated. Above all, and worst lack of all as yet, we have no competent criticism. Hence it is easy for the aspirant after culture to venture on this field without great danger of being brought to account, as he would be if he attempted geology, or physics, or biology. Even a scientific man of high attainments in some other science, in which he well understands what special care, skill, and training are required, will not hesitate to dogmatize about a topic of sociology. A group of half-educated men may be relied upon to attack a social question and to hammer it dead in a few minutes with a couple of commonplaces and a sweeping *a priori* assumption. Above all other topics, social topics lend themselves to the purposes of the diner-out.

Two facts, however, in regard to social phenomena need only be mentioned to be recognized as true. (1) Social phenomena always present themselves to us in very complex combinations, and (2) it is by no means easy to interpret the phenomena. The phenomena are often at three or four removes from their causes. Tradition, prejudice, fashion, habit, and other similar obstacles continually warp and deflect the social forces, and they constitute interferences whose magnitude is to be ascertained separately for each case. It is also impossible for us to set up a social experiment. To do that we should need to dispose of the time and liberty of a certain number of men. It follows that sociology requires a special method, and that probably no science requires such peculiar skill and sagacity in the observer and interpreter of the phenomena which are to be studied. One peculiarity may be especially noted because it shows a very common error of students of social science. A sociologist needs to arrange his facts before he has obtained them; that is to say, he must make a previous classification so as to take up the facts in a certain order. If he does not do this he may be overwhelmed in the mass of his material so that he never can master it. How shall anyone know how to classify until the science itself has made some progress? Statistics furnish us the best illustration at the present time of the difficulty here referred to.

When, now, we take into account these difficulties and requirements, it is evident that the task of sociology is one which will call for especial and long training, and that it will probably be a long time yet before we can train up any body of special students who will be so well trained in the theory and science of society as to be able to form valuable opinions on points of social disease and social remedy. But it is a fact of familiar observation that all popular discussions of social questions seize directly upon points of social disease and social remedies. The diagnosis of some asserted social ill and the prescription of the remedy are undertaken offhand by the first comer, and without reflecting that the diagnosis of a social disease is many times harder than that of a disease in an individual, and that to prescribe for a society is to prescribe for an organism which is immortal. To err in prescribing for a man is at worst to kill him; to err in prescribing for a society is to set in operation injurious forces which extend, ramify, and multiply their effects in ever new combinations throughout an indefinite future. It may pay to experiment with an individual, because he cannot wait for medical science to be perfected; it cannot pay to experiment with a society, because the society does not die and can afford to wait.

If we have to consider the need of sociology, innumerable reasons for studying it present themselves. In spite of all our acquisitions in natural science, the conception of a natural law—which is the most important good to be won from studying natural science—is yet exceedingly vague in the minds of ordinary intelligent people, and is very imperfect even amongst the educated. That conception is hardly yet applied by anybody to social facts and problems. Social questions force themselves upon us in multitudes every year as our civilization advances and our society becomes complex. When such questions arise they are wrangled over and tossed about without any orderly discussion, but as if they were only the sport of arbitrary whims. Is it not then necessary that we enable ourselves, by study of the facts and laws of society, to take up such questions from the correct point of view, and to proceed with the examination of them in such order and method that we can reach solid results, and thus obtain command of an increasing mass of knowledge about social phenomena? The assumption which underlies almost all discussion of social topics is that we men need only to make up our minds what kind of a society we want to have, and that then we can devise means for calling that society into existence. It is assumed that we can decide to live on one spot of the earth's surface or another, and to pursue there one industry or another, and then that we can, by our devices, make that industry as productive as any other could be in that place. People believe that we have only to choose whether we will have aristocratic institutions or democratic institutions. It is believed that statesmen can, if they will, put a people in the way of material prosperity. It is believed that rent on land can be abolished if it is not thought expedient to have it. It is assumed that peasant proprietors can be brought into existence anywhere where it is thought that it would be an advantage to have them. These illustrations might be multiplied indefinitely. They show the need of sociology, and if we should go on to notice the general conceptions of society, its ills and their remedies, which are held by various religious, political, and social sects, we should find ample further evidence of this need.

Let us then endeavor to define the field of sociology. Life in society is the life of a human society on this earth. Its elementary conditions are set by the nature of human beings and the nature of the earth. We have already become familiar, in biology, with the transcendent importance of the fact that life on earth must be maintained by a struggle against nature, and also by a competition with other forms of life. In the latter fact biology and sociology touch. Sociology is a science which deals with one range of phenomena produced by the struggle for existence, while biology deals with another. The forces are the same, acting on different fields and under different conditions. The sciences are truly cognate. Nature contains certain materials which are capable of satisfying human needs, but those materials must, with rare and mean exceptions, be won by labor, and must be fitted to human use by more labor. As soon as any number of human beings are struggling each to win from nature the material goods necessary to support life, and are carrying on this struggle side by side, certain social forces come into operation. The prime condition of this society will lie in the ratio of its numbers to the supply of materials within its reach. For the supply at any moment attainable is an exact quantity, and the number of persons who can be supplied is arithmetically limited. If the actual number present is very much less than the number who might be supported, the condition of all must be ample and easy. Freedom and facility mark all social relations under such a state of things. If the number is larger than that which can be supplied, the condition of all must be one of want and distress, or else a few must be well provided, the others being proportionately still worse off. Constraint, anxiety, possibly tyranny and repression, mark social relations. It is when the social pressure due to an unfavorable ratio of population to land becomes intense that the social forces develop increased activity. Division of labor, exchange, higher social organization, emigration, advance in the arts, spring from the necessity of contending against the harsher conditions of existence which are continually reproduced as the population surpasses the means of existence on any given status.

The society with which we have to deal does not consist of any number of men. An army is not a society. A man with his wife and his children constitutes a society, for its essential parts are all present, and the number more or less is immaterial. A certain division of labor between the sexes is imposed by nature. The family as a whole maintains itself better under an organization with division of labor than it could if the functions were shared so far as possible. From this germ the development of society goes on by the regular steps of advancement to higher organization, accompanied and sustained by improvements in the arts. The increase of population goes on according to biological laws which are capable of multiplying the species beyond any assignable limits, so that the number to be provided for steadily advances and the status of ease and abundance gives way to a status of want and constraint. Emigration is the first and simplest remedy. By winning more land the ratio of population to land is once more rendered favorable. It is to be noticed, however, that emigration is painful to all men. To the uncivilized man, to emigrate means to abandon a mass of experiences and traditions which have been won by suffering, and to go out to confront new hardships and perils. To the civilized man migration means cutting off old ties of kin and country. The earth has been peopled by man at the cost of this suffering.

On the side of the land also stands the law of the diminishing return as a limitation. More labor gets more from the land, but not proportionately more. Hence, if more men are to be supported, there is need not of a proportionate increase of labor, but of a disproportionate increase of labor. The law of population, therefore, combined with the law of the diminishing returns, constitutes the great underlying condition of society. Emigration, improvements in the arts, in morals, in education, in political organization, are only stages in the struggle of man to meet these conditions, to break their force for a time, and to win room under them for ease and enlargement. Ease and enlargement mean either power to support more men on a given stage of comfort or power to advance the comfort of a given number of men. Progress is a word which has no meaning save in view of the laws of population and the diminishing return, and it is quite natural that anyone who fails to understand those laws should fall into doubt which way progress points, whether towards wealth or poverty. The laws of population and the diminishing return, in their combination, are the iron spur which has driven the race on to all which it has ever achieved, and the fact that population ever advances, yet advances against a barrier which resists more stubbornly at every step of advance, unless it is removed to a new distance by some conquest of man over nature, is the guarantee that the task of civilization will never be ended, but that the need for more energy, more intelligence, and more virtue will never cease while the race lasts. If it were possible for an increasing population to be sustained by proportionate increments of labor, we should all still be living in the original home of the race on the spontaneous products of the earth. Let him, therefore, who desires to study social phenomena first learn the transcendent importance for the whole social organization, industrial, political, and civil, of the ratio of population to land.

We have noticed that the relations involved in the struggle for existence are twofold. There is first the struggle of individuals to win the means of subsistence from nature, and secondly there is the competition of man with man in the effort to win a limited supply. The radical error of the socialists and sentimentalists is that they never distinguish these two relations from each other. They bring forward complaints which are really to be made, if at all, against the author of the universe for the hardships which man has to endure in his struggle with nature. The complaints are addressed, however, to society; that is, to other men under the same hardships. The only social element, however, is the competition of life, and when society is blamed for the ills which belong to the human lot, it is only burdening those who have successfully contended with those ills with the further task of conquering the same ills over again for somebody else. Hence liberty perishes in all socialistic schemes, and the tendency of such schemes is to the deterioration of society by burdening the good members and relieving the bad ones. The law of the survival of the fittest was not made by man and cannot be abrogated by man. We can only, by interfering with it, produce the survival of the unfittest. If a man comes forward with any grievance against the order of society so far as this is shaped by human agency, he must have patient hearing and full redress; but if he addresses a demand to society for relief from the hardships of life, he asks simply that somebody else should get his living for him. In that case he ought to be left to find out his error from hard experience.

The sentimental philosophy starts from the first principle that nothing is true which is disagreeable, and that we must not believe anything which is "shocking," no matter what the evidence may be. There are various stages of this philosophy. It touches on one side the intuitional philosophy which proves that certain things must exist by proving that man needs them, and it touches on the other side the vulgar socialism which affirms that the individual has a right to whatever he needs, and that this right is good against his fellow men. To this philosophy in all its grades the laws of population and the diminishing return have always been very distasteful. The laws which entail upon mankind an inheritance of labor cannot be acceptable to any philosophy which maintains that man comes into the world endowed with natural rights and an inheritor of freedom. It is a death-blow to any intuitional philosophy to find out, as an historical fact, what diverse thoughts, beliefs, and actions man has manifested, and it requires but little actual knowledge of human history to show that the human race has never had any ease which it did not earn, or any freedom which it did not conquer. Sociology, therefore, by the investigations which it pursues, dispels illusions about what society is or may be, and gives instead knowledge of facts which are the basis of intelligent effort by man to make the best of his circumstances on earth. Sociology, therefore, which can never accomplish anything more than to enable us to make the best of our situation, will never be able to reconcile itself with those philosophies which are trying to find out how we may arrange things so as to satisfy any ideal of society.

The competition of life has taken the form, historically, of a struggle for the possession of the soil. In the simpler states of society the possession of the soil is tribal, and the struggles take place between groups, producing the wars and feuds which constitute almost the whole of early history. On the agricultural stage the tribal or communal possession of land exists as a survival, but it gives way to private property in land whenever the community advances and the institutions are free to mold themselves. The agricultural stage breaks up tribal relations and encourages individualization. This is one of the reasons why it is such an immeasurable advance over the lower forms of civilization. It sets free individual energy, and while the social bond gains in scope and variety, it also gains in elasticity, for the solidarity of the group is broken up and the individual may work out his own ends by his own means, subject only to the social ties which lie in the natural conditions of human life. It is only on the agricultural stage that liberty as civilized men understand it exists at all. The poets and sentimentalists, untaught to recognize the grand and world-wide cooperation which is secured by the free play of individual energy under the great laws of the social order, bewail the decay of early communal relations and exalt the liberty of the primitive stages of civilization. These notions all perish at the first touch of actual investigation. The whole retrospect of human history runs downwards towards beast-like misery and slavery to the destructive forces of nature. The whole history has been one series of toilsome, painful, and bloody struggles, first to find out where we were and what were the conditions of greater ease, and then to devise means to get relief. Most of the way the motives of advance have been experience of suffering and instinct. It is only in the most recent years that science has undertaken to teach without and in advance of suffering, and as yet science has to fight so hard against tradition that its authority is only slowly winning recognition. The institutions whose growth constitutes the advance of civilization have their guarantee in the very fact that they grew and became established. They suited man's purpose better than what went before. They are all imperfect, and all carry with them incidental ills, but each came to be because it was better than what went before, and each of which has perished, perished because a better one supplanted it.

It follows once and for all that to turn back to any defunct institution or organization because existing institutions are imperfect is to turn away from advance and is to retrograde. The path of improvement lies forwards. Private property in land, for instance, is an institution which has been developed in the most direct and legitimate manner. It may give way at a future time to some other institution which will grow up by imperceptible stages out of the efforts of men to contend successfully with existing evils, but the grounds for private property in land are easily perceived, and it is safe to say that no *a priori* scheme of state ownership or other tenure invented *en bloc* by any philosopher and adopted by legislative act will ever supplant it. To talk of any such thing is to manifest a total misconception of the facts and laws which it is the province of sociology to investigate. The case is less in magnitude but scarcely less out of joint with all correct principle when it is proposed to adopt a unique tax on land, in a country where the rent of land is so low that any important tax on land exceeds it, and therefore becomes indirect, and where also political power is in the hands of small landowners, who hold, without ever having formulated it, a doctrine of absolute property in the soil such as is not held by any other landowners in the world.

Sociology must exert a most important influence on political economy. Political economy is the science which investigates the laws of the material welfare of human societies. It is not its province to teach individuals how to get rich. It is a social science. It was the first branch of sociology which was pursued by man as a science. It is not strange that when the industrial organization of society was studied apart from the organism of which it forms a part it was largely dominated over by arbitrary dogmatism, and that it should have fallen into disrepute as a mere field of opinion, and of endless wrangling about opinions for which no guarantees could be given. The rise of a school of "historical" economists is itself a sign of a struggle towards a positive and scientific study of political economy, in its due relations to other social sciences, and this sign loses none of its significance in spite of the crudeness and extravagance of the opinions of the historical economists, and in spite of their very marked tendency to fall into dogmatism and hobby-riding. Political economy is thrown overboard by all groups and persons whenever it becomes troublesome. When it got in the way of Mr. Gladstone's land-bill he relegated it, by implication, to the planet Saturn, to the great delight of all the fair-traders, protectionists, soft-money men, and others who had found it in the way of their devices. What political economy needs in order to emerge from the tangle in which it is now involved, and to win a dignified and orderly development, is to find its field and its relations to other sciences fairly defined within the wider scope of sociology. Its laws will then take their place not as arbitrary or broken fragments, but in due relation to other laws. Those laws will win proof and establishment from this relation.

For instance, we have plenty of books, some of them by able writers, in which the old-fashioned Malthusian doctrine of population and the Ricardian law of rent are disputed because emigration, advance in the arts, etc., can offset the action of those laws or because those laws are not seen in action in the United States. Obviously no such objections ever could have been raised if the laws in question had been understood or had been put in their proper bearings. The Malthusian law of population and the Ricardian law of rent are cases in which by rare and most admirable acumen powerful thinkers perceived two great laws in particular phases of their action. With wider information it now appears that the law of population breaks the barriers of Malthus' narrower formulae and appears as a great law of biology. The Ricardian law of rent is only a particular application of one of the great conditions of production. We have before us not special dogmas of political economy, but facts of the widest significance for the whole social development of the race. To object that these facts may be set aside by migration or advance in the arts is nothing to the purpose, for this is only altering the constants in the equation, which does not alter the form of the curve, but only its position relatively to some standard line. Furthermore, the laws themselves indicate that they have a maximum point for any society, or any given stage of the arts, and a condition of under-population, or of an extractive industry below its maximum, is just as consistent with the law as a condition of over-population and increasing distress. Hence inferences as to the law of population drawn from the status of an under-populated country are sure to be fallacious. In like manner arguments drawn from American phenomena in regard to rent and wages, when rent and wages are as yet only very imperfectly developed here, lead to erroneous conclusions. It only illustrates the unsatisfactory condition of political economy, and the want of strong criticism in it, that such arguments can find admission to its discussions and disturb its growth.

It is to the pursuit of sociology and the study of the industrial organization in combination with the other organizations of society that we must look for the more fruitful development of political economy. We are already in such a position with sociology that a person who has gained what we now possess of that science will bring to bear upon economic problems a sounder judgment and a more correct conception of all social relations than a person who may have read a library of the existing treatises on political economy. The essential elements of political economy are only corollaries or special cases of sociological principles. One who has command of the law of the conservation of energy as it manifests itself in society is armed at once against socialism, protectionism, paper money, and a score of other economic fallacies. The sociological view of political economy also includes whatever is sound in the dogmas of the "historical school" and furnishes what that school is apparently groping after.

As an illustration of the light which sociology throws on a great number of political and social phenomena which are constantly misconstrued, we may notice the differences in the industrial, political, and

civil organizations which are produced all along at different stages of
the ratio of population to land.

When a country is under-populated newcomers are not competitors,
but assistants. If more come they may produce not only new quotas, but
a surplus besides, to be divided between themselves and all who were
present before. In such a state of things land is abundant and cheap. The
possession of it confers no power or privilege. No one will work for
another for wages when he can take up new land and be his own master.
Hence it will pay no one to own more land than he can cultivate by his
own labor, or with such aid as his own family supplies. Hence, again,
land bears little or no rent; there will be no landlords living on rent and
no laborers living on wages, but only a middle class of yeoman farmers.
All are substantially on an equality, and democracy becomes the political form, because this is the only state on which democracy is based,
is realized as a fact. The same effects are powerfully reenforced by other
facts. In a new and under-populated country the industries which are
most profitable are the extractive industries. The characteristic of these,
with the exception of some kinds of mining, is that they call for only a
low organization of labor and small amount of capital. Hence they allow
the workman to become speedily his own master, and they educate him
to freedom, independence, and self-reliance. At the same time, the social
groups being only vaguely marked off from each other, it is easy to pass
from one class of occupations, and consequently from one social grade,
to another. Finally, under the same circumstances education, skill, and
superior training have but inferior value compared with what they have
in densely populated countries. The advantages lie, in an underpopulated country, with the coarser, unskilled, manual occupations, and not
with the highest developments of science, literature, and art.

If now we turn for comparison to cases of overpopulation we see that
the struggle for existence and the competition of life are intense where
the pressure of population is great. This competition draws out the highest achievements. It makes the advantages of capital, education, talent,
skill, and training tell to the utmost. It draws out the social scale upwards
and downwards to great extremes and produces aristocratic social organizations in spite of all dogmas of equality. Landlords, tenants (i.e.,
capitalist employers), and laborers are the three primary divisions of
any aristocratic order, and they are sure to be developed whenever land
bears rent and whenever tillage requires the application of large capital.
At the same time liberty has to undergo curtailment. A man who has a
square mile to himself can easily do as he likes, but a man who walks

Broadway at noon or lives in a tenement-house finds his power to do as he likes limited by scores of considerations for the rights and feelings of his fellowmen. Furthermore, organization with subordination and discipline is essential in order that the society as a whole may win a support from the land. In an over-populated country the extremes of wealth and luxury are presented side by side with the extremes of poverty and distress. They are equally the products of an intense social pressure. The achievements of power are highest, the rewards of prudence, energy, enterprise, foresight, sagacity, and all other industrial virtues is greatest; on the other hand, the penalties of folly, weakness, error, and vice are most terrible. Pauperism, prostitution, and crime are the attendants of a state of society in which science, art, and literature reach their highest developments. Now it is evident that over-population and under-population are only relative terms. Hence as time goes on any under-populated nation is surely moving forward towards the other status, and is speedily losing its natural advantages which are absolute, and also that relative advantage which belongs to it if it is in neighborly relations with nations of dense population and high civilization; viz., the chance to borrow and assimilate from them the products, in arts and science, of high civilization without enduring the penalties of intense social pressure.

We have seen that if we should try by any measures of arbitrary interference and assistance to relieve the victims of social pressure from the calamity of their position we should only offer premiums to folly and vice and extend them further. We have also seen that we must go forward and meet our problems. We cannot escape them by running away. If then it be asked what the wit and effort of man can do to struggle with the problems offered by social pressure, the answer is that he can do only what his instinct has correctly and surely led him to do without any artificial social organization of any kind, and that is, by improvements in the arts, in science, in morals, in political institutions, to widen and strengthen the power of man over nature. The task of dealing with social ills is not a new task. People set about it and discuss it as if the human race had hitherto neglected it, and as if the solution of the problem was to be something new in form and substance, different from the solution of all problems which have hitherto engaged human effort. In truth, the human race has never done anything else but struggle with the problem of social welfare. That struggle constitutes history, or the life of the human race on earth. That struggle embraces all minor problems which occupy attention here, save those of religion, which reaches beyond this world and finds its objects beyond this life. Every successful effort to widen the power of man over nature is a real victory over poverty, vice, and misery, taking things in general and in the long run. It would be hard to find a single instance of a direct assault by positive effort upon poverty, vice, and misery which has not either failed or, if it has not failed directly and entirely, has not entailed other evils greater than the one which it removed. The only two things which really tell on the welfare of man on earth are hard work and self-denial (in technical language, labor and capital), and these tell most when they are brought to bear directly upon the effort to earn an honest living, to accumulate capital, and to bring up a family of children to be industrious and self-denying in their turn. I repeat that this is the way to work for the welfare of man on earth; and what I mean to say is that the common notion that when we are going to work for the social welfare of man we must adopt a great dogma, organize for the realization of some great scheme, have before us an abstract ideal, or otherwise do anything but live honest and industrious lives, is a great mistake. From the standpoint of the sociologist pessimism and optimism are alike impertinent. To be an optimist one must forget the frightful sanctions which are attached to the laws of right living. To be a pessimist one must overlook the education and growth which are the product of effort and self-denial. In either case one is passing judgment on what is inevitably fixed, and on which the approval or condemnation of man can product no effect. The facts and laws are, once and for all, so, and for us men that is the end of the matter. The only persons for whom there would be any sense in the question whether life is worth living are primarily the yet unborn children, and secondarily the persons who are proposing to found families. For these latter the question would take a somewhat modified form: Will life be worth living for children born of me? This question is, unfortunately, not put to themselves by the appropriate persons as it would be if they had been taught sociology. The sociologist is often asked if he wants to kill off certain classes of troublesome and burdensome persons. No such inference follows from any sound sociological doctrine, but it is allowed to infer, as to a great many persons and classes, that it would have been better for society, and would have involved no pain to them if they had never been born.

In further illustration of the interpretation which sociology offers of phenomena which are often obscure, we may note the world-wide effects of the advances in the arts and sciences which have been made during the last hundred years. These improvements have especially affected transportation and communication; that is, they have lessened the obstacles of time and space which separate the groups of mankind from each other and have tended to make the whole human race a single unit. The distinction between over-populated and under-populated countries loses its sharpness, and all are brought to an average. Every person who migrates from Europe to America affects the comparative status of the two continents. He lessens the pressure in the country he leaves and increases it in the country to which he goes. If he goes to Minnesota and raises wheat there, which is carried back to the country he left as cheap food for those who have not emigrated, it is evident that the bearing upon social pressure is twofold. It is evident, also that the problem of social pressure can no longer be correctly studied if the view is confined either to the country of immigration or the country of emigration, but that it must embrace both. It is easy to see, therefore, that the ratio of population to land with which we have to deal is only in peculiar and limited cases that ratio as it exists in England, Germany, or the United States. It is the ratio as it exists in the civilized world, and every year that passes, as our improved arts break down the barriers between different parts of the earth, brings us nearer to the state of things where all the population of Europe, America, Australasia, and South Africa must be considered in relation to all the land of the same territories, for all that territory will be available for all that population, no matter what the proportion may be in which the population is distributed over the various portions of the territory. The British Islands may become one great manufacturing city. Minnesota, Texas, and Australia may not have five persons to the square mile. Yet all will eat the meat of Texas and the wheat of Minnesota and wear the wool of Australia manufactured on the looms of England. That all will enjoy the maximum of food and raiment under that state of things is as clear as anything possibly can be which is not yet an accomplished fact. We are working towards it by all our instincts of profit and improvement. The greatest obstacles are those which come from prejudices, traditions, and dogmas, which are held independently of any observation of facts or any correct reasoning, and which set the right hand working against the left. For instance, the Mississippi Valley was, a century ago, as unavailable to support the population of France and Germany as if it had been in the moon. The Mississippi Valley is now nearer to France and Germany than the British Islands were a century ago, reckoning distance by the only true standard; viz., difficulty of communication. It is a fair way of stating it to say that the improvements in transportation of the last fifty

years have added to France and Germany respectively a tract of land of
the very highest fertility, equal in area to the territory of those states,
and available for the support of their population. The public men of
those countries are now declaring that this is a calamity, and are devising
means to counteract it.

The social and political effects of the improvements which have been
made must be very great. It follows from what we have said about the
effects of intense social pressure and high competition that the effect of
thus bringing to bear on the great centers of population the new land of
outlying countries must be to relieve the pressure in the oldest countries
and at the densest centers. Then the extremes of wealth and poverty,
culture and brutality, will be contracted and there will follow a general
tendency towards an average equality which, however, must be understood only within very broad limits. Such is no doubt the meaning of
the general tendency towards equality, the decline of aristocratic institutions, the rise of the proletariat, and the ambitious expansion, in short,
which is characteristic of modern civilized society. It would lead me too
far to follow out this line of speculation as to the future, but two things
ought to be noticed in passing. (1) There are important offsets to the
brilliant promise which there is for mankind in a period during which,
for the whole civilized world, there will be a wide margin of ease between the existing population and the supporting power of the available
land. These offsets consist in the effects of ignorance, error, and folly—
the same forces which have always robbed mankind of half what they
might have enjoyed on earth. Extravagant governments, abuses of public
credit, wasteful taxation, legislative monopolies and special privileges,
juggling with currency, restrictions on trade, wasteful armaments on
land and sea, and other follies in economy and statecraft, are capable of
wasting and nullifying all the gains of civilization. (2) The old classical
civilization fell under an irruption of barbarians from without. It is possible that our new civilization may perish by an explosion from within.
The sentimentalists have been preaching for a century notions of rights
and equality, of the dignity, wisdom, and power of the proletariat, which
have filled the minds of ignorant men with impossible dreams. The thirst
for luxurious enjoyment has taken possession of us all. It is the dark
side of the power to foresee a possible future good with such distinctness
as to make it a motive of energy and persevering industry—a power
which is distinctly modern. Now the thirst for luxurious enjoyment,
when brought into connection with the notions of rights, of power, and
of equality, and dissociated from the notions of industry and economy,

produces the notion that a man is robbed of his rights if he has not everything that he wants, and that he is deprived of equality if he sees anyone have more than he has, and that he is a fool if, having the power of the State in his hands, he allows this state of things to last. Then we have socialism, communism, and nihilism; and the fairest conquests of civilization, with all their promise of solid good to man, on the sole conditions of virtue and wisdom, may be scattered to the winds in a war of classes, or trampled underfoot by a mob which can only hate what it cannot enjoy.

It must be confessed that sociology is yet in a tentative and inchoate state. All that we can affirm with certainty is that social phenomena are subject to law, and that the natural laws of the social order are in their entire character like the laws of physics. We can draw in grand outline the field of sociology and foresee the shape that it will take and the relations it will bear to other sciences. We can also already find the standpoint which it will occupy, and, if a figure may be allowed, although we still look over a wide landscape largely enveloped in mist, we can see where the mist lies and define the general features of the landscape, subject to further corrections. To deride or contemn a science in this state would certainly be a most unscientific proceeding. We confess, however, that so soon as we go beyond the broadest principles of the science we have not yet succeeded in discovering social laws, so as to be able to formulate them. A great amount of labor yet remains to be done in the stages of preparation. There are, however, not more than two or three other sciences which are making as rapid progress as sociology, and there is no other which is as full of promise for the welfare of man. That sociology has an immense department of human interests to control is beyond dispute. Hitherto this department has been included in moral science, and it has not only been confused and entangled by dogmas no two of which are consistent with each other, but also it has been without any growth, so that at this moment our knowledge of social science is behind the demands which existing social questions make upon us. We are face to face with an issue no less grand than this: Shall we, in our general social policy, pursue the effort to realize more completely that constitutional liberty for which we have been struggling through modern history, or shall we return to the mediaeval device of functionaries to regulate procedure and to adjust interests? Shall we try to connect with liberty an equal and appropriate responsibility as its essential complement and corrective, so that a man who gets his own way shall accept his own consequences, or shall we yield to the sentimentalism which, after preaching an unlimited liberty, robs those who have been wise out of pity for those who have been foolish? Shall we accept the inequalities which follow upon free competition as the definition of justice, or shall we suppress free competition in the interest of equality and to satisfy a baseless dogma of justice? Shall we try to solve the social entanglements which arise in a society where social ties are constantly becoming more numerous and more subtle, and where contract has only partly superseded custom and status, by returning to the latter, only hastening a more complete development of the former? These certainly are practical questions, and their scope is such that they embrace a great number of minor questions which are before us and which are coming up. It is to the science of society, which will derive true conceptions of society from the facts and laws of the social order,[1] studied without prejudice or bias of any sort, that we must look for the correct answer to these questions. By this observation the field of sociology and the work which it is to do for society are sufficiently defined.

---

[1] It has been objected that no proof is offered that social laws exist in the order of nature. By what demonstration could any such proof be given *a priori*? If a man of scientific training finds his attention arrested, in some group of phenomena, by these sequences, relations, and recurrences which he has learned to note as signs of action of law, he seeks to discover the law. If it exists, he finds it. What other proof of its existences could there be?

# The Forgotten Man

Responding to an invitation from *Harper's Weekly* the previous fall, Sumner drafted eleven short essays during January 1883 for a series on the relations of workers and employers, each being about 2,000 words in length for which he was paid $50 apiece. After appearing in serial form through the early spring, they were collected as *What Social Classes Owe to Each Other* (New York, 1883). An expanded version of two of the essays of which he was especially proud, this address was given before audiences in Brooklyn and New Haven on January 30 and February 8 or 9, 1883, and were reprinted in *Forgotten Man*, ed. Albert Galloway Keller, pp. 465–495.

I propose in this lecture to discuss one of the most subtile and widespread social fallacies. It consists in the impression made on the mind for the time being by a particular fact, or by the interests of a particular group of persons, to which attention is directed while other facts or the interests of other persons are entirely left out of account. I shall give a number of instances and illustrations of this in a moment, and I cannot expect you to understand what is meant from an abstract statement until these illustrations are before you, but just by way of a general illustration I will put one or two cases.

Whenever a pestilence like yellow fever breaks out in any city, our attention is especially attracted towards it, and our sympathies are excited for the sufferers. If contributions are called for, we readily respond. Yet the number of persons who die prematurely from consumption every year greatly exceeds the deaths from yellow fever or any similar disease when it occurs, and the suffering entailed by consumption is very much greater. The suffering from consumption, however, never constitutes a public question or a subject of social discussion. If an inundation takes place anywhere, constituting a public calamity (and an inundation takes place somewhere in the civilized world nearly every year), public attention is attracted and public appeals are made, but the losses by great inundations must be insignificant compared with the losses by runaway horses, which, taken separately, scarcely obtain mention in a local newspaper. In hard times insolvent debtors are a large class. They constitute an interest and are able to attract public attention, so that social philosophers discuss their troubles and legislatures plan measures of relief.

Insolvent debtors, however, are an insignificant body compared with the victims of commonplace misfortune, or accident, who are isolated, scattered, ungrouped and ungeneralized, and so are never made the object of discussion or relief. In seasons of ordinary prosperity, persons who become insolvent have to get out of their troubles as they can. They have no hope of relief from the legislature. The number of insolvents during a series of years of general prosperity, and their losses, greatly exceed the number and losses during a special period of distress.

These illustrations bring out only one side of my subject, and that only partially. It is when we come to the proposed measures of relief for the evils which have caught public attention that we reach the real subject which deserves our attention. As soon as A observes something which seems to him to be wrong, from which X is suffering, A talks it over with B, and A and B then propose to get a law passed to remedy the evil and help X. Their law always proposes to determine what C shall do for X or, in the better case, what A, B and C shall do for X. As for A and B, who get a law to make themselves do for X what they are willing to do for him, we have nothing to say except that they might better have done it without any law, but what I want to do is to look up C. I want to show you what manner of man he is. I call him the Forgotten Man. Perhaps the appellation is not strictly correct. He is the man who never is thought of. He is the victim of the reformer, social speculator and philanthropist, and I hope to show you before I get through that he deserves your notice both for his character and for the many burdens which are laid upon him.

No doubt one great reason for the phenomenon which I bring to your attention is the passion for reflection and generalization which marks our period. Since the printing press has come into such wide use, we have all been encouraged to philosophize about things in a way which was unknown to our ancestors. They lived their lives out in positive contact with actual cases as they arose. They had little of this analysis, introspection, reflection and speculation which have passed into a habit and almost into a disease with us. Of all things which tempt to generalization and to philosophizing, social topics stand foremost. Each one of us gets some experience of social forces. Each one has some chance for observation of social phenomena. There is certainly no domain in which generalization is easier. There is nothing about which people dogmatize more freely. Even men of scientific training in some department in which they would not tolerate dogmatism at all will not hesitate to dogmatize in the most reckless manner about social topics. The truth is, however, that science, as yet, has won less control of social phenomena than of any other class of phenomena. The most complex and difficult subject which we now have to study is the constitution of human society, the forces which operate in it, and the laws by which they act, and we know less about these things than about any others which demand our attention. In such a state of things, over-hasty generalization is sure to be extremely mischievous. You cannot take up a magazine or newspaper without being struck by the feverish interest with which social topics and problems are discussed, and if you were a student of social science, you would find in almost all these discussions evidence, not only that the essential preparation for the discussion is wanting, but that the disputants do not even know that there is any preparation to be gained. Consequently we are bewildered by contradictory dogmatizing. We find in all these discussions only the application of pet notions and the clashing of contradictory "views." Remedies are confidently proposed for which there is no guarantee offered except that the person who prescribes the remedy says that he is sure it will work. We hear constantly of "reform," and the reformers turn out to be people who do not like things as they are and wish that they could be made nicer. We hear a great many exhortations to make progress from people who do not know in what direction they want to go. Consequently social reform is the most barren and tiresome subject of discussion amongst us, except aesthetics.

I suppose that the first chemists seemed to be very hard-hearted and unpoetical persons when they scouted the glorious dream of the alchemists that there must be some process for turning base metals into gold. I suppose that the men who first said, in plain, cold assertion, there is no fountain of eternal youth, seemed to be the most cruel and cold-hearted adversaries of human happiness. I know that the economists who say that if we could transmute lead into gold, it would certainly do us no good and might do great harm, are still regarded as unworthy of belief. Do not the money articles of the newspapers yet ring with the doctrine that we are getting rich when we give cotton and wheat for gold rather than when we give cotton and wheat for iron?

Let us put down now the cold, hard fact and look at it just as it is. There is no device whatever to be invented for securing happiness without industry, economy, and virtue. We are yet in the empirical stage as regards all our social devices. We have done something in science and art in the domain of production, transportation and exchange. But when you come to the laws of the social order, we know very little about them.

Our laws and institutions by which we attempt to regulate our lives under the laws of nature which control society are merely a series of haphazard experiments. We come into collision with the laws and are not intelligent enough to understand wherein we are mistaken and how to correct our errors. We persist in our experiments instead of patiently setting about the study of the laws and facts in order to see where we are wrong. Traditions and formulae have a dominion over us in legislation and social customs which we seem unable to break or even to modify.

For my present purpose I ask your attention for a few moments to the notion of liberty, because the Forgotten Man would no longer be forgotten where there was true liberty. You will say that you know what liberty is. There is no term of more common or prouder use. None is more current, as if it were quite beyond the need of definition. Even as I write, however, I find in a leading review a new definition of civil liberty. Civil liberty the writer declares to be "the result of the restraint exercised by the sovereign people on the more powerful individuals and classes of the community, preventing them from availing themselves of the excess of their power to the detriment of the other classes." You notice here the use of the words "sovereign people" to designate a class of the population, not the nation as a political and civil whole. Wherever "people" is used in such a sense, there is always fallacy. Furthermore, you will recognize in this definition a very superficial and fallacious construction of English constitutional history. The writer goes on to elaborate that construction and he comes out at last with the conclusion that "a government by the people can, in no case, become a paternal government, since its law-makers are its mandataries and servants carrying out its will, and not its fathers or its masters." This, then, is the point at which he desires to arrive, and he has followed a familiar device in setting up a definition to start with which would produce the desired deduction at the end.

In the definition the word "people" was used for a class or section of the population. It is now asserted that if *that* section rules, there can be no paternal, that is, undue, government. That doctrine, however, is the very opposite of liberty and contains the most vicious error possible in politics. The truth is that cupidity, selfishness, envy, malice, lust, vindictiveness, are constant vices of human nature. They are not confined to classes or to nations or particular ages of the world. They present themselves in the palace, in the parliament, in the academy, in the church, in the workshop, and in the hovel. They appear in autocracies, theocracies, aristocracies, democracies, and ochlocracies all alike. They change their masks somewhat from age to age and from one form of society to another. All history is only one long story to this effect: men have struggled for power over their fellow-men in order that they might win the joys of earth at the expense of others and might shift the burdens of life from their own shoulders upon those of others. It is true that, until this time, the proletariat, the mass of mankind, have rarely had the power and they have not made such a record as kings and nobles and priests have made of the abuses they would perpetrate against their fellow-men when they could and dared. But what folly it is to think that vice and passion are limited by classes, that liberty consists only in taking power away from nobles and priests and giving it to artisans and peasants and that these latter will never abuse it! They will abuse it just as all others have done unless they are put under checks and guarantees, and there can be no civil liberty anywhere unless rights are guaranteed against all abuses, as well from proletarians as from generals, aristocrats, and ecclesiastics.

Now what has been amiss in all the old arrangements? The evil of the old military and aristocratic governments was that some men enjoyed the fruits of other men's labor; that some other persons' lives, rights, interests and happiness were sacrificed to other persons' cupidity and lust. What have our ancestors been striving for, under the name of civil liberty, for the last five hundred years? They have been striving to bring it about that each man and woman might live out his or her life according to his or her own notions of happiness and up to the measure of his or her own virtue and wisdom. How have they sought to accomplish this? They have sought to accomplish it by setting aside all arbitrary personal or class elements and introducing the reign of law and the supremacy of constitutional institutions like the jury, the habeas corpus, the independent judiciary, the separation of church and state, and the ballot. Note right here one point which will be important and valuable when I come more especially to the case of the Forgotten Man: whenever you talk of liberty, you must have *two* men in mind. The sphere of rights of one of these men trenches upon that of the other, and whenever you establish liberty for the one, you repress the other. Whenever absolute sovereigns are subjected to constitutional restraints, you always hear them remonstrate that their liberty is curtailed. So it is, in the sense that their power of determining what shall be done in the state is limited below what it was before and the similar power of other organs in the state is widened. Whenever the privileges of an aristocracy are curtailed, there is heard a similar complaint. The truth is that the line of limit or demarcation between classes as regards civil power has been moved and what has been taken from one class is given to another.

We may now, then, advance a step in our conception of civil liberty. It is the status in which we find the true adjustment of rights between classes and individuals. Historically, the conception of civil liberty has been constantly changing. The notion of rights changes from one generation to another and the conception of civil liberty changes with it. If we try to formulate a true definition of civil liberty as an ideal thing towards which the development of political institutions is all the time tending, it would be this: Civil liberty is the status of the man who is guaranteed by law and civil institutions the exclusive employment of all his own powers for his own welfare.

This definition of liberty or civil liberty, you see, deals only with concrete and actual relations of the civil order. There is some sort of a poetical and metaphysical notion of liberty afloat in men's minds which some people dream about which nobody can define. In popular language it means that a man may do as he has a mind to. When people get this notion of liberty into their heads and combine with it the notion that they live in a free country and ought to have liberty, they sometimes make strange demands upon the state. If liberty means to be able to do as you have a mind to, there is no such thing in this world. Can the Czar of Russia do as he has a mind to? Can the Pope do as he has a mind to? Can the President of the United States do as he has a mind to? Can Rothschild do as he has a mind to? Could a Humboldt or a Faraday do as he had a mind to? Could a Shakespeare or a Raphael do as he had a mind to? Can a tramp do as he has a mind to? Where is the man, whatever his station, possessions, or talents, who can get any such liberty? There is none. There is a doctrine floating about in our literature that we are born to the inheritance of certain rights. That is another glorious dream, for it would mean that there was something in this world which we got for nothing. But what is the truth? We are born into no right whatever but what has an equivalent and corresponding duty right alongside of it. There is no such thing on this earth as something for nothing. Whatever we inherit of wealth, knowledge, or institutions from the past has been paid for by the labor and sacrifice of preceding generations; and the fact that these gains are carried on, that the race lives and that the race can, at least within some cycle, accumulate its gains, is one of the facts on which civilization rests. The law of the conservation of energy is not simply a law of physics; it is a law of the whole moral universe, and the order and truth of all things conceivable by man depends upon it. If there were any such liberty as that of doing as you have a mind to, the human race would be condemned to everlasting anarchy and war as these erratic wills crossed and clashed against each other. True liberty lies in the equilibrium of rights and duties, producing peace, order, and harmony. As I have defined it, it means that a man's right to take power and wealth out of the social product is measured by the energy and wisdom which he has contributed to the social effort.

Now if I have set this idea before you with any distinctness and success, you see that civil liberty consists of a set of civil institutions and laws which are arranged to act as impersonally as possible. It does not consist in majority rule or in universal suffrage or in elective systems at all. These are devices which are good or better just in the degree in which they secure liberty. The institutions of civil liberty leave each man to run his career in life in his own way, only guaranteeing to him that whatever he does in the way of industry, economy, prudence, sound judgment, etc., shall redound to his own welfare and shall not be diverted to some one else's benefit. Of course it is a necessary corollary that each man shall also bear the penalty of his own vices and his own mistakes. If I want to be free from any other man's dictation, I must understand that I can have no other man under my control.

Now with these definitions and general conceptions in mind, let us turn to the special class of facts to which, as I said at the outset, I invite your attention. We see that under a regime of liberty and equality before that law, we get the highest possible development of independence, self-reliance, individual energy, and enterprise, but we get these high social virtues at the expense of old sentimental ties which used to unite baron and retainer, master and servant, sage and disciple, comrade and comrade. We are agreed that the son shall not be disgraced even by the crime of the father, much less by the crime of a more distant relative. It is a humane and rational view of things that each life shall stand for itself alone and not be weighted by the faults of another, but it is useless to deny that this view of things is possible only in a society where the ties of kinship have lost nearly all the intensity of poetry and romance which once characterized them. The ties of sentiment and sympathy also have faded out. We have come, under the regime of liberty and equality before the law, to a form of society which is based not on status, but on free contract. Now a society based on status is one in which classes, ranks, interests, industries, guilds, associations, etc., hold men in permanent relations to each other. Custom and prescription create, under status, ties, the strength of which lies in sentiment. Feeble remains of this may be seen in some of our academical societies to-day, and it is unquestionably a great privilege and advantage for any man in our society to win an experience of the sentiments which belong to a strong and close association, just because the chances for such experience are nowadays very rare. In a society based on free contract, men come together as free and independent parties to an agreement which is of mutual advantage. The relation is rational, even rationalistic. It is not poetical. It does not exist from use and custom, but for reasons given, and it does not endure by prescription but ceases when the reason for it ceases. There is no sentiment in it at all. The fact is that, under the regime of liberty and equality before the law, there is no place for sentiment in trade or politics as public interests. Sentiment is thrown back into private life, into personal relations, and if ever it comes into a public discussion of an impersonal and general public question it always produces mischief.

Now you know that "the poor and the weak" are continually put forward as objects of public interest and public obligation. In the appeals which are made, the terms "the poor" and "the weak" are used as if they were terms of exact definition. Except the pauper, that is to say, the man who cannot earn his living or pay his way, there is no possible definition of a poor man. Except a man who is incapacitated by vice or by physical infirmity, there is no definition of a weak man. The paupers and the physically incapacitated are an inevitable charge on society. About them no more need be said. But the weak who constantly arouse the pity of humanitarians and philanthropists are the shiftless, the imprudent, the negligent, the impractical, and the inefficient, or they are the idle, the intemperate, the extravagant, and the vicious. Now the troubles of these persons are constantly forced upon public attention, as if they and their interests deserved especial consideration, and a great portion of all organized and unorganized effort for the common welfare consists in attempts to relieve these classes of people. I do not wish to be understood now as saying that nothing ought to be done for these people by those who are stronger and wiser. That is not my point. What I want to do is to point out the thing which is overlooked and the error which is made in all these charitable efforts. The notion is accepted as if it were not open to any question that if you help the inefficient and vicious you may gain something for society or you may not, but that you lose nothing. This is a complete mistake. Whatever capital you divert to the support of a shiftless and good-for-nothing person is so much diverted from some other employment, and that means from somebody else. I would spend any conceivable amount of zeal and eloquence if I possessed it to try to make people grasp this idea. Capital is force. If it goes one way it cannot go another. If you give a loaf to a pauper you cannot give the same loaf to a laborer. Now this other man who would have got it but for the charitable sentiment which bestowed it on a worthless member of society is the Forgotten Man. The philanthropists and humanitarians have their minds all full of the wretched and miserable whose case appeals to compassion, attacks the sympathies, takes possession of the imagination, and excites the emotions. They push on towards the quickest and easiest remedies and they forget the real victim.

Now who is the Forgotten Man? He is the simple, honest laborer, ready to earn his living by productive work. We pass him by because he is independent, self-supporting, and asks no favors. He does not appeal to the emotions or excite the sentiments. He only wants to make a contract and fulfill it, with respect on both sides and favor on neither side. He must get his living out of the capital of the country. The larger the capital is, the better living he can get. Every particle of capital which is wasted on the vicious, the idle, and the shiftless is so much taken from the capital available to reward the independent and productive laborer. But we stand with our backs to the independent and productive laborer all the time. We do not remember him because he makes no clamor; but I appeal to you whether he is not the man who ought to be remembered first of all, and whether, on any sound social theory, we ought not to protect him against the burdens of the good-for-nothing. In these last years I have read hundreds of articles and heard scores of sermons and speeches which were really glorifications of the good-for-nothing, as if these were the charge of society, recommended by right reason to its care and protection. We are addressed all the time as if those who are respectable were to blame because some are not so, and as if there were an obligation on the part of those who have done their duty towards those who have not done their duty. Every man is bound to take care of himself and his family and to do his share in the work of society. It is totally false that one who has done so is bound to bear the care and charge of those who are wretched because they have not done so. The silly popular notion is that the beggars live at the expense of the rich, but the truth is that those who eat and produce not, live at the expense of those who labor and produce. The next time that you are tempted to subscribe a dollar to a charity, I do not tell you not to do it, because after you have fairly considered the matter, you may think it right to do it, but I do ask you to stop and remember the Forgotten Man and understand that if you put your dollar in the savings bank it will go to swell the capital of the country which is available for division amongst those who, while they earn it, will reproduce it with increase.

Let us now go on to another class of cases. There are a great many schemes brought forward for "improving the condition of the working classes." I have shown already that a free man cannot take a favor. One who takes a favor or submits to patronage demeans himself. He falls under obligation. He cannot be free and he cannot assert a station of equality with the man who confers the favor on him. The only exception is where there are exceptional bonds of affection or friendship, that is, where the sentimental relation supersedes the free relation. Therefore, in a country which is a free democracy, all propositions to do something for the working classes have an air of patronage and superiority which is impertinent and out of place. No one can do anything for anybody else unless he has a surplus of energy to dispose of after taking care of himself. In the United States, the working classes, technically so called, are the strongest classes. It is they who have a surplus to dispose of if anybody has. Why should anybody else offer to take care of them or to serve them? They can get whatever they think worth having and, at any rate, if they are free men in a free state, it is ignominious and unbecoming to introduce fashions of patronage and favoritism here. A man who, by superior education and experience of business, is in a position to advise a struggling man of the wages class, is certainly held to do so and will, I believe, always be willing and glad to do so; but this sort of activity lies in the range of private and personal relations.

I now, however, desire to direct attention to the public, general, and impersonal schemes, and I point out the fact that, if you undertake to lift anybody, you must have a fulcrum or point of resistance. All the elevation you give to one must be gained by an equivalent depression on some one else. The question of gain to society depends upon the balance of the account, as regards the position of the persons who undergo the respective operations. But nearly all the schemes for "improving the condition of the working man" involve an elevation of some working men at the expense of other working men. When you expend capital or labor to elevate some persons who come within the sphere of your influence, you interfere in the conditions of the competition. The advantage of some is won by an equivalent loss of others. The difference is not brought about by the energy and effort of the persons themselves. If it were, there would be nothing to be said about it, for we constantly see people surpass others in the rivalry of life and carry off the prizes which the others must do without. In the cases I am discussing, the difference is brought about by an interference which must be partial, arbitrary, accidental, controlled by favoritism and personal preference. I do not say, in this case, either, that we ought to do no work of this kind. On the contrary, I believe that the arguments for it quite outweigh, in many cases, the arguments against it. What I desire, again, is to bring out the forgotten element which we always need to remember in order to make a wise decision as to any scheme of this kind. I want to call to mind the Forgotten Man, because, in this case also, if we recall him and go to look for him, we shall find him patiently and perseveringly, manfully and independently struggling against adverse circumstances without complaining or begging. If, then, we are led to heed the groaning and complaining of others and to take measures for helping these others, we shall, before we know it, push down this man who is trying to help himself.

Let us take another class of cases. So far we have said nothing about the abuse of legislation. We all seem to be under the delusion that the rich pay the taxes. Taxes are not thrown upon the consumers with any such directness and completeness as is sometimes assumed; but that, in ordinary states of the market, taxes on houses fall, for the most part, on the tenants and that taxes on commodities fall, for the most part, on the consumers, is beyond question. Now the state and municipality go to great expense to support policemen and sheriffs and judicial officers, to protect people against themselves, that is, against the results of their own folly, vice, and recklessness. Who pays for it? Undoubtedly the people who have not been guilty of folly, vice, or recklessness. Out of nothing comes nothing. We cannot collect taxes from people who produce nothing and save nothing. The people who have something to tax must be those who have produced and saved.

When you see a drunkard in the gutter, you are disgusted, but you pity him. When a policeman comes and picks him up you are satisfied. You say that "society" has interfered to save the drunkard from perishing. Society is a fine word, and it saves us the trouble of thinking to say that society acts. The truth is that the policeman is paid by somebody, and when we talk about society we forget who it is that pays. It is the Forgotten Man again. It is the industrious workman going home from a hard day's work, whom you pass without noticing, who is mulcted of a percentage of his day's earnings to hire a policeman to save the drunkard from himself. All the public expenditure to prevent vice has the same effect. Vice is its own curse. If we let nature alone, she cures vice by the most frightful penalties. It may shock you to hear me say it, but when you get over the shock, it will do you good to think of it: a drunkard in the gutter is just where he ought to be. Nature is working away at him to get him out of the way, just as she sets up her processes of dissolution to remove whatever is a failure in its line. Gambling and less mentionable vices all cure themselves by the ruin and dissolution of their victims. Nine-tenths of our measures for preventing vice are really protective towards it, because they ward off the penalty. "Ward off," I say, and that is the usual way of looking at it; but is the penalty really annihilated? By no means. It is turned into police and court expenses and spread over those who have resisted vice. It is the Forgotten Man again who has been subjected to the penalty while our minds were full of the drunkards, spendthrifts, gamblers, and other victims of dissipation. Who is, then, the Forgotten Man? He is the clean, quiet, virtuous, domestic citizen, who pays his debts and his taxes and is never heard of out of his little circle. Yet who is there in the society of a civilized state who deserves to be remembered and considered by the legislator and statesman before this man?

Another class of cases is closely connected with this last. There is an apparently invincible prejudice in people's minds in favor of state regulation. All experience is against state regulation and in favor of liberty. The freer the civil institutions are, the more weak or mischievous state regulation is. The Prussian bureaucracy can do a score of things for the citizen which no governmental organ in the United States can do; and, conversely, if we want to be taken care of as Prussians and Frenchmen are, we must give up something of our personal liberty.

Now we have a great many well-intentioned people among us who believe that they are serving their country when they discuss plans for regulating the relations of employer and employee, or the sanitary regulations of dwellings, or the construction of factories, or the way to behave on Sunday, or what people ought not to eat or drink or smoke. All this is harmless enough and well enough as a basis of mutual encouragement and missionary enterprise, but it is almost always made a basis of legislation. The reformers want to get a majority, that is, to get the power of the state and so to make other people do what the reformers think it right and wise to do. A and B agree to spend Sunday in a certain way. They get a law passed to make C pass it in their way. They determine to be teetotallers and they get a law passed to make C be a teetotaller for the sake of D who is likely to drink too much. Factory acts for women and children are right because women and children are not on an equal footing with men and cannot, therefore, make contracts properly. Adult men, in a free state, must be left to make their own contracts and defend themselves. It will not do to say that some men are weak and unable to make contracts any better than women. Our civil institutions assume that all men are equal in political capacity and all are given equal measure of political power and right, which is not the case with women and children. If, then, we measure political rights by one theory and social responsibilities by another, we produce an immoral and vicious relation. A and B, however, get factory acts and other acts passed regulating the relation of employers and employee and set armies of commissioners and inspectors traveling about to see to things, instead of using their efforts, if any are needed, to lead the free men to make their own conditions as to what kind of factory buildings they will work in, how many hours they will work, what they will do on Sunday and so on. The consequence is that men lose the true education in freedom which is needed to support free institutions. They are taught to rely on government officers and inspectors. The whole system of government inspectors is corrupting to free institutions. In England, the liberals used always to regard state regulation with suspicion, but since they have come to power, they plainly believe that state regulation is a good thing—if *they* regulate—because, of course, they want to bring about good things. In this country each party takes turns, according as it is in or out, in supporting or denouncing the non-interference theory.

Now, if we have state regulation, what is always forgotten is this: Who pays for it? Who is the victim of it? There always is a victim. The workmen who do not defend themselves have to pay for the inspectors who defend them. The whole system of social regulation by boards, commissioners, and inspectors consists in relieving negligent people of the consequences of their negligence and so leaving them to continue negligent without correction. That system also turns away from the agencies which are close, direct, and germane to the purpose, and seeks others. Now, if you relieve negligent people of the consequences of their negligence, you can only throw those consequences on the people who have not been negligent. If you turn away from the agencies which are direct and cognate to the purpose, you can only employ other agencies. Here, then, you have your Forgotten Man again. The man who has been careful and prudent and who wants to go on and reap his advantages for himself and his children is arrested just at that point, and he is told that he must go and take care of some negligent employees in a factory or on a railroad who have not provided precautions for themselves or have not forced their employers to provide precautions, or negligent tenants who have not taken care of their own sanitary arrangements, or negligent house-holders who have not provided against fire, or negligent parents who have not sent their children to school. If the Forgotten Man does not go, he must hire an inspector to go. No doubt it is often worth his while to go or send, rather than leave the thing undone, on account of his remoter interest; but what I want to show is that all this is unjust to the Forgotten Man, and that the reformers and philosophers miss the point entirely when they preach that it is his duty to do all this work. Let them preach to the negligent to learn to take care of themselves. Whenever A and B put their heads together and decide what A, B and C must do for D, there is never any pressure on A and B. They consent to it and like it. There is rarely any pressure on D because he does not like it and contrives to evade it. The pressure all comes on C. Now, who is C? He is always the man who, if let alone, would make a reasonable use of his liberty without abusing it. He would not constitute any social problem at all and would not need any regulation. He is the Forgotten Man again, and as soon as he is brought from his obscurity you see that he is just that one amongst us who is what we all ought to be.

Let us look at another case. I read again and again arguments to prove that criminals have claims and rights against society. Not long ago, I read an account of an expensive establishment for the reformation of crimi-nals, and I am told that we ought to reform criminals, not merely punish them vindictively. When I was a young man, I read a great many novels by Eugene Sue, Victor Hugo, and other Frenchmen of the school of '48, in which the badness of a bad man is represented, not as his fault, but as the fault of society. Now, as society consists of the bad men plus the good men, and as the object of this declaration was to show that the badness of the bad men was not the fault of the bad men, it remains that the badness of the bad men must be the fault of the good men. No doubt, it is far more consoling to the bad men than even to their friends to reach the point of this demonstration.

Let us ask, now, for a moment, what is the sense of punishment, since a good many people seem to be quite in a muddle about it. Every man in society is bound in nature and reason to contribute to the strength and welfare of society. He ought to work, to be peaceful, honest, just, and virtuous. A criminal is a man who, instead of working with and for society, turns his efforts against the common welfare in some way or other. He disturbs order, violates harmony, invades the security and happiness of others, wastes and destroys capital. If he is put to death, it is on the ground that he has forfeited all right to existence in society by the magnitude of his offenses against its welfare. If he is imprisoned, it is simply a judgment of society upon him that he is so mischievous to the society that he must be segregated from it. His punishment is a warning to him to reform himself, just exactly like the penalties inflicted by God and nature on vice. A man who has committed crime is, therefore, a burden on society and an injury to it. He is a destructive and not a productive force and everybody is worse off for his existence than if he did not exist. Whence, then, does he obtain a right to be taught or reformed at the public expense? The whole question of what to do with him is one of expediency, and it embraces the whole range of possible policies from that of execution to that of education and reformation, but when the expediency of reformatory attempts is discussed we always forget the labor and expense and who must pay. All that the state does for the criminal, beyond forcing him to earn his living, is done at the expense of the industrious member of society who never costs the state anything for correction and discipline. If a man who has gone astray can be reclaimed in any way, no one would hinder such a work, but people whose minds are full of sympathy and interest for criminals and who desire to adopt some systematic plans of reformatory efforts are only, once more, trampling on the Forgotten Man.

Let us look at another case. If there is a public office to be filled, of course a great number of persons come forward as candidates for it. Many of these persons are urged as candidates on the ground that they are badly off, or that they cannot support themselves, or that they want to earn a living while educating themselves, or that they have female relatives dependent on them, or for some other reason of a similar kind. In other cases, candidates are presented and urged on the ground of their kinship to somebody, or on account of service, it may be meritorious service, in some other line than that of the duty to be performed. Men are proposed for clerkships on the ground of service in the army twenty years ago, or for customhouse inspectors on the ground of public services in the organization of political parties. If public positions are granted on these grounds of sentiment or favoritism, the abuse is to be condemned on the ground of the harm done to the public interest; but I now desire to point out another thing which is constantly forgotten. If you give a position to A, you cannot give it to B. If A is an object of sentiment or favoritism and not a person fit and competent to fulfill the duty, who is B? He is somebody who has nothing but merit on his side, somebody who has no powerful friends, no political influence, some quiet, unobtrusive individual who has known no other way to secure the chances of life than simply to deserve them. Here we have the Forgotten Man again, and once again we find him worthy of all respect and consideration, but passed by in favor of the noisy, pushing, and incompetent. Who ever remembers that if you give a place to a man who is unfit for it you are keeping out of it somebody, somewhere, who is fit for it?

Let us take another case. A trades-union is an association of journeymen in a certain trade which has for one of its chief objects to raise wages in that trade. This object can be accomplished only by drawing more capital into the trade, or by lessening the supply of labor in it. To do the latter, the trades-unions limit the number of apprentices who may be admitted to the trade. In discussing this device, people generally fix their minds on the beneficiaries of this arrangement. It is desired by everybody that wages should be as high as they can be under the conditions of industry. Our minds are directed by the facts of the case to the men who are in the trade already and are seeking their own advantage. Sometimes people go on to notice the effects of trades-unionism on the employers, but although employers are constantly vexed by it, it is seen that they soon count it into the risks of their business and settle down to it philosophically. Sometimes people go further then and see that, if the employer adds the trades-union and strike risk to the other risks, he submits to it because he has passed it along upon the public and that the public wealth is diminished by trades-unionism, which is undoubtedly the case. I do not remember, however, that I have ever seen in print any analysis and observation of trades-unionism which takes into account its effect in another direction. The effect on employers or on the public would not raise wages. The public pays more for houses and goods, but that does not raise wages. The surplus paid by the public is pure loss, because it is only paid to cover an extra business risk of the employer. If their trades-unions raise wages, how do they do it? They do it by lessening the supply of labor in the trade, and this they do by limiting the number of apprentices. All that is won, therefore, for those in the trade, is won at the expense of those persons in the same class in life who want to get into the trade but are forbidden. Like every other monopoly, this one secures advantages for those who are in only at a greater loss to those who are kept out. Who, then, are those who are kept out and who are always forgotten in all the discussions? They are the Forgotten Men again; and what kind of men are they? They are those young men who want to earn their living by the trade in question. Since they select it, it is fair to suppose that they are fit for it, would succeed at it, and would benefit society by practicing it; but they are arbitrarily excluded from it and are perhaps pushed down into the class of unskilled laborers. When people talk of the success of a trades-union in raising wages, they forget these persons who have really, in a sense, paid the increase.

Let me now turn your attention to another class of cases. I have shown how, in times past, the history of states has been a history of selfishness, cupidity, and robbery, and I have affirmed that now and always the problems of government are how to deal with these same vices of human nature. People are always prone to believe that there is something metaphysical and sentimental about civil affairs, but there is not. Civil institutions are constructed to protect, either directly or indirectly, the property of men and the honor of women against the vices and passions of human nature. In our day and country, the problem presents new phases, but it is there just the same as it ever was, and the problem is only the more difficult for us because of its new phase which prevents us from recognizing it. In fact, our people are raving and struggling against it in a kind of blind way, not yet having come to recognize it. More than half of their blows, at present, are misdirected and fail of their object, but they will be aimed better by and by. There is a great deal of clamor about watering stocks and the power of combined capital, which is not very intelligent or well-directed. The evil and abuse which people are groping after in all these denunciations is jobbery.

By jobbery I mean the constantly apparent effort to win wealth, not by honest and independent production, but by some sort of a scheme for extorting other people's product from them. A large part of our legislation consists in making a job for somebody. Public buildings are jobs, not always, but in most cases. The buildings are not needed at all or are costly far beyond what is useful or even decently luxurious. Internal improvements are jobs. They are carried out, not because they are needed in themselves, but because they will serve the turn of some private interest, often incidentally that of the very legislators who pass the appropriations for them. A man who wants a farm, instead of going out where there is plenty of land available for it, goes down under the Mississippi River to make a farm, and then wants his fellow-citizens to be taxed to dyke the river so as to keep it off his farm. The Californian hydraulic miners have washed the gold out of the hillsides and have washed the dirt down into the valleys to the ruin of the rivers and the farms. They want the federal government to remove this dirt at the national expense. The silver miners, finding that their product is losing value in the market, get the government to go into the market as a great buyer in the hope of sustaining the price. The national government is called upon to buy or hire unsailable ships; to dig canals which will not pay; to educate illiterates in the states which have not done their duty at the expense of the states which have done their duty as to education; to buy up telegraphs which no longer pay; and to provide the capital for enterprises of which private individuals are to win the profits. We are called upon to squander twenty millions on swamps and creeks; from twenty to sixty-six millions on the Mississippi River; one hundred millions in pensions—and there is now a demand for another hundred million beyond that. This is the great plan of all living on each other. The pensions in England used to be given to aristocrats who had political power, in order to corrupt them. Here the pensions are given to the great democratic mass who have the political power, in order to corrupt them. We have one hundred thousand federal office-holders and I do not know how many state and municipal office-holders. Of course public officers are necessary and it is an economical organization of society to set apart some of its members for civil functions, but if the number of persons drawn from production and supported by the producers while engaged in civil functions is in undue proportion to the total population, there is economic loss. If public offices are treated as spoils or benefices or sinecures, then they are jobs and only constitute part of the pillage.

The biggest job of all is a protective tariff. This device consists in delivering every man over to be plundered by his neighbor and in teaching him to believe that it is a good thing for him and his country because he may take his turn at plundering the rest. Mr. Kelley said that if the internal revenue taxes on whisky and tobacco, which are paid to the United States government, were not taken off, there would be a rebellion. Just then it was discovered that Sumatra tobacco was being imported, and the Connecticut tobacco men hastened to Congress to get a tax laid on it for their advantage. So it appears that if a tax is laid on tobacco, to be paid to the United States, there will be a rebellion, but if a tax is laid on it to be paid to the farmers of the Connecticut Valley, there will be no rebellion at all. The tobacco farmers having been taxed for protected manufacturers are now to be taken into the system, and the workmen in the factories are to be taxed on their tobacco to protect the farmers. So the system is rendered more complete and comprehensive.

On every hand you find this jobbery. The government is to give every man a pension, and every man an office, and every man a tax to raise the price of his product, and to clean out every man's creek for him, and to buy all his unsalable property, and to provide him with plenty of currency to pay his debts, and to educate his children, and to give him the use of a library and a park and a museum and a gallery of pictures. On every side the doors of waste and extravagance stand open; and spend, squander, plunder, and grab are the watchwords. We grumble some about it and talk about the greed of corporations and the power of capital and the wickedness of stock gambling. Yet we elect the legislators who do all this work. Of course, we should never think of blaming ourselves for electing men to represent and govern us, who, if I may use a slang expression, give us away. What man ever blamed himself for his misfortune? We groan about monopolies and talk about more laws to prevent the wrongs done by chartered corporations. Who made the charters? Our representatives. Who elected such representatives? We did. How can we get bad law-makers to make a law which shall prevent bad law-makers from making a bad law? That is, really, what we are trying to do. If we are a free, self-governing people, all our misfortunes come right home to ourselves and we can blame nobody else. Is any one astonished to find that men are greedy, whether they are incorporated or not? Is it a revelation to find that we need, in our civil affairs, to devise guarantees against selfishness, rapacity, and fraud? I have ventured to affirm that government has never had to deal with anything else.

Now, I have said that this jobbery means waste, plunder, and loss, and I define it at the outset as the system of making a chance to extort part of his product from somebody else. Now comes the question: Who pays for it all? The system of plundering each other soon destroys all that it deals with. It produces nothing. Wealth comes only from production, and all that the wrangling grabbers, loafers, and jobbers get to deal with comes from somebody's toil and sacrifice. Who, then, is he who provides it all? Go and find him and you will have once more before you the Forgotten Man. You will find him hard at work because he has a great many to support. Nature has done a great deal for him in giving him a fertile soil and an excellent climate and he wonders why it is that, after all, his scale of comfort is so moderate. He has to get out of the soil enough to pay all his taxes, and that means the cost of all the jobs and the fund for all the plunder. The Forgotten Man is delving away in patient industry, supporting his family, paying his taxes, casting his vote, supporting the church and the school, reading his newspaper, and cheering for the politician of his admiration, but he is the only one for whom there is no provision in the great scramble and the big divide.

Such is the Forgotten Man. He works, he votes, generally he prays—but he always pays—yes, above all, he pays. He does not want an office; his name never gets into the newspaper except when he gets married or dies. He keeps production going on. He contributes to the strength of parties. He is flattered before election. He is strongly patriotic. He is wanted, whenever, in his little circle, there is work to be done or counsel to be given. He may grumble some occasionally to his wife and family, but he does not frequent the grocery or talk politics at the tavern. Consequently, he is forgotten. He is a commonplace man. He gives no trouble. He excites no admiration. He is not in any way a hero (like a popular orator); or a problem (like tramps and outcasts); nor notorious (like criminals); nor an object of sentiment (like the poor and weak); nor a burden (like paupers and loafers); nor an object out of which social capital may be made (like the beneficiaries of church and state charities); nor an object for charitable aid and protection (like animals treated with cruelty); nor the object of a job (like the ignorant and illiterate); nor one over whom sentimental economists and statesmen can parade their fine sentiments (like inefficient workmen and shiftless artisans). Therefore, he is forgotten. All the burdens fall on him, or on her, for it is time to remember that the Forgotten Man is not seldom a woman.

When you go to Willimantic, they will show you with great pride the splendid thread mills there. I am told that there are sewing-women who can earn only fifty cents in twelve hours, and provide the thread. In the cost of every spool of thread more than one cent is tax. It is paid not to get the thread, for you could get the thread without it. It is paid to get the Willimantic linen company which is not worth having and which is, in fact, a nuisance, because it makes thread harder to get than it would be if there were no such concern. If a woman earns fifty cents in twelve hours, she earns a spool of thread as nearly as may be in an hour, and if she uses a spool of thread per day, she works a quarter of an hour per day to support the Willimantic linen company, which in 1882 paid 95 per cent dividend to its stockholders. If you go and look at the mill, it will captivate your imagination until you remember all the women in all the garrets, and all the artisans' and laborers' wives and children who are spending their hours of labor, not to get goods which they need, but to pay for the industrial system which only stands in their way and makes it harder for them to get the goods.

It is plain enough that the Forgotten Man and the Forgotten Woman are the very life and substance of society. They are the ones who ought to be first and always remembered. They are always forgotten by sentimentalists, philanthropists, reformers, enthusiasts, and every description of speculator in sociology, political economy, or political science. If a student of any of these sciences ever comes to understand the position of the Forgotten Man and to appreciate his true value, you will find such student an uncompromising advocate of the strictest scientific thinking on all social topics, and a cold and hard-hearted skeptic towards all artificial schemes of social amelioration. If it is desired to bring about social improvements, bring us a scheme for relieving the Forgotten Man of some of his burdens. He is our productive force which we are wasting. Let us stop wasting his force. Then we shall have a clean and simple gain for the whole society. The Forgotten Man is weighted down with the cost and burden of the schemes for making everybody happy, with the cost of public beneficence, with the support of all the loafers, with the loss of all the economic quackery, with the cost of all the jobs. Let us remember him a little while. Let us take some of the burdens off him. Let us turn our pity on him instead of on the good-for-nothing. It will be only justice to him, and society will greatly gain by it. Why should we not also have the satisfaction of thinking and caring for a little about the clean, honest, industrious, independent, self-supporting men and women who have not inherited much to make life luxurious for them, but who are doing what they can to get on in the world without begging from anybody, especially since all they want is to be let alone, with good friendship and honest respect. Certainly the philanthropists and sentimentalists have kept our attention for a long time on the nasty, shiftless, criminal, whining, crawling, and good-for-nothing people, as if they alone deserved our attention.

The Forgotten Man is never a pauper. He almost always has a little capital because it belongs to the character of the man to save something. He never has more than a little. He is, therefore, poor in the popular sense, although in the correct sense he is not so. I have said already that if you learn to look for the Forgotten Man and to care for him, you will be very skeptical toward all philanthropic and humanitarian schemes. It is clear now that the interest of the Forgotten Man and the interest of "the poor," "the weak," and the other petted classes are in antagonism. In fact, the warning to you to look for the Forgotten Man comes the minute that the orator or writer begins to talk about the poor man. That minute the Forgotten Man is in danger of a new assault, and if you intend to meddle in the matter at all, then is the minute for you to look about for him and to give him your aid. Hence, if you care for the Forgotten Man, you will be sure to be charged with *not* caring for the poor.

Whatever you do for any of the petted classes wastes capital. If you do anything for the Forgotten Man, you must secure him his earnings and savings, that is, you legislate for the security of capital and for its free employment; you must oppose paper money, wildcat banking and usury laws and you must maintain the inviolability of contracts. Hence you must be prepared to be told that you favor the capitalist class, the enemy of the poor man.

What the Forgotten Man really wants is true liberty. Most of his wrongs and woes come from the fact that there are yet mixed together in our institutions the old mediaeval theories of protection and personal dependence and the modern theories of independence and individual liberty. The consequence is that the people who are clever enough to get into positions of control, measure their own rights by the paternal theory and their own duties by the theory of independent liberty. It follows that the Forgotten Man, who is hard at work at home, has to pay both ways. His rights are measured by the theory of liberty, that is, he has only such as he can conquer. His duties are measured by the paternal theory, that is, he must discharge all which are laid upon him, as is always the fortune of parents. People talk about the paternal theory of government as if it were a very simple thing. Analyze it, however, and you see that in every paternal relation there must be two parties, a parent and a child, and when you speak metaphorically, it makes all the difference in the world who is parent and who is child. Now, since we, the people, are the state, whenever there is any work to be done or expense to be paid, and since the petted classes and the criminals and the jobbers cost and do not pay, it is they who are in the position of the child, and it is the Forgotten Man who is the parent. What the Forgotten Man needs, therefore, is that we come to a clearer understanding of liberty and to a more complete realization of it. Every step which we win in liberty will set the Forgotten Man free from some of his burdens and allow him to use his powers for himself and for the commonwealth.

# The Survival of the Fittest

In the May 1884 issue of the *Index*, editor William J. Potter charged that Sumner used the term "fittest" in contradictory ways. In response, Sumner confronted the implications of the "fittest-unfittest" phrasemaking he had engaged in several times in the previous few years. When Potter rejoined the controversy in the June issue, Sumner replied with a promise of a fuller explanation at another time, but one never appeared. Coming on the heels of the controversy with Noah Porter over Herbert Spencer and the sometimes hostile reviews of *What Social Classes Owe to Each Other*, this exchange apparently persuaded Sumner that the offending phrase was more trouble than it was worth. When, two years later, the editor of *Popular Science* requested an essay titled "The Survival of the Fittest," Sumner provided an article that deliberately avoided the phrase, and henceforth dropped it from his speeches and writings. From "The Survival of the Fittest," *Index* n.s., 4 (May 29, 1884), 567; and "The Doctrine of Survival Again," *Index* n.s., 4 (June 19, 1884), 603–604.

## The Survival of the Fittest

At the meeting of the Liberal Union Club at which I read a paper, it seemed to me that there was some misapprehension in regard to the doctrine of the survival of the fittest. Such misapprehension is very common in spite of many efforts of the leading evolutionists to correct it. It is supposed that the doctrine is that the *best* survive. This is an error, and it forms the basis for all disputes about evolution and ethics. For the word "best" implies moral standards, a moral stand-point, etc.; and, if the doctrine were affirmed in that form, it would not be scientific at all, but would be theological, for it would involve the notion that man is the end of creation and that his notions of things are the standard to which things must conform. The doctrine is that those survive who are fittest to survive. Hence, rattlesnakes may survive where horses perish, or a highly cultivated white man may die where Hottentots flourish.

Mr. Potter quotes my remark that the only alternative to the survival of the fittest is the survival of the unfittest, and objects that there is a third possibility,—namely, "that the fittest shall strive to transform the unfit into a fitness to survive." This is not a third thing, but a restatement of the survival of the unfittest. A moralist preaches to John and William that they "ought" to do so and so. Why? Because, as he tells them, life, health, happiness, etc., depend on doing as he says. "Well," says William, "I do not believe you. Your doctrine is untrue, and you are a bore. Life, health, and happiness come for pleasure. I choose that course." "I," says John, "believe you, and will do as you teach. As I understand you, I shall, by obeying you, enjoy a long youth and a green old age; I shall acquire a competence; I shall have healthy and intelligent offspring; I shall be able to start them well in life; I shall, with others who likewise obey you, form a peaceful and prosperous commonwealth, in which they and I will enjoy the social advantages which such a commonwealth can secure to all its members. If I understand your doctrine, William here will, on his plan of life, acquire no capital, found no prosperous family, contribute to no sound commonwealth, win no true friends, but, becoming less and less fit to survive in a modern civilized and industrial society as time goes on, he will be cut off by disease, poverty, vice, or crime. I shall acquire capital, health, friends, and other resources and guarantees by which men arm themselves against the hardships of life. I shall be one of the fittest to survive, and shall survive accordingly. Have I understood you correctly?" "No," says the teacher. "You will be one of the fittest to survive, and William will become one of the unfittest; but the outcome of your faithful obedience to me will be that you will *ipso facto* fall under an obligation to 'transform' William by the use of the resources which you will have acquired into a fitness to survive."

Plainly, if this doctrine is true, the resources by which survival is assured being diverted from John, his survival is imperilled and curtailed, and the same resources being applied in favor of William his survival is secured; that is, Mr. Potter's third possibility is only the second branch of my alternative, and he has only furnished a proof that, if we do not like the survival of the fittest, we can only substitute for it the survival of the unfittest.

Mr. Potter goes on to say that there is a fallacy of logic in applying the doctrine of the survival of the fittest to men. There certainly is such a fallacy, if, "when we come to man, we invest the word 'fitness' with moral qualities"; for we have then arbitrarily altered a definition, while trying to carry on the same line of reasoning.

## The Doctrine of Survival Again

I must study brevity for other reasons than considerations in favor of space, proper as the latter are, but I will reply briefly to Mr. Potter's courteous rejoinder.

He looks at William (the unfittest) and will not look at John; and he will not look at all until William is in misery and an object of altruism. I look at John; and I confess that, after William has decided to neglect instruction, I care nothing about him. My interest and attention are given to the point of time at which they are deciding what they will do. After William chooses his course, using his personal liberty and choice, I say he ought to take the responsibility and bear the consequences; and I maintain that it is immoral and mischievous for John to bear his penalty.

In Mr. Potter's view of the matter, has William no duties to his neighbor? Are all the rights on the side of the idle, shiftless spendthrifts, and all the duties on the side of the honest, industrious, and frugal? Mr. Potter sets aside "utilitarianism"; but, on his theory, John should be good, only in order to win strength enough to seek the delights of altruism. William likes that doctrine. He says: "I will do as I please—marry, beget children, spend, drink, be merry. There is John plodding away to get ready to take care of us—to educate my children, support my wife, and provide for me when my troubles come upon me. He will want an object for his altruism, or he cannot be altruistic. I will have a first-rate object ready for him against the time when he is ready to pay for it."

I hold that William has a great duty to John. Not an altruistic duty, but plain, old-fashioned homely justice. That duty is to take care of himself, and bear his own share in the struggle for existence. The "ethics" which are aimed at John are unjust and insulting. Mr. Potter argues that John ought to "transform" William, because otherwise harm will come to John; that is, that because William has gone wrong or failed of his duty to John, whereby John suffers, William has become endowed, not with the just penalty of wrong-doing, but with a claim to redemption at John's expense.

It is easy to assume that John is a millionnaire and can pension off William without knowing that his superfluities are curtailed; but that is not the case. Either John is one of the great average of good citizens with an expensive family, so that his "charities" cut into his books, or his recreation, or his travel, or the comforts and advantageous luxuries of his family; or, if he is a millionnaire, William is not one, but a thousand—

perhaps ten thousand—and, if John secures their survival, he limits his own. The proposition will only be more firmly established by more study—that, if we do not like the survival of the fittest, our only alternative is the survival of the unfittest.

The "economic harmonies" are a great subject. I do not hold the doctrine as Mr. Potter seems to hold it, and I do not deny it as some economists do. I hope some time to publish my notion in its proper detail.

# Laissez-Faire

Keller dated this fragment to the late 1880s. Reference in deleted portions to a recent economic conference in England of 1885, and to early debate over railway legislation in the United States, suggests that it was written in 1886. In another omitted reference, and in mention of the "historical school," Sumner revealed that much of the argument concerning *laissez-faire* continued to be directed against the German *Verein für Socialpolitik*, the model of many economists who formed the American Economic Association in 1885. Sumner insisted that *laissez-faire* did not mean the "unrestrained action of nature," and, indeed, was less a scientific theory than a practical caution. This insistence probably reflected a desire to answer some of the more hostile criticisms of the previous years. MS. ca.1886, reprinted with permission from *Essays of William Graham Sumner*, eds. Albert Galloway Keller and Maurice R. Davie, vol. II, pp. 468–477.

Among the many terms and phrases of social science which are ill-understood and lightly and incorrectly used, no instance is more remarkable than *laissez-faire*. It will be profitable to define and illustrate its meaning.

The story goes that a certain French minister of state, desiring to exert himself for the benefit of the governed, called the merchants of Paris to a conference. He asked them what he could do for them. His idea of doing something for them was not as new as he supposed it was. In fact, they had had a large experience of that sort of thing already. They therefore answered "*Laissez-nous faire.*" Their answer has passed into a proverb and a maxim.

It seems to be widely believed that this phrase means "Do not do anything at all to interfere with nature." The current English translation of it is "Let alone." The translation, however, is so inadequate as to be incorrect and the lack of any equally terse expression in English which will render all the force of the original is the reason why the French phrase has been retained and naturalized.

A fair rendering of the answer of the French merchants would be: "Let us manage for ourselves." They did not propose to do without management. There is no sign in what they said or in what they did that they thought that brains could not be applied to trade and industry so as to develop and improve them. What they dreaded and declined with thanks was the proposition to define lines of action for them according to the wisdom of a statesman. Even if he took them into counsel they could not be induced to cooperate in the work of laying down rules for themselves which must, in the nature of the case, be rigid, arbitrary, hard to change, dictated by some dogma or ideal, and not such as the development of trade and industry would from time to time call for.

What the merchants meant by *laissez-faire* is a matter of only historical importance, but I know of no scientific writer who maintains the doctrine of *laissez-faire* in any other sense than that in which it was originally used. Anyone who gets his notion of *laissez-faire* from the rendering of it in the writings of the professorial socialists may well suppose that it is something very different from this, but that is only one of the features of the situation of political economy at the moment.

*Laissez-faire* is so far from meaning the unrestrained action of nature without any intelligent interference by man, that it really means the only rational application of human intelligence to the assistance of natural development. The best illustration of the perfect application of *laissez-faire* is a garden in which art has done its utmost to aid nature in that course of development which fits the interests and purposes of man. If we find such a garden anywhere and investigate the methods by which it has been brought into existence, do we find that the gardener has first made up his mind what he wants nature to give and has then proceeded by the method of trial and failure to try to make her come up to his ideal? There have been such gardeners and their successes have been more complete demonstrations of the folly of their method than even the failures. The Dutch gardeners who trimmed trees to represent beasts and birds, spoiling trees without making animals, illustrate very fairly what those statesmen have done to society who have tried to proceed by first forming ideals and then devising schemes to realize them. The gardener who wants a good garden and not a miserable imitation of a menagerie guards himself well against forming any ideals at all, and still more against putting any coercion on nature. He begins with a submission of himself to the investigation of nature. He abstains most carefully from meddling with her until he has observed her lines of independent action, because he knows that if he interferes sooner he will spoil the clearness and distinctness of the information which she will give him. He wants to find out her laws and he knows that, if he interferes with her action before the manifestation of the law is complete, he will not get that pure and simple expression of it which is his most priceless acquisition. His attitude therefore is one of obedience, of subordination, of following, and his chief folly would be conceit and "regulation." When he has a fund of information about the laws of nature, however, he does not use it to impose any purposes of his own on nature. He has only found out what is the range and what are the limitations of the plant world and by what laws nature produces her results within that range. He then selects, not what is better for the plant, but what suits his purposes. Then his whole task consists in furnishing to nature what she needs to help her and in removing all the obstacles which would hinder her in concentrating her forces on the things which men like to the exclusion of the things they do not like.

This illustration furnishes a complete parallel to what art may do to aid nature in society. The social case is infinitely more difficult for a great variety of reasons, but there are plenty of people who, while they would never dream of laying down rules for the management of a garden, are ready enough to prescribe regulations for society. Others propose to get some "statistics" and solve the problem at once. This is in some respects the funniest superstition of our time. A gardener might as well hope to learn how to raise cabbages by learning how many cabbages were raised in the country in a year. The fallacy would be the same.

*Laissez-faire* is the only true corrective of dogmatism and *a prior* reasoning. History and statistics are not the opposites or the correctives of those abuses. On the contrary, history and statistics are the very best cloaks of dogmatism. I have a large collection of passages from the writings of the "historical school," as it calls itself, in proof of this. An uncritical reader, having in hand an historical or statistical treatise, is likely to accept generalizations or assertions as in some way guaranteed by the positive material in the context, when a moment's examination would show that it stands entirely upon itself.

To give one instance: Jannasch, in an article on the movement of population into the great cities of Germany at the expense of the small cities and rural districts, says that the German great cities do not have specialized industries like those of England, but have a "higher mission on behalf of culture." He then tries to work out his pronouncement by a few assertions about the class of small independent handicraftsmen who migrate into German cities and by generalizations about independent craftsmen as compared with wage-earners. All this is absolutely without foundation or evidence. The assertions are only part of the articles of faith of a pseudopatriotism. They are open to plain contradiction on appropriate evidence. These generalizations are only the accepted and certainly erroneous commonplaces of an economic sect. Especially, however, I desire to point out that the alleged comparison of German and English cities, in a statistical article of a statistical periodical, is as purely dogmatic as if it appeared in a treatise on metaphysics.

Did space permit I should be glad to go into an analysis to show what dogmatism is and to distinguish its mischievous from its useful and necessary forms. A similar analysis needs to be made of speculation and generalization. These terms are all used nowadays in a flippant way by ill-educated men, to the great harm of science.

The doctrine and precept of *laissez-faire* do not preclude the attainment of positive results from investigation, nor the formulation of accurate statements of those results, nor the most elaborate verification of those results. The students of the *laissez-faire* school have done nearly all that ever has yet been done in the way of actual achievement under all these heads. *Laissez-faire* means: Do not meddle; wait and observe. Do not regulate; study. Do not give orders; be teachable. Do not enter upon any rash experiments; be patient until you see how it will work out.

The contrary temper is plainly manifested in our day on every hand. A man who has studied into any social question far enough to be nonplussed by its difficulties will propose some form of legislation about it. *Laissez-faire* would teach: At this time and under such a state of the question, the last thing to do is to legislate about it. When a half-dozen large and delicate interests are involved in a matter like transportation, in such a way that no human intelligence can possibly comprehend and adjust them, least of all by a piece of legislation which must be inelastic and arbitrary, this state of things is made a reason, not for letting the matter alone, but for passing legislation by way of experiment. Nothing could reveal more astoundingly the prevailing ignorance of what a society is and what methods of dealing with it are rational; for it is not possible to experiment with a society and just drop the experiment whenever we choose. The experiment enters into the life of the society and never can be got out again. Therefore, whenever there is a mania for interference, the doctrine of non-interference is the highest wisdom. It does not involve us in any argument with the people who know that the way to national prosperity is through plenty of greenbacks, or another dose of tariff, or who see what direful results will flow from lack of money if we do not have a "double standard." It does not compel us to argue that everything now is ideally good. It simply means that, whatever may be unsatisfactory in the world, we know we would rather take our chances of managing for ourselves than to submit our interests to the manipulation of social doctors.

The social doctor who, having become possessed by a pet notion, has deduced from it a world of bliss is not the worst variety of the species. The Germans have invented a thing which they call *Socialpolitik*. The cruelest blow that can be aimed at one of these German phrases is to translate it into English, for then all the flatulency is let out of it. I early learned that when a German notion was stated in compound and abstract nouns in *heit* and *keit*, so that it seemed to say something very profound, it was well, before accepting it, to sit down and translate it into everyday English. It is astonishing how often what seemed a profound piece of philosophy turned out to be a bathos. "Social policy" in English does not mean anything. "Statecraft," says Bamberger, "has been defined as the science of the possible. This new 'craft' [*Socialpolitik*], consisting in statecraft plus a new series of social functions which the state is to assume, constitutes a science of the impossible, so long as it is a science of the unproved," *i.e.*, of ends whose attainability has not been shown and whose appropriate means have not been ascertained or tested.

A man who has become interested in some one scheme of social improvement, although in his general standpoint unfavorable to interference, will resist the seduction of state interference as a means of accomplishing his object. A man who has been employed in administering some form of government interference is almost sure to become an advocate of that form of interference.

Let anyone notice, whenever a social question is brought into discussion, how inevitably the conversation or debate will run to the aspect of the matter which comes under the question: What can we do about it? or What can we make the tax-payer do about it? It is scarcely possible to get attention for an economic or sociological analysis of the matter which would aim to answer the question: What is the trouble? Is there any trouble? What are the social and economic causes of it? By what free cooperation of the parties concerned, under better knowledge and better temper, could any evil which exists be remedied? The greatest obstacle to any rational and true social improvement at this moment is the well-founded alarm excited by every proposition to do something by legislation—which compels all sober men to insist upon *laissez-faire* as an absolute principle of safety. In the face of those who are elaborating a social policy for us, there is often nothing to do but prevent anything from being done. Nearly all the machinery of Congress is an elaborate mechanism for preventing anything from being done, and although it stops many measures which a great many of us might think it very advisable to pass, we cheerfully do without them lest some of the others should get through likewise. The only fault with the mechanism is that it is not perfect enough. It fails when there is great clamor out of doors, for there is always cowardice inside, and then a Bland Bill or something of that sort can get a two-thirds vote and rise above the barrier of obstruction.

*Laissez-faire* is a maxim of policy. It is not a rule of science. Here we have another point of cardinal importance in the social wrangle of the day. No sound thinking is possible if we fail to distinguish correctly the domain of art from that of science. Science deals with what is true. The laws which it discovers admit of no exceptions, and when correctly stated cannot be overstated. The scientific man has reached the limit of his domain when he has laid down what he has found to be true. It is immaterial whether anybody believes it or profits by it or not. Here there is no room for maxims. There is nothing approximate or rough that is not imperfect, needing more work put on it. When, however, we go over to the domain of art, that is, of the application of scientific laws by human intelligence to the fulfillment of our purposes, we have come upon an entirely different domain. The limitations of our intelligence and the complications of natural phenomena as they actually occur prevent all clear, absolute, and unmodified rules. Maxims alone are in order over the whole domain of art. They embody long experience of mankind in the work or art, that is, in getting along as well as is practically possible towards the goal we want to reach under the circumstances in which we find ourselves and with the means at our disposal. For instance, if we are dealing with the phenomena of exchange, it belongs to science to analyze those phenomena and find out their laws. We talk about supply and demand very easily, but supply and demand are less understood today than the most difficult and abstruse laws of physics. The text-books present a weary waste of contradiction and whimsical assertion. I am ashamed of political economy whenever I put the chapter on value in Laughlin's "Mill" before my students. Sidgwick's treatment of the same subject is a "mush of concession" to every notion which has ever been put forward in sufficiently metaphysical form to strike the mind of the author. If the economists have no other function than to tell the public that there is no such thing as political economy, and to wrangle with each other about the method by which they shall prove this, whether deductively or inductively, then a man of common sense would best cease to be an economist and seek a respectable means of livelihood. If they say to the statesman: We have no laws of the industrial order which we can give you as the results of our science to guide you in your work; we have no science and cannot get any results which we can affirm with confidence; the field is open for your experiments—if this, I say, is their position, then all men of sense will send political economy to Saturn as Mr. Gladstone did before he began his colossal experiment in Ireland. If, however, there are laws of exchange and value, it is the duty of economists to find them out. The laws which they may discover will be laws in the only scientific sense of the word. When we go over to statecraft, we go over to art—to the domain, not of truth but of expediency, not of scientific laws but of maxims. The statesman then may well be guided by maxims drawn from history and experience. No maxim is more than approximately wise, for wisdom cannot be put into absolute statements and injunctions.

Statecraft is to be guided all the time by the active reason and intelligent conscience. This is the domain of ethics also. *Laissez-faire* belongs here, where it had its birth and where alone, so far as I know, the English economists, who have given us all the political economy we possess, have used it. If the statesman proposes to interfere with exchange, then *laissez-faire* comes in as a general warning, not as an absolute injunction: Let them manage for themselves. *Laissez-faire* is the only maxim which allows of the correct use of history and statistics to secure such knowledge as shall properly guide the statesman in his task.

# The State as an "Ethical Person"

The notion that the State (usually capitalized) was more than the sum of its parts found support in German Idealist philosophy and American post-Civil War nationalism. Influenced by one or both, Sumner himself argued in the early 1870s that the State was "not a machine but an organism—a *person* with a consciousness." However, Sumner later rejected this idea, now updated in the work of Thomas Hill Green and other British idealists as an argument for increased governmental power. "My notion of the state has dwindled with growing experience of life," he wrote in *What Social Classes Owe to Each Other*. "As an abstraction the state is to me only All-of-us." Originally printed in the *Independent* (October 6, 1887); reprinted in *Challenge of Facts*, ed. Albert Galloway Keller, pp. 201–204.

We meet often, in current social discussion, with the assertion that "the state is an ethical person." This is not a proposition concerning a relation of things, which is said to be true, nor is it an observation of fact which can be verified by a new examination; it is an assertion in regard to the standpoint which should be adopted or the mode of conceiving of the matter which should be accepted. Such assertions are, no doubt, extremely useful and fruitful when they are correct; but they are also very easily made, which implies that they are very liable to be incorrect, and they furnish broad ground for fallacious deductions. Let us examine this one.

The student of social welfare finds that the limit of social well-being of the society in the progress of time depends on the possibility of increasing the capital faster than the numbers increase. But so soon as he comes to consider the increase of capital, he finds himself face to face with ethical facts and forces. Capital is the fruit of industry, temperance, prudence, frugality, and other industrial virtues. Here then the welfare of society is found to be rooted in moral forces, and the relation between ethical and social phenomena is given in terms of actual facts and not of rhetorical abstractions. It comes to this: that the question how well off we can be depends at last on the question how rational, virtuous, and enlightened we are. Hence the student of society finds that if the society has developed all the social and economic welfare which its existing moral development will justify or support, then there is no way to get any more welfare, save by advancing the moral development. It is possible that there may be obstacles in the political or social organization which prevent the actual moral power of the people from attaining its maximum result in social and material welfare. In any existing society there are such obstacles, and the field of reform lies in dealing with them. But if we may imagine such obstacles to be removed and all the social machinery to be perfect, we should then have distinctly before us the fact that for every increase of social well-being we must provide by ourselves becoming better men.

It is only putting the same statement in another form to say that whatever deficiencies there are in our society which are important or radical—that is to say, which surpass in magnitude the harm which comes from defects in the social machinery—are due to deficiencies in our moral development. We are as well off as we deserve to be. We are as well off as such moral creatures as we are can be. The solidarity of society holds us together so that, although some of us are better than others in industrial virtue, we must all go together.

Now arises the interesting question: Where can we get any more moral power? Where is there any spring or source of it which we have not yet used? What new stimulus can be applied to the development of moral energy to quicken or intensify it? When, therefore, we are told that the state is an ethical person, the question we have to ask is this: Is the state a source of moral energy which can contribute what is needed? Can it bring to us from some outside source that which, by the facts of the case, we lack? If it can, then indeed it is the most beneficent patron we possess; it has a function which is on the same plane with that ascribed by some theological doctrines to the Holy Spirit. Or, if not that, then it has a function similar to that of the church and the school, only far more elevated and incomparably more direct and effective; and it executes this function, not by acting on the minds and hearts of men, but by mechanical operations, regulations, and ceremonial activities. If the assertion that the state is an ethical person does not mean this, if it does not mean that, in the midst of our social struggles and perplexities, the state is an independent source of power which can be called in to help, by contributing the ethical energy which we need, then that assertion is an empty jingle of words, or, at most, it refers vaguely to the general advantage of the association and co-operation of men with each other. It appears, therefore, that the assertion that we ought to conceive of the state as an ethical person does not rest upon any such solid analysis of the facts of life and the nature of the state as would make it a useful and fruitful proposition for further study of social phenomena, but that it is a product of the phrase-mill. It is one of those mischievous dicta which seem to say something profound; but, upon examination, prove to say nothing which will bear analysis. In current discussion, especially of state interference, this proposition is always invoked just when the real crisis of discussion comes, and it serves to cover the lack of true analysis and sound thinking.

If we turn aside from the special field of social discussion for a moment to call up accepted principles of ethics and of sound thinking, we shall find it undisputed that the source of ethical energy is in the hearts and minds of human beings and not anywhere else. Institutions of which the family, the church, and the school are the chief, which have for their purpose the development of ethical energy in the rising generation, cost energy and give it back. The institution itself produces nothing. It is like any other machine; it only gives direction and combination or division to the forces which are put into it. It is the moral force of the parent and teacher which develops the moral force of the child; the institution is only a convenient arrangement or apparatus for bringing the one to bear on the other. The institution is at its best when it allows this personal contact and relationship to be most direct and simple—that is, when the institution itself counts for the least possible. When we turn to the state, we find that it is not even in nature and purpose, or pretence, an institution like those mentioned. It has its purposes, which are high and important, and for these it needs moral power and consumes moral power. The family, the church, and the school are preparing men and women of moral power for the service of the state; they hand them over, such as they are, to be citizens and members of the commonwealth. In that position their moral capacities are drawn upon; speaking of the society as a whole, we must say that they are used up. The practice of virtue increases virtue, whether it be in the state or the store, the profession or the handicraft; but there is no more reason on that account to call the state an ethical person than there is to apply the same high-sounding epithet to trades or professions. There is no sense in which it may be properly used in the one case in which it would not equally well apply to the other.

# Liberty

Although Sumner often equated liberty and rights in his early lectures, he gradually introduced an important if not always clear distinction between them. Existing in the shifting realm of politics, rights were relative. Liberty, in contrast, was or should be absolute because it is basic to economic well-being. Liberty, he explained in 1880, "means simply a free chance to get as good a living as one can by one's own industry and economy." He added that property was basic to liberty, not as a right, but as a precondition of freedom, contrasting his view with that of the Belgian socialist Émile de Laveleye. Originally published as "Liberty and Responsibility," "Liberty and Discipline," "Liberty and Property," "The Disappointment of Liberty," in a series of fourteen articles that appeared in the *Independent* from 1887 to 1889; reprinted in *Earth Hunger*, ed. Albert Galloway Keller, pp. 156–161, 166–171, 171–176, 198–203.

## Liberty and Responsibility

From one end to the other of history, from one extreme to the other of the social scale, we can find no status in which men realize the kind of liberty which consists in doing as one pleases, or in unrestrainedness of action. If we should go on to consider the case of the learned man, or the statesman, or the monarch, or any other class and position, we should find the same. The Emperor Nicholas of Russia, who left the reputation of a military autocrat behind, complained that his Minister took a position before the chimney, and, to everything which the Emperor proposed, simply answered: "It is not permitted to do it." Liberty to do as one pleases is not of this world, for the simple reason that all human and earthly existence is conditioned on physical facts. The life of man is surrounded and limited by the equilibrium of the forces of nature, which man can never disturb, and within the bounds of which he must find his chances.

If that seems too ponderous and abstract for the reader, it may be interpreted as follows. Man must get his living out of the earth. He must, in so doing, contend with the forces which control the growth of trees, the production of animals, the cohesion of metals in ores; he must meet conditions of soil and climate; he must conform to the conditions of the social organization, which increases the power of a body of men to extort

237

their living from the earth, but at the price of mutual concessions and inevitable subordination. Organization means more power, but it also means constraint, and, at every step of advancing civilization, while we seem to get nearer to this form of liberty, the means of emancipation proves a new bond. Such being the case, it is a plain delusion to suppose that we can ever emancipate ourselves from earth while we are upon it.

Yet men have, in all the higher forms of civilization, been determined that they would have this liberty. They have, as it were, determined that they would fly. They have made liberty a dream, a poetic illusion, by which to escape, at least for an hour, from the limitations of earth; they have put liberty at the beginning of all things, in the "state of nature," or far on in the future, in a millennium. Within the last century, especially, they have elaborated notions of liberty as a natural endowment, belonging to everybody, a human birthright. Their experience has been that they did not get it, and, when this clashed with the smooth doctrines in which they had been educated, they have become enraged.

Now it will be most advantageous to notice that this notion of liberty has a certain historical justification, and, when historically considered, a relative truth.

The mediaeval social and political system consisted of a complex of customs and institutions such that, when we come to analyze them, and find out their philosophy, we find they imply all the time that men are, but for political institutions and social arrangements, under universal servitude. The point of departure of administration and legislation was that a man had no civil rights or social liberty, but what was explicitly conferred by competent authority, and that the sum of rights which any person had were not such as belonged generally to all members of the society, but such as each, by his struggles and those of his ancestors, had come to possess. The modern view gets its interpretation, and its relative justification, by reference to and in antagonism to this; the doctrine of natural liberty as an antecedent status of general non-restraint was a revolt against the doctrine just stated. It meant to affirm that laws and state institutions ought to be built upon an assumption that men were, or would be but for law, not all unfree, but all free, and that freedom ought to be considered, not a product of social struggle and monarchical favor or caprice, but an ideal good which states could only limit, and that they ought not to do this except for good and specific reason, duly established. The nineteenth-century state is built on this construction. We are obliged all the time to assume, in all our studies, certain constructions, of which we say only that things act as if they were under such and such a formula, although we cannot prove that that formula is true. Institutions grow under conditions into certain forms which can be explained and developed only by similar constructions.

Modern civil institutions have been developed as if man had been, anterior to the state, and but for the state, in a condition of complete non-restraint. The notion has been expanded by the most pitiless logic, and at this moment a score, or perhaps a hundred, eager "reforms" are urged upon grounds which are only new and further deductions from it. At this point, like the other great eighteenth-century notions which are also true relatively when referred back to the mediaeval notions which they were intended to combat, the notion of abstract liberty turns into an independent dogma claiming full philosophical truth and authority. In that sense, as we have seen, it is untrue to fact.

When we turn to test the dogma of liberty by history and experience, we find immediately that the practical reason why no man can do as he likes in a human society is that he cannot get rid of responsibility. It is responsibility which fetters an autocrat, unless he is a maniac. It is that which binds the millionaire, which limits the savage who is responsible to his tribe, which draws narrow lines about the statesman, and which will just as inevitably fetter a democratic majority unless such a majority proposes social suicide. Responsibility rises up by the side of liberty, correlative, commensurate, and inevitable. Responsibility to nature is enforced by disease, poverty, misery, and death; responsibility to society is enforced by discord, revolution, national decay, conquest, and enslavement. Within the narrow limits of human institutions, liberty and responsibility are made equal and co-ordinate whenever the institutions are sound. If they are not equal and co-ordinate, then he who has liberty without responsibility incurs a corresponding loss of liberty, or servitude. Those men and classes who at any time have obtained a measure of abstract liberty to do as they like on earth, have got it in this way—at the expense of the servitude of somebody else. Thousands of men died that Napoleon Bonaparte might, in a measure, have his way; great aristocracies have won wide unrestraint by displacing the lives and property of thousands of others, when the aristocracies have been built up by a remission of responsibility.

The worst modern political and social fallacies consist in holding out to the mass of mankind hopes and affirmations of right according to which they are entitled by prerogative to liberty without responsibility. The current political philosophy, having fallen under the dominion of romanticism (except as to war and diplomacy), has apparently no power to do more than to follow and furnish platitudes for the popular tendency, or to oppose all forms of liberty in the interest of socialistic equality. The prosecution of that line of criticism, however, lies aside from my present purpose.

I have now arrived at the point where the true idea of liberty, as the greatest civil good, can be brought forward. The link between liberty and responsibility can be established and upheld only by law; for this reason, civil liberty, the only real liberty which is possible or conceivable on earth, is a matter of law and institutions. It is not metaphysical at all. Civil liberty is really a great induction from all the experience of mankind in the use of civil institutions; it must be defined, not in terms drawn from metaphysics, but in terms drawn from history and law. It is not an abstract conception; it is a series of concrete facts. These facts go to constitute a status—the status of a freeman in a modern jural state. It is a product of institutions; it is embodied in institutions; it is guaranteed by institutions. It is not a matter of resolutions, or "declarations," as they seemed to think in the last century. It is unfriendly to dogmatism. It pertains to what a man shall do, have, and be. It is unfriendly to all personal control, to officialism, to administrative philanthropy and administrative wisdom, as much as to bureaucratic despotism or monarchical absolutism. It is hostile to all absolutism, and people who are well-trained in the traditions of civil liberty are quick to detect absolutism in all its new forms. Those who have lost the traditions of civil liberty accept phrases.

The questions in regard to civil liberty are: do we know what it is? do we know what it has cost? do we know what it is worth? do we know whether it is at stake?

## Liberty and Discipline

The proposition that "every man should be free to do as he likes, without encroaching on the similar liberty of every other man," is commonly used as if it were a simple and final definition of social and civil liberty. It is not so, however. It is only one of those formulas which we get into the habit of using because they save us the trouble of thinking, not because they are real solutions. Evidently any two men might easily disagree as to the limits set by this formula to their respective spheres of right and liberty—if so they would quarrel and fight. Law, peace, and order would not therefore be guaranteed; that is to say, the problem would not be solved.

Civil liberty must therefore be an affair of positive law, of institutions, and of history. It varies from time to time, for the notion of rights is constantly in flux. The limiting line between the rights and duties of each man, up to which each may go without trenching on the same rights and liberty of others, must be defined at any moment of time by the constitution, laws, and institutions of the community. People often deny this, and revolt at it, because they say that one's notions of rights and liberty are not set for him by the laws of the state. The first man you meet will undoubtedly tell you that there are a number of laws now in force in the United States which he does not think are consistent with liberty and (natural) rights—I who write this would say so of laws restricting immigration, laying protective taxes, etc. But it is to be observed that behind the positive law existing at any time, there is the moral reflection of the community which is at work all the time. This is the field of study, debate, and reflection, on which moral convictions are constantly being formed, and when they are formed; they find their way into laws, constitutions, and institutions, provided that the political institutions are free, so as to allow this to take place. If not, there is opened a gap between the positive law and the moral convictions of the people, and social convulsions ensue. It is a constant phenomenon of all exaggerated philosophers of the state, that they obscure this distinction between public morals and positive law. The older abuse was to suppress public morals in the name of positive law; the later abuse is to introduce public morals into positive law directly and immaturely.

If now we turn to individual liberty, still it is true that all liberty is under law. The whole life of man is under law—it is impossible to conceive of it otherwise. It is impossible to understand society except we think of it as held and governed by forces which maintain equilibrium in it, just as we have learned to conceive of nature. The objections which are made to this notion are exactly parallel to those which were formerly brought against the same conception of physics, and it is impossible to argue against them, because, if they were true, there would be no thinking or arguing possible. If social science deals only with matters of expediency, then there is no social science. It is a question of expediency whether there shall be two Houses in the Legislature or one; whether the Cabinet ministers shall have seats in Congress; whether men shall work ten hours a day or eight; whether we should use more or less paper money inside the requirement of the country; whether university education should be based on Greek; whether women should have the suffrage; and so on. If all the questions of social science are of this nature, there is no social science; there is nothing to find out. All that can be said is: "Go on and try it"; and the people who have "views" may be listened to if they show what they think to be the advantages of one or another arrangement.

In truth, however, the field of expediency is very circumscribed. It is surrounded by the domain of forces, so that when we seem most free to adopt such plans as we please, we find ourselves actually controlled by facts in the nature of man and of the earth, and we find that it is the sum of our wisdom to find out those facts and to range ourselves under them and in obedience to them. Then our science and our art have their proper places and fall into due relation to each other.

Thus we come to this: that there is no liberty for the intelligent man as an individual, or in voluntary co-operation with others, except in intelligent obedience to the laws of right living. His first task is to know the world in which he finds himself. He must work and he must study. He is not turned out to riot in self-indulgence because he is free; he must conform to the conditions in which he finds himself. He must obey. When he has broken all the bonds of old institutions, of superstition and human tyranny, he wakes to find that he can have no liberty unless he subdues himself; labor and self-control are the conditions of welfare. He must not cry out that liberty is only a delusion and a juggle; he must understand that what liberty properly means for the individual, is intelligent acceptance of the conditions of earthly life, conformity to them, and manful effort to make life a success under them.

Not to follow this line of thought into the domain of private morals, I turn back to the relation of individual liberty to civil liberty. Civil and political liberty cannot release a man from state burdens. It is interesting and instructive to notice that free yeomen in the United States have to take up, of their own accord, many of those burdens which, in the Middle Ages, were regarded as the heaviest feudal obligations. The farmers in a New England township have to maintain roads and bridges, do police duty, and maintain all public institutions as much as if they lived upon a manor. A farmer who works out his taxes on a road does not know how near he comes to reproducing a mediaeval villain. The burdens are there, because society is there; and they must be borne. If the state does them on a larger scale than the township, then they must be paid for; and when we see men eager to work them out if they can, we must infer that the burden is increased, not lessened, by being turned into taxes.

When the peasant obtains freedom, therefore, and sets up a democratic republic, he finds that that means only that he must turn about and do again voluntarily, as an intelligent citizen, what he did before under human compulsion. When he gets self-government, he finds that it still means government; only that now it is turned into personal discipline instead of being governmental compulsion. If he gets his personal liberty, then civil liberty is nothing but a guarantee that, in doing his best to learn the laws of right living and to obey them, to the end that his life may be a success, no one else shall be allowed to interfere with him or to demand a share in the product of his efforts. That is what the function of the state is; and if it does more or less it fails of its function.

Discipline, therefore, is the great need of our time. It should be the first object of education. By it we mean something much more than the mental training about which we used to hear so much. We mean training of thought, feeling, and emotions, so as to apprehend and appreciate all things correctly; and habits of self-control so as to hold one's self within the limits which enable free men in a free society to live in harmony and pursue their ends successfully without encroaching on each other. Our children need it. Their freedom and fearlessness give them spirit and courage; but they lack form and training—they would not be any less free if they were considerably chastened. We need it as parents; we should discharge our responsibilities in that relationship much better if we were schooled to more patience and to more rational methods of exercising authority or instruction. We need it in social relations, because it is only by virtue of discipline that men can co-operate with each other. The notion that co-operation is a power which can take the place of the intelligence of well-trained men, is itself a product and proof of undisciplined thinking. Men increase their power indefinitely by co-operation and organization; but in order to co-operate they must make concessions. The prime condition is concord, and it is only disciplined men who are capable of attaining to that. It has often been said that men have to surrender their liberty in order to organize; but it is better stated that they gain new power consistently with liberty by organizing. We need better discipline in science, at least in social science. There is a great luxuriance in the production of "views" and notions in this field; and the greatest need is of a set of guarantees and criteria by which this exuberance could be trimmed down. There is one set of persons whose

liberty would certainly gain by the production of such tests and guarantees, viz., those who are now likely to have to pay the expense of all
the social speculation which is on foot, if any of it should be put to
experiment. We need more discipline in public affairs. Our freedom
would lose nothing if it were more sober, and if a great many abuses
which the law cannot reach were more under the ban of public opinion.

Thus liberty in a free state, and for intelligent men, is limited, first by
responsibility, and second by discipline.


## Liberty and Property

M. de Laveleye says: "Property is the essential complement of liberty.
Without property man is not truly free." It will be worth while, taking
this dictum as a text, to unravel it and distinguish its elements of truth
and falsehood; for it is as pretty a specimen as could well be found of
the sort of social philosophy in which confusion of terms and unclear-
ness of thinking set apothegms in circulation which easily pass as the
profoundest wisdom, when they are really null, or, still worse, are true
or false just as you take them.

The specimen before us may mean either of two things. It may mean
that every man has a right to be, and expects to be, a free man, that to
be such he must have some property, and that, therefore, the authority
which is responsible for securing him his freedom is bound to see to it
that he gets some property; or, it may mean that freedom is a thing which
every man should seek to win and acquire, that it is not possible to
acquire it without property, and that, therefore, every sober, industrious,
and socially ambitious man should properly seek to get property. Which
of these two does the proposition mean? By its terms it is impossible to
decide. It is a proposition which two persons might understand and
employ at the same time in the two opposite senses with perfect good
faith, and thereby lay the foundation for a "social discussion" of great
magnitude, the only fruit of which would be to find out at last how they
had misunderstood each other from the beginning. We have seen numerous instances of this kind and it can hardly be disputed that the
propositions which admit of such differences of interpretation are extremely mischievous.

If the proposition is taken in the former sense, the notion of a "free
man" is taken to be something simple and definite, which can be made
the basis of deductions, and upon which obligations of social duty can

be constructed, aimed especially at the state, which guarantees liberty as a political right. Property then becomes a right of the individual, in his relation with society or the state. He would not forfeit this right to have property unless he should get some property by his own effort—if he did that he would fall under the "duties of wealth," the first of which, as we learn from current discussion, is to subscribe to or contribute the fund by which the state makes others free.

If the proposition is taken in the latter sense, the notion of a free man cannot be set up *a priori*. A free man is such a man as results under the limitation of earthly life, when he has individual and social power sufficient to bear up against the difficulties which harass us here. The proposition would then say that no man can do this without property—property would, therefore, be a duty, not a right. A man could not lay claims to it against anybody else; he would be bound to produce it from his own energy, and by the use of his own resources. Property would, therefore, arise in the social organization from the obligation of every man to pay his way in the body of which he is a member, and to carry the burden of others for whom he is responsible—first of all, of his wife and children. It would not arise, as under the first interpretation, from the fact that he needs something which he has not.

According to these two interpretations, the proposition contains neither one nor the other of the two great philosophies which are now in dispute on the social domain. They might, in fact, be defined as affirming, one, that property is a right of him who has it not and a duty of him who has it, looking always simply at the distribution of that which is; the other, that property is a right of him who has it, and a duty of him who has it not, *viz.*, a duty to work and produce some.

We need not stop for any long discussion of the definition of property, for it does not seem to be involved in the issue before us. By property I mean the sum of things which serve the wants of men, and the appropriation of which to individual use and enjoyment is assured by the power of society. Such, also, seems to be the sense in which the word is taken in the passage quoted, so that we are at least free from the constant confusion between property, the metaphysical notion of property, the right of property, and the moral justification of property. The author of this thesis has not, therefore, a balloon at hand, so that when he is beaten on the ground he can take to the clouds. The property which a man needs to make him free is food, clothes, shelter, and fuel to release him from the slavery of want. These are material things, goods, wealth, products of labor and capital, objects of appropriation, sources of exclusive satisfaction to him who consumes them on himself; they are therefore objects of strife, occasions of crime, definitions of *meum* and *tuum*, things about which law turns, chief subjects of the moral law, leading facts in the history of civilization, having their origin far back before it was sufficiently developed to leave traces which we can follow. That is what is meant by property when it is said that without property a man cannot be free, no matter which interpretation we give to that proposition.

One of the best mediaeval scholars of this century, Guerard, wrote: "Liberty and property entered the hut of the serf together"; "Liberty and property increased together and justified each other"; and he often repeats statements to the same effect. Another scholar, Pigeonneau, has written that in the boroughs which were built up around the seats of bishops, princes, and abbots, commerce created wealth, and wealth created liberty. The history of the Middle Ages, when studied objectively and not romantically, fully sustains these dicta. The history of modern civilization from the ninth and eleventh centuries, about which these writers were speaking, down to the present time, reveals the course by which liberty and property have been developed together; but at the same time it reveals that they have grown together only when property has been secure, and the right of property has been strictly maintained, and that nothing has ever been more fatal to liberty than socialistic abuse of property.

In the view of liberty which I have tried to present, liberty is a conquest. It does not lie at the beginning of history and of the struggle of the human race on this earth; it lies at the end of it, and it is one of the richest and finest fruits of civilization. We should not, therefore, if we gave up civilization, fall back into permanent rest in the primeval state of "natural liberty"; we should, on the contrary, lose liberty, if we lost civilization. It is liberty which is unstable and always in jeopardy, and which can be maintained only by virtue and diligence. The two great means by which men have won liberty in the course of civilization have been property and knowledge; whenever the distribution of property has been arbitrarily interfered with, either because the state became too strong or too weak, liberty has declined. Civilization has not always suffered, because, as in the formation of the great states, under certain circumstances, civilization might win, although liberty was arrested—civilization will win any time at the expense of liberty, if discipline and coercion are necessary to the security of property. Therefore the truth is that liberty and property go together, and sustain each other in a glorious accord, but only in the highest and best civilization which men have yet attained; and to maintain them both together, or to maintain that order of society in which they are consonant and co-operative, is a task which mankind has never yet succeeded in accomplishing save in a most imperfect way.

The serf first obtained chattels and then land in property; on them he won his first power, and that meant his first liberty—meaning thereby his personal liberty. His title to these things, that is, his right to appropriate them to his own exclusive use and enjoyment, and to be sustained by the power of the state in so doing, was his first step in civil liberty. It was by this movement that he ceased to be a serf. This movement has produced the great middle class of modern times; and the elements in it have been property, science, and liberty. The first and chief of these, however, is property; there is no liberty without property, because there is nothing else without property on this earth. How can any one dispute this who will think for a moment that property means food and shelter— the first things necessary that we may exist at all; and that we use the word property rather than wealth or goods when we mean to refer to their appropriation to the exclusive use of individuals? Therefore liberty and property are not inseparable, and if they are separated it is property which is fundamental and permanent, and not liberty.

Hence the proposition which we undertook to examine does not bear analysis well. The dictum that no man can be free without property is entirely true or false as we construe it one way or another. Freedom and property, I say, are not inseparable, and if they are separated, it is liberty and not property which is the adjunct. If they are united, they do not simply coalesce, but their combination belongs to a new and higher order of civilization, calling for new social knowledge and for wisdom to maintain it.

## The Disappointment of Liberty

As we probe the idea of liberty on one side and another, distinctions are brought to light. First we have revolutionary or anarchistic liberty, the notion of which is that a free man is emancipated from the struggle for existence, and assured everything he needs (wants), by virtue of his liberty, on terms which he shall not regard as onerous. Secondly, we have personal liberty, which is the chance to fight the struggle for existence for one's self, to the best of one's will and ability, within the bounds

of one's personal circumstances, for which other men are not responsible, without any risk of being compelled to fight the struggle for anybody else, and without any claim to the assistance of anybody else in
one's own. Third, we have civil liberty, which is a status produced by
laws and civil institutions, in which the personal liberty of individuals
is secured; it is a status in which all rights and duties are in equilibrium.

Objection has been made to the second and third definitions that a
man might steal, by way of liberty to pursue the struggle for existence
on his own behalf. The objection only illustrates the difficulty of this
order of discussion. It is conceivable that laws and institutions might
tolerate stealing, for they have done it; but as there can be no robber
without a robbed, and as the definition must apply equally to all individuals in the society, the definition absolutely excluded stealing or
other invasion of personal rights. The objection is therefore futile, and
does not call for any modification of the definition.

As we go on with the discussion, we also see that in one view of the
case all human strength seems to lie in liberty, while in another view it
all seems to lie in discipline. At this point a pitfall lies on either side.
Anarchists and Nihilists, accepting the notion that in liberty is all
strength, elevate revolution to the highest function as a redeeming and
reforming force; to destroy and tear down becomes a policy of wisdom
and growth; everything which is in the way; everything which has grown
as an institution is an obstacle to that ideal of primitive purity and
simplicity, combined with liberty, to which we would be eager to return.
Hence liberty of the first species is sought, in practise, by universal
negation and reckless destruction. But society cannot sustain itself without stringent organization—organization which coerces its members.
Liberty, on this view, is therefore social suicide, for it is war of the society
against the most essential conditions of its own existence.

On the other side, the notion that discipline is the secret of all strength
is easily convertible into the notion that subordination, submission,
obedience to one's fellow-men, is the secret of all strength. That is the
fallacy of authoritative absolutism in all its forms. A man without discipline is a boor and a barbarian, but a man who has submitted his will
to another mortal's will has broken the spring of moral power. The effect
of sound discipline is that it never breaks the spring, but strengthens it,
because the individual character reacts with new energy on account of
new moral forces which are brought into play, viz., critical reflection
and independent conviction. The question which arises at every new
crisis in which a man is freed from control is this: if others let go of you

will you take hold of yourself? A spoiled boy or man is one in whom a succession of these crises has been decided the wrong way.

At this point the moral problem comes in. It consists in the combination of the two elements of liberty and discipline; and they must be combined according to circumstances. The problem is not, therefore, capable of definite or final solution; it defies analysis and rule. Like other moral problems, it is only a fragment of the great problem of living.

The more widely and thoroughly we explore the field of social fact and relations in which liberty falls, the more are we convinced that liberty in the sense of the first of the above definitions is the grandest of human delusions. That notion of liberty is a part of the great dream that our situation on earth is, to a great extent, a matter of our own choice and decision, or, as the current fashion expresses it, that social questions are ethical. With the growth of social science the old wrangle about free will has been transferred to this domain, and the question whether we make our social phenomena or our social phenomena make us, whether the man is a function of the state or the state is a function of the man, is the question whether social science can throw off the thraldom of metaphysics or not. At present we have to note that our studies of liberty, in all its phases and applications, have forced us again and again to observe that there is no real liberty but that which is an affair of history, law, and institutions. It is therefore positive, and so is capable of historical study and scientific analysis.

The dream of liberty has taken possession of men's minds within the last century to the exclusion of other dreams except that of equality—and with good reason, for if the dream of emancipation from the heavy weight of the struggle for existence were realizable it would supersede all other dreams. Then, again, there has been an unprecedented opening of new chances to mankind, which chances have permitted the human race at the same time to increase in numbers and to advance in comfort of living. Political institutions have advanced at the same time and have been assumed to be the cause of the advance in average comfort. This claim has been almost universally admitted, and has produced the natural inference that political devices can do all for us that we can possibly desire. This is the latest Utopianism and it surpasses all previous phases of Utopianism in pure silliness. Then, again, any period of advancing comfort is sure to be one of advancing sentimentalism; men who are struggling each for himself, under the pressure of dire necessity, will spare little sympathy on each other—it is when they are at ease that they have sympathy to spare. Distress dissolves the social bond; comfort strengthens it. All these things, then, have concurred within a century to raise and intensify the dream of liberty.

It is not strange that this movement has issued and is issuing in disappointment, neither is it strange that the disappointment should be vented on constitutional liberty, the only true liberty, and never should reach the delusive and fallacious liberty at all. Human history is full of just such errors as that. The last thing in the world to which we attribute our misfortunes is our pet delusions; they stand firm through all.

I say that it is not strange that the dream of liberty should issue in disappointment and revolt, because this liberty has been promised as a cause and guarantee of bliss on earth, and it has failed to give what it promised. Civil and personal liberty help on the evolution of society; they produce growth of individuals and societies. They are not revolutionary, but are hostile to revolution; they stand related to the revolutionary liberty as the truth to the caricature. It stands, therefore, as one of the tasks before our social science to distinguish these two notions of liberty from each other as sharply as possible, and while manifesting the strength and value of the one to show the error and falsity of the other.

Everything, however, which is evolutionary aims to produce the utmost possible, in the next stage, out of the antecedents which lie in the last stage. Evolutionary methods, therefore, have nothing to do with ideals; they aim always at the best possible under the circumstances. Under such methods, therefore, there can be no dreams of universal bliss at all; neither can there be hope in brutal destruction, or unintelligent negation, for any sober reform.

It is most natural that this reduction of all the enthusiastic dreams of the last century to the test of positive truth should be regarded as "cold" and unsympathetic; that a wider and wider gulf should open between "ethical aspirations" and the products of scientific method applied to social phenomena; and that the point at which the cleft opens should be the doctrine of liberty. Any student of social science who accepts the anarchistic notion of liberty will find himself lost in the new forms of the mist of free-will. No such notion of liberty can be tolerated in a scientific discussion, but only that notion which, being a product of social growth, is within the field of the science itself. On every ground and at every point the domain of social science must be defended against the alleged authority of ethical dicta, which cannot be subjected to any verification whatever.

# The Absurd Effort to Make the World Over

Sumner wrote this essay in the midst of one of the nation's worst economic depressions, two years after overwork and a near-breakdown had persuaded him to accept private support for an overseas sabbatical. Twitting the many Americans who pictured Germany as a model of efficiency and organization, he suggested that German railways could use some capitalist know-how. He also took aim at Edward Bellamy's Utopian novel, *Looking Backward* (1888), directly and in the reference to "slate and pencil" in his final sentence. Originally published in the *Forum* 17 (March 1894), 92–102; reprinted in *War*, ed. Albert Galloway Keller, pp. 195–210.

It will not probably be denied that the burden of proof is on those who affirm that our social condition is utterly diseased and in need of radical regeneration. My task at present, therefore, is entirely negative and critical: to examine the allegations of fact and the doctrines which are put forward to prove the correctness of the diagnosis and to warrant the use of the remedies proposed.

The propositions put forward by social reformers nowadays are chiefly of two kinds. There are assertions in historical form, chiefly in regard to the comparison of existing with earlier social states, which are plainly based on defective historical knowledge, or at most on current stock historical dicta which are uncritical and incorrect. Writers very often assert that something never existed before because they do not know that it ever existed before, or that something is worse than ever before because they are not possessed of detailed information about what has existed before. The other class of propositions consists of dogmatic statements which, whether true or not, are unverifiable. This class of propositions is the pest and bane of current economic and social discussion. Upon a more or less superficial view of some phenomenon a suggestion arises which is embodied in a philosophical proposition and promulgated as a truth. From the form and nature of such propositions they can always be brought under the head of "ethics." This word at least gives them an air of elevated sentiment and purpose, which is the only warrant they possess. It is impossible to test or verify them by any investigation or logical process whatsoever. It is therefore very difficult for anyone who feels a high responsibility for historical statements, and who absolutely rejects any statement which is unverifiable, to find a common platform for discussion or to join issue satisfactorily in taking the negative.

When anyone asserts that the class of skilled and unskilled manual laborers of the United States is worse off now in respect to diet, clothing, lodgings, furniture, fuel, and lights; in respect to the age at which they can marry; the number of children they can provide for; the start in life which they can give to their children, and their chances of accumulating capital, than they ever have been at any former time, he makes a reckless assertion for which no facts have been offered in proof. Upon an appeal to facts, the contrary of this assertion would be clearly established. It suffices, therefore, to challenge those who are responsible for the assertion to make it good.

If it is said that the employed class are under much more stringent discipline than they were thirty years ago or earlier, it is true. It is not true that there has been any qualitative change in this respect within thirty years, but it is true that a movement which began at the first settlement of the country has been advancing with constant acceleration and has become a noticeable feature within our time. This movement is the advance in the industrial organization. The first settlement was made by agriculturists, and for a long time there was scarcely any organization. There were scattered farmers, each working for himself, and some small towns with only rudimentary commerce and handicrafts. As the country has filled up, the arts and professions have been differentiated and the industrial organization has been advancing. This fact and its significance has hardly been noticed at all; but the stage of the industrial organization existing at any time, and the rate of advance in its development, are the absolutely controlling social facts. Nine-tenths of the socialistic and semi-socialistic, and sentimental or ethical, suggestions by which we are overwhelmed come from failure to understand the phenomena of the industrial organization and its expansion. It controls us all because we are all in it. It creates the conditions of our existence, sets the limits of our social activity, regulates the bonds of our social relations, determines our conceptions of good and evil, suggests our life-philosophy, molds our inherited political institutions, and reforms the oldest and toughest customs, like marriage and property. I repeat that the turmoil of heterogeneous and antagonistic social whims and speculations in which we live is due to the failure to understand what the industrial organization is and its all-pervading control over human life, while the traditions of our school of philosophy lead us always to approach the industrial organization, not from the side of objective study, but from that of philosophical doctrine. Hence it is that we find that the method of measuring what we see happening by what are called ethical standards, and of proposing to attack the phenomena by methods thence deduced, is so popular.

The advance of a new country from the very simplest social coordination up to the highest organization is a most interesting and instructive chance to study the development of the organization. It has of course been attended all the way along by stricter subordination and higher discipline. All organization implies restriction of liberty. The gain of power is won by narrowing individual range. The methods of business in colonial days were loose and slack to an inconceivable degree. The movement of industry has been all the time toward promptitude, punctuality, and reliability. It has been attended all the way by lamentations about the good old times; about the decline of small industries; about the lost spirit of comradeship between employer and employee; about the narrowing of the interests of the workman; about his conversion into a machine or into a "ware," and about industrial war. These lamentations have all had reference to unquestionable phenomena attendant on advancing organization. In all occupations the same movement is discernible—in the learned professions, in schools, in trade, commerce, and transportation. It is to go on faster than ever, now that the continent is filled up by the first superficial layer of population over its whole extent and the intensification of industry has begun. The great inventions both make the intension of the organization possible and make it inevitable, with all its consequences, whatever they may be. I must expect to be told here, according to the current fashions of thinking, that we ought to control the development of the organization. The first instinct of the modern man is to get a law passed to forbid or prevent what, in his wisdom, he disapproves. A thing which is inevitable, however, is one which we cannot control. We have to make up our minds to it, adjust ourselves to it, and sit down to live with it. Its inevitableness may be disputed, in which case we must re-examine it; but if our analysis is correct, when we reach what is inevitable we reach the end, and our regulations must apply to ourselves, not to the social facts.

Now the intensification of the social organization is what gives us greater social power. It is to it that we owe our increased comfort and abundance. We are none of us ready to sacrifice this. On the contrary, we want more of it. We would not return to the colonial simplicity and the colonial exiguity if we could. If not, then we must pay the price. Our life is bounded on every side by conditions. We can have this if we will agree to submit to that. In the case of industrial power and product the great condition is combination of force under discipline and strict co-ordination. Hence the wild language about wage-slavery and capitalistic tyranny.

In any state of society no great achievements can be produced without great force. Formerly great force was attainable only by slavery aggregating the power of great numbers of men. Roman civilization was built on this. Ours has been built on steam. It is to be built on electricity. Then we are all forced into an organization around these natural forces and adapted to the methods or their application; and although we indulge in rhetoric about political liberty, nevertheless we find ourselves bound tight in a new set of conditions, which control the modes of our existence and determine the directions in which alone economic and social liberty can go.

If it is said that there are some persons in our time who have become rapidly and in a great degree rich, it is true; if it is said that large aggregations of wealth in the control of individuals is a social danger, it is not true.

The movement of the industrial organization which has just been described has brought out a great demand for men capable of managing great enterprises. Such have been called "captains of industry." The analogy with military leaders suggested by this name is not misleading. The great leaders in the development of the industrial organization need those talents of executive and administrative skill, power to command, courage, and fortitude, which were formerly called for in military affairs and scarcely anywhere else. The industrial army is also as dependent on its captains as a military body is on its generals. One of the worst features of the existing system is that the employees have a constant risk in their employer. If he is not competent to manage the business with success, they suffer with him. Capital also is dependent on the skill of the captain of industry for the certainty and magnitude of its profits. Under these circumstances there has been a great demand for men having the requisite ability for this function. As the organization has advanced, with more impersonal bonds of coherence and wider scope of operations, the value of this functionary has rapidly increased. The possession of the requisite ability is a natural monopoly. Consequently, all the conditions have concurred to give to those who possessed this monopoly excessive and constantly advancing rates of remuneration.

Another social function of the first importance in an intense organization is the solution of those crises in the operation of it which are

called the conjuncture of the market. It is through the market that the lines of relation run which preserve the system in harmonious and rhythmical operation. The conjuncture is the momentary sharper mis-adjustment of supply and demand which indicates that a redistribution of productive effort is called for. The industrial organization needs to be insured against these conjunctures, which, if neglected, produce a crisis and a catastrophe; and it needs that they shall be anticipated and guarded against as far as skill and foresight can do it. The rewards of this function for the bankers and capitalists who perform it are very great. The captains of industry and the capitalists who operate on the conjuncture, therefore, if they are successful, win, in these days, great fortunes in a short time. There are no earnings which are more legitimate or for which greater services are rendered to the whole industrial body. The popular notions about this matter really assume that all the wealth accumulated by these classes of persons would be here just the same if they had not existed. They are supposed to have appropriated it out of the common stock. This is so far from being true that, on the contrary, their own wealth would not be but for themselves; and besides that, millions more of wealth, many-fold greater than their own, scattered in the hands of thousands, would not exist but for them.

Within the last two years I have traveled from end to end of the German Empire several times on all kinds of trains. I reached the conviction, looking at the matter from the passenger's standpoint, that, if the Germans could find a Vanderbilt and put their railroads in his hands for twenty-five years, letting him reorganize the system and make twenty-five million dollars out of it for himself in that period, they would make an excellent bargain.

But it is repeated until it has become a commonplace which people are afraid to question, that there is some social danger in the possession of large amounts of wealth by individuals. I ask, Why? I heard a lecture two years ago by a man who holds perhaps the first chair of political economy in the world. He said, among other things, that there was great danger in our day from great accumulations; that this danger ought to be met by taxation, and he referred to the fortune of the Rothschilds and to the great fortunes made in America to prove his point. He omitted, however, to state in what the danger consisted or to specify what harm has ever been done by the Rothschild fortunes or by the great fortunes accumulated in America. It seemed to me that the assertions he was making, and the measures he was recommending, ex-cathedra, were very serious to be thrown out so recklessly. It is hardly to be expected that novelists, popular magazinists, amateur economists, and politicians will be more responsible. It would be easy, however, to show what good is done by accumulations of capital in a few hands—that is, under close and direct management, permitting prompt and accurate application; also to tell what harm is done by loose and unfounded denunciations of any social component or any social group. In the recent debates on the income tax the assumption that great accumulations of wealth are socially harmful and ought to be broken down by taxation was treated as an axiom, and we had direct proof how dangerous it is to fit out the average politician with such unverified and unverifiable dogmas as his warrant for his modes of handling the direful tool of taxation.

Great figures are set out as to the magnitude of certain fortunes and the proportionate amount of the national wealth held by a fraction of the population, and eloquent exclamation-points are set against them. If the figures were beyond criticism, what would they prove? Where is the rich man who is oppressing anybody? If there was one, the newspapers would ring with it. The facts about the accumulation of wealth do not constitute a plutocracy, as I will show below. Wealth, in itself considered, is only power, like steam, or electricity, or knowledge. The question of its good or ill turns on the question how it will be used. To prove any harm in aggregations of wealth it must be shown that great wealth is, as a rule, in the ordinary course of social affairs, put to a mischievous use. This cannot be shown beyond the very slightest degree, if at all.

Therefore, all the allegations of general mischief, social corruption, wrong, and evil in our society must be referred back to those who make them for particulars and specifications. As they are offered to us we cannot allow them to stand, because we discern in them faulty observation of facts, or incorrect interpretation of facts, or a construction of facts according to some philosophy, or misunderstanding of phenomena and their relations, or incorrect inferences, or crooked deductions.

Assuming, however, that the charges against the existing "capitalistic"—that is, industrial—order of things are established, it is proposed to remedy the ill by reconstructing the industrial system on the principles of democracy. Once more we must untangle the snarl of half ideas and muddled facts.

Democracy is, of course, a word to conjure with. We have a democratic-republican political system, and we like it so well that we are prone to take any new step which can be recommended as "democratic" or which will round out some "principle" of democracy to a fuller fulfillment. Everything connected with this domain of political thought is crusted over with false historical traditions, cheap philosophy, and undefined terms, but it is useless to try to criticize it. The whole drift of the world for five hundred years has been toward democracy. That drift, produced by great discoveries and inventions, and by the discovery of a new continent, has raised the middle class out of the servile class. In alliance with the crown they crushed the feudal classes. They made the crown absolute in order to do it. Then they turned against the crown and, with the aid of the handicraftsmen and peasants, conquered it. Now the next conflict which must inevitably come is that between the middle capitalist class and the proletariat, as the word has come to be used. If a certain construction is put on this conflict, it may be called that between democracy and plutocracy, for it seems that industrialism must be developed into plutocracy by the conflict itself. That is the conflict which stands before civilized society to-day. All the signs of the times indicate its commencement, and it is big with fate to mankind and to civilization.

Although we cannot criticise democracy profitably, it may be said of it, with reference to our present subject, that up to this time democracy never has done anything, either in politics, social affairs, or industry, to prove its power to bless mankind. If we confine our attention to the United States, there are three difficulties with regard to its alleged achievements, and they all have the most serious bearing on the proposed democratization of industry.

1. The time during which democracy has been tried in the United States is too short to warrant any inferences. A century or two is a very short time in the life of political institutions, and if the circumstances change rapidly during the period the experiment is vitiated.

2. The greatest question of all about American democracy is whether it is a cause or a consequence. It is popularly assumed to be a cause, and we ascribe to its beneficent action all the political vitality, all the easiness of social relations, all the industrial activity and enterprise which we experience and which we value and enjoy. I submit, however, that, on a more thorough examination of the matter, we shall find that democracy is a consequence. There are economic and sociological causes for our political vitality and vigor, for the ease and elasticity of our social relations, and for our industrial power and success. Those causes have also produced democracy, given it success, and have made its faults and errors innocuous. Indeed, in any true philosophy, it must be held that in the economic forces which control the material prosperity of a

population lie the real causes of its political institutions, its social class-adjustments, its industrial prosperity, its moral code, and its world-philosophy. If democracy and the industrial system are both products of the economic conditions which exist, it is plainly absurd to set democracy to defeat those conditions in the control of industry. If, however, it is not true that democracy is a consequence, and I am well aware that very few people believe it, then we must go back to the view that democracy is a cause. That being so, it is difficult to see how democracy, which has had a clear field here in America, is not responsible for the ills which Mr. Bellamy and his comrades in opinion see in our present social state, and it is difficult to see the grounds of asking us to intrust it also with industry. The first and chief proof of success of political measures and systems is that, under them, society advances in health and vigor and that industry develops without causing social disease. If this has not been the case in America, American democracy has not succeeded. Neither is it easy to see how the masses, if they have undertaken to rule, can escape the responsibilities of ruling, especially so far as the consequences affect themselves. If, then, they have brought all this distress upon themselves under the present system, what becomes of the argument for extending the system to a direct and complete control of industry?

3. It is by no means certain that democracy in the United States has not, up to this time, been living on a capital inherited from aristocracy and industrialism. We have no pure democracy. Our democracy is limited at every turn by institutions which were developed in England in connection with industrialism and aristocracy, and these institutions are of the essence of our system. While our people are passionately democratic in temper and will not tolerate a doctrine that one man is not as good as another, they have common sense enough to know that he is not; and it seems that they love and cling to the conservative institutions quite as strongly as they do to the democratic philosophy. They are, therefore, ruled by men who talk philosophy and govern by the institutions. Now it is open to Mr. Bellamy to say that the reason why democracy in America seems to be open to the charge made in the last paragraph, of responsibility for all the ill which he now finds in our society, is because it has been infected with industrialism (capitalism); but in that case he must widen the scope of his proposition and undertake to purify democracy before turning industry over to it. The socialists generally seem to think that they make their undertakings easier when they widen their scope, and make them easiest when they propose to

remake everything; but in truth social tasks increase in difficulty in an enormous ratio as they are widened in scope.

The question, therefore, arises, if it is proposed to reorganize the social system on the principles of American democracy, whether the institutions of industrialism are to be retained. If so, all the virus of capitalism will be retained. It is forgotten, in many schemes of social reformation in which it is proposed to mix what we like with what we do not like, in order to extirpate the latter, that each must undergo a reaction from the other, and that what we like may be extirpated by what we do not like. We may find that instead of democratizing capitalism we have capitalized democracy—that is, have brought in plutocracy. Plutocracy is a political system in which the ruling force is wealth. The denunciation of capital which we hear from all the reformers is the most eloquent proof that the greatest power in the world to-day is capital. They know that it is, and confess it most when they deny it most strenuously. At present the power of capital is social and industrial, and only in a small degree political. So far as capital is political, it is on account of political abuses, such as tariffs and special legislation on the one hand and legislative strikes on the other. These conditions exist in the democracy to which it is proposed to transfer the industries. What does that mean except bringing all the power of capital once for all into the political arena and precipitating the conflict of democracy and plutocracy at once? Can anyone imagine that the masterfulness, the overbearing disposition, the greed of gain, and the ruthlessness in methods, which are the faults of the master of industry at his worst, would cease when he was a functionary of the State, which had relieved him of risk and endowed him with authority? Can anyone imagine that politicians would no longer be corruptly fond of money, intriguing, and crafty when they were charged, not only with patronage and government contracts, but also with factories, stores, ships, and railroads? Could we expect anything except that, when the politician and the master of industry were joined in one, we should have the vices of both unchecked by the restraints of either? In any socialistic state there will be one set of positions which will offer chances of wealth beyond the wildest dreams of avarice; viz., on the governing committees. Then there will be rich men whose wealth will indeed be a menace to social interests, and instead of industrial peace there will be such war as no one has dreamed of yet: the war between the political ins and outs—that is, between those who are on the committee and those who want to get on it.

We must not drop the subject of democracy without one word more. The Greeks already had occasion to notice a most serious distinction between two principles of democracy which lie at its roots. Plutarch says that Solon got the archonship in part by promising equality, which some understood of esteem and dignity, others of measure and number. There is one democratic principle which means that each man should be esteemed for his merit and worth, for just what he is, without regard to birth, wealth, rank, or other adventitious circumstances. The other principle is that each one of us ought to be equal to all the others in what he gets and enjoys. The first principle is only partially realizable, but, so far as it goes, it is elevating and socially progressive and profitable. The second is not capable of an intelligible statement. The first is a principle of industrialism. It proceeds from and is intelligible only in a society built on the industrial virtues, free endeavor, security of property, and repression of the baser vices; that is, in a society whose industrial system is built on labor and exchange. The other is only a rule of division for robbers who have to divide plunder or monks who have to divide gifts. If, therefore, we want to democratize industry in the sense of the first principle, we need only perfect what we have now, especially on its political side. If we try to democratize it in the sense of the other principle, we corrupt politics at one stroke; we enter upon an industrial enterprise which will waste capital and bring us all to poverty, and we set loose greed and envy as ruling social passions.

If this poor old world is as bad as they say, one more reflection may check the zeal of the headlong reformer. It is at any rate a tough old world. It has taken its trend and curvature and all its twists and tangles from a long course of formation. All its wry and crooked gnarls and knobs are therefore stiff and stubborn. If we puny men by our arts can do anything at all to straighten them, it will only be by modifying the tendencies of some of the forces at work, so that, after a sufficient time, their action may be changed a little and slowly the lines of movement may be modified. This effort, however, can at most be only slight, and it will take a long time. In the meantime spontaneous forces will be at work, compared with which our efforts are like those of a man trying to deflect a river, and these forces will have changed the whole problem before our interferences have time to make themselves felt. The great stream of time and earthly things will sweep on just the same in spite of us. It bears with it now all the errors and follies of the past, the wreckage of all the philosophies, the fragments of all the civilizations, the wisdom of all the abandoned ethical systems, the debris of all the institutions, and the penalties of all the mistakes. It is only in imagination that we stand by and look at and criticize it and plan to change it. Everyone of us is a child of his age and cannot get out of it. He is in the stream and is swept along with it. All his sciences and philosophy come to him out of it. Therefore the tide will not be changed by us. It will swallow up both us and our experiments. It will absorb the efforts at change and take them into itself as new but trivial components, and the great movement of tradition and work will go on unchanged by our fads and schemes. The things which will change it are the great discoveries and inventions, the new reactions inside the social organism, and the changes in the earth itself on account of changes in the cosmical forces. These causes will make of it just what, in fidelity to them, it ought to be. The men will be carried along with it and be made by it. The utmost they can do by their cleverness will be to note and record their course as they are carried along, which is what we do now, and is that which leads us to the vain fancy that we can make or guide the movement. That is why it is the greatest folly of which a man can be capable, to sit down with a slate and pencil to plan out a new social world.

# V

## Anti-Imperialist

# The Fallacy of Territorial Extension

By mid-1896, the United States was involved with overseas expansion in the Pacific and the Caribbean. In Hawaii, American sugar planters had been at odds with the ruling native government since the ascension to the throne of Queen Liliuokalani in 1891. In 1893, the United States Minister to Hawaii called in the marines to protect American property and, without U.S. State Department permission, proclaimed the islands a U.S. protectorate. Although an independent Republic of Hawaii was recognized in 1894 after a protracted battle over annexation in the U.S. Senate, calls for annexation continued.

To the south, native insurrection against Spanish rule in Cuba in early 1895 revived American interest in the island. In early 1896, the U.S. Congress, by concurrent resolution, recognized the Cuban revolutionaries and offered its assistance to Spain in creating an independent Cuba. Published originally in the *Forum* 21 (June 1896), 414–419; reprinted in *War*, ed. Albert Galloway Keller, pp. 285–296.

The traditional belief is that a state aggrandizes itself by territorial extension, so that winning new land is gaining in wealth and prosperity, just as an individual would gain if he increased his land possessions. It is undoubtedly true that a state may be so small in territory and population that it cannot serve the true purposes of a state for its citizens, especially in international relations with neighboring states which control a large aggregate of men and capital. There is, therefore, under given circumstances, a size of territory and population which is at the maximum of advantage for the civil unit. The unification of Germany and Italy was apparently advantageous for the people affected. In the nineteenth century there has been a tendency to create national states, and nationality has been advocated as the true basis of state unity. The cases show, however, that the national unit does not necessarily coincide with the most advantageous state unit, and that the principle of nationality cannot override the historical accidents which have made the states. Sweden and Norway, possessing unity, threaten to separate. Austro-Hungary, a conglomerate of nationalities largely hostile to each other, will probably he held together by political necessity. The question of expedient size will always be one for the judgment and good sense of statesmen. The opinion may be risked that Russia has carried out a policy of territorial extension which has been harmful to its internal integration. For three hundred years it has been reaching out after more territory and has sought the grandeur and glory of conquest and size. To this it has sacrificed the elements of social and industrial strength. The autocracy has been confirmed and established because it is the only institution which symbolizes and maintains the unity of the great mass, and the military and tax burdens have distorted the growth of the society to such an extent as to produce disease and weakness.

Territorial aggrandizement enhances the glory and personal importance of the man who is the head of a dynastic state. The fallacy of confusing this with the greatness and strength of the state itself is an open pitfall close at hand. It might seem that a republic, one of whose chief claims to superiority over a monarchy lies in avoiding the danger of confusing the king with the state, ought to be free from this fallacy of national greatness, but we have plenty of examples to prove that the traditional notions are not cut off by changing names and forms.

The notion that gain of territory is gain of wealth and strength for the state, after the expedient size has been won, is a delusion. In the Middle Ages the beneficial interest in land and the jurisdiction over the people who lived on it were united in one person. The modern great states, upon their formation, took to themselves the jurisdiction, and the beneficial interest turned into full property in land. The confusion of the two often reappears now, and it is one of the most fruitful causes of fallacy in public questions. It is often said that the United States owns silver-mines, and it is inferred that the policy of the state in regard to money and currency ought to be controlled in some way by this fact. The "United States," as a subject of property rights and of monetary claims and obligations, may be best defined by calling it the "Fiscus." This legal person owns no silver-mines. If it did, it could operate them by farming them or by royalties. The revenue thus received would lower taxes. The gain would inure to all the people in the United States. The body politic named the United States has nothing to do with the silver-mines except that it exercises jurisdiction over the territory in which they lie. If it levies taxes on them it also incurs expenses for them, and as it wins no profits on its total income and outgo, these must be taken to be equal. It renders services for which it exacts only the cost thereof. The beneficial and property interest in the mines belongs to individuals, and they win profits only by conducting the exploitation of the mines with an expenditure of labor and capital. These individuals are of many nationalities. They alone own the product and have the use and enjoyment of it. No other individuals, American or others, have any interest, right, duty, or responsibility in the matter. The United States has simply provided the protection of its laws and institutions for the mine-workers while they were carrying on their enterprise. Its jurisdiction was only a burden to it, not a profitable good. Its jurisdiction was a boon to the mine-workers and certainly did not entail further obligation.

It is said that the boundary between Alaska and British America runs through a gold field, and some people are in great anxiety as to who will "grab it." If an American can go over to the English side and mine gold there for his profit, under English laws and jurisdiction, and an Englishman can come over to the American side and mine gold there for his profit, under American laws and jurisdiction, what difference does it make where the line falls? The only case in which it would make any difference is where the laws and institutions of the two states were not on equal stages of enlightenment.

This case serves to bring out distinctly a reason for the old notion of territorial extension which is no longer valid. In the old colonial system, states conquered territories or founded colonies in order to shut them against all other states and to exploit them on principles of subjugation and monopoly. It is only under this system that the jurisdiction is anything but a burden.

If the United States should admit Hawaii to the Union, the Fiscus of the former state would collect more taxes and incur more expenses. The circumstances are such that the latter would probably be the greater. The United States would not acquire a square foot of land in property unless it paid for it. Individual Americans would get no land to till without paying for it and would win no products from it except by wisely expending their labor and capital on it. All that they can do now. So long as there is a government on the islands, native or other, which is competent to guarantee peace, order, and security, no more is necessary, and for any outside power to seize the jurisdiction is an unjustifiable aggression. That jurisdiction would be the best founded which was the most liberal and enlightened, and would give the best security to all persons who sought the islands upon their lawful occasions. The jurisdiction would, in any case, be a burden, and any state might be glad to see any other state assume the burden, provided that it was one which could be relied upon to execute the charge on enlightened principles for the good of all. The best case is, therefore, always that in which the resident population produce their own state by the institutions of self-government.

What private individuals want is free access, under order and security, to any part of the earth's surface, in order that they may avail themselves of its natural resources for their use, either by investment or commerce.

If, therefore, we could have free trade with Hawaii while somebody else had the jurisdiction, we should gain all the advantages and escape all the burdens. The Constitution of the United States establishes absolute free trade between all parts of the territory under its jurisdiction. A large part of our population was thrown into indignant passion because the Administration rejected the annexation of Hawaii, regarding it like the act of a man who refuses the gift of a farm. These persons were generally those who are thrown into excitement by any proposition of free trade. They will not, therefore, accept free trade with the islands while somebody else has the trouble and burden of the jurisdiction, but they would accept free trade with the islands eagerly if they could get the burden of the jurisdiction too.

Canada has to deal with a race war and a religious war, each of great virulence, which render governmental jurisdiction in the Dominion difficult and hazardous. If we could go to Canada and trade there our products for those of that country, we could win all for our private interests which that country is able to contribute to the welfare of mankind, and we should have nothing to do with the civil and political difficulties which harass the government. We refuse to have free trade with Canada. Our newspaper and congressional economists prove to their own satisfaction that it would be a great harm to us to have free trade with her now, while she is outside the jurisdiction under which we live, but, within a few months, we have seen an eager impulse of public opinion toward a war of conquest against Canada. If, then, we could force her to come under the same jurisdiction, by a cruel and unprovoked war, thus bringing on ourselves the responsibility for all her civil discords and problems, it appears to be believed that free trade with her would be a good thing.

The case of Cuba is somewhat different. If we could go to the island and trade with the same freedom with which we can go to Louisiana, we could make all the gains, by investment and commerce, which the island offers to industry and enterprise, provided that either Spain or a local government would give the necessary security, and we should have no share in political struggles there. It may be that the proviso is not satisfied, or soon will not be. Here is a case, then, which illustrates the fact that states are often forced to extend their jurisdiction whether they want to do so or not. Civilized states are forced to supersede the local jurisdiction of uncivilized or half-civilized states, in order to police the territory and establish the necessary guarantees of industry and commerce. It is idle to set up absolute doctrines of national ownership in the soil which would justify a group of population in spoiling a part of the earth's surface for themselves and everybody else. The island of Cuba may fall into anarchy. If it does, the civilized world may look to the United States to take the jurisdiction and establish order and security there. We might be compelled to do it. It would, however, be a great burden, and possibly a fatal calamity to us. Probably any proposition that England should take it would call out a burst of jingo passion against which all reasoning would be powerless. We ought to pray that England would take it. She would govern it well, and everybody would have free access to it for the purposes of private interest, while our Government would be free from all complications with the politics of the island. If we take the jurisdiction of the island, we shall find ourselves in a political dilemma, each horn of which is as disastrous as the other: either we must govern it as a subject province, or we must admit it into the Union as a state or group of states. Our system is unfit for the government of subject provinces. They have no place in it. They would become seats of corruption, which would react on our own body politic. If we admitted the island as a state or group of states, we should have to let it help govern us. The prospect of adding to the present senate a number of Cuban senators, either native or carpet-bag, is one whose terrors it is not necessary to unfold. Nevertheless it appears that there is a large party which would not listen to free trade with the island while any other nation has the jurisdiction of it, but who are ready to grab it at any cost and to take free trade with it, provided that they can get the political burdens too.

This confederated state of ours was never planned for indefinite expansion or for an imperial policy. We boast of it a great deal, but we must know that its advantages are won at the cost of limitations, as is the case with most things in this world. The fathers of the Republic planned a confederation of free and peaceful industrial commonwealths, shielded by their geographical position from the jealousies, rivalries, and traditional policies of the Old World and bringing all the resources of civilization to bear for the domestic happiness of the population only. They meant to have no grand statecraft or "high politics," no "balance of power" or "reasons of state," which had cost the human race so much. They meant to offer no field for what Benjamin Franklin called the "pest of glory." It is the limitation of this scheme of the state that the state created under it must forego a great number of the grand functions of European states; especially that it contains no methods and apparatus of conquest, extension, domination, and imperialism. The plan of the fathers would have no controlling authority for us if it had been proved by experience that that plan was narrow, inadequate, and mistaken. Are we prepared to vote that it has proved so? For our territorial extension has reached limits which are complete for all purposes and leave no necessity for "rectification of boundaries." Any extension will open questions, not close them. Any extension will not make us more secure where we are, but will force us to take new measures to secure our new acquisitions. The preservation of acquisitions will force us to reorganize our internal resources, so as to make it possible to prepare them in advance and to mobilize them with promptitude. This will lessen liberty and require discipline. It will increase taxation and all the pressure of government. It will divert the national energy from the provision of self-maintenance and comfort for the people, and will necessitate stronger and more elaborate governmental machinery. All this will be disastrous to republican institutions and to democracy. Moreover, all extension puts a new strain on the internal cohesion of the pre-existing mass, threatening a new cleavage within. If we had never taken Texas and Northern Mexico we should never have had secession.

The sum of the matter is that colonization and territorial extension are burdens, not gains. Great civilized states cannot avoid these burdens. They are the penalty of greatness because they are the duties of it. No state can successfully undertake to extend its jurisdiction unless its internal vitality is high, so that it has surplus energy to dispose of. Russia, as already mentioned, is a state which has taken upon itself tasks of this kind beyond its strength, and for which it is in no way competent. Italy offers at this moment the strongest instance of a state which is imperiling its domestic welfare for a colonial policy which is beyond its strength, is undertaken arbitrarily, and has no proper motive. Germany has taken up a colonial policy with great eagerness, apparently from a notion that it is one of the attributes of a great state. To maintain it she must add a great navy to her great military establishment and increase the burdens of a population which is poor and heavily taxed and which has not in its territory any great natural resources from which to draw the strength to bear its burdens. Spain is exhausting her last strength to keep Cuba, which can never repay the cost unless it is treated on the old colonial plan as a subject province to be exploited for the benefit of the mother-country. If that is done, however, the only consequence will be another rebellion and greater expenditure. England, as a penalty of her greatness, finds herself in all parts of the world face to face with the necessity of maintaining her jurisdiction and of extending it in order to maintain it. When she does so she finds herself only extending law and order for the benefit of everybody. It is only in circumstances like hers that the burdens have any compensation.

# The Conquest of the United States by Spain

Sumner presented this address on January 16, 1899, before a packed house in the old College Street Hall, New Haven. With the sinking of the *Maine*, the battle of Manila Bay, and Theodore Roosevelt's charge up San Juan Hill already in the past, Sumner represented a small but vociferous band of anti-imperialists who continued to oppose the Spanish-American War and its foreseeable consequences. Standing ramrod straight, his head thrust slightly forward, he delivered his remarks, well aware that most in the audience supported the side he was opposing. For his efforts, he received finally a vigorous ovation. Originally published in *Yale Law Journal*, 1898; reprinted in *War*, ed. Albert Galloway Keller, pp. 297–334.

During the last year the public has been familiarized with descriptions of Spain and of Spanish methods of doing things until the name of Spain has become a symbol for a certain well-defined set of notions and policies. On the other hand, the name of the United States has always been, for all of us, a symbol for a state of things, a set of ideas and traditions, a group of views about social and political affairs. Spain was the first, for a long time the greatest, of the modern imperialistic states. The United States, by its historical origin, its traditions, and its principles, is the chief representative of the revolt and reaction against that kind of a state. I intend to show that, by the line of action now proposed to us, which we call expansion and imperialism, we are throwing away some of the most important elements of the American symbol and are adopting some of the most important elements of the Spanish symbol. We have beaten Spain in a military conflict, but we are submitting to be conquered by her on the field of ideas and policies. Expansionism and imperialism are nothing but the old philosophies of national prosperity which have brought Spain to where she now is. Those philosophies appeal to national vanity and national cupidity. They are seductive, especially upon the first view and the most superficial judgment, and therefore it cannot be denied that they are very strong for popular effect. They are delusions, and they will lead us to ruin unless we are hard-headed enough to resist them. In any case the year 1898 is a great landmark in the history of the United States. The consequences will not be all good or all bad, for such is not the nature of societal influences. They are always mixed of good and ill, and so it will be in this case. Fifty years from now the historian, looking back to 1898, will no doubt see, in the course which things will have taken, consequences of the proceedings of that year and of this present one which will not all be bad, but you will observe that that is not a justification for a happy-go-lucky policy; that does not affect our duty to-day in all that we do to seek wisdom and prudence and to determine our actions by the best judgment which we can form.

War, expansion, and imperialism are questions of statesmanship and of nothing else. I disregard all other aspects of them and all extraneous elements which have been intermingled with them. I received the other day a circular of a new educational enterprise in which it was urged that, on account of our new possessions, we ought now to devote especial study to history, political economy, and what is called political science. I asked myself, Why? What more reason is there for pursuing these studies now on behalf of our dependencies than there was before to pursue them on behalf of ourselves? In our proceedings of 1898 we made no use of whatever knowledge we had of any of these lines of study. The original and prime cause of the war was that it was a move of partisan tactics in the strife of parties at Washington. As soon as it seemed resolved upon, a number of interests began to see their advantage in it and hastened to further it. It was necessary to make appeals to the public which would bring quite other motives to the support of the enterprise and win the consent of classes who would never consent to either financial or political jobbery. Such appeals were found in sensational assertions which we had no means to verify, in phrases of alleged patriotism, in statements about Cuba and the Cubans which we now know to have been entirely untrue.

Where was the statesmanship of all this? If it is not an established rule of statecraft that a statesman should never impose any sacrifices on his people for anything but their own interests, then it is useless to study political philosophy any more, for this is the alphabet of it. It is contrary to honest statesmanship to imperil the political welfare of the state for party interests. It was unstatesmanlike to publish a solemn declaration that we would not seize any territory, and especially to characterize such action in advance as "criminal aggression," for it was morally certain that we should come out of any war with Spain with conquered territory on our hands, and the people who wanted the war, or who consented to it, hoped that we should do so.

We talk about "liberty" all the time in a big and easy way, as if liberty was a thing that men could have if they want it, and to any extent to which they want it. It is certain that a very large part of human liberty consists simply in the choice either to do a thing or to let it alone. If we decide to do it, a whole series of consequences is entailed upon us in regard to which it is exceedingly difficult, or impossible, for us to exercise any liberty at all. The proof of this from the case before us is so clear and easy that I need spend no words upon it. Here, then, you have the reason why it is a rule of sound statesmanship not to embark on an adventurous policy. A statesman could not be expected to know in advance that we should come out of the war with the Philippines on our hands, but it belongs to his education to warn him that a policy of adventure and of gratuitous enterprise would be sure to entail embarrassments of some kind. What comes to us in the evolution of our own life and interests, that we must meet; what we go to seek which lies beyond that domain is a waste of our energy and a compromise of our liberty and welfare. If this is not sound doctrine, then the historical and social sciences have nothing to teach us which is worth any trouble.

There is another observation, however, about the war which is of far greater importance: that is, that it was a gross violation of self-government. We boast that we are a self-governing people, and in this respect, particularly, we compare ourselves with pride with older nations. What is the difference after all? The Russians, whom we always think of as standing at the opposite pole of political institutions, have self-government, if you mean by it acquiescence in what a little group of people at the head of the government agree to do. The war with Spain was precipitated upon us headlong, without reflection or deliberation, and without any due formulation of public opinion. Whenever a voice was raised in behalf of deliberation and the recognized maxims of statesmanship, it was howled down in a storm of vituperation and cant. Everything was done to make us throw away sobriety of thought and calmness of judgment and to inflate all expressions with sensational epithets and turgid phrases. It cannot be denied that everything in regard to the war has been treated in an exalted strain of sentiment and rhetoric very unfavorable to the truth. At present the whole periodical press of the country seems to be occupied in tickling the national vanity to the utmost by representations about the war which are extravagant and fantastic. There will be a penalty to be paid for all this. Nervous and sensational newspapers are just as corrupting, especially to young people, as nervous and sensational novels. The habit of expecting that all mental pabulum shall be highly spiced, and the corresponding loathing for whatever is soberly truthful, undermines character as much as any other vice. Patriotism is being prostituted into a nervous intoxication which is fatal to an apprehension of truth. It builds around us a fool's paradise, and it will lead us into errors about our position and relations just like those which we have been ridiculing in the case of Spain.

There are some now who think that it is the perfection of statesmanship to say that expansion is a fact and that it is useless to discuss it. We are told that we must not cross any bridges until we come to them; that is, that we must discuss nothing in advance, and that we must not discuss anything which is past because it is irretrievable. No doubt this would be a very acceptable doctrine to the powers that be, for it would mean that they were relieved from responsibility, but it would be a marvelous doctrine to be accepted by a self-governing people. Senator Foraker has told us that we are not to keep the Philippines longer than is necessary to teach the people self-government. How one man can tell what we are to do before the constitutional authorities have decided it, I do not know. Perhaps it is a detail in our new method of self-government. If his assurances are to be trusted, we are paying $20,000,000 for the privilege of tutoring the Tagals up to liberty and self-government. I do not believe that, if the United States undertakes to govern the islands, it will ever give them up except to superior force, but the weakening of imperialism shown by this gentleman's assurances, after a few days of mild debate in the senate, shows that agitation of the subject is not yet in vain. Then again, if we have done anything, especially if we have acted precipitately, it is a well-recognized course of prudent behavior to find out where we are, what we have done, and what the new situation is into which we have come. Then, too, we must remember that when the statesman lays a thing down the historian takes it up, and he will group it with historical parallels and contrasts. There is a set of men who have always been referred to, in our Northern states, for the last thirty years, with especial disapproval. They are those Southerners who, in 1861, did not believe in secession, but, as they said, "went with their states." They have been condemned for moral cowardice. Yet within a year it has become almost a doctrine with us that patriotism requires that we should hold our tongues while our interests, our institutions, our most sacred traditions, and our best established maxims have been trampled underfoot. There is no doubt that moral courage is the virtue which is more needed than any other in the modern democratic state, and that truckling to popularity is the worst political vice. The press, the platform, and the pulpit have all fallen under this vice, and there is evidence that the university also, which ought to be the last citadel of truth, is succumbing to it likewise. I have no doubt that the conservative classes of this country will yet look back with great regret to their acquiescence in the events of 1898 and the doctrines and precedents which have been silently established. Let us be well assured that self-government is not a matter of flags and Fourth of July orations, nor yet of strife to get offices. Eternal vigilance is the price of that as of every other political good. The perpetuity of self-government depends on the sound political sense of the people, and sound political sense is a matter of habit and practice. We can give it up and we can take instead pomp and glory. That is what Spain did. She had as much self-government as any country in Europe at the beginning of the sixteenth century. The union of the smaller states into one big one gave an impulse to her national feeling and national development. The discovery of America put into her hands the control of immense territories. National pride and ambition were stimulated. Then came the struggle with France for world-dominion, which resulted in absolute monarchy and bankruptcy for Spain. She lost self-government and saw her resources spent on interests which were foreign to her, but she could talk about an empire on which the sun never set and boast of her colonies, her gold-mines, her fleets and armies and debts. She had glory and pride, mixed, of course, with defeat and disaster, such as must be experienced by any nation on that course of policy; and she grew weaker in her industry and commerce and poorer in the status of the population all the time. She has never been able to recover real self-government yet. If we Americans believe in self-government, why do we let it slip away from us? Why do we barter it away for military glory as Spain did?

There is not a civilized nation which does not talk about its civilizing mission just as grandly as we do. The English, who really have more to boast of in this respect than anybody else, talk least about it, but the Phariseeism with which they correct and instruct other people has made them hated all over the globe. The French believe themselves the guardians of the highest and purest culture, and that the eyes of all mankind are fixed on Paris, whence they expect oracles of thought and taste. The Germans regard themselves as charged with a mission, especially to us Americans, to save us from egoism and materialism. The Russians, in their books and newspapers, talk about the civilizing mission of Russia in language that might be translated from some of the finest paragraphs in our imperialistic newspapers. The first principle of Mohammedanism is that we Christians are dogs and infidels, fit only to be enslaved or butchered by Moslems. It is a corollary that wherever Mohammedanism extends it carries, in the belief of its votaries, the highest blessings, and that the whole human race would be enormously elevated if Mohammedanism should supplant Christianity everywhere. To come, last, to Spain, the Spaniards have, for centuries, considered themselves the most zealous and self-sacrificing Christians, especially charged by the Almighty, on this account, to spread true religion and civilization over the globe. They think themselves free and noble, leaders in refinement and the sentiments of personal honor, and they despise us as sordid money-grabbers and heretics. I could bring you passages from peninsular authors of the first rank about the grand role of Spain and Portugal in spreading freedom and truth. Now each nation laughs at all the others when it observes these manifestations of national vanity. You may rely upon it that they are all ridiculous by virtue of these pretensions, including ourselves. The point is that each of them repudiates the standards of the others, and the outlying nations, which are to be civilized, hate all the standards of civilized men. We assume that what we like and practice, and what we think better, must come as a welcome blessing to Spanish-Americans and Filipinos. This is grossly and obviously untrue. They hate our ways. They are hostile to our ideas. Our religion, language, institutions, and manners offend them. They like their own ways, and if we appear amongst them as rulers, there will be social discord in all the great departments of social interest. The most important thing which we shall inherit from the Spaniards will be the task of suppressing rebellions. If the United States takes out of the hands of Spain her mission, on the ground that Spain is not executing it well, and if this nation in its turn attempts to be school-mistress to others, it will shrivel up into the same vanity and self-conceit of which Spain now presents an example. To read our current literature one would think that we were already well on the way to it. Now, the great reason why all these enterprises which begin by saying to somebody else, We know what is good for you better than you know yourself and we are going to make you do it, are false and wrong is that they violate liberty; or, to turn the same statement into other words, the reason why liberty, of which we Americans talk so much, is a good thing is that it means leaving people to live out their own lives in their own way, while we do the same. If we believe in liberty, as an American principle, why do we not stand by it? Why are we going to throw it away to enter upon a Spanish policy of dominion and regulation?

The United States cannot be a colonizing nation for a long time yet. We have only twenty-three persons to the square mile in the United

States without Alaska. The country can multiply its population by thirteen; that is, the population could rise above a billion before the whole country would be as densely populated as Rhode Island is now. There is, therefore, no pressure of population, which is the first condition of rational expansion, unless we could buy another territory like the Mississippi Valley with no civilized population in it. If we could do that it would postpone the day of over-population still further, and make easier conditions for our people in the next generations. In the second place, the islands which we have taken from Spain never can be the residence of American families, removing and settling to make their homes there. The climatic conditions forbid it. Although Spaniards have established themselves in Spanish America, even in the tropics, the evils of Spanish rule have largely arisen from the fact that Spaniards have gone to the colonies as adventurers, eager to make fortunes as quickly as possible, that they might return to Spain to enjoy them. That the relation of our people to these possessions will have that character is already apparent. It is, therefore, inaccurate to speak of a colonial system in describing our relation to these dependencies, but as we have no other term, let us use this one and inquire *what kind of a colonial system we are to establish.*

# I

Spain stands, in modern history, as the first state to develop and apply a colonial system to her outlying possessions. Her policy was to exclude absolutely all non-Spaniards from her subject territories and to exploit them for the benefit of Spain, without much regard for the aborigines or the colonists. The cold and unnecessary cruelty of the Spaniards to the aborigines is appalling, even when compared with the treatment of the aborigines by other Europeans. A modern economist stands aghast at the economic measures adopted by Spain, as well in regard to her domestic policy as to her colonies. It seems as if those measures could only have been inspired by some demon of folly, they were so destructive to her prosperity. She possesses a large literature from the last three centuries, in which her publicists discuss with amazement the question whether it was a blessing or a curse to get the Indies, and why, with all the supposed conditions of prosperity in her hands, she was declining all the time. We now hear it argued that she is well rid of her colonies, and that, if she will devote her energies to her internal development and rid her politics of the corruption of colonial officials and interests, she may be regenerated. That is a rational opinion. It is the best diagnosis of her condition and the best prescription of a remedy which the occasion has called forth. But what, then, will happen to the state which has taken over her colonies? I can see no answer except that that nation, with them, has taken over the disease and that *it* now is to be corrupted by exploiting dependent communities just as she has been. That it stands exposed to this danger is undeniable.

It would not be becoming to try, in a paragraph, to set forth the causes of the decadence of Spain, and although the economic history of that country has commanded such attention from me as I could give to it consistently with other obligations, yet I could not feel prepared to do any justice to that subject; but one or two features of the history can be defined with confidence, and they are such as are especially instructive for us.

In the first place Spain never intended, of set purpose, to ruin the material prosperity of herself or her colonies. Her economic history is one long lesson to prove that any prosperity policy is a delusion and a path to ruin. There is no economic lesson which the people of the United States need to take to heart more than that. In the second place the Spanish mistakes arose, in part, from confusing the public treasury with the national wealth. They thought that, when gold flowed into the public treasury, that was the same as an increase of wealth of the people. It really meant that the people were bearing the burdens of the imperial system and that the profits of it went into the public treasury; that is, into the hands of the king. It was no wonder, then, that as the burdens grew greater the people grew poorer. The king spent the revenues in extending the imperial system in Germany, Italy, and the Netherlands, so that the revenues really became a new cause of corruption and decay. The only people who were well off, in the midst of the increasing distress, were the ecclesiastics and nobles, who were protected by entails and charters, which, in their turn, were a new cause of restriction and destruction to the industries of the country. As to the treatment of the aborigines in the outlying possessions of Spain, the orders from the home government were as good as could possibly be desired. No other European government issued any which were nearly so enlightened or testified to such care about that matter. Spanish America is still covered with institutions founded by Spain for the benefit of the aborigines, so far as they have not been confiscated or diverted to other uses. Nevertheless the Spanish rule nearly exterminated the aborigines in one hundred and fifty years. The Pope gave them into servitude to the Spaniards. The Spaniards regarded them as savages, heretics, beasts, not entitled to human consideration. Here you have the great explanation of man's inhumanity to man. When Spaniards tortured and burned Protestants and Jews it was because, in their minds, Protestants and Jews were heretics; that is to say, were beyond the pale, were abominable, were not entitled to human consideration. Humane men and pious women felt no more compunctions at the sufferings of Protestants and Jews than we would at the execution of mad dogs or rattlesnakes. There are plenty of people in the United States to-day who regard negroes as human beings, perhaps, but of a different order from white men, so that the ideas and social arrangements of white men cannot be applied to them with propriety. Others feel the same way about Indians. This attitude of mind, wherever you meet with it, is what causes tyranny and cruelty. It is this disposition to decide off-hand that some people are not fit for liberty and self-government which gives relative truth to the doctrine that all men are equal, and inasmuch as the history of mankind has been one long story of the abuse of some by others, who, of course, smoothed over their tyranny by some beautiful doctrines of religion, or ethics, or political philosophy, which proved that it was all for the best good of the oppressed, therefore the doctrine that all men are equal has come to stand as one of the corner-stones of the temple of justice and truth. It was set up as a bar to just this notion that we are so much better than others that it is liberty for them to be governed by us.

The Americans have been committed from the outset to the doctrine that all men are equal. We have elevated it into an absolute doctrine as a part of the theory of our social and political fabric. It has always been a domestic dogma in spite of its absolute form, and as a domestic dogma it has always stood in glaring contradiction to the facts about Indians and negroes and to our legislation about Chinamen. In its absolute form it must, of course, apply to Kanakas, Malays, Tagals, and Chinese just as much as to Yankees, Germans, and Irish. It is an astonishing event that we have lived to see American arms carry this domestic dogma out where it must be tested in its application to uncivilized and half-civilized peoples. At the first touch of the test we throw the doctrine away and adopt the Spanish doctrine. We are told by all the imperialists that these people are not fit for liberty and self-government; that it is rebellion for them to resist our beneficence; that we must send fleets and armies to kill them if they do it; that we must devise a government for them and administer it ourselves; that we may buy them or sell them as we please, and dispose of their "trade" for our own advantage. What is that but the policy of Spain to her dependencies? What can we expect as a consequence of it? Nothing but that it will bring us where Spain is now.

But then, if it is not right for us to hold these islands as dependencies, you may ask me whether I think that we ought to take them into our Union, at least some of them, and let them help to govern us. Certainly not. If *that* question is raised, then the question whether they are, in our judgment, fit for self-government or not is in order. The American people, since the Civil War, have to a great extent lost sight of the fact that this state of ours, the United States of America, is a confederated state of a very peculiar and artificial form. It is not a state like the states of Europe, with the exception of Switzerland. The field for dogmatism in our day is not theology, it is political philosophy. "Sovereignty" is the most abstract and metaphysical term in political philosophy. Nobody can define it. For this reason it exactly suits the purposes of the curbstone statesman. He puts into it whatever he wants to get out of it again, and he has set to work lately to spin out a proof that the United States is a great imperialistic state, although the Constitution, which tells us just what it is and what it is not, is there to prove the contrary.

The thirteen colonies, as we all know, were independent commonwealths with respect to each other. They had little sympathy and a great deal of jealousy. They came into a union with each other upon terms which were stipulated and defined in the Constitution, but they united only unwillingly and under the pressure of necessity. What was at first only a loose combination or alliance has been welded together into a great state by the history of a century. Nothing, however, has altered that which was the first condition of the Union; viz., that all the states members of it should be on the sample plane of civilization and political development; that they should all hold the same ideas, traditions, and political creed; that their social standards and ideals should be such as to maintain cordial sympathy between them. The Civil War arose out of the fact that this condition was imperfectly fulfilled. At other times actual differences in standpoint and principle, or in ideals and opinion, have produced discord within the confederation. Such crises are inevitable in any confederated state. It is the highest statesmanship in such a system to avoid them, or smooth them over, and above all, never to take in voluntarily any heterogeneous elements. The prosperity of such a state depends on closer and closer sympathy between the parts in order that differences which arise may be easily harmonized. What we need is more intension, not more extension.

It follows, then, that it is unwisdom to take into a State like this any foreign element which is not congenial to it. Any such element will act as a solvent upon it. Consequently we are brought by our new conquests face to face with this dilemma: we must either hold them as inferior possessions, to be ruled and exploited by us after the fashion of the old colonial system, or we must take them in on an equality with ourselves, where they will help to govern us and to corrupt a political system which they do not understand and in which they cannot participate. From that dilemma there is no escape except to give them independence and to let them work out their own salvation or go without it. Hayti has been independent for a century and has been a theater of revolution, tyranny, and bloodshed all the time. There is not a Spanish-American state which has proved its capacity for self-government as yet. It is a fair question whether any one of them would have been worse off than it is to-day if Spanish rule had been maintained in it. The chief exception is Mexico. Mr. Lummis, an American, has recently published a book on Mexico, in which he tells us that we would do well to go to school to Mexico for a number of important public interests, but Mexico has been, for ten or fifteen years, under a dictator, and the republican forms have been in abeyance. What will happen there when the dictator dies nobody knows. The doctrine that we are to take away from other nations any possessions of theirs which we think that we could manage better than they are managing them, or that we are to take in hand any countries which we do not think capable of self-government, is one which will lead us very far. With that doctrine in the background, our politicians will have no trouble to find a war ready for us the next time that they come around to the point where they think that it is time for us to have another. We are told that we must have a big army hereafter. What for; unless we propose to do again by and by what we have just done? In that case our neighbors have reason to ask themselves whom we will attack next. They must begin to arm, too, and by our act the whole western world is plunged into the distress under which the eastern world is groaning. Here is another point in regard to which the conservative elements in the country are making a great mistake to allow all this militarism and imperialism to go on without protest. It will be established as a rule that, whenever political ascendency is threatened, it can be established again by a little war, filling the minds of the people with glory and diverting their attention from their own interests. Hard-headed old Benjamin Franklin hit the point when, referring back to the days of Marlborough, he talked about the "pest of glory." The thirst for glory is an epidemic which robs a people of their judgment, seduces their vanity, cheats them of their interests, and corrupts their consciences.

This country owes its existence to a revolt against the colonial and navigation system which, as I have said, Spain first put in practice. The English colonial system never was even approximately so harsh and tyrannical as that of Spain. The first great question which arose about colonies in England was whether they were parts of the possessions of the king of England or part of the dominion of the crown. The constitutional difference was great. In the one case they were subject to the king and were not under the constitutional guarantees; in the other case they were subject to the Parliament and were under the constitutional guarantees. This is exactly the same question which arose in the middle of this century in this country about territories, and which helped to bring on the Civil War. It is already arising again. It is the question whether the Constitution of the United States extends over all men and territory owned by the United States, or whether there are to be grades and planes of rights for different parts of the dominions over which our flag waves. This question already promises to introduce dissensions amongst us which will touch the most vital elements in our national existence.

The constitutional question, however, goes even deeper than this. Of the interpretation of clauses in the Constitution I am not competent to speak, but the Constitution is the organic law of this confederated state in which we live, and therefore it is the description of it as it was planned and as it is. The question at stake is nothing less than the integrity of this state in its most essential elements. The expansionists have recognized this fact by already casting the Constitution aside. The military men, of course, have been the first to do this. It is of the essence of militarism that under it military men learn to despise constitutions, to sneer at parliaments, and to look with contempt on civilians. Some of the imperialists are not ready to go quite so fast as yet. They have remonstrated against the military doctrine, but that only proves that the military men see the point at issue better than the others do. Others say that if the legs of the Constitution are too short to straddle the gulf between the old policy and the new, they can be stretched a little, a view of the matter which is as flippant as it is in bad taste. It would require too much time to notice the various contemptuous and jaunty references to the Constitution which every day brings to our notice, and from the same class, at least, who, two years ago, were so shocked at a criticism of the *interpretation* of the Constitution which was inserted in the Chicago platform.

The question of imperialism, then, is the question whether we are going to give the lie to the origin of our own national existence by establishing a colonial system of the old Spanish type, even if we have to sacrifice our existing civil and political system to do it. I submit that it is a strange incongruity to utter grand platitudes about the blessings of liberty, etc., which we are going to impart to these people, and to begin by refusing to extend the Constitution over them, and still more, by throwing the Constitution into the gutter here at home. If you take away the Constitution, what is American liberty and all the rest? Nothing but a lot of phrases.

Some will answer me that they do not intend to adopt any Spanish colonial system; that they intend to imitate the modern English policy with respect to colonies. The proudest fact in the history of England is that, since the Napoleonic wars, she has steadily corrected abuses, amended her institutions, redressed grievances, and so has made her recent history a story of amelioration of all her institutions, social, political, and civil. To do this she has had to overcome old traditions, established customs, vested rights, and all the other obstacles which retard or prevent social improvement. The consequence is that the traditions of her public service, in all its branches, have been purified, and that a body of men has grown up who have a noble spirit, high motives, honorable methods, and excellent standards. At the same time the policy of the country has been steadily growing more and more enlightened in regard to all the great interests of society. These triumphs of peace are far greater than any triumphs of war. It takes more national grit to correct abuses than to win battles. England has shown herself very willing indeed to learn from us whatever we could teach, and we might learn a great deal from her on matters far more important than colonial policy. Her reform of her colonial policy is only a part, and perhaps a consequence, of the improvements made elsewhere in her political system.

We have had some experience this last summer in the attempt to improvise an army. We may be very sure that it is equally impossible to improvise a colonial system. The present English colonial system is aristocratic. It depends upon a large body of specially trained men, acting under traditions which have become well established, and with a firm *esprit de corps*. Nobody can get into it without training. The system is foreign to our ideas, tastes, and methods. It would require a long time

and radical changes in our political methods, which we are not as yet
at all disposed to make, to establish any such thing here, and then it
would be an imitation. Moreover, England has three different colonial
systems, according to the development of the resident population in
each colony or dependency, and the selection of the one of these three
systems which we will adopt and apply involves all the difficulties
which I have been discussing.

There is, however, another objection to the English system. A great
many people talk about the revenue which we are to get from these
possessions. If we attempt to get any revenues from them we shall repeat
the conduct of England towards her colonies against which they revolted. England claimed that it was reasonable that the colonies should
pay their share of imperial expenses which were incurred for the benefit
of all. I have never been able to see why that was not a fair demand. As
you know, the colonies spurned it with indignation, on the ground that
the taxation, being at the discretion of a foreign power, *might* be made
unjust. Our historians and publicists have taught us that the position of
the colonists was right and heroic, and the only one worthy of freemen.
The revolt was made on the *principle* of no taxation, not on the size of
the tax. The colonists would not pay a penny. Since that is so, we cannot
get a penny of revenue from the dependencies, even for their fair share
of imperial expenditures, without burning up all our histories, revising
all the great principles of our heroic period, repudiating our great men
of that period, and going over to the Spanish doctrine of taxing dependencies at the discretion of the governing State. Already one of these
dependencies is in arms struggling for liberty against us. Read the threats
of the imperialists against these people, who dare to rebel against us,
and see whether I am misstating or exaggerating the corruption of imperialism on ourselves. The question is once more, whether we are prepared to repudiate the principles which we have been insisting on for
one hundred and fifty years, and to embrace those of which Spain is the
oldest and most conspicuous representative, or not.

In regard to this matter of taxation and revenue, the present English
colonial system is as unjust to the mother-country as the old system was
the colonies, or more so. The colonies now tax the mother-country. She
pays large expenses for their advantage, for which they return nothing.
They set up tax barriers against her trade with them. I do not believe
that the United States will ever consent to any such system, and I am
clear in the opinion that they never ought to. If the colonies ought not
to be made tributary to the mother-country, neither ought the mother-

country to be made tributary to them. The proposition to imitate England's colonial policy is evidently made without the necessary knowledge of what it means, and it proves that those who thrust aside prudent objections by declaring off-hand that we will imitate England have not any serious comprehension of what it is that they propose to us to do.

The conclusion of this branch of the subject is that it is fundamentally antagonistic to our domestic system to hold dependencies which are unfit to enter into the Union. Our system cannot be extended to take them in or adjusted to them to keep them out without sacrificing its integrity. If we take in dependencies which, as we now agree, are not fit to come in as states, there will be constant political agitation to admit them as states, for such agitation will be fomented by any party which thinks that it can win votes in that way. It was an enormous blunder in statecraft to engage in a war which was sure to bring us into this predicament.

## II

It seems as if this new policy was destined to thrust a sword into every joint in our historical and philosophical system. Our ancestors revolted against the colonial and navigation system, but as soon as they got their independence, they fastened a navigation system on themselves. The consequence is that our industry and commerce are to-day organized under a restrictive system which is the direct offspring of the old Spanish restrictive system, and is based on the same ideas of economic policy; viz., that statesmen can devise a prosperity policy for a country which will do more for it than a spontaneous development of the energy of the people and the resources of the territory would do. On the other hand, inside of the Union we have established the grandest experiment in absolute free trade that has ever existed. The combination of the two is not new, because it is just what Colbert tried in France, but it is original here and is an interesting result of the presence in men's minds of two opposite philosophies, the adjustment of which has never yet been fought out. The extension of our authority over these new territories forces the inconsistency between our internal and our external policy out of the field of philosophy into that of practical politics. Wherever the boundary line of the national system falls we have one rule inside of it and another outside of it. Are the new territories to be taken inside or to be treated as outside? If we develop this dilemma, we shall see that it is of the first importance.

If we treat the dependencies as inside the national system, we must have absolute free trade with them. Then if, on the policy of the "open door," we allow all others to go to them on the same terms as ourselves, the dependencies will have free trade with all the world, while we are under the restrictive system ourselves. Then, too, the dependencies can obtain no revenues by import duties.

If we take the other branch of the dilemma and treat the dependencies as outside of our national policy, then we must shut out their products from our market by taxes. If we do this on the policy of the "open door," then any taxes which the islands lay upon imports from elsewhere they must also lay upon imports from us. Then they and we will be taxing each other. If we go upon the protectionist policy, we shall determine our taxes against them and theirs against other nations, and we shall let them lay none against us. That is exactly the Spanish system. Under it the colonies will be crushed between the upper and the nether millstone. They will revolt against us for just the same reason for which they revolted against Spain.

I have watched the newspapers with great interest for six months, to see that indications were presented of the probable currents of opinion on the dilemma which I have described. There have been but few. A few extreme protectionist newspapers have truculently declared that our protective system was to be extended around our possessions, and that everybody else was to be excluded from them. From a number of interviews and letters, by private individuals, I select the following as expressing well what is sure to be the view of the unregenerate man, especially if he has an interest to be protected as this writer had.

"I am opposed to the 'open door' policy, as I understand it. To open the ports of our new territories free to the world would have the effect of cheapening or destroying many of the benefits of territorial acquisition, which has cost us blood and money. As a nation we are well qualified to develop and handle the trade of our new possessions, and by permitting others to come in and divide the advantages and profits of this trade we not only wrong our own citizens, who should be given preference, but exhibit a weakness that ill becomes a nation of our prominence."

This is exactly the view which was held in Spain, France, Holland, and England in the eighteenth century, and upon which the navigation system, against which our fathers revolted, was founded. If we adopt this view we may count upon it that we shall be embroiled in constant wars with other nations, which will not consent that we should shut them out of parts of the earth's surface until we prove that we can do it by force. Then we shall be parties to a renewal of all the eighteenth century wars for colonies, for supremacy on the sea, for "trade," as the term is used, for world supremacy, and for all the rest of the heavy follies from which our fathers fought to free themselves. That is the policy of Russia and France at the present time, and we have before our eyes proofs of its effect on the peace and welfare of mankind.

Our modern protectionists have always told us that the object of their policy is to secure the home market. They have pushed their system to an extravagant excess. The free traders used to tell them that they were constructing a Chinese wall. They answered that they wished we were separated from other nations by a gulf of fire. Now it is they who are crying out that they are shut in by a Chinese wall. When we have shut all the world out, we find that we have shut ourselves in . The protective system is applied especially to certain selected lines of production. Of course these are stimulated out of proportion to the requirements of the community, and so are exposed to sharp fluctuations of high profits and over-production. At great expense and loss we have carried out the policy of the home market, and now we are called upon at great expense and loss to go out and conquer territory in order to widen the market. In order to have trade with another community the first condition is that we must produce what they want and they must produce what we want. That is the economic condition. The second condition is that there must be peace and security and freedom from arbitrary obstacles interposed by government. This is the political condition. If these conditions are fulfilled, there will be trade, no matter whether the two communities are in one body politic or not. If these conditions are not fulfilled, there will be no trade, no matter what flag floats. If we want more trade we can get it any day by a reciprocity treaty with Canada, and it will be larger and more profitable than that of all the Spanish possessions. It will cost us nothing to get it. Yet while we were fighting for Puerto Rico and Manila, and spending three or four hundred millions to get them, negotiations with Canada failed through the narrow-mindedness and bigotry which we brought to the negotiation. Conquest can do nothing for trade except to remove the political obstacles which the conquered could not, or would not, remove. From this it follows that the only justification for territorial extension is the extension of free and enlightened policies in regard to commerce. Even then extension is an irksome necessity. The question always is, whether you are taking an asset or a liability. Land grabbing means properly taking territory and shutting all the rest of the world out of it, so as to exploit it ourselves. It is not land grabbing to take it and police it and throw it open to all. This is the policy of the "open door." Our external commercial policy is, in all its principles, the same as that of Spain. We had no justification, on that ground, in taking anything away from her. If we now seek to justify ourselves, it must be by going over to the free policy; but, as I have shown, that forces to a crisis the contradiction between our domestic and our external policy as to trade. It is very probable, indeed, that the destruction of our restrictive system will be the first good result of expansion, but my object here has been to show what a network of difficulties environ us in the attempt to establish a commercial policy for these dependencies. We have certainly to go through years of turmoil and political bitterness, with all the consequent chances of internal dissension, before these difficulties can be overcome.

## III

Another phenomenon which deserves earnest attention from the student of contemporaneous history and of the trend of political institutions is the failure of the masses of our people to perceive *the inevitable effect of imperialism on democracy*. On the twenty-ninth of last November [1898] the Prime Minister of France was quoted in a cable dispatch as follows: "For twenty-eight years we have lived under a contradiction. The army and democracy subsist side by side. The maintenance of the traditions of the army is a menace to liberty, yet they assure the safety of the country and its most sacred duties."

That antagonism of democracy and militarism is now coming to a crisis in France, and militarism is sure to win, because the French people would make any other sacrifice rather than diminish their military strength. In Germany the attempt has been going on for thirty years to establish constitutional government with parliamentary institutions. The parts of the German system are at war with each other. The Emperor constantly interferes with the operation of the system and utters declarations which are entirely personal. He is not responsible and cannot be answered or criticized. The situation is not so delicate as in France, but it is exceedingly unstable. All the desire of Germans for self-government and civil liberty runs out into socialism, and socialism is repressed by force or by trickery. The conservative classes of the country acquiesce in the situation while they deplore it. The reason is because the Emperor is the war lord. His power and authority are essential to the military strength of the State in face of its neighbors. That is the preponderating consideration to which everything else has to yield, and the consequence of it is that there is to-day scarcely an institution in Germany except the army.

Everywhere you go on the continent of Europe at this hour you see the conflict between militarism and industrialism. You see the expansion of industrial power pushed forward by the energy, hope, and thrift of men, and you see the development arrested, diverted, crippled, and defeated by measures which are dictated by military considerations. At the same time the press is loaded down with discussions about political economy, political philosophy, and social policy. They are discussing poverty, labor, socialism, charity, reform, and social ideals, and are boasting of enlightenment and progress, at the same time that the things which are done are dictated by none of these considerations, but only by military interests. It is militarism which is eating up all the products of science and art, defeating the energy of the population and wasting its savings. It is militarism which forbids the people to give their attention to the problems of their own welfare and to give their strength to the education and comfort of their children. It is militarism which is combating the grand efforts of science and art to ameliorate the struggle for existence.

The American people believe that they have a free country, and we are treated to grandiloquent speeches about our flag and our reputation for freedom and enlightenment. The common opinion is that we have these things because we have chosen and adopted them, because they are in the Declaration of Independence and the Constitution. We suppose, therefore, that we are sure to keep them and that the follies of other people are things which we can hear about with complacency. People say that this country is like no other; that its prosperity proves its exceptionality, and so on. These are popular errors which in time will meet with harsh correction. The United States is in a protected situation. It is easy to have equality where land is abundant and where the population is small. It is easy to have prosperity where a few men have a great continent to exploit. It is easy to have liberty when you have no dangerous neighbors and when the struggle for existence is easy. There are no severe penalties, under such circumstances, for political mistakes. Democracy is not then a thing to be nursed and defended, as it is in an old country like France. It is rooted and founded in the economic circumstances of the country. The orators and constitution-makers do not make democracy. They are made by it. This protected position, however, is sure to pass away. As the country fills up with population, and the task of getting a living out of the ground becomes more difficult, the struggle for existence will become harder and the competition of life more severe. Then liberty and democracy will cost something, if they are to be maintained.

Now what will hasten the day when our present advantages will wear out and when we shall come down to the conditions of the older and densely populated nations? The answer is: war, debt, taxation, diplomacy, a grand governmental system, pomp, glory, a big army and navy, lavish expenditures, political jobbery—in a word, imperialism. In the old days the democratic masses of this country, who knew little about our modern doctrines of social philosophy, had a sound instinct on these matters, and it is no small ground of political disquietude to see it decline. They resisted every appeal to their vanity in the way of pomp and glory which they knew must be paid for. They dreaded a public debt and a standing army. They were narrow-minded and went too far with these notions, but they were, at least, right, if they wanted to strengthen democracy.

The great foe of democracy now and in the near future is plutocracy. Every year that passes brings out this antagonism more distinctly. It is to be the social war of the twentieth century. In that war militarism, expansion and imperialism will all favor plutocracy. In the first place, war and expansion will favor jobbery, both in the dependencies and at home. In the second place, they will take away the attention of the people from what the plutocrats are doing. In the third place, they will cause large expenditures of the people's money, the return for which will not go into the treasury, but into the hands of a few schemers. In the fourth place, they will call for a large public debt and taxes, and these things especially tend to make men unequal, because any social burdens bear more heavily on the weak than on the strong, and so make the weak weaker and the strong stronger. Therefore expansion and imperialism are a grand onslaught on democracy.

The point which I have tried to make in this lecture is that expansion and imperialism are at war with the best traditions, principles, and interests of the American people, and that they will plunge us into a network of difficult problems and political perils, which we might have avoided, while they offer us no corresponding advantage in return.

Of course "principles," phrases, and catch-words are always invented to bolster up any policy which anybody wants to recommend. So in this case. The people who have led us on to shut ourselves in, and who now want us to break out, warn us against the terrors of "isolation." Our ancestors all came here to isolate themselves from the social burdens and inherited errors of the old world. When the others are all over ears in trouble, who would not be isolated in freedom from care? When the others are crushed under the burden of militarism, who would not be isolated in peace and industry? When the others are all struggling under debt and taxes, who would not be isolated in the enjoyment of his own earnings for the benefit of his own family? When the rest are all in a quiver of anxiety, lest at a day's notice they may be involved in a social cataclysm, who would not be isolated out of reach of the disaster? What we are doing is that we are abandoning this blessed isolation to run after a share in the trouble.

The expansionists answer our remonstrances on behalf of the great American principles by saying that times have changed and that we have outlived the fathers of the republic and their doctrines. As far as the authority of the great men is concerned, that may well be sacrificed without regret. Authority of persons and names is a dangerous thing. Let us get at the truth and the right. I, for my part, am also afraid of the great principles, and I would make no fight on their behalf. In the ten years before the Revolution our ancestors invented a fine lot of "principles" which they thought would help their case. They repudiated many of them as soon as they got their independence, and the rest of them have since made us a great deal of trouble. I have examined them all critically, and there is not one of them which I consider sound, as it is popularly understood. I have been denounced as a heretic on this account by people who now repudiate them all in a sentence. But this only clears the ground for the real point. There is a consistency of character for a nation as well as for a man. A man who changes his principles from week to week is destitute of character and deserves no confidence. The great men of this nation were such because they embodied and expressed the opinion and sentiments of the nation in their time. Their names are something more than clubs with which to knock an opponent down when it suits one's purpose, but to be thrown away with contempt when they happen to be on the other side. So of the great principles; whether some of us are skeptical about their entire validity and want to define and limit them somewhat is of little importance. If the nation has accepted them, sworn by them, founded its legislation on them, embedded them in the decisions of its courts, and then if it throws them away at six months' warning, you may depend upon it that that nation will suffer in its moral and political rectitude a shock of the severest kind. Three years ago we were ready to fight Great Britain to make her arbitrate a quarrel which she had with Venezuela. The question about the *Maine* was one of the fittest subjects for arbitration that ever arose between two nations, and we refused to listen to such a proposition. Three years ago, if you had said that any proposition put forth by anybody was "English," he might have been mobbed in the streets. Now the English are our beloved friends, and we are going to try to imitate them and adopt their way of doing things. They are encouraging us to go into difficulties, first because our hands will be full and we shall be unable to interfere elsewhere, and secondly, because if we are in difficulties we shall need allies, and they think that they will be our first choice as such. Some of our public journals have been pouring out sentimental drivel for years about arbitration, but last summer they turned around and began to pour out sentimental drivel about the benefits of war. We congratulate ourselves all the time on the increased means of producing wealth, and then we take the opposite fit and commit some great folly in order to prove that there is something grander than the pursuit of wealth. Three years ago we were on the verge of a law to keep immigrants out who were not good enough to be in with us. Now we are going to take in eight million barbarians and semi-barbarians, and we are paying twenty million dollars to get them. For thirty years the negro has been in fashion. He has had political value and has been petted. Now we have made friends with the Southerners. They and we are hugging each other. We are all united. The negro's day is over. He is out of fashion. We cannot treat him one way and the Malays, Tagals, and Kanakas another way. A Southern senator two or three days ago thanked an expansionist senator from Connecticut for enunciating doctrines which proved that, for the last thirty years, the Southerners have been right all the time, and his inference was incontrovertible. So the "great principles" change all the time; or, what is far more important, the phrases change. Some go out of fashion, others come in, but the phrase-makers are with us all the time. So when our friends the expansionists tell us that times have changed, what it means is that they have a whole set of new phrases which they want to force into the place of the old ones. The new ones are certainly no more valid than the old ones. All the validity that the great principles ever had they have now. Anybody who ever candidly studied them and accepted them for no more than they were really worth can stand by them now as well as ever. The time when a maxim or principle is worth something is when you are tempted to violate it.

Another answer which the imperialists make is that Americans can do anything. They say that they do not shrink from responsibilities. They are willing to run into a hole, trusting to luck and cleverness to get out. There are some things that Americans cannot do. Americans cannot make $2 + 2 = 5$. You may answer that that is an arithmetical impossibility and is not in the range of our subject. Very well; Americans cannot collect two dollars a gallon tax on whiskey. They tried it for many years and failed. That is an economic or political impossibility, the roots of which are in human nature. It is as absolute an impossibility on this domain as the former on the domain of mathematics. So far as yet appears, Americans cannot govern a city of one hundred thousand inhabitants so as to get comfort and convenience in it at a low cost and without jobbery. The fire department of this city is now demoralized by political jobbery—and Spain and all her possessions are not worth as much to you and me as the efficiency of the fire department of New Haven. The Americans in Connecticut cannot abolish the rotten borough system. The English abolished their rotten borough system seventy years ago, in spite of nobles and landlords. We cannot abolish ours in spite of the small towns. Americans cannot reform the pension list. Its abuses are rooted in the methods of democratic self-government, and no one dares to touch them. It is very doubtful indeed if Americans can keep up an army of one hundred thousand men in time of peace. Where can one hundred thousand men be found in this country who are willing to spend their lives as soldiers; or if they are found, what pay will it require to induce them to take this career? Americans cannot disentangle their currency from the confusion into which it was thrown by the Civil War, and they cannot put it on a simple, sure, and sound basis which would give stability to the business of the country. This is a political impossibility. Americans cannot assure the suffrage to negroes throughout the United States; they have tried it for thirty years and now, contemporaneously with this war with Spain, it has been finally demonstrated that it is a failure. Inasmuch as the negro is now out of fashion, no further attempt to accomplish this purpose will be made. It is an impossibility on account of the complexity of our system of State and Federal government. If I had time to do so, I could go back over the history of negro suffrage and show you how curbstone arguments, exactly analogous to the arguments about expansion, were used to favor it, and how objections were thrust aside in this same blustering and senseless manner in which objections to imperialism are met. The ballot, we were told, was an educator and would solve all difficulties in its own path as by magic.

Worse still, Americans cannot assure life, liberty, and the pursuit of happiness to negroes inside of the United States. When the negro post-master's house was set on fire in the night in South Carolina, and not only he, but his wife and children, were murdered as they came out, and when, moreover, this incident passed without legal investigation or punishment, it was a bad omen for the extension of liberty, etc., to Malays and Tagals by simply setting over them the American flag. Upon a little serious examination the off-hand disposal of an important question of policy by the declaration that Americans can do anything proves to be only a silly piece of bombast, and upon a little reflection we find that our hands are quite full at home of problems by the solution of which the peace and happiness of the American people could be greatly increased. The laws of nature and of human nature are just as valid for Americans as for anybody else, and if we commit acts we shall have to take consequences, just like other people. Therefore prudence demands that we look ahead to see what we are about to do, and that we gauge the means at our disposal, if we do not want to bring calamity on ourselves and our children. We see that the peculiarities of our system of government set limitations on us. We cannot do things which a great centralized monarchy could do. The very blessings and special advantages which we enjoy, as compared with others, bring disabilities with them. That is the great fundamental cause of what I have tried to show throughout this lecture, that we cannot govern dependencies consistently with our political system, and that, if we try it, the State which our fathers founded will suffer a reaction which will transform it into another empire just after the fashion of all the old ones. That is what imperialism means. That is what it will be; and the democratic republic, which has been, will stand in history, like the colonial organization of earlier days, as a mere transition form.

And yet this scheme of a republic which our fathers formed was a glorious dream which demands more than a word of respect and affection before it passes away. Indeed, it is not fair to call it a dream or even an ideal; it was a possibility which was within our reach if we had been wise enough to grasp and hold it. It was favored by our comparative isolation, or, at least, by our distance from other strong states. The men who came here were able to throw off all the trammels of tradition and established doctrine. They went out into a wilderness, it is true, but they took with them all the art, science, and literature which, up to that time, civilization had produced. They could not, it is true, strip their minds of the ideas which they had inherited, but in time, as they lived on in the new world, they sifted and selected these ideas, retaining what they chose. Of the old-world institutions also they selected and adopted what they chose and threw aside the rest. It was a grand opportunity to be thus able to strip off all the follies and errors which they had inherited, so far as they chose to do so. They had unlimited land with no feudal restrictions to hinder them in the use of it. Their idea was that they would never allow any of the social and political abuses of the old world to grow up here. There should be no manors, no barons, no ranks, no prelates, no idle classes, no paupers, no disinherited ones except the vicious. There were to be no armies except a militia, which would have no functions but those of police. They would have no court and no pomp; no orders, or ribbons, or decorations, or titles. They would have no public debt. They repudiated with scorn the notion that a public debt is a public blessing; if debt was incurred in war it was to be paid in peace and not entailed on posterity. There was to be no grand diplomacy, because they intended to mind their own business and not be involved in any of the intrigues to which European statesmen were accustomed. There was to be no balance of power and no "reason of state" to cost the life and happiness of citizens. The only part of the Monroe doctrine which is valid was their determination that the social and political systems of Europe should not be extended over any part of the American continent, lest people who were weaker than we should lose the opportunity which the new continent gave them to escape from those systems if they wanted to. Our fathers would have an economical government, even if grand people called it a parsimonious one, and taxes should be no greater than were absolutely necessary to pay for such a government. The citizen was to keep all the rest of his earnings and use them as he thought best for the happiness of himself and his family; he was, above all, to be insured peace and quiet while he pursued his honest industry and obeyed the laws. No adventurous policies of conquest or ambition, such as, in the belief of our fathers, kings and nobles had forced, for their own advantage, on European states, would ever be undertaken by a free democratic republic. Therefore the citizen here would never be forced to leave his family or to give his sons to shed blood for glory and to leave widows and orphans in misery for nothing. Justice and law were to reign in the midst of simplicity, and a government which had little to do was to offer little field for ambition. In a society where industry, frugality, and prudence were honored, it was believed that the vices of wealth would never flourish.

We know that these beliefs, hopes, and intentions have been only partially fulfilled. We know that, as time has gone on and we have grown numerous and rich, some of these things have proved impossible ideals, incompatible with a large and flourishing society, but it is by virtue of this conception of a commonwealth that the United States has stood for something unique and grand in the history of mankind and that its people have been happy. It is by virtue of these ideals that we have been "isolated," isolated in a position which the other nations of the earth have observed in silent envy; and yet there are people who are boasting of their patriotism, because they say that we have taken our place now amongst the nations of the earth by virtue of this war. My patriotism is of the kind which is outraged by the notion that the United States never was a great nation until in a petty three months' campaign it knocked to pieces a poor, decrepit, bankrupt old state like Spain. To hold such an opinion as that is to abandon all American standards, to put shame and scorn on all that our ancestors tried to build up here, and to go over to the standards of which Spain is a representative.

# War

Intrigued by the role of increasing organization in human affairs, Sumner sought during the 1890s to clarify the role of competition and cooperation. Humans in society, he decided, fought the struggle of existence, not as individuals, but in groups, a process he termed "antagonistic cooperation." Throughout history, the "competition of life" was likewise a struggle, not among individuals, but between "in-groups" and "out-groups." For this reason, "war has always existed and always will." Drawing on a wealth of anthropological literature, Sumner was also influenced by the *Realpolitik* of Ludwig Gumplowicz, a representative of the Austrian "conflict school" of sociology. In this version, Sumner's extensive notes are eliminated. Lecture delivered presumably in New Haven, 1903, reprinted in *War*, ed. Albert Galloway Keller, pp. 3–40.

We have heard our political leaders say from time to time that "War is necessary," "War is a good thing." They were trying to establish a major premise which would suggest the conclusion, "Therefore let us have a little war now," or "It is wise, on general principles, to have a war once in a while." That argument may be taken as the text of the present essay. It has seemed to me worth while to show from the history of civilization just what war has done and has not done for the welfare of mankind.

In the eighteenth century it was assumed that the primitive state of mankind was one of Arcadian peace, joy, and contentment. In the nineteenth century the assumption went over to the other extreme—that the primitive state was one of universal warfare. This, like the former notion, is a great exaggeration. Man in the most primitive and uncivilized state known to us does not practice war all the time; he dreads it; he might rather be described as a peaceful animal. Real warfare comes with the collisions of more developed societies.

If we turn to facts about the least civilized men we find proofs that they are not warlike and do not practice war if they can help it. The Australians have no idea of conquest or battle. Their fights do not lead to slaughter or spoils or other consequences of victory. Sometimes a fight takes the form of a friendly trial of skill with weapons between two parties who, one by one, cast their weapons at each other. Quarrels between tribes are sometimes settled by a single combat between chiefs.

"Real fighting rarely takes place unless the women arouse the men," and even then it is only carried on by taunts and wrestling. "The first wound ends the combat." It is often followed by a war of words, hair-pulling, and blows with yam-sticks between the women. The Australians have no war because they have no property that is worth pillaging; no tribe has anything to tempt the cupidity of another. They have no political organization, so there can be no war for power. Each group appropriates hunting grounds, and over these war arises only with the increase of population. An Englishman who knew them well said that he knew of serious wounds, but he had known of but one death from their affrays.

Neither are the Papuans of New Guinea warlike in all parts of the island. Like other men on the same grade of civilization, they may be assassins, but they are not warriors, and if two bodies of them meet in hostility, we are told that "there is a remarkably small death-roll at the end of the battle." Of another group of them we are told that they have no offensive weapons at all, but live without disturbance from neighbors and without care for the future. Their children rarely quarrel at play, and if they do, it ends in words. We are told that they lack the courage, temper, and concentration of will which would be necessary for a good schoolboy fight. Perhaps the converse would be true: they have no schoolboy fights and therefore have no courage, temper, and concentration of will. We are not astonished to hear that they develop excessive tyranny and cruelty to those who are weaker than themselves, especially to women, and even to their mothers. These people are excessively distrustful of each other and villages but a little distance apart have very little intercourse. This is attributed in great part to head-hunting and cannibalism. In general they know the limits of their own territory and observe them, but they quarrel about women. The people in German Melanesia are of the same kind; they are cowardly and mean, make raids on each other's land to destroy and plunder, when they think they can do it safely, but they will not join battle. On some of the small islands war is entirely unknown.

The Chatham Islanders sometimes quarreled over booty won in pursuing seals or whales, but they had a law that the first drop of blood ended the fight. The Khonds in Madras became insubordinate a few years ago and a police force was sent against them; they prepared stones to roll down the hill in front of their village, but left the rear unguarded, and when the police entered by the rear the Khonds protested against the unfairness of this movement after they had taken such precautions in front. The Rengmahs on the Assam hills attach to the body a tail of wood eighteen inches long, curved upwards, which they use to wag defiance at an enemy. Such people evidently could never have had much experience of war. The Mrú on the Chittagong hills are peaceable, timid, and simple; in a quarrel they do not fight, but call in an exorcist to take the sense of the spirits on the matter.

Livingstone says that the tribes in the interior of South Africa, where no slave trade existed, seldom had any war except about cattle, and some tribes refused to keep cattle in order not to offer temptation. In one case only had he heard of war for any other reason; three brothers, Barolongs, fought over one woman, and their tribe had remained divided, up to the time of writing, into three parties. During his residence in the Bechuana country he never saw unarmed men strike each other. They quarrel with words, but generally both parties burst into a laugh and that ends it. By an exception among the Canary islanders, the people of Hierro knew no war and had no weapons, although their long leaping-poles could be used as such when occasion demanded.

A Spanish priest, writing an account, in 1739, of the Aurohuacos of Colombia, says that they have no weapons of offense or defense. If two quarrel they go out to a big rock or tree and each with his staff beats the rock or tree with vituperations. The one whose staff breaks first is the victor; then they embrace and return home as friends. Even our American Indians, who appear in our legends to be so bloodthirsty and war-like, always appreciated the blessings of peace. Wampum strings and belts were associated with peace-pacts and with prayers for peace.

In contrast with these cases we find others of extreme warlikeness which account for the current idea that primitive men love war and practice it all the time. But if we examine the cases of peacefulness or unwarlikeness which have been cited, we see that only two or three seem to present evidence of Arcadian peace and simplicity, such as, in the imagination of the eighteenth century philosophers, characterized men in a state of nature. Probably if we had fuller knowledge these few instances would be much modified. What we see is that men have always quarreled. The cases which have been selected are some of them also those of people who have been defeated, broken, and cowed down. Another set of examples consists of those in which abstinence from war is due to cowardice, and with it go the vices of cowardice—tyranny and cruelty to the weak. These cases are calculated to delight the hearts of the advocates of strenuosity. What our testimonies have in common is this: they show that we cannot postulate a warlike character or a habit of fighting as a universal or even characteristic trait of primitive man.

When we undertake to talk about primitive society we should conceive of it as consisting of petty groups scattered separately over a great territory. I speak of groups because I want a term of the widest significance. The group may consist, as it does amongst Australians and Bushmen, of a man with one or possibly two wives and their children, or it may have a few more members, or it may be a village group as in New Guinea, or a tribe or part of a tribe as amongst our own Indians. It is to be observed that this ultimate unit is a group and not an individual. Every individual excludes every other in the competition of life unless they can by combining together win more out of nature by joint effort than the sum of what they could win separately. This combination is what makes groups and brings about industrial organization. When a man and woman unite in the most elementary group known, they do it for economic reasons, because they can carry on the struggle for existence better together than apart. In time this turns into a kin-group, united "by blood." This remains undivided as long as its organization gives advantages, but breaks up when it grows too big for the existing economic system. As soon as it breaks, the fractions begin to compete with each other. If by greater culture a higher organization becomes possible, two groups coalesce by intermarriage or conquest, competition gives way to combination again, and the bigger unit enters into competition with other composite units. Thus at all stages throughout the history of civilization competition and combination forever alternate with each other.

These groups are independent of each other, their size being determined by their mode of life, because the number who can live together economically is limited by the possibilities of the food quest. When a group outgrows this limit, it breaks up and scatters. The fact of former association is long remembered and there is a bond of kinship and alliance which may at times draw former associates together again for festivals and religious observances, but after they separate the tendency is to become entirely independent and to fall under the type just described; *viz.*, scattered groups each with its individuality, yet in a certain neighborhood to each other. Their remoter relationship does not keep them from quarreling and fighting. In the book of Judges we see cases of war between tribes of Israel in spite of the higher bond which united them with each other and separated them from the Gentiles.

All the members of one group are comrades to each other, and have a common interest against every other group. If we assume a standpoint in one group we may call that on the "we-group" or the "in-group"; then every other group is to us an "others-group" or an "out-group." The sentiment which prevails inside the "we-group," between its members, is that of peace and cooperation; the sentiment which prevails inside of a group towards all outsiders is that of hostility and war. These two sentiments are perfectly consistent with each other; in fact, they necessarily complement each other. Let us see why that is so.

War arises from the competition of life, not from the struggle for existence. In the struggle for existence a man is wrestling with nature to extort from her the means of subsistence. It is when two men are striving side by side in the struggle for existence, to extort from nature the supplies they need, that they come into rivalry and a collision of interest with each other takes place. This collision may be light and unimportant, if the supplies are large and the number of men small, or it may be harsh and violent, if there are many men striving for a small supply. This collision we call the competition of life. Of course men are in the competition of life with beasts, reptiles, insects, and plants—in short, with all organic forms; we will, however, confine our attention to men. The greater or less intensity of the competition of life is a fundamental condition of human existence, and the competition arises between those ultimate unit groups which I have described. The members of the unit group work together. The Australian or Bushman hunter goes abroad to seek meat food, while the woman stays by the fire at a trysting place, with the children, and collects plant food. They cooperate in the struggle for existence, and the size of the group is fixed by the number who can work together to the greatest advantage under their mode of life. Such a group, therefore, has a common interest. It must have control of a certain area of land; hence it comes into collision of interest with every other group. The competition of life, therefore, arises between groups, not between individuals, and we see that the members of the in-group are allies and joint-partners in one interest while they are brought into antagonism of interest with all outsiders. It is the competition of life, therefore, which makes war, and that is why war always has existed and always will. It is in the conditions of human existence. In the cases which have been cited of nature peoples who have no war, we have heard mention already of division of hunting grounds and of quarrels which arise about them. Wherever there is no war, there we find that there is no crowding, as among the scattered Eskimo, or that, after long fighting, treaties and agreements have been made to cover all relations of interest between the groups. These we call peace-pacts, and it is evident that they consist in conventional agreements creating some combination between the groups which are parties to the agreement.

Each group must regard every other as a possible enemy on account of the antagonism of interests, and so it views every other group with suspicion and distrust, although actual hostilities occur only on specific occasion. Every member of another group is a stranger; he may be admitted as a guest, in which case rights and security are granted him, but if not so admitted he is an enemy. We can now see why the sentiments of peace and cooperation inside are complementary to sentiments of hostility outside. It is because any group, in order to be strong against an outside enemy, must be well disciplined, harmonious, and peaceful inside; in other words, because discord inside would cause defeat in battle with another group. Therefore the same conditions which made men warlike against outsiders made them yield to the control of chiefs, submit to discipline, obey law, cultivate peace, and create institutions inside. The motion of rights grows up in the in-group from the usages established there securing peace. There was a double education, at the same time, out of the same facts and relations. It is no paradox at all to say that peace makes war and that war makes peace. There are two codes of morals and two sets of mores, one for comrades inside and the other for strangers outside, and they arise from the same interests. Against outsiders it was meritorious to kill, plunder, practice blood revenge, and to steal women and slaves; but inside none of these things could be allowed because they would produce discord and weakness. Hence, in the in-group, law (under the forms of custom and taboo) and institutions had to take the place of force. Every group was a peace-group inside and the peace was sanctioned by the ghosts of the ancestors who had handed down the customs and taboos. Against outsiders religion sanctioned and encouraged war; for the ghosts of the ancestors, or the gods, would rejoice to see their posterity and worshipers once more defeat, slay, plunder, and enslave the ancient enemy.

The Eskimos of Bering Strait think it wrong to steal from people in the same village or tribe; a thief is publicly reproached and forced to return the thing stolen. But to steal from an outsider is not wrong unless it brings harm on one's own tribe. Strabo says of the Scythians that they were just and kind to each other, but very savage towards all outsiders. The sentiment of cohesion, internal comradeship, and devotion to the in-group, which carries with it a sense of superiority to any out-group and readiness to defend the interests of the in-group against the out-group, is technically known as ethnocentrism. It is really the sentiment of patriotism in all its philosophic fullness; that is, both in its rationality and in its extravagant exaggeration. The Mohaves and the Seri of southern California will have no relations of marriage or trade with any other people; they think themselves superior. The Mohaves are wild and barbarous and the Seri are on a lower grade of civilization than any other tribe in America. Therefore, we see that ethnocentrism has nothing to do with the relative grade of civilization of any people. The Seri think that "the brightest virtue is the shedding of alien blood, while the blackest crime in their calendar is alien conjugal union." Perhaps nine-tenths of all the names given by savage tribes to themselves mean "Men," "The Only Men," or "Men of Man"; that is, We are men, the rest are something else. A recent etymology of the word Iroquois makes it mean "I am the real man." In general Indians held that they were a favored race, due to a special creation. Nansen gives a letter written by an Eskimo in 1756 when he heard of the war between England and France. He burst into a rhapsody about Greenland. "Your unfruitfulness makes us happy and saves us from molestation." The writer was surprised that the Christians had not learned better manners amongst the Eskimo, and he proposed to send missionaries to them. A traveler in Formosa says that the Formosans thought foreigners barbarians, "civilization being solely within the dominion of the Celestial Emperor. All the rest of the world—if there was any poor remainder—was benighted, and but the home of 'barbarians,' not 'men.' " This is the language of ethnocentrism; it may be read in the newspapers of any civilized country to-day.

We find then that there are two sentiments in the minds of the same men at the same time. These have been called militancy and industrialism. The latter term does not seem to be a good one and it is not apt until we reach high civilization; what we want is a term to express the peace sentiment in antithesis to militancy, but industrialism has obtained currency and it has this much justification, even for savage life, that, inside the group, the needs of life must be provided for by productive labor. Generally that is left to the women and the men practice militarism.

It would not be possible for neighboring groups to remain really isolated from each other. One has in its territory stone or salt, water or fuel, limited fruits, melons, nuts, fish, or perhaps other natural materials which the others need. They also take wives from each other, generally, but now always. Hence arise treaties of *commercium* and *connubium*, which bring about a middle state of things between war and peace. These treaties are the origin of international law. A comparison of modern municipal and international law will show that the difference between the relations of members of the in-group with each other, and of the groups with each other, still exists.

If now we turn back to the question with which I started, whether men began in a state of peace or a state of war, we see the answer. They began with both together. Which preponderated is a question of the intensity of the competition of life at the time. When that competition was intense, war was frequent and fierce, the weaker were exterminated or absorbed by the stronger, the internal discipline of the conquerors became stronger, chiefs got more absolute power, laws became more stringent, religious observances won greater authority, and so the whole societal system was more firmly integrated. On the other hand, when there were no close or powerful neighbors, there was little or no war, the internal organization remained lax and feeble, chiefs had little power, and a societal system scarcely existed.

The four great motives which move men to social activity are hunger, love, vanity, and fear of superior powers. If we search out the causes which have moved men to war we find them under each of these motives or interests. Men have fought for hunting grounds, for supplies which are locally limited and may be monopolized, for commerce, for slaves, and probably also for human flesh. These motives come under hunger, or the food-quest, or more widely under the economic effort to win subsistence. They have fought for and on account of women, which we must put partly under love, although the women were wanted chiefly as laborers and so, along with the slaves, would come under the former head. They have fought to win heads, or scalps, or other trophies, and for honor or dignity, or purely for glory; this comes under the operation of vanity. They have fought for blood revenge, to prevent or punish sorcery, and to please their gods; these motives belong under the fear of superior powers. It was reserved for modern civilized men to fight on account of differences of religion, and from this motive the fiercest and most persistent wars have been waged.

Is there anything grand or noble in any of these motives of war? Not a bit. But we must remember that the motives from which men act have nothing at all to do with the consequences of their action. Where will you find in history a case of a great purpose rationally adopted by a great society and carried through to the intended result and then followed by the expected consequences in the way of social advantage? You can find no such thing. Men act from immediate and interested motives like these for which they have waged war, and the consequences come out of the forces which are set loose. The consequences may be advantageous or disadvantageous to men. The story of these acts and consequences makes up human history. So it has been with war. While men were fighting for glory and greed, for revenge and superstition, they were building human society. They were acquiring discipline and cohesion; they were learning cooperation, perseverance, fortitude, and patience. Those are not savage virtues; they are products of education. War forms larger social units and produces states; of the North American Indians, those had the intensest feeling of unity who were the most warlike. The Netherlands form a striking example in modern history of the weakness of a state which is internally divided; the best historian of Dutch civilization tells us that the internal disintegration was always greatest in times of truce or of peace. There can be no doubt that the Germans of to-day owe their preeminence in industry and science to the fact that they are a highly disciplined nation. A Portuguese sociologist says that "War is the living fountain from which flows the entire society." If we fix our minds on the organic growth and organization of society, this assertion is not exaggerated. An American sociologist says that "in spite of the countless miseries which follow in its train, war has probably been the highest stimulus to racial progress. It is the most potent excitant known to all the faculties." The great conquests have destroyed what was effete and opened the way for what was viable. What appalls us, however, is the frightful waste of this process of evolution by war— waste of life and waste of capital. It is this waste which has made the evolution of civilization so slow.

Here, then, let us turn back and see how the peace-element develops alongside the war-element. We shall find that peace-rules and peace-institutions have been established, from the earliest civilization, even for the relations of groups with each other. House-peace is perhaps the simplest form. The nature-people very often bury a man under his own fireplace, and from this usage radiate various customs, all of which go to associate the ghosts of the dead with the hearthstone of the living. It follows that quarreling, brawling, or violence near the hearth is an insult to the ghosts. Hence arises a notion of religious sacredness about the hearth an atmosphere of peace is created, and the women who live in the house and work at the hearth profit by it. The house-holder has a dignity and prerogative in his house, however humble his social position may be; hence the maxim that a man's house is his castle goes back to the beginning of civilization. It may be only a wind-shelter, but the ghosts protect it; and any stranger, fugitive, suppliant, even an enemy, if admitted, comes under the house protection and hospitality while there. As the house becomes larger and better the peace-taboo extends from the fireplace to the whole house and then to the yard or enclosure. This is the house-peace.

If any group which possesses deposits of salt, flint-stone fit for implements, pipe-stone, water supply, or special foods should try to prevent others from having access to the same, all others would join in war against that one until an agreement was made and established by usage. This agreement is either one of peaceful access to natural supplies or one of trade. Tribes also agree to take wives from each other. We often have reason to be astonished at the institution-making power of nature-men when disagreeable experience has forced them to find relief. The Tubu of the Sahara are warlike and distrustful even of each other to such an extent that they scarcely form a society; even in their villages they quarrel and fight. It is a very noteworthy feature that these people have no notion of rights. It is the in-group as a peace-group which is the school of rights; as we have seen there can be peace and order inside only by law (using this term in its broadest sense); but a law creates and enforces rights. Now these Tubu have been forced to make a law that inside the village no weapons may be worn, so that here already we find an institutional arrangement to limit warlikeness. When Nachtigal, visiting the Tubu, complained of their ill usage of himself and threatened to go away, they pointed out to him that as soon as he had left their territory he would be at their mercy. This shows that even they had an idea of some rights of a guest inside their group as compared with his status outside, when he would be protected by nothing. The Beduin have the same notion. They are ruthless robbers and murderers, but a guest in the tent is perfectly safe and entitled to their best hospitality. When he leaves it he is fair game, whether enemy, friend, or neighbor.

The West-Australians have a usage that any man who has committed a wrong according to their code must submit to a flight of spears from all who think themselves aggrieved, or he must allow a spear to be thrust through his leg or arm. There is a tariff of wounds as penalties for all common crimes. We understand that this is an in-group usage. It is a common custom in Australia that a man who has stolen a wife from an out-group must submit to a flight of spears from her group-comrades; this is now only a ceremony, but it is a peace-institution which has set aside old warfare on account of stolen women. As we have seen, the Australians live in very small groups, but they assemble from time to time in large kin-groups for purposes of festivals of a religious character. The kin-groups are not peace-groups, because they are loose and have no common life. At the assemblies all the sacred objects are brought into the ceremonial ground, but on account of the danger of quarrels, no display of arms is allowed anywhere near the sacred objects. Bearers of messages from one tribe to another are regarded as under a peace-taboo in eastern Australia; women are under a peace-taboo and hence are employed as ambassadors to arrange disputes between tribes. After a quarrel there is a corroboree, to make and confirm peace. These usages are institutional. They are positive rules of an arbitrary character, depending upon agreement and usage, but are devised to satisfy expediency. In Queensland no fighting at all is allowed at night in camp; those who want to fight must go outside, and after a fight the victor must show to his comrades that he had a real grievance. If he does not convince them of this they force him to submit to the same mutilation from his victim that he has inflicted. The women fight with their yam-sticks, which are about four feet long. One woman allows the other to strike her on the head; the second must then submit to a blow; thus they go on until one does not want any more. What we have to notice here is that the fight, inside the group, is under regulations, which fact makes it institutional. The duel is a similar case of a conventionalized fight in the midst of a peaceful civil order. In all these cases we see that war is admitted inside of a peace-group when individuals are wronged or offended by comrades, but only in conventionalized and regulated form, so that it is a kind of lawful war.

We also find war between groups under some regulation and conventionalization when there is a bond of kinship or religion uniting the two groups. It appears that this is the origin of the rules of war by which its horrors are reduced. On the island of Tanna in the New Hebrides the eight thousand inhabitants are divided into two groups, one at each end of the island, and each group is subdivided into villages. If two villages in the same division fight, as they often do, the fighting is not intense and there is no cannibalism; but between the two big divisions there is blood revenge, and if they fight there is no limit to the ferocity, cannibalism being then practiced. On the Mortlock Islands when two tribes go to war each warrior must select as his antagonist on the other side one who is not in the same kin-group with himself. Amongst certain Sumatrans if a man of one village has a grievance against a man of another, the men of the former go into the fields of the other, where they are met by the local chief, who asks their errand. They answer that they have come to destroy the plantation of the man in the village who has injured a man of theirs. The chief admits that this is just, but proposes to avoid violence; so he brings to them fruit from the plantation of the offender and, if the offense was great, he allows them to destroy a certain number of trees on it. They also burn down the offender's house "ceremonially"—a little hut is built of light material on his field and with triumphant cries is set on fire by the offended party. Generally an agreement is reached, but if not, long hostilities endure between two neighboring villages.

The Christian states have always professed to moderate somewhat the horrors of war when they went to fighting with each other, and so we have laws of war which are good between the states agreeing to them, but not with outsiders. This makes a limited peace-group of all the states which unite now to make international law. Let us follow these peace-institutions up into higher civilization.

The Scandinavian people spread in small bodies over their territory, and these bodies often engaged in war with each other. They had a common sanctuary at Upsala at which there were annual festivals. This religious bond kept up a certain sense of national unity, which, however, has never produced national sympathy. At the festivals at Upsala peace was enforced for the time and place; disputes were settled and fairs held, and there were also feasts and conferences. The Swedes in the thirteenth century formed kin-groups which adopted rules of mutual succor and defense. The dwellings of kings also came to have in so far the character of sanctuaries that peace was maintained around them. The ancient Germans maintained by law and severe penalties peace for women as to person and property; the penalties for wrong to a woman varied in the laws of the different German nations, but were two or three times as great as for wrongs to men. The house-peace was also very fully developed in German law. The Peace of God was perhaps the most remarkable case in history of a law to establish a time-taboo against war and violence. In the tenth century the church tried to curb the robber barons and to protect merchants; the attempts were often repeated with little result, but the "Truce of God" was at last established in 1041 by the Bishop of Arles and the Abbot of Cluny, and it won some acceptance throughout France. There was to be no fighting between Wednesday evening and Monday morning; later these limits were changed. No such law was ever obeyed with any precision and it never became a custom, much less an institution, but it had some influence. As the kings gained real power and prestige in the feudal states they made the king's peace a great reality; it went with the development of the modern state. The king's peace was a name for a central civil authority which could put down all private war and violations of public order and establish a peace-group over a great extent of territory, within which rights, law, and civil authority should be secured by competent tribunals. In the Holy Roman Empire of the German nation the public general peace of the empire was introduced in 1495, but the emperors never had the means to enforce it, and it did not exist until 1873. We can see how the king's peace grew by the following case: Canute the Dane made a law in England that, if any unknown man was found dead, he should be assumed to be a Dane and a special tax, called *murdrum*, should be paid for him to the king. William the Conqueror followed this example, only the unknown man was assumed to be a Norman; if it could be proved that he was an Englishman ("proving his Englishry") then the murderer or the hundred had nothing to pay to the king but only the legal compensation to the family of the deceased, if he had one. This means that the king first extended his peace over his own countrymen by a special penalty on the murder of one of them, while Englishmen were left only under the old law of composition for blood revenge; but in time equal protection was extended to all his subjects. Again, at the time of the Conquest all crimes committed on the roads which ran through a city (Canterbury, for instance) were crimes against the king's peace—which also extended one league, three perches, and three feet beyond the city gate. This means that the high roads which ran through a town were first brought under the king's peace, and this peace also extended beyond the royal burgh for an extent which was measured with droll accuracy. What was a crime elsewhere was a greater crime there, and what was not a crime elsewhere might be a crime there. King Edmund forbade blood revenge in his burgh; that is, he delimited an in-group in which there must be law and an administration of justice by his tribunal; Jews and merchants bought the protection of the king's peace throughout his realm. From this germ grew up the state as a peace-group and the king's peace as the law of the land; we Americans call it the peace of the people.

One of the most remarkable examples of a peace-group which could be mentioned is the League of the Iroquois which was formed in the sixteenth century; it deserves to be classed here with the peace-institutions of civilized states. This league was a confederation of five, afterwards six tribes of Indians, to maintain peace. By Indian usage blood revenge was a duty; but the Iroquois confederation put a stop to this, as between its members, by substituting laws and civil authority.

It was, for its stage, fully as marvelous a production of statesmanship as are these United States—themselves a great peace-confederation. Compared with Algonkins and Sioux the Iroquois were an industrial society. They tried to force others to join the confederacy—that is, to come into the peace-pact or to make an alliance with it; if they would do neither, war arose and the outside people was either exterminated or absorbed. Hiawatha was the culture-hero to whom the formation of the league was attributed. The constitution was held in memory by strings of wampum, and at annual festivals there were confessions and exhortations. The duties inculcated were those of a warrior towards outsiders and of tribal brotherhood towards insiders. "The duty of living in harmony and peace, of avoiding evil-speaking, of kindness to the orphan, of charity to the needy and of hospitality to all, would be among the prominent topics brought under consideration" at the annual assemblies.

We have now found a peace of the house, of the sanctuary, of religion, of the market, of women, of the popular assembly, and of the king, all of which were legal and institutional checks upon war and an introduction of rational and moral methods in the place of force. Let us see next what has been the relation between religion on the one side and peace or war on the other.

Those who perform the rites of worship towards the same ancestors or the same gods come into the same cult-group, but no religion has ever succeeded in making its cult-group into a peace-group, although they all try to do it. The salutation of members of a cult-group to each other is very generally "Peace," or something equivalent. Quakers call themselves "Friends" and always have a closer bond to each other than to the outside world. Such a peace-group is only an ideal for all who profess the same religion; in most of the great religions down to the seventeenth century, dissenters or heretics were always treated with great severity, because it was thought that they would bring down the wrath of the ghost or the god not only on themselves but also on the whole community. The New England Puritans had this notion that the sins of some would bring down the wrath of God on the whole. Religion has always intensified ethnocentrism; the adherents of a religion always think themselves the chosen people or else they think that their god is superior to all others, which amounts to the same thing. The Jews looked down upon all non-Jews as Gentiles; the Mohammedans despise all infidels— their attitude towards non-Mussulmans is one leading to aggression, plunder, and annihilation. The Greeks looked down on all non-Greeks as barbarians, but in their case the sentiment was only partly religious;

they themselves were never united by their own religion. In the thirteenth and fourteenth centuries, when Mohammedanism threatened to overwhelm Christendom, Latin Christians were inflamed with greater rage against Greek Christians than against Mohammedans. Nicholas V in 1452 gave to Alfonso V of Portugal authority to subjugate any non-Christians, having in view especially people of the west coast of Africa, and to reduce them to servitude (*illorum personas in servitutem*), which probably did not mean slavery, but subjection. The Spaniards and Portuguese of the sixteenth century treated all aborigines with ruthlessness because the aborigines were outside of Christianity and entitled to no rights or consideration. When the American colonies revolted, the English were amazed that the colonists could ally themselves with Frenchmen against the mother-country, although the French were Roman Catholics in religion, absolutists in the state, and of an alien nationality. Buddhism is characterized by a pervading peacefulness, but no religion has ever kept its adherents from fighting each other. The instances which have been cited suffice to show that religion has been quite as much a stimulus to war as to peace; and religious wars are proverbial for ruthlessness and ferocity.

Christianity has always contained an ideal of itself as a peace-group. The mediaeval church tried to unite all Christendom into a cult- and peace-group which should reach over all the disintegration and war of the feudal period. This was the sense of mediaeval Catholicity. Churches, convents, and ecclesiastical persons were put under a peace-taboo. The church, however, at the same time, entered into an alliance with the feudal nobles and adopted militant methods; heretics were dealt with as outside the fold. The modern state, as it began to take definite form, entered into a contest with the church for the control of society and for the guardianship of peace, because the church had failed to secure peace.

The United States presents us a case quite by itself. We have here a confederated state which is a grand peace-group. It occupies the heart of a continent; therefore there can be no question of balance of power here and no need of war preparations such as now impoverish Europe. The United States is a new country with a sparse population and no strong neighbors. Such a state will be a democracy and a republic, and it will be "free" in almost any sense that its people choose. If this state becomes militant, it will be because its people choose to become such; it will be because they think that war and warlikeness are desirable in themselves and are worth going after. On their own continent they need never encounter war on their path of industrial and political development up to any standard which they choose to adopt. It is a very remarkable fact, and one which has had immense influence on the history of civilization, that the land of the globe is divided into two great sections, the mass of Europe, Asia, and Africa on the one side and these two Americas on the other, and that one of these worlds remained unknown to the other until only four hundred years ago. We talk a great deal about progress and modern enlightenment and democracy and the happiness of the masses, but very few people seem to know to what a great extent all those things are consequences of the discovery of the new world. As to this matter of war which we are now considering, the fact that the new world is removed to such a distance from the old world made it possible for men to make a new start here. It was possible to break old traditions, to revise institutions, and to think out a new philosophy to fit an infant society, at the same time that whatever there was in the inheritance from the old world which seemed good and available might be kept. It was a marvelous opportunity; to the student of history and human institutions it seems incredible that it ever could have been offered. The men who founded this republic recognized that opportunity and tried to use it. It is we who are now here who have thrown it away; we have decided that instead of working out the advantages of it by peace, simplicity, domestic happiness, industry and thrift, we would rather do it in the old way by war and glory, alternate victory and calamity, adventurous enterprises, grand finance, powerful government, and great social contrasts of splendor and misery. Future ages will look back to us with amazement and reproach that we should have made such a choice in the face of such an opportunity and should have entailed on them the consequences—for the opportunity will never come again.

Some illustration of our subject has, however, been furnished by the internal history of our peace-group. The aborigines of this continent have never been taken into our peace-bond, and our law about them is, consequently, full of inconsistencies. Sometimes they have been treated as comrades in the in-group; sometimes as an out-group with which our group was on a footing of hostility. Another question seems to be arising with respect to the negroes; we have been trying, since the Civil War, to absorb them into our peace-bond, but we have not succeeded. They are in it and not of it now, as much as, or more than, in the days of slavery, for the two races live more independently of each other now than they did in those former days. The Southern States do not constitute true societies because they lack unity of interest and sentiment, on account of the race difference which divides them. This discord may prove worse and more fatal to the internal integrity of the peace-group than such old antagonisms of interest as disturb Ireland, the national antagonisms which agitate Austria-Hungary, or the religious antagonisms which distract Belgium. In short, a state needs to be a true peace-group in which there is sufficient concord and sympathy to overcome the antagonisms of nationality, race, class, etc., and in which are maintained institutions adequate to adjust interests and control passions. Before even the great civilized states have reached this model, there is yet much to be done.

If we look at these facts about peace-laws and institutions and the formation of peace-groups in connection with the facts previously presented about the causes of war and the taste for war, we see that militancy and peacefulness have existed side by side in human society from the beginning just as they exist now. A peaceful society must be industrial because it must produce instead of plundering; it is for this reason that the industrial type of society is the opposite of the militant type. In any state on the continent of Europe to-day these two types of societal organization may be seen interwoven with each other and fighting each other. Industrialism builds up; militancy wastes. If a railroad is built, trade and intercourse indicate a line on which it ought to run; military strategy, however, overrules this and requires that it run otherwise. Then all the interests of trade and intercourse must be subjected to constant delay and expense because the line does not conform to them. Not a discovery of invention is made but the war and navy bureaus of all the great nations seize it to see what use can be made of it in war. It is evident that men love war; when two hundred thousand men in the United States volunteer in a month for a war with Spain which appeals to no sense of wrong against their country, and to no other strong sentiment of human nature, when their lives are by no means monotonous or destitute of interest, and where life offers chances of wealth and prosperity, the pure love of adventure and war must be strong in our population. Europeans who have to do military service have no such enthusiasm for war as war. The presence of such a sentiment in the midst of the most purely industrial state in the world is a wonderful phenomenon. At the same time the social philosophy of the modern civilized world is saturated with humanitarianism and flabby sentimentalism. The humanitarianism is in the literature; by it the reading public is led to suppose that the world is advancing along some line which they call "progress" towards peace and brotherly love. Nothing could be more mistaken. We read of fist-law and constant war in the Middle Ages and think that life must have been full of conflicts and bloodshed then; but modern warfare bears down on the whole population with a frightful weight through all the years of peace. Never, from the day of barbarism down to our own time, has every man in a society been a soldier until now; and the armaments of to-day are immensely more costly than ever before. There is only one limit possible to the war preparations of a modern European state; that is, the last man and the last dollar it can control. What will come of the mixture of sentimental social philosophy and warlike policy? There is only one thing rationally to be expected, and that is a frightful effusion of blood in revolution and war during the century now opening.

It is said that there are important offsets to all the burden and harm of this exaggerated militancy. That is true. Institutions and customs in human society are never either all good or all bad. We cannot adopt either peacefulness or warlikeness as a sole true philosophy. Military discipline educates; military interest awakens all the powers of men, so that they are eager to win and their ingenuity is quickened to invent new and better weapons. In history the military inventions have led the way and have been afterwards applied to industry. Chemical inventions were made in the attempt to produce combinations which would be destructive in war; we owe some of our most useful substances to discoveries which were made in this effort. The skill of artisans has been developed in making weapons, and then that skill has been available for industry. The only big machines which the ancients ever made were battering-rams, catapults, and other engines of war. The construction of these things familiarized men with mechanical devices which were capable of universal application. Gunpowder was discovered in the attempt to rediscover Greek fire; it was a grand invention in military art but we should never have had our canals, railroads, and other great works without such explosives. Again, we are indebted to the chemical experiments in search of military agents for our friction matches.

War also develops societal organization; it produces political institutions and classes. In the past these institutions and classes have been attended by oppression and by the exploitation of man by man; nevertheless, the more highly organized society has produced gains for all its members, including the oppressed or their posterity. The social exploitation is not essential to the organization, and it may be prevented by better provisions. In long periods of peace the whole societal structure becomes fixed in its adjustments and the functions all run into routine.

Vested interests get an established control; some classes secure privileges and establish precedents, while other classes form habits of acquiescence. Traditions acquire a sacred character and philosophical doctrines are taught in churches and schools which make existing customs seem to be the "external order of nature." It becomes impossible to find a standing-ground from which to attack abuses and organize reform. Such was the case in France in the eighteenth century. By war new social powers break their way and create a new order. The student is tempted to think that even a great social convulsion is worth all it costs. What other force could break the bonds and open the way? But that is not the correct inference, because war and revolution never produce what is wanted, but only some mixture of the old evils with new ones; what is wanted is a peaceful and rational solution of problems and situations—but that requires great statesmanship and great popular sense and virtue. In the past the work has been done by war and revolution, with haphazard results and great attendant evils. To take an example from our own history: the banking and currency system of the United States, in 1860, was at a deadlock; we owe the national bank system, which was a grand reform of currency and banking, to the Civil War. It is impossible to see how else we could have overcome the vested interests and could have extricated ourselves from our position. It was no purpose of the war to reform the currency, but it gave an incidental opportunity and we had to win from it what we could.

There is another effect of war which is less obvious but more important. During a period of peace, rest, and routine, powers are developed which are in reality societal variations, among which a certain societal selection should take place. Here comes in the immense benefit of real liberty, because, if there is real liberty, a natural selection results; but if there is social prejudice, monopoly, privilege, orthodoxy, tradition, popular delusion, or any other restraint on liberty, selection does not occur. War operates a rude and imperfect selection. Our Civil War may serve as an example; think of the public men who were set aside by it and of the others who were brought forward by it, and compare them in character and ideas. Think of the doctrines which were set aside as false, and of the others which were established as true; also of the constitutional principles which were permanently stamped as heretical or orthodox. As a simple example, compare the position and authority of the president of the United States as it was before and as it has been since the Civil War. The Germans tell of the ruthless and cruel acts of Napoleon in Germany, and all that they say is true; but he did greater services to

Germany than any other man who can be mentioned. He tore down the relics of mediaevalism and set the powers of the nation to some extent free from the fetters of tradition; we do not see what else could have done it. It took another war in 1870 to root out the traditional institutions and make way for the new ones. Of course the whole national life responded to this selection. The Roman state was a selfish and pitiless subjugation of all the rest of mankind. It was built on slavery, it cost inconceivable blood and tears, and it was a grand system of extortion and plunder, but it gave security and peace under which the productive powers of the provinces expanded and grew. The Roman state gave discipline and organization and it devised institutions; the modern world has inherited societal elements from it which are invaluable. One of the silliest enthusiasms which ever got control of the minds of a great body of men was the Crusades, but the Crusades initiated a breaking up of the stagnation of the Dark Ages and an emancipation of the social forces of Europe. They exerted a selective effect to destroy what was barbaric and deadening and to foster what had new hope in it by furnishing a stimulus to thought and knowledge.

A society needs to have a ferment in it; sometimes an enthusiastic delusion or an adventurous folly answers the purpose. In the modern world the ferment is furnished by economic opportunity and hope of luxury. In other ages it has often been furnished by war. Therefore some social philosophers have maintained that the best course of human affairs is an alternation of peace and war. Some of them also argue that the only unity of the human race which can ever come about must be realized from the survival of the fittest in a war of weapons, in a conflict of usages, and in a rivalry issuing in adaptability to the industrial organization. It is not probable that aborigines will ever in the future be massacred in masses, as they have been in the past, but the case is even worse when, like our Indians for instance, they are set before a fatal dilemma. They cannot any longer live in their old way; they must learn to live by unskilled labor or by the mechanic arts. This, then, is the dilemma: to enter into the civilized industrial organization or to die out. If it had been possible for men to sit still in peace without civilization, they never would have achieved civilization; it is the iron spur of the nature-process which has forced them on, and one form of the nature-process has been the attack of some men upon others who are weaker than they.

We find, then, that in the past as a matter of fact war has played a great part in the irrational nature-process by which things have come to pass.

But the nature-processes are frightful; they contain no allowance for the feelings and interests of individuals—for it is only individuals who have feelings and interests. The nature-elements never suffer and they never pity. If we are terrified at the nature-processes there is only one way to escape them; it is the way by which men have always evaded them to some extent; it is by knowledge, by rational methods, and by the arts. The facts which have been presented about the functions of war in the past are not flattering to the human reason or conscience. They seem to show that we are as much indebted for our welfare to base passion as to noble and intelligent endeavor. At the present moment things do not look much better. We talk of civilizing lower races, but we never have done it yet; we have exterminated them. Our devices for civilizing them have been as disastrous to them as our firearms. At the beginning of the twentieth century the great civilized nations are making haste, in the utmost jealousy of each other, to seize upon all the outlying parts of the globe; they are vying with each other in the construction of navies by which each may defend its share against the others. What will happen? As they are preparing for war they certainly will have war, and their methods of colonization and exploitation will destroy the aborigines. In this way the human race will be civilized—but by the extermination of the uncivilized—unless the men of the twentieth century can devise plans for dealing with aborigines which are better than any which have yet been devised. No one has yet found any way in which two races, far apart in blood and culture, can be amalgamated into one society with satisfaction to both. Plainly, in this matter which lies in the immediate future, the only alternatives to force and bloodshed are more knowledge and more reason.

Shall any statesman, therefore, ever dare to say that it would be well, at a given moment, to have a war, lest the nation fall into the vices of industrialism and the evils of peace? The answer is plainly: No! War is never a handy remedy, which can be taken up and applied by routine rule. No war which can be avoided is just to the people who have to carry it on, to say nothing of the enemy. War is like other evils; it must be met when it is unavoidable, and such gain as can be got from it must be won. In the forum of reason and deliberation war never can be anything but a makeshift, to be regretted; it is the task of the statesman to find rational means to the same end. A statesman who proposes war as an instrumentality admits his incompetency; a politician who makes use of war as a counter in the game of parties is a criminal.

Can peace be universal? There is no reason to believe it. It is a fallacy to suppose that by widening the peace-group more and more it can at last embrace all mankind. What happens is that, as it grows bigger, differences, discords, antagonisms, and war begin inside of it on account of the divergence of interests. Since evil passions are a part of human nature and are in all societies all the time, a part of the energy of the society is constantly spent in repressing them. If all nations should resolve to have no armed ships any more, pirates would reappear upon the ocean; the police of the seas must be maintained. We could not dispense with our militia; we have too frequent need of it now. But police defense is not war in the sense in which I have been discussing it. War, in the future will be the clash of policies of national vanity and selfishness when they cross each other's path.

If you want war, nourish a doctrine. Doctrines are the most frightful tyrants to which men ever are subject, because doctrines get inside a man's own reason and betray him against himself. Civilized men have done their fiercest fighting for doctrines. The reconquest of the Holy Sepulcher, "the balance of power," "no universal dominion," "trade follows the flag," "he who holds the land will hold the sea," "the throne and the altar," the revolution, the faith—these are the things for which men have given their lives. What are they all? Nothing but rhetoric and phantasms. Doctrines are always vague; it would ruin a doctrine to define it, because then it could be analyzed, tested, criticized, and verified; but nothing ought to be tolerated which cannot be so tested. Somebody asks you with astonishment and horror whether you do not believe in the Monroe Doctrine. You do not know whether you do or not, because you do not know what it is; but you do not dare to say that you do not, because you understand that it is one of the things which every good American is bound to believe in. Now when any doctrine arrives at that degree of authority, the name of it is a club which any demagogue may swing over you at any time and apropos of anything. In order to describe a doctrine we must have recourse to theological language. A doctrine is an article of faith. It is something which you are bound to believe, not because you have some rational grounds for believing it true, but because you belong to such and such a church or denomination. The nearest parallel to it in politics is the "reason of state." The most frightful injustice and cruelty which has ever been perpetrated on earth has been due to the reason of state. Jesus Christ was put to death for the reason of state; Pilate said that he found no fault in the accused, but he wanted to keep the Jews quiet and one man crucified more or less was of no consequence. None of these metaphysics ought to be tolerated in a free state. A policy in a state we can understand; for instance it was the policy of the United States at the end of the eighteenth century to get the free navigation of the Mississippi to its mouth, even at the expense of war with Spain. That policy had reason and justice in it; it was founded in our interests; it had positive form and definite scope. A doctrine is an abstract principle; it is necessarily absolute in its scope and abstruse in its terms; it is a metaphysical assertion. It is never true, because it is absolute, and the affairs of men are all conditioned and relative. The physicists tell us now that there are phenomena which appear to present exceptions to gravitation which can be explained only by conceiving that gravitation requires time to get to work. We are convinced that perpetual motion is absolutely impossible within the world of our experiences, but it now appears that our universe taken as a whole is a case of perpetual motion.

Now, to turn back to politics, just think what an abomination in statecraft an abstract doctrine must be. Any politician or editor can, at any moment, put a new extension on it. The people acquiesce in the doctrine and applaud it because they hear the politicians and editors repeat it, and the politicians and editors repeat it because they think it is popular. So it grows. During the recent difficulty between England and Germany on one side and Venezuela on the other, some newspapers here began to promulgate a new doctrine that no country ought to be allowed to use its naval force to collect private debts. This doctrine would have given us standing-ground for interference in that quarrel. That is what it was invented for. Of course it was absurd and ridiculous, and it fell dead unnoticed, but it well showed the danger of having a doctrine lying loose about the house, and one which carries with it big consequences. It may mean anything or nothing, at any moment, and no one knows how it will be. You accede to it now, with the vague limits of what you suppose it to be; therefore you will have to accede to it to-morrow when the same name is made to cover something which you never have heard or thought of. If you allow a political catchword to go on and grow, you will awaken some day to find it standing over you, the arbiter of your destiny, against which you are powerless, as men are powerless against delusions.

The process by which such catchwords grow is the old popular mythologizing. Your Monroe Doctrine becomes an entity, a being, a lesser kind of divinity, entitled to reverence and possessed of prestige, so that it allows of no discussion or deliberation. The President of the United States talks about the Monroe Doctrine and he tells us solemnly that it is true and sacred, whatever it is. He even undertakes to give some definition of what he means by it; but the definition which he gives binds nobody, either now or in the future, any more than what Monroe and Adams meant by it binds anybody now not to mean anything else. He says that, on account of the doctrine, whatever it may be, we must have a big navy. In this, at least, he is plainly in the right; if we have the doctrine, we shall need a big navy. The Monroe Doctrine is an exercise of authority by the United States over a controversy between two foreign states, if one of them is in America, combined with a refusal of the United States to accept any responsibility in connection with the controversy. That is a position which is sure to bring us into collision with other States, especially because it will touch their vanity, or what they call their honor—or it will touch our vanity, or what we call our honor, if we should ever find ourselves called upon to "back down" from it. Therefore it is very true that we must expect to need a big navy if we adhere to the doctrine. What can be more contrary to sound statesmanship and common sense than to put forth an abstract assertion which has no definite relation to any interest of ours now at stake, but which has in it any number of possibilities of producing complications which we cannot foresee, but which are sure to be embarrassing when they arise!

What has just been said suggests a consideration of the popular saying, "In time of peace prepare for war." If you prepare a big army and navy and are all ready for war, it will be easy to go to war; the military and naval men will have a lot of new machines and they will be eager to see what they can do with them. There is no such thing nowadays as a state of readiness for war. It is a chimera, and the nations which pursue it are falling into an abyss of wasted energy and wealth. When the army is supplied with the latest and best rifles, someone invents a new field gun; then the artillery must be provided with that before we are ready. By the time we get the new gun, somebody has invented a new rifle and our rival nation is getting that; therefore we must have it, or one a little better. It takes two or three years and several millions to do that. In the meantime somebody proposes a more effective organization which must be introduced; signals, balloons, dogs, bicycles, and every other device and invention must be added, and men must be trained to use them all. There is no state of readiness for war; the notion calls for never-ending sacrifices. It is a fallacy. It is evident that to pursue such a motion with any idea of realizing it would absorb all the resources and activity of the state; this the great European states are now proving by experiment. A wiser rule would be to make up your mind soberly what you want, peace or war, and then to get ready for what you want; for what we prepare for is what we shall get.

# VI

## Sociologist

# Purposes and Consequences

Crucial to the development of a behavioristic or objectivist perspective in social science was a view of human activity as a response to stimuli and the conviction that "behavior" could be considered apart from "intentions." Foreshadowing this development, Sumner's divorce of the "purposes" and "consequences" of public policy revealed the role of his disillusionment over American imperialism and domestic politics in shaping this outlook. Manuscript ca. 1900–1906, reprinted in *Earth Hunger*, ed. Albert Galloway Keller, pp. 67–75.

The observation that motives and purposes have nothing to do with consequences is a criterion for distinguishing between the science of society and the views, whims, ideals, and fads which are current in regard to social matters, but especially for distinguishing between socialism and sociology. Motives and purposes are in the brain and heart of man. Consequences are in the world of fact. The former are infected by the human ignorance, folly, self-deception, and passion; the latter are sequences of cause and effect dependent upon the nature of the forces at work. When, therefore, a man acts, he sets forces in motion, and the consequences are such as those forces produce under the conditions existing. They are entirely independent of any notion, will, wish, or intention in the mind of any man or men. Consequences are facts in the world of experience. If one man discharges a gun at another and kills him, he may say afterwards that he "did not know that it was loaded." He did not mean to kill. The consequences remain; they are such as follow from the structure of a gun, the nature of explosives, and the relative adjustment of the men and the things. Of course this proposition is so simple and obvious that no demonstration can add to it. Why is there any such thing as wisdom, unless there is a distinction between a correct and an incorrect apprehension of existing conditions and of the effects which certain forces will produce? How could anybody ever make a "mistake" if his purposes would determine the consequences of his acts? Why should we try to get experience of life and to know how to act under given circumstances, unless it is because the causes and effects will follow their own sequences and we, instead of controlling them by our mental operations, are sure to be affected by them in our interests and welfare? Why, in short, is there any need of education if things in this world will follow our motives and purposes— since education aims to inform us of the order of things in this world to which we are subject?

Since consequences are entirely independent of motives and purposes, ethics have no application to consequences. Ethics apply only to motives and purposes. This is why the whole fashion, which is now so popular and which most people think so noble, of mixing ethics into economics and politics, is utterly ignorant and mischievous. All policies are deliberate choices of series of acts; whether we wish good or ill, when we choose our acts, is of no importance. The only important thing is whether we know what the conditions are and what will be the effects of our acts. To act from notions, pious hopes, benevolent intentions, or ideals is sentimentalism, because the mental states and operations lack basis in truth and reality. Policies, therefore, which have not been tested by all the criteria which science provides are not to be discussed at all. Somebody's notion that they would work well and give us a gain, or that there is great need of them, because he thinks he sees a great evil at present, are no grounds of action for sober-minded men. The protective tariff is a case, so far as it is a policy of prosperity. The silver policy which was urged in 1896 and 1900 was another example. We live in the midst of a mass of illustrations of the fact that laws do not produce the consequences which the legislator intended. They give rise to other consequences, such, namely, as the forces which they set in operation, under the conditions which exist, necessarily produce.

Acts of the legislature work on the cupidity, envy, and ambition of men; as soon as a law is passed each man affected by it takes his attitude to it. Mass phenomena result from the concurrent action of many. What results is what must result from the actions, acting as causes, under the conditions; if the actions are of a certain kind, institutions are undermined, men are miseducated, the public conscience is corrupted, false standards are set up; frivolity, idleness, love of pleasure, sycophancy, will become traits of the society. That the legislator intended to promote education, temperance, industry, and purity is entirely aside from the case. In 1899 the press of the United States constantly reiterated the assertion that the motives of the United States in the war with Spain were noble, humanitarian, and ethical, and that it never entered into expectation that the Philippine Islands were to come into our possession. All this was entirely idle; when a war is begun it will run its course and bring its consequences. What the intention was makes no difference.

This, of course, is the reason why no serious statesman will enter upon a war if he can help it, or will ever engage in an adventurous policy, that is, a policy whose course and consequences are not open to his view so far as the utmost training and effort of human reason will enable him to see.

Whenever any policy is adopted, all the consequences of it must be accepted—those which are unwelcome as well as those which are welcome. This works both ways, for there are good consequences of an evil policy as well as bad consequences of a good policy. It is clear, however, that in the adoption of a policy the considerations which should be taken into account are those which are deduced from the conditions existing and from the relations of cause and effect in the world of experience. They are not ethical at all, and the introduction of ethical notions or dogmas can never do anything but obscure the study of the facts and relations which alone should occupy attention.

The explanation of the popular confusion between motives and consequences is easy. We men are daily compelled to act. We cannot desist from activity. Therefore we have to make decisions and go forward. Hence, in our judgment of each other, if the act turns out to have evil consequences, we have to grant excuse and indulgence to each other, if the intention was honest and the motive pure. It is no doubt necessary and right so to do, but that does not affect the reality of the consequences or the suffering and loss attendant upon them. Therefore we turn back to our educational operations, and to science, in order to learn more about the world of fact and the play of forces in it, for what we want is, not to judge or excuse each other, but to avoid suffering and loss.

Here, then, is the great gulf between all the sentimental, ethical, humanitarian, and benevolent views about social matters and the scientific view of the same. The former start out from some mental states or emotions produced by impressions from occurrences; the latter starts out from the desire to know the truth about facts and relations in the world of experience. In all the dictionaries definitions of socialism are given which try to express the sense of socialism in terms of the pious hope or benevolent intention by which socialists claim to be animated. All these definitions appear to be colored by a desire on the part of the persons who made them to give definitions which would be satisfactory to socialists. The definitions are substantially alike. Not one of them contains an idea; that is to say, not one of them expresses a true definition, if by a definition is understood the expression in language of a single complete and well-rounded concept. An aspiration for better

things is common to all philosophies and systems; it is not a definition
of any one. It is a diffused sentiment and nothing more. These definitions, however, are all true to the reality of the case in one respect; they
are all attempts to bring within the compass of a formula what is really
a nebulous state of mind with respect to the phenomena of human society. The only positive characteristic of this state of mind is that it is
one of disapproval and dislike. The suggestion of contrast with some
other phenomena which would be approved and liked is, of course, a
dispersion of thought to the infinite variety of subjective phantasms
which might float in the imagination of an indefinite number of men.
The point is, for the present purpose, that all this belongs on the side of
motives, purposes, hopes, intentions, ideals, and has nothing to do with
realities, forces, laws, consequences, facts, conditions, relations. The
science of society finds its field in exploring the latter; it has nothing at
all to do with the former. This is why it is true, although socialists are
annoyed by the assertion, that socialism is not a subject for discussion
by serious students of the science of society. An economist or sociologist
who discusses socialism is like a physicist who discusses Jules Verne's
novels. He does not prove his own breadth of mind; he proves that he
does not understand the domain of his own vocation.

Poetry and other forms of the fine arts express sentiments, states of
mind, and emotional reactions on experience. As new stimuli they affect
the imagination and produce new states of thought and emotion. For the
greatest part their effect is dissipated and exhausted in these subjective
experiences, not without residual effect on character. As motives of action, these impulses of the emotions produced by artistic devices do not
stand in good repute in the experience of mankind. Why? Because they
contain no knowledge or foresight, and therefore no guarantee of consequences. It belongs to education to train men and women to criticize
and withstand impulses of this class. Pictures of scenes or objects, instead of inciting to action, ought to act upon an educated person as
warnings to distrust the influence to which he is exposed. It is not possible to cross-examine a picture, even if it is a photograph.

A good education would, in a similar manner, teach its pupils to resist
the magnetism of a crowd and the seductions of popularity. When a
crowd, of which one is a member, are enthused with a common sentiment and purpose, it is impossible to resist the influence of it. Hence
the well-known fact that men who act in a crowd often look back later
in astonishment at their own actions; they cannot understand how they
came to participate in the things which were done. Education ought to

train us so that when we are in a crowd which is being swept away by a motive, we should refuse to join, and should instead go away to think over the probable consequences. In like manner popularity, which seems now to be the grand standard of action, is always to be distrusted. "Woe unto you when all men speak well of you." That is the time to take warning that you are probably going astray. It is very smooth and easy to run with the current and it involves no responsibility for the consequences. Who then will consider the consequences? They will come. All our reason, study, science, and education are turned to scorn and ridicule if popularity is a proper and adequate motive of action.

In fact the judgment of probable consequences is the only real and sound ground of action. It is because men have been ignorant of the probable consequences, or have disregarded them, that human history presents such a picture of the devastation and waste of human energy and of the wreck of human hopes. If there is any salvation for the human race from woe and misery it is in knowledge and in training to use knowledge. Every investigation of the world in which we live is an enlargement of our power to judge of probable consequences when cases arise in which we shall be compelled to act. The difference between motives and consequences, therefore, is seen to be a gulf between the most divergent notions of human life and of the way to deal with its problems. It is most essential that all of us who believe in the scientific view of life and its problems should extricate ourselves completely from the trammels of the sentimental view, and should understand the antagonism between them, for the sentimental view has prevailed in the past and we live now in a confusion between the two.

It is a still more positive vice to act from an intention to attain ideals. Ideals are necessarily phantasms. They have no basis in fact. Generally ideals are formed under the stress of difficulty along the hard road of positive endeavor. Then the imagination takes wing and, disregarding conditions and forces, revels in constructions which are not limited by anything. The ideal for mankind would be to have material supplies without limit and without labor and to reproduce without care or responsibility. Minor ideals are but details or fractions which are not worth attention. If ideals have any power or value, it is as easy to use them for the whole as for any part. Dogmatic ideals like perfect liberty, justice, or equality, especially if economic and not political liberty, justice, and equality are meant, can never furnish rational or scientific motives of action or starting-points for rational effort. They never can enter into scientific thinking since they admit of no analysis and can be tested by no canons of truth. They have no footing in reality. Anybody who says that "we want to build a republic of educated labor" is not defining a rational program of action. He is only manufacturing turgid phrases. He who says that the state "ought to balance the motives of interest and benevolence" is not contributing to any sober discussion. He is talking nonsense, since an analysis of "state," "interest," and "benevolence" would cause the proposition to fall into contradictions and absurdities. The vice and fallacy of this way of looking at things is that it assumes that men can by thinking things call them into being; or that men can add by thinking to the existing conditions some element which is not in them. All who talk about the "power of ideas" are more or less under this fallacy. It is a relic of the sympathetic magic of savage men. Serious study of human society shows us that we can never do anything but use and develop the opportunities which are offered to us by the conditions and conjunctures of the moment.

Other motives of action are derived from the authoritative or dogmatic precepts of some sect of philosophy or religion. These are what is commonly called ethics. In the ordinary course of life it is best and is necessary that for most of us, and for all of us most of the time, these current rules of action which are traditional and accepted in our society should be adopted and obeyed. This is true, however, only because it is impossible for nearly all of us to investigate for ourselves and win personal convictions, and it is impossible for any of us to do so except in a few special matters. Nevertheless, all this sets out only in so much clearer light the pre-eminent value of science, because science extends, over the whole domain of human experience, a gradually wider and wider perception of those relations of man to earth and man to man on which human welfare depends. Science is investigation of facts by sound methods, and deduction of inferences by sound processes. The further it goes the more it enlightens us as to consequences which must ensue if acts are executed by which things and men are brought into the relations which science has elucidated. At the present moment civilized society stands at a point in the development of the applications of science to human interests, at which the thing of the highest importance is the subjection of societal phenomena to scientific investigation, together with the elimination of metaphysics from this entire domain.

# The Scientific Attitude of Mind

Late in his career, the philosopher Charles S. Pierce coined the term "pragmaticism" to distance himself from popularizations of pragmatism by William James and others. With similar motive, Sumner adopted the term "societology" as preferable to "sociology" or even "social science." Although he earlier likened the laws of society to those of physics, he continued to waver between contrasting conceptions of science. In one view, science was merely the study of perceived regularities. Scientific truth was thus relative, a necessarily tentative consensus of a community of observers based on available evidence. In the other view, science grasped the reality behind appearances. Its truth was therefore absolute.

In this statement concerning scientific method, Sumner betrayed his still imperfect grasp of this issue. In his path-breaking *The Grammar of Science* (1892), the Englishman Karl Pearson warned scientists not to probe the "real world"—Kant's *Ding an sich*—or to conceptualize experience under the category of causation. A thoroughgoing nominalist, Pearson instead offered a "looser" form of "cause" in statistical correlation. Scientific truth, so viewed, consisted of measurements made by those trained as scientists, not some deeper understanding of an underlying reality. Appearing to accept this view, Sumner at one point argued that the "highest test of truth" lay in the "opinions and methods" of trained observers. But to this he joined the insistence that science's ultimate goal was "knowledge of reality," a legacy of the Baconian realism that permeated his thought. Address to the initiates of the Sigma Xi Society, May 4, 1905; reprinted in *Earth Hunger*, ed. Albert Galloway Keller, pp. 17–28.

I have undertaken the duty of addressing you for a few moments in order to welcome you to this society and also to make some suggestions which seem appropriate to the beginning of your connection with it. What we expect this society to do for you is, that it shall confirm your devotion to true science and help to train you in scientific methods of thought and study.

Let us begin by trying to establish a definite idea of what science is. The current uses of the term are both very strict and very loose or vague. Some people use the term as a collective term for the natural sciences; others define science as orderly knowledge. Professor Karl Pearson, in his Grammar of Science, does not offer any definition of science, but he tells the aim of science and its function.

"The classification of facts and the formation of absolute judgments upon the basis of this classification—judgments independent of the idiosyncrasies of the individual mind—is peculiarly the *scope and method of modern science.* The scientific man has above all things, to strive at self-elimination in his judgments, to provide an argument which is as true for each individual mind as for his own. *The classification of facts, the recognition of their sequence and relative significance is the function of science,* and the habit of forming a judgment upon those facts unbiased by personal feelings is characteristic of what we shall term the scientific frame of mind." These statements we may gladly accept so far as they go, but they are not definitions of science.

I should want to make the definition of science turn upon the *method* employed, and I would propose as a definition: knowledge of reality acquired by methods which are established in the confidence of men whose occupation it is to investigate truth. In Pearson's book, he refers constantly to the opinions and methods of scientific scholars as the highest test of truth. I know of no better one; I know of none which we employ as constantly as we do that one; and so I put it in the definition. I propose to define science as knowledge of reality because "truth" is used in such a variety of senses. I do not know whether it is possible for us ever to arrive at a knowledge of "the truth" in regard to any important matters. I doubt if it is possible. It is not important. It is the pursuit of truth which gives us life, and it is to that pursuit that our loyalty is due.

What seems to me most important is that we should aim to get knowledge of realities, not of phantasms or words. By a phantasm I mean a mental conception which is destitute of foundation in fact, and of relations to the world of the senses. In the Middle Ages all men pursued phantasms; their highest interest was in another world which was a phantasm, and they were anxious about their fate in that world. They tried to provide for it by sacraments and rites which were fantastic in their form, and in their assumed relation to the desired end. They built up a great church corporation and endowed it with a large measure of control of human affairs so that it could provide for welfare in the other world. It had special functions which were fantastic with reference to the end which they were to accomplish because they contained no rational connection between means and ends. All the societal power which the church did not have was given to the Emperor, because in a certain text of Scripture mention was made of "two swords." The historical period was spent in a war between the Pope and the Emperor to see which should rule the other. The Crusades were an attempt to realize a great phantasm. Chivalry and the devotion to women were phantasms. The societal system was unreal; it assumed that men were originally in a state of slavery and that all rights which they had were due to gift from some sovereign. It resulted that only two men in the world, the Pope and the Emperor, had original and independent rights. The relation of classes, parties, and corporations in the society were therefore both loose and complicated. It is amazing to notice the effect of all this attention to unrealities on all the products of the Middle Ages. People had no idea of reality. Their poetry dealt with arbitrary inventions and demanded of the reader that he should accept tiresome conventions and stereotyped forms. They formed ideas of Cathay such as we meet in the *Arabian Nights,* and they were ready to believe that there might be, in Cathay, any animal form which anybody's imagination could conceive, and any kind of a human figure, for instance, one with a countenance on the elbows or the knees. Theologians quarreled about whether Jesus and his disciples abjured property and lived by beggary, and whether the blood which flowed from the side of Jesus remained on earth or was taken up to heaven with him. The most noticeable fact is that all the disputants were ready to go to the stake, or to put the other party to the stake, according as either should prove to have the power. It was the rule of the game as they understood it and played it. It was another striking manifestation of the temper of the times that within a few days after the capture of Antioch, the poets in the several divisions of the successful army began to write the history of the conflict, not according to facts, but each glorifying the great men of his own group by ascribing to them great deeds such as the current poetry ascribed to legendary heroes. What could more strikingly show the absence of any notion of historic reality?

Now, if you compare our world of ideas with that of the Middle Ages, the greatest difference is that we want *reality* beyond everything else. We do not demand the truth because we do not know where or how to get it. We do not want rationalism, because that is only a philosophy, and it has limitations like any other philosophy. We do not demand what is natural or realistic in the philosophical sense, because that would imply a selection of things, in operation all the time, before the things were offered to us. In zoology and anthropology we want to know all forms which really exist, but we have no patience with invented and imaginary forms. In history we do not allow documents to be prepared which will serve a purpose; to us, such documents would have the character of lies. That they would be edifying or patriotic does not

excuse them. Probably modern men have no harder task than the application of the historic sense to cases in those periods of history when
it was not thought wrong to manufacture such documents as one's cause
required.

The modern study of nature has helped to produce this way of looking
at things, and the way of looking at things has made science possible. I
want to have the notion of science built on this thirst for reality, and
respond to it at every point. There may be knowledge of reality whose
utility we do not know, but it would be overbold for any one to say that
any knowledge of reality is useless.

Since our ancestors devoted so much attention to phantasms and left
us piles of big books about them, one great department of science must
be criticism, by which we discern between the true and the false. There
is one historical case of this requirement which always rises before
my mind whenever I think of the need of criticism—that is witch-
persecution. Although the church had a heavy load of blame for this
frightful abuse, yet the jurists were more to blame. As to the church also,
the Protestants, especially the Puritans of Scotland, were as bad as the
Roman Catholics. Witch-persecution is rooted in demonism, which is
the oldest, widest, and most fundamental form of religion. Whenever
religion breaks down there is always produced a revival of demonism.
The developments of it may be traced from early Chaldaea. It was believed that demons and women fell in love and begot offspring. Nightmare, especially in the forms experienced on mountains, led to notions
of midnight rides, and Walpurgis-Nacht assemblies; then the notion of
obscene rites was added. It was believed that witches could provoke
great storms and convulsions of nature; all remarkable instances of calamity or good luck, especially if it affected one or a few, were ascribed
to them. Especially hail-storms and tornadoes, which sometimes destroy
crops over a very limited area, but spare all the rest, were thought to be
their work. It was believed that they could transfer good crops from their
neighbors' fields to their own. Here we see how phantasms grow. The
bulls of popes summed up and affirmed the whole product as fact. Then,
too, all the apparatus of pretended investigation and trial which the
Inquisition had developed was transferred to the witch-trials. As women
chiefly were charged with witchcraft, the result was that all this accumulation of superstition, folly, and cruelty was turned against them. If
we try to form an idea of the amount of suffering which resulted, our
hearts stand still with horror.

Now there are some strong reasons for the faith in witchcraft. Everybody believed that witches existed, that they could enter into contracts with demons, and could get supernatural aid to carry out their purposes in this world. All the accused witches believed this. It was held to be wicked to make use of witches or demons, but it was believed that there were possible ways of accomplishing human purposes by employing them. Consequently when men or women wanted wealth, or office, or honor, or great success, or wanted to inspire love, or to gratify hate, envy, and vengeance, or wanted children or wanted to prevent other people from having children, this way was always supposed to be open. No doubt very many of them tried it, at least in homely and silly ways— when put to the torture they confessed it. Then, too, somnambulism, dreams, and nightmare took forms which ran on the lines of popular superstition, and many a woman charged with witchcraft did not know but she had been guilty of it to some extent and without conscious knowledge. Again, the Scripture argument for demonism and witchcraft was very strong. It was this pitfall which caught the Protestants; how could they deny that there are any witches when the Bible says: "Thou shalt not suffer a witch to live." Witches were persons who had gone over to the side of Satan and his hosts in their war on God; they were enemies of the human race. The deductions from the primary fantastic notion of demons were all derived on direct and indisputable lines, and those deductions ruled the thought of Christian Europe for five hundred years.

What was wanted to put a stop to the folly and wickedness was criticism. The case shows us that we men, including the greatest and best of us, may fall at any time under the dominion of such a mania, unless we are trained in methods of critical thinking. A series of great sceptics from Montaigne to Voltaire met the witch doctrines with scorn and derision. They were not afraid to deny the existence of demons. It appears also that the so-called common-sense of the crowd revolted at the absurdities of witchcraft. Every person who was executed as a witch named, under torture, others, who were then arrested, tortured, and executed; each of these named others, and so the witch-judges found that they were driven on, by judicial execution of the most cruel form, to depopulate a whole territory. It was a critical revolt when they saw this construction of their own conduct and turned against it. When we read the story we are amazed that good and honest men could have gone on for centuries inflicting torture of the extremest kind on old women without the bit of critical reflection which should have led them to ask themselves what they were doing.

Let us not make the mistake of supposing that all follies and manias of this kind are permanently overcome and need not be feared any longer. The roots of popular error are ineradicable; they lie at the bottom of human nature; they can produce new growth and new fruits at any time. In this twentieth century the probable line on which the deductions will be drawn is in politics and civil institutions. The modern world has rejected religious dogmatism, but it has taken up a great mass of political dogmatism, and this dogmatism is intertwined with the interests of groups of men. If you accept the political dogmas of the eighteenth century and begin to build deductions on them you will reach a construction as absurd and false as that of witchcraft. The only security is the constant practice of critical thinking. We ought never to accept fantastic notions of any kind; we ought to pursue all propositions until we find out their connection with reality. That is the fashion of thinking which we call scientific in the deepest and broadest sense of the word. It is, of course, applicable over the whole field of human interests, and the habit of mind which insists on finding realities is the best product of an education which may be properly called scientific. I have no doubt that, in your lifetime, you will see questions arise out of popular notions and faiths, which call for critical thinking such as has never been required before, especially as to social relations, political institutions, and economic interests.

Here I may notice, in passing, the difference between science and religion in regard to the habits of thought which each encourages. No religion ever offers itself except as a complete and final answer to the problems of life. No religion ever offers itself as a tentative solution. A religion cannot say: I am the best solution yet found, but I may be superseded tomorrow by new discoveries. But that is exactly what every science must say. Religions do not pretend to grow; they are born complete and fully correct and our duty in regard to them is to learn them in their integrity. Hence Galton says that "the religious instructor, in every creed, is one who makes it his profession to saturate his pupils with prejudice."

Every science contains the purpose and destiny of growth as one of its distinguishing characteristics; it must always be open to re-examination and must submit to new tests if such are proposed. Consequently the modes and habits of thought developed by the study of science are very different from those developed by the study of religion. This is the real cause, I think, of the antagonism between science and religion which is vaguely felt in modern times, although the interest is lacking which would bring the antagonism into an open conflict. I cannot believe that this attitude will remain constant. I am prepared to believe that some of you may live to see new interest infused into our traditional religion which will produce an open conflict. At present scientific methods are largely introduced into history, archaeology, the comparison of religions, and Biblical interpretation, where their effect is far more destructive than the mass of people yet know. When the antagonism develops into open conflict, parties will take sides. It is evident that the position of the parties on all the great faiths and interests of men will differ very widely and that each position will have to be consistent with the fundamental way of looking at the facts of life on which it is founded. It does not seem possible that a scientist and a sacramentarian could agree about anything.

There is another form of phantasm which is still in fashion and does great harm, that is, faith in ideals. Men who rank as strong thinkers put forward ideals as useful things in thought and effort. Every ideal is a phantasm; it is formed by giving up one's hold on reality and taking a flight into the realm of fiction. When an ideal has been formed in the imagination the attempt is made to spring and reach it as a mode of realizing it. The whole process seems to me open to question; it is unreal and unscientific; it is the same process as that by which Utopias are formed in regard to social states, and contains the same fallacies; it is not a legitimate mental exercise. There is never any correct process by which we can realize an ideal. The fashion of forming ideals corrupts the mind and injures character. What we need to practise, on the contrary, is to know, with the greatest exactitude, what is, and then plan to deal with the case as it is by the most approved means.

Let me add a word about the ethical views which go with the scientific-critical way of looking at things. I have mentioned already our modern view of manufactured documents, which we call forged. In regard to history it seems to me right to say that history has value just on account of the truth which it contains and not otherwise. Consequently the historian who leaves things out, or puts them in, for edifying, patriotic, or other effect, sins against the critical-scientific method and temper which I have described. In fact, patriotism is another root of non-reality, and the patriotic bias is hostile to critical thinking.

It must be admitted that criticism is pessimistic. I say that it must be admitted, because, in our time, optimism is regarded as having higher

merit and as a duty; that which is pessimistic is consequently regarded
as bad and wrong. That is certainly an error. Pessimism includes caution,
doubt, prudence, and care; optimism means gush, shouting, boasting,
and rashness. The extreme of pessimism is that life is not worth living;
the extreme of optimism is that everything is for the best in the best of
worlds. Neither of these is true, but one is just as false as the other. The
critical temper will certainly lead to pessimism; it will develop the great
element of loss, disaster, and bad luck which inheres in all human enterprises. Hence it is popularly considered to consist in fault-finding.
You will need to guard against an excess of it, because if you yield to it,
it will lame your energies and deprive you of courage and hope. Nevertheless I cannot doubt that the popular feeling in our time and country
needs toning down from a noisy and heedless optimism. Professor Giddings, a few years ago, made a very interesting analysis and classification
of books published in this country, from which he thought that he
proved, statistically, that the temper of our people now is between ideo-
emotional and dogmatic-emotional. By ideo-emotional he means in-
quiring or curious, and convivial; by dogmatic-emotional he means
domineering and austere. We must notice, as limiting this test, that the
book-market can bear testimony only to the taste of the "reading public,"
which is but a very small part of the population, and does not include
the masses. Professor Giddings found that 50 per cent of the books published aimed to please and appealed to emotion or sentiment; 40 per
cent aimed to convert, and appealed to belief, ethical emotion, or self-
interest; 8 per cent aimed to instruct, were critical, and appealed to
reason. The other 2 per cent contained all the works of high technical
or scientific value, lost really in an unclassified residuum. This means
that our literature is almost entirely addressed to the appetite for romance and adventure, probable or improbable, to sentimentalism, to
theoretical interest in crime, marital infelicity, and personal misfortune,
and to the pleasure of light emotional excitement, while a large part of
it turns on ethical emotion and ignorant zeal in social matters. This
accords with the impression one gets from the newspapers as to what
the people like. The predominance of the emotional element in popular
literature means that people are trained by it away from reality. They
lose the power to recognize truth. Their power to make independent
ethical judgments is undermined, and all value is taken out of their
collective opinion on social and political topics. They are made day-
dreamers, or philistines, or ready victims of suggestion, to be operated
upon by religious fakers, or politicians, or social innovators. What they

need is criticism, with all the pessimism which it may bring in its train. Ethics belong to the folkways of the time and place; they can be kept sound and vigorous only by the constant reaction between the traditional rule and the individual judgment. What we must have, on this domain also, is a demand for reality and a trained power to perceive the relation between all human interests and the facts of reality at the time existing.

These are the ideas which it seemed to me most desirable to suggest to you at this moment when you are joining this society. I hope that you will here, by your work, your influence on each other, and all the exercises of the society, develop your zeal for scientific truth, and all the virtues of mind and character which common pursuit of reality may be expected to produce. We cannot welcome you to grand halls and old endowments. You cannot carry on your work under fine paintings, with beautiful furniture, or a rich society library. I will say frankly that I wish you could do so; I wish that we had all the accumulations of time and money which such conveniences would present. I do not doubt, however, that your youth and zeal will suffice for you and we expect that you will make up for all deficiencies by your earnest work. It should be the spirit with which you enter the society to make your connection with it tell on your education. You have been selected as men of earnest purpose and industry. You can do much for each other. Common interest in the same line of work will draw you together. I wish you all prosperity and success.

# Mores and Statistics

About 1902, Albert G. Keller began to tutor his mentor on the implications of Darwinian theory, including natural selection, the finer points of which Sumner remained innocent. Among possible implications was a probabilistic or statistical view of natural and social development, a position developed in the "new statistics" of the Englishmen Francis Galton and Karl Pearson. Toying with this conception, Sumner expressed interest in what he termed the "aleatory element" (or chance) in human affairs. In *Folkways*, he discussed briefly the Galtonian conception of a genetic group as a variety of traits distributed about a mean, leaving open the possibility that the mores were simply probability predictions concerning the way individuals in fact respond under changing conditions and thus were capable of "statistical specification." In this unpublished essay, he put these questions to rest. Luck remained a term to describe occurrences where the "facts" were not known, not an occasion for redefining natural law as a statement of probabilities. Keller eventually agreed in "The Luck Element," *Scientific Monthly* 4 (1917), 145–150. MS. fragment, ca. 1900–1906, Sumner Papers, Yale, New Haven, Connecticut.

The mores are the class of societal phenomena which is most peculiar, and the most especial object of study in society. They are group phenomena. They are not like vital phenomena; they are not controlled specifically by physical facts. They cannot therefore be treated by statistics as insurance is. If we use current language we must say that the mores contain a "moral" element. The mores differ from civic institutions and laws in that the latter contain a large element of arbitrary invention; they differ also from language and from many usages which we have put under the head of public morality, because these are conventional and formulated, in which respects they differ from mores. To what extent are the mores controlled by probability? To what extent are they capable of statistical specification? The answer is that the pure mores are not capable of such treatment at all. It is not until the mores have taken on some concrete institutional character that they can be reduced to statistics at all and then only imperfectly. Attempts to reduce them to statistics fail because the categories never fit, and there is always need to go further and take in other factors or to make distinctions and to lose one's self in details.

Census makers have tried to seize the mores in their statistical machines and they do well for if we could get statistics of the mores they would far transcend in value any others. But this is always in vain; in portraying the mores a census would become a library and its categories would require descriptive chapters. Travelers try to describe the mores, but who ever does justice to them? Suppose that a foreigner tries to describe the mores of New England; can he ever present in language a picture of the ways of New England which will carry, to a foreign reader, a just apprehension and appreciation of them? The difficulty is that there is an element which seems to us accidental and capricious, which we cannot observe or analyze. It seems to be hidden in the opinions and will of "the people" of a past generation, but what ones are responsible for it, or how and when they acted, we cannot tell. Popular explanations are "the agency of great men" (this is the old barbaric notion over again) or "agitation." But no agitation ever gains ground in a community against the mores of that community; you can agitate against slavery in Massachusetts and against the tariff in South Carolina but not vice versa. Slavery and tariff are not mores, but mores go with them. The pulpit, platform, and press can cause people to cease to keep decanters all the time on the sideboard, but whether a man shall be entitled to indulgence if he drinks too much wine at a dinner party is decided by something else. In colonial days a widow or a widower would remarry in a few months; what has changed the public taste to make that seem unseemly and to bring down social penalties on one who should do it now?

If we go on to a real case of pure mores, we shall see how unknown the agency and the manner of the origin of the mores are. "Sacramental" monogamy is now dominant in our mores by the side of somewhat easy divorce, although the two are absolutely antagonistic. Who raised the sentiment about pair marriage to this height, and when and how? All illicit sex relations are absolutely tabooed and must be concealed; the mores contain no toleration or compromise for them. The Puritans rejected ecclesiastical marriage; what made them all turn back to it so that their descendants now all look upon it as the correct mode and do not know that it ever was a party doctrine of their ancestors to oppose it? Who ever caused relaxation of the Puritan Sunday; when and how did the change come about? No agitation or discussion in favor of pair marriage or against Sunday observance ever took place. We could get statistics of the period within which remarriages take place in Connecticut, but they would not express the public taste as to the proper length of mourning. We could get statistics of the families who never have spirits, wine, or liquor in the house, but some have one and not another of these; some have one or another sometimes; some very rarely, others often; some do not have them on hand but have no principle against them, and so on. How could we get statistics which would express the usage of families in regard to this matter? We can get statistics of marriages and divorces but we can get no statistics of unhappy marriages and these last are what we need to test the marriage institution as it exists amongst us. How, then, could we sum up in statistics a measure of the intensity of respect for pair marriage and adherence to it throughout all classes and how could we express in statistics what is now the balance of feeling in the population between pair marriage and divorce? Yet these last measures are what we should need for a statistical summation of the mores. If we cannot get these first arithmetical data, how can we apply mathematical processes to the mores at all, that is, how can we treat them scientifically? And yet anyone who refuses to believe in "accidents" will be sure of the interdependence of the phenomena and of their relation to economic and political phenomena; and a study of the mores shows that there is no element of personal caprice in them. It is one of their characteristic features that they start and grow unconsciously. The mores are a domain of insight, sagacity, trained judgment, and the conclusions we reach must always remain qualitative only.

# Science and Mores

In this fragment of his uncompleted "Science of Society," Sumner argued that scientific theory entered the mores only through their practical application in discoveries and invention. Even the rhetoric of evolution entered the popular mind because of its imagined relation to religion, he insisted, probably reflecting his current interest in Darwinism. Concluding with his familiar distinction between scientific methods and theories ("discoveries"), Sumner showed how the hoped-for benefits of a scientific attitude tempered his perennial pessimism concerning the "masses." MS., ca. 1900–1906, Sumner Papers, Yale, New Haven, Connecticut.

Science[1] never directly influences the mores. The most profound discovery in mathematics, e.g. the differential calculus has never directly influenced the ways, ideas, faiths, and practices of any group. The same may be said of the law of the conservation of energy which is the highest formula of science yet attained. The same was true of all the discoveries in electricity and magnetism. Not until the art, the telegraph, was invented were mores affected. Without the differential calculus all the discoveries and inventions in physics of the last two hundred years would have been difficult or impossible. The Röntgen rays are a case of a discovery which was immediately applicable in disease, one of the most universal interests of mankind, but they were at the end of a long series of discoveries of which the crowd knows nothing. Discoveries must become arts and be included in the routine of life before they affect mores. Pure science therefore must always go through the stage of application before it can affect mores. Here a gulf is opened between men of scientific education and the crowd.[2] The minds of the former are trained to work on scientific processes and to value scientific truth entirely aside from its applications. It is known that the application of today's abstract principle will come tomorrow.

[1] In the margin, Sumner wrote: "Science is critical and systematic knowledge of realities acquired by processes which have been developed and approved by the most successful investigators."

[2] In the margin, Sumner wrote: "History affects mores only through patriotism, myth, etc. Political economy as science does not affect mores. The crowd invents its own dogmas to join [?] its passions and prejudices. Literature affects mores. Crowd does not see applications of political economy."

Crook's discoveries[3] interested scientific men as much as Röntgen's. Here is the real gulf between the practical man and the theorist. It is a profound fault of our society to underrate theory and exalt the practical man. The latter is always boasting that he is up with the times when the most noteworthy fact about him is that he is *not* up with the times.

Evolution on account of its supposed possible bearing on religion has interested the crowd. The jargon of evolution (development, survival of the fittest, struggle for existence, etc.) has got into literature and has affected all the thinking of the age. To realize this one should note that the ecclesiastics at the Council of Trent were not able to conceive that what they had received from the last preceding generation had not all been given just so by Jesus Christ himself. These were men whose minds had not been trained on evolution at all.

Apprehension of scientific truth never can affect the mass of any group in any way at all. What has science, then, to do with the mores?

The first impression produced on the mind by phenomena is almost always erroneous. It is necessary to train the mind to resist the first impression and to look deeper. It is necessary to investigate and verify, to form judgments, and thus to accumulate knowledge and develop mental power. That the sun moves from east to west is a fact open to everybody's perception. The true relation of things can only be understood by mental effort. The leading minds for centuries were employed to find out the truth. The concepts connected with it are beyond the grasp of untrained men. We must, therefore, recognize the fact that phenomena envelop man in delusion to begin with, and his own mind betrays him. Only by very long and painful effort does he rise above these conditions so as to find out "the truth." He started off with the grand phantasm of goblinism as his world-philosophy, and he may be said to have found his way out of it to the world-philosophy which we now hold by advancing backwards; he has modified and corrected the notions which came down to him by tradition; he has never, until within a century or two, faced forwards to find out by free investigation of problems posed independently of tradition. He has had to correct and recorrect by criticism his apprehension of the world around him. These processes of criticism and investigation constitute science. No man can do more than investigate a little bit of the field of knowledge for himself. For the rest

[3]Sumner's reference here may have been to Sir William Crookes (1832–1919), the English chemist whose discoveries included thallium and other breakthroughs in the application of scientific theory.

he must accept the authority of his colleagues. There are vested interests of church and state, the guardians of which are sure to meet him with all possible opposition. The masses hold, in the mores, all the traditional errors. They dislike to be forced to change their notions. Knowledge can be used and enjoyed by those who have it and it gives them power and superiority. This goes far to account for the "inequalities" in modern society. It is when discoveries affect life-philosophy that they necessarily pervade the society. Then the fact becomes important that the masses can be imbued with new philosophy only very slowly, and from the top downwards.

We must also notice that men have always practiced artificial delusion on each other, both innocently and intentionally. Enthusiasts, dreamers, crafty men, politicians, and demagogs have ruled the masses by suggesting to them utopias and other dreams of bliss, or by exciting their fears of unknown ills. They have always played upon the imaginative element. They can affect the masses far more than the master of science with his demonstrations. Defence against fraud requires the same arms and armor as defence against delusion.

Scientific discoveries never enter into the mores, but scientific methods do. The upper sections of the masses have become so habituated to those methods that they are familiar with new truths and readjustments of old concepts. They are not frightened by the results but are receptive to them. They trust and use the methods in respect to all the interests of life. This last is the most important point for the mores. The same habits of thought spread to lower strata slowly but steadily. So far as this takes place the mores are affected and science has then effected its most important results. The masses get a popular and approximate notion of the difference between reality and unreality. They acquire instinctive habits of criticism and investigation. The old world-philosophies, with their fantastic conceptions, are displaced from their control of the mores. The outlook upon the world is changed. The notion of what are real "interests" is entirely changed. Therefore the motives which will move the men, and which can be appealed to with a certainty of response, are changed. It is a fact of the mores that the evolution philosophy has so largely entered into the current language and affected the popular thinking of our time, although of course the notions which are current are crass and erroneous, and the current phrases are very imperfectly understood. However imperfectly evolution may be apprehended, it controls, so far as it goes, the concept of interests and therefore the whole attitude of men to life, its activities, and its problems. In the

Middle Ages demonism and otherworldliness controlled the notion of interests, or traversed the primary notions of interest which each should work to realize for himself, during his earthly career, so far as he could. Under the evolution philosophy there are no transcendental interests. Interests must be defined in terms of the struggle for existence and the competition of life. Science has supplanted all transcendental philosophy in the second step of the schedule—act, thought, act. It tends all the time, as it (science) becomes a more universal possession or habit of mind of members of the group, to raise the mores to a more rational and purified character.

# On Mores and Progress

Although his youthful belief in providential design and his observations of material prosperity in the post-Civil War era disposed Sumner to accept the prevailing faith in progress, he increasingly had his doubts. After Henry George made an issue of it in *Progress and Poverty* (1879), he returned to the subject repeatedly, and, by the turn of the century, had rejected the 19th century view. In one unpublished fragment, "The Glacier," he developed a metaphor of mankind buffeted by uncontrollable forces, an image he repeated in this essay. In a speech to the Yale Anthropology Club in 1905, he explicitly denied that social evolution was progressive. Elsewhere, although sporadically, he accepted a cyclical view of history—a perennial refuge of the disaffected. In the following transcriptions Sumner's sketchy citations of sources are omitted. Selection from Sumner's uncompleted "Science of Society" MS., ca. 1900–1906, Sumner Papers, Yale, New Haven, Connecticut.

What all the ethical philosophers aim at is an external and imperative principle or dogmatic basis. They find none which is not, by a circle in reasoning, a part of the selected world-philosophy which each of them has accepted. All agree in denouncing egoism and selfishness. The current fashion favors the social-happiness theory (the welfare of society); that is, under democratic institutions, the welfare of the majority; that is, the welfare of the masses; that is, the welfare of non-possessors, laborers technically so-called, the uneducated and uncultivated classes. The notion is elusive and is not on the plane of actuality except in the last form: that morals are the precepts of right action which are deduced from the purpose of the society to promote the welfare (satisfaction, enjoyment) of the class of uneducated non-possessors. On this code morals are systematically defined by the end assumed for the society. No such thing has ever existed anywhere as a society whose energies were bent to the welfare of non-possessors. No society has ever existed anywhere which was not in fact controlled in the disposition of its force by a few. Large expenditure of effort and capital is now made voluntarily by the cultured and possessing classes on behalf of the numerous non-possessing and uncultured classes in every civilized state. Such efforts lie in the mores and it is a part of the accepted code of morals that they are a part of the duty of the said classes. Also in democracies (United States, English colonies) the ruling few, as a part of their policy, impose upon the whole, concession, patronage, beneficence, petting, indulgence, towards the non-possessors, by whose suffrages and in whose name they exercise power. This they do amply in phrases and to a degree in fact. If the procedure is sincere, it is a delusion; if it is insincere, it is humbug and fraud. One or the other any happiness policy must be and the theory of ethics based on societal happiness is far more bankrupt than that based on individual happiness, because happiness is not a real idea. Inasmuch as happiness is entirely subjective and individual no group operation can give it to a number of men at once, but it is at least conceivable that, for a moment, an individual might experience it according to his notion of it. Perhaps every man gets near enough to it at moments in his life to get a glimpse of its glistening radiance, but no one ever lives long in its light. What happens to us is that we recognize its delusion and settle down to fact and habit. How then can it give us laws of morals or define the end of societal effort? The ruling few, after providing for paying toll to the masses, direct state effort to their own happiness and welfare, as they construe and hope for these.

A far more plausible theory of morals is that which construes them with respect to the evolution of society. The evolution philosophy has won dominion over the thinking of our age. If it is true, every individual who is born is caught up into the immense current which is moving on from what is to what is to be and he serves the movement whether he will or no, whether he dies within an hour or lives a century, whether he is an imbecile or a genius, whether he is supported all his life by society or becomes one of the greatest masters of industry of his time. If this view is correct, the moral sense of human existence must lie in it and ethical relations must be deduced from it. What then are they? Can we discern any end to which the movement of evolution tends? What men try to imagine for it is some end the contemplation of which would yield some satisfaction to each of us as he sees his existence swept into the stream, if he should contribute his willing and intelligent effort to the process in which he is involved. There is no such end. The outcome of the whole universe may be, so far as we can find out, another nebulous mass like the one from which, so far as we can find out, it came. We fondly think of all the geological, biological, historical and all other changes as a "progress" fitting the earth for us. Evolution has its popular delusions as well as endaimonism.[1] Evolution does not tend to what is

---

[1]This is Sumner's Hellenized spelling of "eudaemonism," referring to the doctrine that moral obligations be based in the tendency of right actions to produce happiness.

better, for better implies a human judgment about consequent compared with antecedent and when we say that the former is better what we mean is that it suits our interests better. The current notion of "progress" seems to be that the whole universe is enthused by a set or drift towards nicer things for men so that they can have a better time here without so much trouble.

In the nineteenth century a notion became popular and very current that there is in the affairs of earth and of men an innate tendency forward and upward which gives the law to the details of human and national existence. This notion is called progress and it fell in with and helped the popular optimism, the theory of a good time coming, the expectation of prosperity and happiness for everybody, the notion of a gratuitous benefaction for mankind in the nature of things and the world-philosophy according to which "mind rules matter," meaning that men form notions of what they want and bring those things to pass by voluntary mass action; that is, by declarations of the rights of man, etc., by resolutions in convention, by constitutions and other enactments, and by acts of legislation. There never were wanting dissenters from this conception of men and their status on earth. It has been asserted that, if there is any progress, it is progress on a spiral line, and it has been pointed out that the conception itself was easily accounted for by the popular misconception of evolution, by the economic effect of great inventions, producing prosperity, by the economic facts in new countries, etc. One effect of this philosophy has been a great error in regard to the effect of contact between high and low civilization or between good and evil influences in society. It has been believed that one or a few civilized men could civilize a group of savages; that women, being morally superior to men, could by taking a share in political affairs raise the moral tone of politics, etc. The facts are all against these notions. Colonies of Phoenicians, Carthaginians, Greeks, and other civilized people which once existed in Africa and outlying countries around the Mediterranean disappeared entirely in the surrounding uncivilization. If, as is well believed, Europeans in small numbers must have been carried over to America by storm and accident, or by Scandinavian enterprise, before Columbus, they disappeared leaving no societal effect. The Boers in South Africa regressed so fast and so far from the civilization of Holland which existed in the times when their ancestors left that country that it is probable that, if left alone, they would have disappeared like the Phoenician colonies. The French in Canada lost ground from the seventeenth century to the nineteenth. There are tribes of Indians which have a tradition of a time when they were agricultural but which turned into prairie tribes living in tepees and following the buffalo. The Anglo-American colonists used the term "indianizing" for the fact of their experience and observation that white men by contact with Indians ran down to Indian mores. The most shocking and useless fact of this class was the adoption by white men of the custom of scalping. Facts of this kind could be multiplied. They show plainly that both the physical environment (mode of food supply) and the societal environment (organization and mores of the larger society) exert an action on everybody.

There is no tendency at all in evolution to produce what we think better or to serve our interests. Evolution produces numberless consequences which are inferior to what existed before. If Eskimos or Bushmen are pushed off by superior tribes into a bad habitat they degenerate in obedience to evolution just as much as Indo-Europeans have advanced by it. Sir Issac Newton would die in a few days in the wilds of Tasmania where a Tasmanian savage would flourish, both in obedience to evolution. If European troops go to a warm and damp climate they find flint lock better than percussion lock guns and this is a case of evolution.

Especially it [evolution] overwhelms the work and pains and hopes of men. It is part of evolution when a glacier readvances into a Swiss valley and destroys the meadow pastures so that what was a thriving community of men disappears and a mass of ice fills the place. One might have dilated a few years before on the beneficence of nature which had set the glacier to grind the rocks, and the stream to carry down the dust and build the meadow and cover it with grass from the early geologic ages in order to offer homes and a chance of life to the men of a human community. Such is the current way of talking about "progress" and construing all the knowledge we gain into consoling and flattering theories with which to cajole ourselves. Glaciers readvance under the same forces by which they recede and their readvance is just as much a part of the progress of evolution. When this movement is complete we see that what happened was that men, taking advantage of an interlude in the great process of the universe which chanced to offer in that valley a period of rest and an expanse of verdure which could be made to serve their self-realization, entered upon it and enjoyed it. The case shows us the construction which we ought to put on man's whole relation to the earth and of the period within which he can enjoy it between the time when it was not possible to live here and the coming time when it will not be possible for him to live here. All the "changes" are but the successive phases of the movement from one of these states to the other. Where does the idea of progress come in?

The whole existence of the earth presents itself as a wave which begins at a zero line, moves through a maximum, and returns to the zero line. It is, however, interrupted by minor wave motions of rise and fall and the view of men, even if it includes all history, encompasses but the minor fluctuations on a certain extent of the great wave of earth existence. We call the movements of a century progress, which means only that they are different from some other movements. Nations appear and disappear. States rise and fall. Doctrines prevail and are forgotten. Institutions flourish and decay. Where is the progress? It consists only in the fact that all which happens belongs to the great cycle which is to be completed and is nearer completion with every moment which passes. Even then it will perhaps all recommence and run the same course again. Progress can never be more than a relation of certain things within a horizon of thought assumed for the purpose to be actually defined. In the sixteenth century the existing civilized men of Europe found a new world. They went out to seize and use it. They have been living on it since. It is as if a family suddenly inherited a fortune and lived well upon it until they had used it up. They would experience great progress. In another view progress is like the experience of a man who has lain on a rock until he is all lame and sore on one side. He rolls over and for a time feels great relief. That is progress, but he gets sore after awhile on the other side. The world rejected feudalism and trampled it in scorn. It turned to equality and liberty and capitalism. It is beginning to weary of these and to sneer at them. So it will go on forever. Spiral line.

If a man is twenty-five years of age, why does he go on to become thirty? Is it because he expects to be "happy" when he reaches that age? Or because he will have advanced towards some end at that age? Evidently it is not. He will approach no end but death for, if he accomplishes a minor purpose, it will be by labor, not by the passage of time, and happiness we have already disposed of. He goes on to thirty because he is alive and with the progress of time he must go on through his span of earthly existence. The only alternative is suicide. The world goes on for the same reason. Existence means that with time phases of successive change must be traversed without end. From the end or purpose or from the process of this evolution no deductions as to man's duty can be made except possibly his duty to live on and not commit suicide. All the ethical relations are to be deduced from the *terminus a quo* not from the *terminus ad quem*, and here we come back from speculation to the individual, to facts, to history and to the range of experience. That is, to what we know. The mores are the voice of preceding generations (history) speaking to the new generation the outcome of their experience as to the art of living. That part of the mores which we call morals are the injunctions which dictate the societal laws under which the struggle for existence and the competition of life may best be carried on (so far as the ancestors have found out). These laws are really a fluctuating compromise between the numbers and the quality of the society under the life-conditions. The individual with his career before him must construe it as a task of self-realization because otherwise it has for him no sense or law. He must at any moment of time deal with the case next at hand, and his duty comes out of the conditions of the case in which he finds himself and out of his relations to the comrades in cooperation with whom he must solve it. There must be give and take in an organization because the task is to be performed in society, not isolated. It is not selfishness for a man to devote himself to his career. There would be no selfishness unless, when receiving cooperation in the organization, he refused to give cooperation in it. No man can derive his duty, overlooking all the conditions around him, from notions about the world evolution which is going on. He cannot afford to dispense with the support of the mores. The strongest must lean on them. What is the "right" thing to do at each juncture is a far larger question than the "right and wrong" of current morals. It is the question what, at this point, self-realization calls for under the total of existing conditions, physical and social. The world-process, so far as it is social, issues out of the being and doing of all these men in the course of time, and men contribute to its course when they fulfill as well as they can the immediate tasks of existence from moment to moment so that for each, as life passes, a sum is attained which is his self-realization. What the outcome of the world-process will be we do not know. It does not matter. It may be that we cannot change it by anything that we may do and that our propositions which imply that we ought to do right because so we shall shape it are only delusions of ours. The point is that our *duty* is not derived from that result of the world-process. It is derived from what each of us is by his antecedents and from his position at present in the process. For almost all men the subjective result is not happiness but resignation.

For the civilized and educated man all the glamour of mythology and world-philosophy as an explanation and sanction of his duty fades away. "To do one's duty in that state in life in which it has pleased God to call me" expresses it as well as any words can. I am here; I am face to face with this case; I must meet it as well as I can and as well as I know how. The utmost reach of moral philosophy is to inculcate resignation to the laws of human life and to the limitations on individual liberty (self-determination) which are set by societal order; to give intelligent recognition of the compensations in societal order for the constraint which must be endured; to teach patience with civil regulations and institutions in spite of their crudeness and the often cruel friction with which they act on individuals; and to produce a sense of the value of organization and cooperation in peace. The world-philosophy of an age ceases to verify, if it ever did do so, from the standpoint of a time. Another is devised and adopted and runs the same course. Moses, Solon, Lycurgus, Mohammed promulgated systems which probably suited their times or at least set things forward for the time being. The systems fell far short of the needs of later ages when the authority and prestige of their first success maintained them as fitter until they were broken or became superseded. Are these phases of a progressive movement from what is less "true" to what is more "true"? That is, of a movement towards a final goal of rest in a conclusive result? They certainly are not. They are only temporary readjustments of societal interests which relieve special stresses and strains which have arisen. But similar discomfort recurs, new struggles begin and the process is repeated forever.

We have found reason to doubt the nineteenth century notion of progress as a process of successive changes in a direction which man would call from worse to better, especially with regard to man's satisfaction with his earthly experience. Biological forms show us a series of changes, in time, from the more simple to the more complex. Civilization shows us serial changes in man and in his active and passive relations to the environment which are advancing in the sense that man has steadily gained in power over nature. By virtue of this gain he has made a square mile of land support more and more men. This process has been attended also by a series of changes in the industrial organization to take advantage of this power over nature, which changes have in nearly all cases entailed a limitation of population. The consequence of these two changes taken together has been an improvement in the quality of the men. No other notion of progress than this will verify. The rest is all a part of the delusions of speculative optimism, product of the invincible demand of mankind to hear prophecies of smooth things and to be cajoled with dreams. These characteristics of human nature have been cultivated in modern times by the relaxation of the harsher sanctions of evolution which has been due to the discovery of the New World. That discovery did not become really very effective until the beginning of the nineteenth century, and the inventions in transportation and the communication of intelligence of that century have thrown the great gain into the hands of the last three generations. The struggle for existence and the competition of life, especially the latter, have been greatly softened by this immense addition to the land which living men could use. Eighteenth century social and political philosophy, the product of a long revolt against medievalism, seemed to get a verification for its theories of world-beatification from the experiences of the nineteenth century. Men are not aware that they are enjoying conditions which must forever remain most exceptional in human history. They accept the facts as in the external order of nature or they attribute them to philosophical notions or democratic theories. The effect has been to give anything but contentment and happiness. Where the gain has been greatest and most obvious there the effect has been most pronounced to cause discontent and unhappiness. This is, in fact, perfectly true to human nature. When a man gets something the effect is to make him want something more. To win or succeed opens his mind to new hopes and ambitions without end. There is incomparably more discontent and unhappiness in Europe than in Asia and more still in America. "Progress" therefore does not make happiness, although we constantly reason as if the two were identical. It stimulates desire and makes men work. That serves evolution, but not happiness. And we hear men cry out that they are strapped fast to the machine which they started and that they cannot stop it although it is crushing them. The result is gnashing of teeth over the experience at the same time that the demand for fulfillment of the optimistic delusions grows louder and louder. Progress in learning does not make a man happy. It removes him from human sympathy. He sees error and cannot consent to it or stop it. If he is wrong that does not make it less true that it destroys his happiness. It is not the most miserable who revolt but those who are well off. Progress always *costs*. Waste and pain of it. We cannot renounce it. We cannot stay boys. The great sin is sin against culture.

In strongest contrast with the success of man in winning power over nature and in cultivating his mental powers to fit those gains stands the weakness which he has shown in societal organization (political organization). The political organization of modern states is face to face with the same problems which were presented in Greece and which received a partial solution at Rome, upon which the modern states have advanced but little. Within fifty years the inadequacy of the modern state for the tasks which have been thrown upon it by the industrial and commercial expansion has been made more and more evident in every civilized state. Yet there is a school of social philosophers who favor the commitment of industry to state control. Such a step would sacrifice the industry and finally corrupt the state. As it is, the peril of society is from the unequal development of the industrial and political organizations. The abuse of political power for pecuniary gain through industrial legislation by all classes and parties (plutocracy and labor sin) is a symptom of the inadequacy of the political organization to maintain its independent function. The great societal conflict of the twentieth century will be between plutocracy and democracy, between wealth and numbers.

As the outlying parts of the earth fill up with population, the present favorable conditions for non-possessors will pass away and the generations which grow up will find disappointment in respect to the optimistic assurances which have become traditional. They will regard this disappointment as due to the plutocrats who have seized all the wealth. The disposition of the forces for this battle is already to be seen and the war cries may already be heard. Special legislation on one side and legislative strikes on the other are the opening of the battle. In the meantime politics is supposed to be the arena for phrases and metaphysical dogmas about liberty, equality, the sovereignty of the people, the rights of man, etc., etc. Men are taught to look for societal welfare to political doctrines and acts, not to economic effort, and the function of the state to provide a civil organization which is able to support the industrial organization by adequate institutions of peace, order, security, justice, and the restraint of social abuses is neglected because it does not seem to be duly recognized. The economic outlook is optimistic in the extreme but societal catastrophes threaten from the lack of knowledge and power in the political domain to meet political strain which the economic development necessarily brings with itself. This is the real point in the present relation of economics and politics.

It also throws great light on current notions to notice that we are passing through a period in which power has passed from the church to the state and then from the rank-classes to the masses. All political struggle is a struggle for power. One party has been defeated, another has won but has not yet consolidated its power. In this interval there is a special opportunity for broad and general theories of justice and equal rights, as if societal interest groups could settle down side by side contented with the distribution and seeking not by strife to win power over each other. Since the former powers have been dethroned their methods and instrumentalities have fallen into disuse and become abominations. However, men have always been cruel, if they had social power, against those whom they suspected of a purpose to take it away from them. The Inquisition was an organ chiefly of worldly power. The Greek democracies, Venice and the other Italian republics, the rebels of Ghent in Charles Fifth's time, showed that ruling factions in republics and democracies can be as suspicious and jealous and, when frightened, as pitilessly cruel as any despot. There is no security that, if the new ruling classes win established power and a demagogical oligarchy organizes this power in its own hands, the era of toleration, humanitarianism, and a political philosophy of justice, equality, etc. will not give way to terroristic methods of the old type for maintaining power. The suggestion, however, has value only as it raises the question whether the predominance of broad sentiments in the political philosophy of the present time is not due to the fact that we live in a period when societal power is passing from one depositary to another.

# Folkways

In 1899, Sumner began to organize materials from lectures and essays into a long-planned "Science of Society," one proposed chapter of which grew into *Folkways* (1906). In two opening chapters he defined and characterized the "mores" and "folkways," the key concepts of the work. Building upon Jacob Burckhardt's *Civilization of the Renaissance* (1859), among others, Sumner reflected in a final chapter on the implications of his analysis for understanding the contest of the "virtue" and "success" policies in modern western history. The following sections are from *Folkways*, ch. 1 (§ 1, 2, 34, 36, 37, 38, 43, 52, 57, 58, 65, 66, 72); ch. 2 (§ 80); and ch. 20 (§ 712, 718, 721, 726, 728). Although Sumner identified the sources of his quotations in the original text, his footnotes are here omitted.

## Fundamental Notions of the Folkways and of the Mores

### DEFINITION AND MODE OF ORIGIN OF THE FOLKWAYS

If we put together all that we have learned from anthropology and ethnography about primitive men and primitive society, we perceive that the first task of life is to live. Men begin with acts, not with thoughts. Every moment brings necessities which must be satisfied at once. Need was the first experience, and it was followed at once by a blundering effort to satisfy it. It is generally taken for granted that men inherited some guiding instincts from their beast ancestry, and it may be true, although it has never been proved. If there were such inheritances, they controlled and aided the first efforts to satisfy needs. Analogy makes it easy to assume that the ways of beasts had produced channels of habit and predisposition along which dexterities and other psychophysical activities would run easily. Experiments with newborn animals show that in the absence of any experience of the relation of means to ends, efforts to satisfy needs are clumsy and blundering. The method is that of trial and failure, which produces repeated pain, loss, and disappointments. Nevertheless, it is a method of rude experiment and selection. The earliest efforts of men were of this kind. Need was the impelling force. Pleasure and pain, on the one side and the other, were the rude constraints which defined the line on which efforts must proceed. The ability to distinguish between pleasure and pain is the

357

only psychical power which is to be assumed. Thus ways of doing things were selected, which were expedient. They answered the purpose better than other ways, or with less toil and pain. Along the course on which efforts were compelled to go, habit, routine, and skill were developed. The struggle to maintain existence was carried on, not individually, but in groups. Each profited by the other's experience; hence there was concurrence towards that which proved to be most expedient. All at last adopted the same way for the same purpose; hence the ways turned into customs and became mass phenomena. Instincts were developed in connection with them. In this way folkways arise. The young learn them by tradition, imitation, and authority. The folkways, at a time, provide for all the needs of life then and there. They are uniform, universal in the group, imperative, and invariable. As time goes on, the folkways become more and more arbitrary, positive, and imperative. If asked why they act in a certain way in certain cases, primitive people always answer that it is because they and their ancestors always have done so. A sanction also arises from ghost fear. The ghosts of ancestors would be angry if the living should change the ancient folkways (see sec. 6).

## THE FOLKWAYS ARE A SOCIETAL FORCE

The operation by which folkways are produced consists in the frequent repetition of petty acts, often by great numbers acting in concert or, at least, acting in the same way when face to face with the same need. The immediate motive is interest. It produces habit in the individual and custom in the group. It is, therefore, in the highest degree original and primitive. By habit and custom it exerts a strain on every individual within its range; therefore it rises to a societal force to which great classes of societal phenomena are due. Its earliest stages, its course, and laws may be studied; also its influence on individuals and their reaction on it. It is our present purpose so to study it. We have to recognize it as one of the chief forces by which a society is made to be what it is. Out of the unconscious experiment which every repetition of the ways includes, there issues pleasure or pain, and then, so far as the men are capable of reflection, convictions that the ways are conducive to societal welfare. These two experiences are not the same. The most uncivilized men, both in the food quest and in war, do things which are painful, but which have been found to be expedient. Perhaps these cases teach the sense of social welfare better than those which are pleasurable and favorable to welfare. The former cases call for some intelligent reflection on experience. When this conviction as to the relation to welfare is added to the folkways they are converted into mores, and, by virtue of the philosophical and ethical element added to them, they win utility and importance and become the source of the science and the art of living.

## DEFINITION OF THE MORES

When the elements of truth and right are developed into doctrines of welfare, the folkways are raised to another plane. They then become capable of producing inferences, developing into new forms, and extending their constructive influence over men and society. Then we call them the mores. The mores are the folkways, including the philosophical and ethical generalizations as to societal welfare which are suggested by them, and inherent in them, as they grow.

## NO PRIMITIVE PHILOSOPHIZING; MYTHS; FABLES; NOTION OF SOCIETAL WELFARE

It is not to be understood that primitive men philosophize about their experience of life. That is our way; it was not theirs. They did not formulate any propositions about the causes, significance, or ultimate relations of things. They made myths, however, in which they often presented conceptions which are deeply philosophical, but they represented them in concrete, personal, dramatic and graphic ways. They feared pain and ill, and they produced folkways by their devices for warding off pain and ill. Those devices were acts of ritual which were planned upon their vague and crude faiths about ghosts and the other world. We develop the connection between the devices and the faiths, and we reduce it to propositions of a philosophic form, but the primitive men never did that. Their myths, fables, proverbs, and maxims show that the subtler relations of things did not escape them, and that reflection was not wanting, but the method of it was very different from ours. The notion of societal welfare was not wanting, although it was never consciously put before themselves as their purpose. It was pestilence, as a visitation of the wrath of ghosts on all, or war, which first taught this idea, because war was connected with victory over a neighboring group. The Bataks have a legend that men once married their fathers' sisters' daughters, but calamities followed and so those marriages were tabooed. This inference and the cases mentioned in sec. 28 show a conception of societal welfare and of its relation to states and acts as conditions.

## THE IMAGINATIVE ELEMENT

The correct apprehension of facts and events by the mind, and the correct inferences as to the relations between them, constitute knowledge, and it is chiefly by knowledge that men have become better able to live well on earth. Therefore the alternation between experience or observation and the intellectual processes by which the sense, sequence, interdependence, and rational consequences of facts are ascertained, is undoubtedly the most important process for winning increased power to live well. Yet we find that this process has been liable to most pernicious errors. The imagination has interfered with the reason and furnished objects of pursuit to men, which have wasted and dissipated their energies. Especially the alternations of observation and deduction have been traversed by vanity and superstition which have introduced delusions. As a consequence, men have turned their backs on welfare and reality, in order to pursue beauty, glory, poetry, and dithyrambic rhetoric, pleasure, fame, adventure, and phantasms. Every group, in every age, has had its "ideals" for which it has striven, as if men had blown bubbles into the air, and then, entranced by their beautiful colors, had leaped to catch them. In the very processes of analysis and deduction the most pernicious errors find entrance. We note our experience in every action or event. We study the significance from experience. We deduce a conviction as to what we may best do when the case arises again. Undoubtedly this is just what we ought to do in order to live well. The process presents us a constant reiteration of the sequence,—act, thought, act. The error is made if we allow suggestions of vanity, superstition, speculation, or imagination to become confused with the second stage and to enter into our conviction of what is best to do in such a case. This is what was done when goblinism was taken as the explanation of experience and the rule of right living, and it is what has been done over and over again ever since. Speculative and transcendental notions have furnished the world philosophy, and the rules of life policy and duty have been deduced from this and introduced at the second stage of the process,—act, thought, act. All the errors and fallacies of the mental processes enter into the mores of the age. The logic of one age is not that of another. It is one of the chief useful purposes of a study of the mores to learn to discern in them the operation of traditional error, prevailing dogmas, logical fallacy, delusion, and current false estimates of goods worth striving for.

## THE ETHICAL POLICY OF THE SCHOOLS AND THE SUCCESS POLICY

Although speculative assumptions and dogmatic deductions have produced the mischief here described, our present world philosophy has come out of them by rude methods of correction and purification, and "great principles" have been deduced which now control our life philosophy; also ethical principles have been determined which no civilized man would now repudiate (truthfulness, love, honor, altruism). The traditional doctrines of philosophy and ethics are not by any means adjusted smoothly to each other or to modern notions. We live in a war of two antagonistic ethical philosophies: the ethical policy taught in the books and the schools, and the success policy. The same man acts at one time by the school ethics, disregarding consequences, at another time by the success policy, in which the consequences dictate the conduct; or we talk the former and act by the latter.

## WHY USE THE WORD MORES

"Ethica," in the Greek sense, or "ethology," as above defined, would be good names for our present work. We aim to study the ethos of groups, in order to see how it arises, its power and influence, the modes of its operation on members of the group, and the various attributes of it (ethica). "Ethology" is a very unfamiliar word. It has been used for the mode of setting forth manners, customs, and mores in satirical comedy. The Latin word "mores" seems to be, on the whole, more practically convenient and available than any other for our purpose, as a name for the folkways with the connotations of right and truth in respect to welfare, embodied in them. The analysis and definition above given show that in the mores we must recognize a dominating force in history, constituting a condition as to what can be done, and as to the methods which can be employed.

## THE MASSES AND THE MORES

In connection with the mores the masses are of very great importance. The historical or selected classes are those which, in history, have controlled the activities and policy of generations. They have been differentiated at one time by one standard, at another time by another. The position which they held by inheritance from early society has given them prestige and authority. Merit and societal value, according to the standards of their time, have entered into their status only slightly and incidentally. Those classes have had their own mores. They had the power to regulate their lives to some extent according to their own choice, a power which modern civilized men eagerly desire and strive for primarily by the acquisition of wealth. The historical classes have, therefore, selected purposes, and have invented ways of fulfilling them. Their ways have been imitated by the masses. The classes have led the way in luxury, frivolity, and vice, and also in refinement, culture, and the art of living. They have introduced variation. The masses are not large classes at the base of a social pyramid; they are the core of the society. They are conservative. They accept life as they find it, and live on by tradition and habit. In other words, the great mass of any society lives a purely instinctive life just like animals. We must not be misled by the conservatism of castes and aristocracies, who resist change of customs and institutions by virtue of which they hold social power. The conservatism of the masses is of a different kind. It is not produced by interests, but it is instinctive. It is due to inertia. Change would make new effort necessary to win routine and habit. It is therefore irksome. The masses, moreover, have not the power to reach out after "improvements," or to plan steps of change by which needs might be better satisfied. The mores of any society, at a period, may be characterized by the promptness or reluctance of the masses to imitate the ways of the classes. It is a question of the first importance for the historian whether the mores of the historical classes of which he finds evidence in documentary remains penetrated the masses or not. The masses are the real bearers of the mores of the society. They carry tradition. The folkways are their ways. They accept influence or leadership, and they imitate, but they do so as they see fit, being controlled by their notions and tastes previously acquired. They may accept standards of character and action from the classes, or from foreigners, or from literature, or from a new religion, but whatever they take up they assimilate and make it a part of their own mores, which they then transmit by tradition, defend in its integrity, and refuse to discard again. Consequently the writings of the literary class may not represent the faiths, notions, tastes, standards, etc., of the masses at all. The literature of the first Christian centuries shows us scarcely anything of the mores of the time, as they existed in the faith and practice of the masses. Every group takes out of a new religion which is offered to it just what it can assimilate with its own traditional mores. Christianity was a very different thing amongst Jews, Egyptians, Greeks, Germans, and Slavs. It would be a great mistake to suppose that any people ever accepted and held philosophical or religious teaching as it was offered to them, and as we find it recorded in the books of the teachers. The mores of the masses admit of no such sudden and massive modification by doctrinal teaching. The process of assimilation is slow, and it is attended by modifying influences at every stage. What the classes adopt, be it good or ill, may be found pervading the mass after generations, but it will appear as a resultant of all the vicissitudes of the folkways in the interval. "It was the most frightful feature of the corruption of ancient Rome, that it extended through every class in the community." "As in the Renaissance, so now [in the Catholic reaction] vice trickled downward from above, infiltrating the mass of the people with its virus." It is the classes who produce variation; it is the masses who carry forward the traditional mores.

### THE COMMON MAN

Every civilized society has to carry below the lowest sections of the masses a dead weight of ignorance, poverty, crime, and disease. Every such society has, in the great central section of the masses, a great body which is neutral in all the policy of society. It lives by routine and tradition. It is not brutal, but it is shallow, narrow-minded, and prejudiced. Nevertheless it is harmless. It lacks initiative and cannot give an impulse for good or bad. It produces few criminals. It can sometimes be moved by appeals to its fixed ideas and prejudices. It is affected in its mores by contagion from the classes above it. The work of "popularization" consists in bringing about this contagion. The middle section is formed around the mathematical mean of the society, or around the mathematical mode, if the distribution of the subdivisions is not symmetrical. The man on the mode is the "common man," the "average man," or the "man in the street." Between him and the democratic political institutions—the pulpit, the newspapers, and the public library—there is a constant reaction by which mores are modified and preserved. The aim of all the institutions and literature in a modern state is to please him. His aim is to get out of them what suits him. The yellow newspapers thrive and displace all the others because he likes them. The trashy novels pay well because his wife and daughters like them. The advertisements in the popular magazines are addressed to him. They show what he wants. The "funny items" are adjusted to his sense of humor. Hence all these things are symptoms. They show what he "believes in," and they strengthen his prejudices. If all art, literature, legislation, and political power are to be cast at his feet, it makes some difference who and what he is. His section of society determines the mores of the whole.

### "THE PEOPLE." POPULAR IMPULSES

In a democratic state the great middle section would rule if it was organized independently of the rest. It is that section which constitutes "the people" in the special technical sense in which that expression is current in political use. It is to it that the Jeffersonian doctrines about the "wisdom" of the people would apply. That section, however, is never organized independently; that is to say, "the people" never exist as a body exercising political power. The middle section of a group may be enthused by an impulse which is adapted to its ways and notions. It clings to persons, loves anecdotes, is fond of light emotions, and prides itself on its morality. If a man wins popularity in that section, the impulse which his name can give to it may be irresistible (Jefferson, Jackson). The middle section is greatly affected by symbolism. "The flag" can be developed into a fetich. A cult can be nourished around it. Group vanity is very strong in it. Patriotic emotions and faiths are its favorite psychological exercises, if the conjuncture is favorable and the material well-being is high. When the middle section is stirred by any spontaneous and consentaneous impulses which arise from its nature and ways, it may produce incredible results with only a minimum of organization. "A little prosperity and some ideas, as Aristotle saw, are the ferment which sets the masses in ebullition. This offers an opportunity. A beginning is made. The further development is unavoidable."

### WHAT IS GOODNESS OR BADNESS OF THE MORES

It is most important to notice that, for the people of a time and place, their own mores are always good, or rather that for them there can be no question of the goodness or badness of their mores. The reason is because the standards of good and right are in the mores. If the life conditions change, the traditional folkways may produce pain and loss, or fail to produce the same good as formerly. Then the loss of comfort and ease brings doubt into the judgment of welfare (causing doubt of the pleasure of the gods, or of war power, or of health), and thus disturbs the unconscious philosophy of the mores. Then a later time will pass judgment on the mores. Another society may also pass judgment on the mores. In our literary and historical study of the mores we want to get from them their educational value, which consists in the stimulus or warning as to what it is, in its effects, societally good or bad. This may lead us to reject or neglect a phenomenon like infanticide, slavery, or witchcraft, as an old "abuse" and "evil," or to pass by the Crusades as a folly which cannot recur. Such a course would be a great error. Everything in the mores of a time and place must be regarded as justified with regard to that time and place. "Good" mores are those which are well adapted to the situation. "Bad" mores are those which are not so adapted. The mores are not so stereotyped and changeless as might appear, because they are forever moving towards more complete adaptation to conditions and interests, and also towards more complete adjustment to each other. People in mass have never made or kept up a custom in order to hurt their own interests. They have made innumerable errors as to what their interests were and how to satisfy them, but they have always aimed to serve their interests as well as they could. This gives the standpoint for the student of the mores. All things in them come before him on the same plane. They all bring instruction and warning. They all have the same relation to power and welfare. The mistakes in them are component parts of them. We do not study them in order to approve some of them and condemn others. They are all equally worthy of attention from the fact that they existed and were used. The chief object of study in them is their adjustment to interests, their relation to welfare, and their coordination in a harmonious system of life policy. For the men of the time there are no "bad" mores. What is traditional and current is the standard of what ought to be. The masses never raise any question about such things. If a few raise doubts and questions, this proves that the folkways have already begun to lose firmness and the regulative element in the mores has begun to lose authority. This indicates that the folkways are on their way to a new adjustment. The extreme of folly, wickedness, and absurdity in the mores is witch persecutions, but the best men of the seventeenth century had no doubt that witches existed, and that they ought to be burned. The religion, statecraft, jurisprudence, philosophy, and social system of that age all contributed to maintain that belief. It was rather a culmination than a contradiction of the current faiths and convictions, just as the dogma that all men are equal and that one ought to have as much political power in the state as another was the culmination of the political dogmatism and social philosophy of the nineteenth century. Hence our judgments of the good and evil consequences of folkways are to be kept separate from our study of the historical phenomena of them, and of their strength and the reasons for it. The judgments have their place in plans and doctrines for the future, not in a retrospect.

## MORE EXACT DEFINITION OF THE MORES

We may now formulate a more complete definition of the mores. They are the ways of doing things which are current in a society to satisfy human needs and desires, together with the faiths, notions, codes, and standards of well living which inhere in those ways, having a genetic connection with them. By virtue of the latter element the mores are traits in the specific character (ethos) of a society or a period. They pervade and control the ways of thinking in all the exigencies of life, returning from the world of abstractions to the world of action, to give guidance and to win revivification. "The mores [Sitten] are, before any beginning of reflection, the regulators of the political, social, and religious behavior of the individual. Conscious reflection is the worst enemy of the mores, because mores begin unconsciously and pursue unconscious purposes, which are recognized by reflection only after long and circuitous processes, and because their expediency often depends on the assumption that they will have general acceptance and currency, uninterfered with by reflection." "The mores are usage in any group, in so far as it, on the one hand, is not the expression or fulfillment of an absolute natural necessity [e.g., eating or sleeping], and, on the other hand, is independent of the arbitrary will of the individual, and is generally accepted as good and proper, appropriate and worthy."

## MIGHT AND RIGHT

Modern civilized states of the best form are often called jural states because the concept of rights enter so largely into all their constitutions and regulations. Our political philosophy centers around that concept, and all our social discussions fall into the form of propositions and disputes about rights. The history of the dogma of rights has been such that rights have been believed to be self-evident and self-existent, and as having prevailed especially in primitive society. Rights are also regarded as the opposite of force. These notions only prove the antagonism between our mores and those of earlier generations. In fact, it is a char-

acteristic of our mores that the form of our thinking about all points of
political philosophy is set for us by the concept of rights. Nothing but
might has ever made right, and if we include in might (as we ought to)
elections and the decisions of courts, nothing but might makes right
now. We must distinguish between the anterior and the posterior view
of the matter in question. If we are about to take some action, and are
debating the right of it, the might which can be brought to support one
view of it has nothing to do with the right of it. If a thing has been done
and is established by force (that is, no force can reverse it), it is right in
the only sense we know, and rights will follow from it which are not
vitiated at all by the force in it. There would be no security at all for
rights if this were not so. We find men and parties protesting, declaiming,
complaining of what is done, and which they say is not "right," but only
force. An election decides that those shall have power who will execute
an act of policy. The defeated party denounces the wrong and wickedness of the act. It is done. It may be a war, a conquest, a spoliation; every
one must help to do it by paying taxes and doing military service or
other duty which may be demanded of him. The decision of a lawsuit
leaves one party protesting and complaining. He always speaks of
"right" and "rights." He is forced to acquiesce. The result is right in the
only sense which is real and true. It is more to the purpose to note that
an indefinite series of consequences follow, and that they create or condition rights which are real and just. Many persons now argue against
property that it began in force and therefore has no existence in right
and justice. They might say the same of marriage or religion. Some do
say the same of the state. The war of the United States with Mexico in
1845 is now generally regarded as unjustified. That cannot affect the
rights of all kinds which have been contracted in the territory then ceded
by Mexico or under the status created on the land obtained by the treaty
of peace with that country. The whole history of mankind is a series of
acts which are open to doubt, dispute, and criticism, as to their right
and justice, but all subsequent history has been forced to take up the
consequences of those acts and go on. The disputants about "rights"
often lose sight of the fact that the world has to go on day by day and
dispute must end. It always ends in force. The end always leaves some
complaining in terms of right and rights. They are overborne by force of
some kind. Therefore might has made all the right which ever has existed
or exists now. If it is proposed to reverse, reform, or change anything
which ever was done because we now think that it was wrong, that is a
new question and a new case, in which the anterior view alone is in

place. It is for the new and future cases that we study historical cases and form judgments on them which will enable us to act more wisely. If we recognize the great extent to which force now enters into all which happens in society, we shall cease to be shocked to learn the extent to which it has been active in the entire history of civilization. The habit of using jural concepts, which is now so characteristic of our mores, leads us into vague and impossible dreams of social affairs, in which metaphysical concepts are supposed to realize themselves, or are assumed to be real.

## Characteristics of the Mores

### THE MORES HAVE THE AUTHORITY OF FACTS

The mores come down to us from the past. Each individual is born into them as he is born into the atmosphere, and he does not reflect on them, or criticize them any more than a baby analyzes the atmosphere before he begins to breathe it. Each one is subjected to the influence of the mores, and formed by them, before he is capable of reasoning about them. It may be objected that nowadays, at least, we criticize all traditions, and accept none just because they are handed down to us. If we take up cases of things which are still entirely or almost entirely in the mores, we shall see that this is not so. There are sects of free-lovers amongst us who want to discuss pair marriage (sec. 374). They are not simply people of evil life. They invite us to discuss rationally our inherited customs and ideas as to marriage, which, they say, are by no means so excellent and elevated as we believe. They have never won any serious attention. Some others want to argue in favor of polygamy on grounds of expediency. They fail to obtain a hearing. Others want to discuss property. In spite of some literary activity on their part, no discussion of property, bequest, and inheritance has ever been opened. Property and marriage are in the mores. Nothing can ever change them but the unconscious and imperceptible movement of the mores. Religion was originally a matter of mores. It became a societal institution and a function of the state. It has now to a great extent been put back into the mores. Since laws with penalties to enforce religious creeds or practices have gone out of use any one may think and act as he pleases about religion. Therefore it is not now "good form" to attack religion. Infidel publications are now tabooed by the mores, and are more effectually repressed than ever before. They produce no controversy. Democracy is in our American mores. It is a product of our physical and economic conditions. It is impossible to discuss or criticize it. It is glorified for popularity, and is a subject of dithyrambic rhetoric. No one treats it with complete candor and sincerity. No one dares to analyze it as he would aristocracy or autocracy. He would get no hearing and would only incur abuse. The thing to be noticed in all these cases is that the masses oppose a deaf ear to every argument against the mores. It is only in so far as things have been transferred from the mores into laws and positive institutions that there is discussion about them or rationalizing upon them. The mores contain the norm by which, if we should discuss the mores, we should have to judge the mores. We learn the mores as unconsciously as we learn to walk and eat and breathe. The masses never learn how we walk, and eat, and breathe, and they never know any reason why the mores are what they are. The justification of them is that when we wake to consciousness of life we find them facts which already hold us in the bonds of tradition, custom, and habit. The mores contain embodied in them notions, doctrines, and maxims, but they are facts. They are in the present tense. They have nothing to do with what ought to be, will be, may be, or once was, if it is not now.

## Life Policy. Virtue vs. Success

### LIFE POLICY

Some primitive or savage groups are very truthful, both in narrative and in regard to their promises or pledged word. Other groups are marked by complete neglect of truthfulness. Falsehood and deceit are regarded as devices by which to attain success in regard to interests. The North American Indians generally regarded deceit by which an enemy was outwitted as praiseworthy; in fact it was a part of the art of war. It is still so regarded in modern civilized warfare. It is, however, limited by rules of morality. There was question whether the deception by which Aguinaldo was captured was within the limit. In sport also, which is a sort of mimic warfare, deception and "jockeying" are more or less recognized as legitimate. Samoan children are taught that it is "unsamoan" to tell the truth. It is stupid, because it sacrifices one's interest. It does not appear that the experience of life teaches truthfulness on any of the lower stages. The truthful peoples are generally the isolated, unwarlike, and simple. Warfare and strength produce cunning and craft. It is only at the highest stage of civilization that deceit is regarded with contempt, and is thought not to pay. That honesty is the best policy is current doctrine, but not established practice now. It is a part of a virtue policy, which is inculcated as right and necessary, but whether it is a success policy is not a closed question.

## SUCCESS POLICY IN THE ITALIAN RENAISSANCE

The historical period in which the success policy was pursued most openly and unreservedly was the Italian Renaissance. The effect on all virtue, especially on truthfulness of speech and character, was destructive, and all the mores of the period were marked by the choice of the code of conduct which disregards truth. The most deep-lying and far-reaching cause of societal change was the accumulation of capital and the development of a capitalistic class. New developments in the arts awakened hope and enterprise, and produced a "boundless passion for discovery" in every direction. The mediaeval church system did not contain much obscurantism in Italy as in some other countries, and the interests of the Italians were intertwined with the hierarchical interests of Rome in many ways. It flattered Italian pride and served Italian interests that Rome should be the center of the Christian world. Every person had ties with the church establishment either directly or by relatives. In spite of philosophic freedom of thought or moral contempt for the clergy, "it was a point of good society and refined taste to support the church." "It was easy for Germans and Englishmen to reason calmly about dethroning the papal hierarchy. Italians, however they might loathe the temporal power, could not willingly forego the spiritual primacy of the civilized world." Thus the Renaissance pursued its aims, which were distinctly worldly, with a superficial good-fellowship towards the church institution. "The attitude of the upper and middle classes of Italy towards the church, at the height of the Renaissance, is a combination of deep and contemptuous dislike with accommodation towards the hierarchy as a body deeply interwoven with actual life, and with a feeling of dependence on sacraments and ritual. All this was crossed, too, by the influence of great and holy preachers."

## THE HUMANISTS

The humanists of Italy are a class by themselves, without historical relations. They had no trade or profession and could make no recognized career. Their controversies had a large personal element. They sought to exterminate each other. Three excuses have been suggested for them. The excessive petting and spoiling they met with when luck favored them; the lack of a guarantee for their physical circumstances, which depended on the caprice of patrons and the malice of rivals; and the delusive influence of antiquity, or of their notions about it. The last destroyed their Christian morality without giving them a substitute. Their careers were such generally that only the strongest moral natures could endure them without harm. They plunged onto changeful and wearing life, in which exhaustive study, the duties of a household tutor, a secretary, or a professor, service near a prince, deadly hostility and danger, enthusiastic admiration and extravagant scorn, excess and poverty, followed each other in confusion. The humanist needed to know how to carry a great erudition and to endure a succession of various positions and occupations. To these were added on occasion stupefying and disorderly enjoyment, and when the basest demands were made on him he had to be indifferent to all morals. Haughtiness was a certain consequence in character. The humanists needed it to sustain themselves, and the alternation of flattery and hatred strengthened them in it. They were victims of subjectiveness. The admiration of classical antiquity was so extravagant and mistaken that all the humanists were subject to excessive suggestion which destroyed their judgment.

THE CULT OF SUCCESS

This deep depravation of all social interests by the elevation of success to a motive which justified itself has the character of an experiment. Amongst ourselves now, in politics, finance, and industry, we see the man-who-can-do-things elevated to a social hero whose success overrides all other considerations. Where that code is adopted it calls for arbitrary definitions, false conventions, and untruthful character.

MORAL ANARCHY

The antagonism between a virtue policy and a success policy is a constant ethical problem. The Renaissance in Italy shows that although moral traditions may be narrow and mistaken, any morality is better than moral anarchy. Moral traditions are guides which no one can afford to neglect. They are in the mores and they are lost in every great revolution of the mores. Then the men are morally lost. Their notions, desires, purposes, and means become false, and even the notion of crime is arbitrary and untrue. If all try the policy of dishonesty, the result will be the firmest conviction that honesty is the best policy. The mores aim always to arrive at correct notions of virtue. In so far as they reach correct results the virtue policy proves to be the only success policy.

# VII

## Prophet

# The Bequests of the Nineteenth Century to the Twentieth

As the new century dawned, Sumner weighed the advantages and liabilities of increases in organized power and popular rule during the previous hundred years. After predicting that the 20th century would be "full of war," he directed most of his attention to the ongoing battle between "democracy" and "plutocracy." When Albert G. Keller discovered this manuscript accidentally twenty-three years after Sumner's death, he concluded that it was written in 1901 and later revised. A reference to the "dying century," however, suggests that it may initially have been written a year earlier. First published posthumously in the *Yale Review* 22 (1933), 732–754.

Many have invited us to a proud review of the increased inheritance of economic power which the nineteenth century hands down to the twentieth. The talent which was received from the eighteenth century is bequeathed with grand usury. The increase is so great that what the nineteenth century got from the eighteenth seems insignificant. The new powers and devices, which are just in their infancy, are a legacy at whose ultimate value we can only guess. The outlying parts of the earth are made available and stand open to the use of the next generations. The nineteenth century bequeaths to the twentieth new land and new arts, which are the prime conditions of material welfare. The capital at the disposal of the human race is immensely greater per capita than it ever was before. There are inexhausted improvements all over the globe which the nineteenth century undertook and paid for, the gain of which will come to the twentieth. Science has a mass of acquired knowledge and processes to confide to the coming generation whose power and value in the struggle for existence are beyond imagination. There are acquisitions in the higher branches of pure mathematics, which are fruitless at present but which are certain to prove of inestimable value to sustain the development of the applications of electricity. The population of the globe is far below the number which it could support with the present resources. Consequently men are in demand. The conjuncture favors numbers. While numbers increase, the comfort per capita will increase. Popular education will pay. The life-conditions will improve. The chances for those who inherit nothing will be good provided that they are industrious, prudent, and temperate. The competition of life is so mild that men are hardly conscious of it. So far as we can see ahead there is every reason for even rash optimism in regard to the material or economic welfare of mankind.

No one will deny that the enterprises of territorial acquisition on the part of the great states which are now being undertaken or which will be undertaken in the twentieth century are very likely to bring them into collision with each other. Already England finds Russia, Germany, and France arrayed in more or less hostile attitude to her because she has priority and advantage in this scramble. Other combinations will be formed in which the United States will be a party. The probability is great that war will result, and even that the century will be as full of war as the eighteenth century was and of the same reasons. The case of China is already actual, and the course of things suggests doubt and fear of the future. The possibilities of disturbance and mischief are very great, and they will so far as they occur traverse the realization of economic welfare which the economic powers and organization promise. It is not, however, the purpose of the present article to dwell upon this outlook of practical international politics, for in that domain one could at best predict and speculate. The prospect that the program of action will cause war touches upon our subject only so far as it is political. Our present purpose is to notice those elements in the social and political world of to-day which we are handing down together with the above described elements of economic gain, and which are certain to affect the realization of the optimistic prospects above described.

Along with all economic knowledge and industrial effort there must go always decisions of industrial policy. Success in industrial production and success in the selection of wise lines of policy are two very different things. The questions of policy are generally nowadays questions of politics, and here is where the existing conditions contain elements of peril. Pessimistic views of the situation from the side of politics are as thoroughly justified as optimistic views from the side of economic power. A mere optimist is an idiot who will not think, or be prudent, or listen to reason. He seems to be in fashion just now, and in the popular use pessimist is a term of opprobrium. Every man of sense is a pessimist; that is to say, he is cautious. He knows that he must expect some bad luck and that things never turn out all smooth and easy as they are planned—he tries to prepare for evil contingencies by precautions and an "anchor to windward."

These decisions must nowadays be made by the concurrence of large bodies of men because the industrial organization is so large and complex. The decisions of policy affect the relations of parties in the industrial organization, that is to say, they affect rights. The decisions also call into being institutions or provide for ways of using existing institutions by methods which are due to "understandings" or agreements. In the majority of cases these decisions must be made by the legislature and take the form of law. They then affect the interests of the whole population and the rights of individuals and groups. The problem of justice in these cases is a serious one. It is rendered more serious by the speed with which the changes occur, on account of which there is not time to revise and correct one policy before another supersedes it. The coercion of the state to enforce a policy decided upon by the legislature is indispensable. The state is an organization of force. In its origin it was an organization of force for conquest and subjugation, and it produced plunder, slavery, and the exploitation of one group by another. In its highest form it has become an organization of force to enforce rights and to give efficiency to institutions according to the views and policy which prevail in the community at the time. The co-operation of the state, therefore, with industrial enterprise, to maintain peace and order, to ensure the regular operation of civil institutions, and to guarantee rights is indispensable to industry. This is the connection of economics and politics.

During the nineteenth century the state, as it was inherited from the eighteenth century, has undergone great improvement. The nineteenth century inherited from the eighteenth vague notions of political beatification. To abolish kings and get a "republic" would, it was expected, bring universal and endless peace and happiness. Then the idea was to get the "rights of man" declared and sworn to. Then the result was to come from universal suffrage in the republic. Then democracy was to be the realizer of hope and faith. It was thought that a democracy never would be warlike or extravagant in expenditure. Then faith was put in constitutional government, whether republican or monarchical. Next hope turned to representative institutions as the key to the right solution. The century ends with despondency as to each and all of these notions. Now social democracy and state socialism seem to be the divinities which are to beatify us. The faith that beatification is possible and that some piece of political machinery can get it for us seems to be as strong as ever. In the details of life and practice much has been gained in regard to peace, security, conditions of welfare, and actual experience in the body politic, beyond what existed a hundred years ago. The security of life, property, and honor, for men and women, is greater in all civilized countries than it was.

Wherever there is a force in human society the problem is to use it and regulate it; to get the use and prevent the abuse of it. The state is no exception; on the contrary, it is the chief illustration. In all the forms of the state which have ever existed families, groups, classes, corporations have struggled with each other to get into their hands the power of the state. To get control of this power is to win the industrial products (wealth), after other people have made them, without labor of one's own. This is the real objection to all class government, and it is just as strong to-day against the democratic mass or the middle class joint stock company as it ever was against king or aristocracy. The great and standing abuse of the political organization is the control of it by a clique or faction so that they can use it to serve their own interests at the expense of everybody else. No state has ever existed which has not been subject to this abuse, for, in practice, the power of the state must be in the hands of some group of men. The theory of the state is that this group is to use the power for the welfare of all. In practice they have always used the power for their own advantage.

The nineteenth century bequeaths to the twentieth a state organization which is still infected with this vice under new forms which conform to the middle class constitutional state with representative institutions, whether it is monarchical or republican, aristocratic or democratic. In fact, the immense increase in all facilities of transportation and communication has made it not only possible but necessary to organize industry in co-operative combinations which reach over state boundaries and embrace the whole globe. It is idle to criticise or bewail this fact. The genii whom we call up will obey, but there are consequences of using genii and he who uses them must take the consequences. If we use steam and electricity we must get space for their evolutions, and we must adjust our plans to their incidental effects. Organization on a grand scale is a necessary consequence of steam and electricity. The little independent man is forced into a place in a great organization where he may win more but will lose his independence. It is as inevitable as the introduction of machinery and the consequences of machinery.

The corresponding function of the state and the importance of the political element (legislation) have increased in equal degree. The modern industrial state transfers millions on a punctuation mark in an act of the legislature. To get the legislative machine into one's control is worth ever so much more than it ever was before. To get the use and avoid the abuse of the state is harder than it ever was before. It is harder in the democratic republic than in any other form of the state. There are thousands of men in public life or in the lobby who suppose that this is all as it should be. They suppose that to elect a legislature and then work bills through it which will be to somebody's profit is the regular order of things. That, they suppose, is what it is all for. There is not a civilized state with parliamentary institutions which has not had a financial scandal within ten years.

It is a great mistake to say, as we hear people say every day, that this abuse is perpetrated by capitalists and corporations. It is perpetrated by everybody. Capitalists try to get a protective tariff. They turn to the laborers and say the tariff will raise their wages, and the laborers respond at once to the pocket argument. Everybody who can get a pension votes for pensions regardless of justice, right, truth, public welfare, and all those other noble things. Socialistic schemes are without exception appeals to the greed of the masses, for the propositions all mean taking from those who have and giving to them who have not. Policemen, teachers, and other employees organize politically to further their pecuniary interests at the public expense.

Populism or social democracy is the abuse of democracy which is parallel to the older abuses of earlier forms of the state. In democracy the power resides in the masses. In social democracy the masses are organized to win materialistic advantages for themselves by the use of their political power. In all our discussions we talk as if political functions ought to be exercised in obedience to some abstract notions of political and societal welfare. In practice they are exercised to serve interests. Debtors *vs.* creditors, tenants *vs.* landlords, shippers *vs.* transporters, wage receivers *vs.* wage givers, passengers *vs.* carriers, *et cetera* are, of course, antagonistic in their interests. Their antagonism is in the industrial organization. They have recourse to political enginery that they try to direct against each other for victory in their economic battles. If a group of us are passengers, let us get passage rates fixed by law. Why then may not the carriers at the next session get a majority and advance their own interests at the expense of passengers? The temperance people took to politics to crush the saloon. The saloon organized politically first for defense, then for aggression, and it became a permanent power in politics. This retaliation or reaction is to be counted upon, and it results in turning politics into a scramble of interests. The interstate commerce

law was thought to be a great gain when it was passed. It was planned
to satisfy certain views and to override and destroy certain usages. The
assailed interests defended themselves and sought escape. Whoever
imagined that the law would have the effect which it has had on the
railroad organization of the country, although it was fully predicted that
its effects would be far other than those which were expected and intended? The lawmaker who goes to work with his face in one direction
expecting to advance on a chosen line will find that he always has reactions to deal with and that they may be far stronger than his purpose.

Evidently all this tends towards an alternative question. Can the state
find anywhere power to repel all the special interests and keep uppermost the one general interest or the welfare of all? Will the state itself
degenerate into the instrument of an attack on property, and will it
cripple wealth-making or will the wealth-making interest, threatened
by the state, rise up to master it, corrupt it, and use it? This is the alternative which the twentieth century must meet. It is the antagonism of
democracy and plutocracy. It is the most momentous antagonism which
has ever arisen in human society because it is internal; it is in the vitals
of society. We have had a foretaste of it in the last two presidential
elections in which the voters have shown that they would disregard
everything else in order to secure property interests and the public order
which is essential to wealth production.

The problem would be far easier to solve if it were not for the easy
political optimism which is another of the bequests of the nineteenth
century to the twentieth. We are told to "trust the people"; that the
people will decide all questions wisely; that the people will protect its
institutions and will correct all abuses. Who is "the people" as the term
is used in these hard-worn phrases? Where does it stay? How can it be
reached? Where does it utter its oracles? How can we test and verify
what is asserted about the people? We have been trained in a habit of
"wanting to know" on all the other fields. Why may we not demand to
be allowed to employ the same processes here? The people is what is
called nowadays a "political symbol." It is a mythological product and
has no definition. It is an object of reverence and faith like Fate or Destiny. We know that it is not the population. It is a part of the population
but an undefined part, a lost part absorbed or immanent somewhere in
the total. The word is one of the counters with which party editors,
politicians, and half-educated platform orators juggle. Why does not the
people do some of the things which we are told that it can do, so that
we might believe in it? There are tasks enough undone, which are the
people's business. The people is said to rule in a democratic republic.

It fills no offices. We see it nowhere. It has reserved to itself the function of selecting legislative bodies from time to time. This is the way in which it rules. The rest of the time it is quiescent. We go into the legislatures, and we see what kind of men the people have selected. We see then how it has performed this function.

The eighteenth-century republicans were sure that if the people elected the legislature, it would select men of brains, character, virtue, independence, and so forth. We have found that this expectation was a delusion as much as the notion that democracies would be unwarlike and frugal. The point now is, however, that it is the legislature which the people elects which has got to meet the assaults of special interests which were described above. The root of all our troubles at present and in the future is in the fact that the people fails of what was assumed about it and attributed to it. If the people is (as the newspapers say it is) angry at the raids of plutocrats on the legislatures, why does not the people elect legislatures which cannot be raided? He who rules is responsible, be it Tsar, Pope, Emperor, Aristocracy, Oligarchy, or Demos. Some people wax very indignant against anybody who, as they say, bribes a legislator. It takes two to perpetrate bribery. The relation between the two may vary through a very wide scale. It is possible that a man may buy a legislature to get what he ought not to have. It is also possible that a legislature may blackmail a man before giving him what he ought to have. There are many grades between these two extremes. The bribee is in any case more base than the briber, for he betrays a public trust. Why does not the people elect legislators who will do their duty and not take bribes at all? The indignant denouncers of bribers stand with their backs to the truth. No one would ever bribe a legislator if he could get what he wanted without it and could not get what he wanted even with it. Of course this is no apology for the briber. It is an attempt to analyze the case in order to see the real elements in it and their relation to each other. Our popular preachers and teachers will not entertain the possibility that the people is at fault. In fact, the people is altogether at fault. It has not done its first duty in the premises, and therefore the whole institution has gone astray.

The current answer which is given with confidence is that the people is controlled by politicians. It is true, but it is a fatal answer. What shall be said of an oracle which pleads that somebody deceived it? What shall be said of a sovereign who says that he was dictated to by somebody?

Democracy is another "political symbol." It is unanalyzed. The term is used as if it had a single and simple definition. Democracy includes Jacobinism, Sansculottism, Social Democracy or Populism, Mobocracy, besides two or three legitimate forms. When it is glorified in orations and books one kind is meant. When it is in operation another kind is at work. Before the twentieth century is out, men will know more about democracy. It answers our present purpose to note only that democracy is the power of numbers. It assumes that numbers have a right in the nature of things to rule. Of course that is entirely untrue. There is nobody who, in the nature of things, ought to rule. The doctrine that the "voice of the people is the voice of God," is just as silly as the doctrine that the voice of the autocrat is the voice of God. We have had the fetish man (king priest) and the fetish book. Now we have the fetish crowd. The sum of superstition in the world seems to be a constant quantity. The divine right of a big (or bigger) number to rule is just as false as the divine right of one to rule. No one has a right to rule. It is all a question of expediency to get our affairs carried on satisfactorily. Why not have done with "natural right," and "divine authority," and the rest? We have got rid of them in metaphysics and theology. Why should a hard-headed and practical people transfer all this old superstition over into politics? Why get up a new political mythology and a new apparatus of fictions and humbugs? Why not look at things as they are; not at words? Democracy is like every other --ocracy, a dogmatic system; and we are surfeited with phrases, catchwords, cant, dogmas about democracy which are false. The trouble with them is that they are popular. People like them. They know that they are falsehoods, but they are flattering to human nature. There is a great deal of pathos about democracy, using pathos in the original Greek sense. It is surrounded with a halo of sentiment and emotion, and is enveloped in affectionate concessions which protect it from scrutiny. It is a pet notion which is in fashion, and so there are penalties against anyone who touches it rudely as he might touch monarchy or aristocracy. It is elevated into the plane of a social religion and is given the prestige of political orthodoxy.

It is in the nature of things that a set of conventional falsehoods and stereotyped dogmas should produce false institutions. You begin by attributing to numbers an authority which numbers never possess and cannot exercise, and you end with a legislature which has not the brains or the integrity to stand a raid by the lobby. You look for some representation of *all* which shall defend all against some. This, as has been shown above, is the great need in any and every form of the state. You find agents of all ready to betray all to some. Democracy is jealous of the power of wealth. It denies the right of wealth to political power and ostracizes it. What happens? Wealth is power. Everybody knows it. It is a just social power. In modern society wealth (capital) is the power which has supplanted rank and which moves the world. Its power in society is even made subject of exaggeration and denunciation. This surely is recognition of it. Socialism, denouncing property, is only trying to get property (other peoples'—that of the rich to give it to the poor). All schemes of social amelioration or improvement aim to make poor people richer. It always has been so. Plutocracy has existed in all society in all ages. In truth, it is not as efficient now as in any former age, assertions to the contrary notwithstanding. The jealousy and hostility of democracy to plutocracy are due to the fact that democracy recognizes its adversary.

The economic state of the world at the present time, as described at the beginning of this article, is the cause of the power of democracy. Numbers are now economically demanded. The man is superior, for the time being, to the dinner or the dollar. In other states of things men will be present in greater supply than the demand will employ. Then the dinner will be greater than the man, as it has been many and many a time in the course of human history. During the twentieth century the men will be in demand, and democracy will be strong, but the wealth, denied recognition and legitimate power in politics, will do what we now see it do; it will exert an illicit and corrupting power because its processes will be secret and unavowable. It is amusing to hear "publicity" advocated as a cure when secrecy is a minor symptom only of the disease. Plutocracy is not every form of the power of wealth, much less is the word properly used when, as often occurs, it is used for great wealth and luxury. Plutocracy means properly a form of societal organization in which wealth is the ruling power. Hence a democracy turns into a plutocracy not when it recognizes wealth as a legitimate form of social power in any state but when after trying to exclude it from any power a state of things is produced in which wealth is the real power by secret, illicit, and corrupt operation.

The state of things which results is well known to us, but the current discussion of it is very one-sided. No one appears to admit that democracy can be at fault. What are the facts? Legislative strikes, "hold ups," and special legislation are complementary forms of abuse. The kind of legislature which "the people" elects goes to work to threaten wealth, especially corporate wealth, with hostile legislation or, when asked to pass acts which are needed to organize industry, it makes interested opposition. The men to whom great corporate interests are entrusted have to meet the situation. If they did not attend to the matter before the legislature was elected they find themselves in calamity a little later. This aspect of the matter is either ignored or denied; but one must have little knowledge of affairs as they go on to dispute the truth of it. The next development is the boss. The money interests would never meddle with legislation if they could help it. It is dangerous. They prefer to deal with a boss who holds no office, who is an individual, who can be held responsible to them but not to the public, who wants only campaign funds. This is a new and very evident corruption of the democracy, for it strengthens the evolution of the boss. When the money interests and the boss have formed their alliance, it is available to enable the plutocrats to get what they ought not to have. The action and reaction of these operations is disastrous to the political system; and this reaction is exactly what forms the chief part of legislative activity to-day. The twentieth century inherits it as a system in full operation whose consequences the next generations must meet and whose remedy they must find. There ought to be a free and pitiless exposition of democracy, as a political system and philosophy, which would show just what it is and is not.

The evolution of democracy has produced a type of person in the nineteenth century which is now to be bequeathed to the twentieth. This is the man-on-the-curbstone. He is now in full control, and his day of glory will be the twentieth century. He is ignorant, noisy, self-sufficient, dogmatic, and impatient of opposition or remonstrance. He is ready to talk at any time about anything, but he prefers to talk of public affairs. He talks a great deal. Often he edits a newspaper. The newspapers bow down to him, flatter him, and treat him as the specimen type of "the people." It is in the name of that venerated "symbol" that he commonly speaks. When he wants to say a thing he says that the people says it. When he wants a thing he says that the people wants it. Taine called him the *cuistre*, for he is well known in France, where he is almost always an editor. He is also in authority in England. He is the typical person who is referred to as the common man, the average citizen, and who is credited with superhuman insight and wisdom. His cleverness is put in especially strong contrast with that of the learned. The doctrine seems to be that if a man who once was humble and ignorant uses all the means mortals have in order to try to find out something, the result is that he knows less than his humble and ignorant comrades who never made any such attempt. The man-on-the-curbstone is not one of the quiet people who go about their own affairs and who, since they make no noise, are neglected. He puts himself in evidence, and seeks opportunity to make demonstrations with badges, with shouts and cries. He responds very promptly to the military appeal. That is exactly in his line. There is no need to know or think much. The affair is one of noise and hurrah, bells and trumpets, flags and drums, speeches and poetry. He is always great on patriotism. He supposes that patriotism is an affair of enthusiasm and brag and bluster. He calls the flag "Old Glory" and wants a law that it shall be raised on all schoolhouses. Such matters as this occupy his mind. He has taken us in hand since the Spanish War and has fixed the destiny of this country. The people who knew better have nearly all thought it policy not to oppose the popular current set by this type of person. The newspapers have taken their cue from him, and our destiny has been settled without any reason or sense, without regard to history or political philosophy. That the press, the pulpit, the universities, the magazines could have so given up their functions and prostrated themselves before this organ of folly, for fear of falling out of sympathy with the man-on-the-curbstone, would have been incredible if we had not lived through it. What is the use of trying to learn anything? What is the use of preaching to young men that they should stick to what they think is true and should act from principle not from popularity? Their parents and teachers do not do it. What is the use of bewailing "commercialism" and the power of money? It is all humbug, if we know that everybody does and will act from gain or policy when the occasion arises. What is the use of talking about making good citizens in our universities when our young men see that what every-body does is to listen for the keynote from the man-on-the-curbstone and then begin to shout it as hard as he can without regard to anything else. All humbug is shameful and disgusting. If commercialism is the code, let us avow it.

The man-on-the-curbstone is not a speechmaker. His method is em-phatic conversation with anyone who comes along. He writes frequent letters to the newspapers which appear in the column of "Letters from the People." No one who ever reads that column will be able to retain "trust in the people." Perhaps the most remarkable display of what the man-on-the-curbstone is capable of was his letters to the newspapers on the Sampson-Schley controversy, in which he stated his valuable opinion on the strategy of the naval battle of Santiago. He (and his wife) assails legislatures with fads about the naval canteen, vivisec-tion, text-books of physiology, the age of consent, for he prides himself on being a reformer and a man of moral motives. This is the ruling class in the United States. He is one of the most marked products of the nineteenth century, and the twentieth will have its woes before it has done with him.

The eighteenth century bequeathed to the nineteenth notions of the state of nature, natural rights, social compact, equality of all men, sovereignty of the people, fighting doctrines. The nineteenth century is bequeathing to the twentieth a large assortment of popular or semi-popular notions about economic facts and relations. It is current doctrine in large circles of the ruling classes that the laborer (wage class) is entitled to the whole of the product; that all the wealth which the rich accumulate is taken away from others, especially from the poor; that land is a gratuitous gift of God which never ought to be appropriated by anybody; that God provided a fund (viz. the unearned increment from land) to pay the expenses of the civil organization; that there is some danger from large aggregations of capital; that it is not the man who creates the wealth which he accumulates but the society around him so that this society may justly confiscate it when he dies; that there is some innate tendency in things which is called progress, meaning a tendency all the time to become more and more as men would like to have them. The natural and necessary effect of the increased material comfort of the nineteenth century is to increase discontent. This is perfectly correct in human nature. The contented man is he who never has anything and never had any expectation that he ever could get anything. To get something opens the mind to hope for more and produces discontent. The countries in which the gain has been greatest are those in which the discontent is greatest. A writer who knew Russia said that there was no discontent there except amongst those who expected an order or title on the last royal birthday and did not get it. The social and political philosophy which has been spread abroad in the nineteenth century has nourished a doctrine that if a man wants anything which he has not got it is the fault of somebody else who ought to be found and compelled to give it to him. The age is fond of phrases. It cajoles itself with words. Its literary and rhetorical purveyors treat it as if it would take nothing but honey and pie. The future historian, if he ever reads the newspapers of to-day, will wonder whether the American people of to-day really were so unwilling to listen to reason that it was necessary to feed them all the time with flattery, appeals to national vanity, gratification of their ill-educated prejudices, and reiterated assurances of their greatness, wisdom, and virtue. The real interests of the country and these matters with which popular attention is all the time occupied stand in glaring contrast to each other. It is the combination of all these tendencies which gives significance to the above mentioned economic notions. The United States has its peculiar phases, but other states suffer from the same popular delusions. The rage of disillusion and disappointment will have to be met by the inheriting century.

The bequest of economic and social confusion and contradiction, not to say fallacy, which the dying century leaves to the coming one is a formidable charge of peril and societal burden.

The mode of thought according to which popularity is a test of truth, right, or wisdom leads people to say that few believe in a certain proposition or hold a certain opinion, as if that was conclusive as to the truth or correctness of the proposition or opinion. No one could seriously believe this. The number of people who believe a thing to be true does not even create a presumption about it one way or the other. If it did, why not open the polls and get the oracle to solve some of the hard questions in the domain of science, for instance, the monogenistic or polygenistic origin of the human race. Are political and social questions so easy that the poll plan may be applicable to them and not to abstruse scientific questions? Quite the contrary. The questions of social policy which are mooted to-day are the hardest questions with which we have to deal because we have no positive and specific processes by which to solve them. They also bear the heaviest weight of consequences for the weal or woe of men. But the great point in connection with this matter of popularity is this—What is the use of education, learning, training, discipline, if the numbers can solve the questions? or if numbers hold the ultimate test by which to revise and verify the results? Of course we have no ultimate tests of truth and wisdom. That is a reason for caution and study; it is not a reason for throwing every interest into the street to be kicked around in a crowd and amongst the newspapers, to be caught up by politicians, when it has got a certain vogue, so that they think they can make capital out of it, and to be embodied in crude and hasty legislation whose consequences will be utterly different from what was expected. The history of every year which passes is full of cases of this kind.

Everybody is passing judgment on the way in which his neighbors choose to live. Why not let each other be happy each in his own way? Every man, every group resents the criticism and regulation when he or they are affected by it. The farmers want an oleomargarine law, but if a dairy law is proposed they resist it with all the doctrines of the "let alone" policy. What everybody wants for himself is "peace and quiet." It is what the age needs for the recuperation of its nerves, but society is full of schemers eager to "get a majority" so as to use it to meddle with some other people's way of living their lives. The young century inherits turmoil and clamor with little knowledge or sense. The newspapers are, according to the conditions of the case, forced to catch everything as it flies. They have no time for quiet and sober reflection. They never finish anything. They never go deeply into anything and never go back to correct mistakes. The methods are those of haste and superficiality, and what tells is the most striking phase of a matter which at the critical moment happens to be uppermost. In the turmoil and clamor what is most effective is anything which can capture attention and hold it for a moment before the chance passes. Hence the point of what is here said is not, for instance, the question whether the imperialists or the anti-imperialists are right; it is whether what is done either way shall be decided by sober knowledge and reason and whether the discussion of the matter shall be conducted on a plane of considerations which are appropriate for an enlightened society. The popular talk about "Destiny" and "Providence" has this much sense in it, that it recognizes and ex-presses the fact that we have been whirled along by quite other methods than these, at the sport of forces which we set loose but cannot control, and loaded with consequences which we find it hard to bear.

The opposite of the popularity theory of truth, wisdom, and right is the expert theory. According to this we must look for truth and wisdom to the specialists in each case, and the work of society is to be carried on by combining the knowledge which they all bring to the common stock. Every man of sense acts on this theory except in politics. Popular discussions are generally carried on in the form of submitting the facts and leaving the hearers to form their own opinions. Is it true that "form-ing opinions" is the easy part which anyone can do for himself? Quite the contrary. The greatest astronomer living, if he wanted to know what to think about a question in biology, would go to a biologist and ask him what he ought to think about it. Of course he could not do otherwise since he would have questions in chemistry, physics, political economy, and so on without end, and he would need a hundred lifetimes in which to "form opinions" on them all. "Authority" is out of date, but everyone must know that competent authority (on everything but political and social questions) is what we have to live by. All that has helped mankind to gain anything (what is commonly called progress) is *knowledge* of the world in which we live. The masses have never won knowledge. Instead of numbers, it has always been individuals who have won knowledge. It has not come of itself to "those who eddy round and round." It has cost toil and sacrifice. In every domain except politics the authority of the specialist and expert is being more and more definitely acknowledged. Especially in the arts, as they go on to more complex development, the scientific training is more essential and is commanding its authority. Are political and social affairs any proper exception? As they become grander and the interests affected by them become greater, the forces of greed, vanity, chicane, passion which enter into them are, as we see, more powerful. How shall our affairs prosper in this domain except by knowledge and special training? The new century may well complain that the last one hands down to it political institutions and machinery which are in irrational contrast to other societal developments and to the tasks which are handed down at the same time.

The man-on-the-curbstone resents expert advice and the whole theory of special knowledge. He says that it is un-democratic, un-American, and that it shows distrust of the people. He is conscious of the issue which it raises, for the expert theory of human affairs would dethrone him from his position. He cannot afford to take expert advice, for he would confess his own incapacity for the functions which he has undertaken. He is like an incompetent autocrat who must be acted upon by a clever minister, by suggestion and insinuation, so that he may believe or at least pretend that the ideas originated in his own mind. Our politicians treat the man-on-the-curbstone in the same way. Civil service reform is the first positive measure in which the expert theory and the numbers theory have come in collision, and the history of that effort is instructive for the understanding of the issue and the obstacles which it will meet. The more the economic system expands and the greater its power to produce wealth becomes, the greater also the responsibilities and tasks of the state become by territorial expansion, the greater will be the harm from institutions and usages built on delusive dogmas of political power and wisdom. The young century will have a right to complain that the penalty of all these dogmas and usages has been passed down upon it.

It is very easy to take sides in regard to the antagonisms which have been noted and to say that, of course, the other side is doing wrong and therefore is to blame for all the trouble. Democracy and plutocracy make each other worse by their conflict. That democratic institutions are corrupted to their core by the plutocratic legislation which has been described is obvious. There is nothing left of democracy when politicians squeeze money out of capitalists and corporations with which to win elections and pay it back by jobbing legislation. The most essential interests of everybody who has any property, from the man who has a hundred dollars in the savings bank up to the millionaire, are imperilled by legislative strikes and jobs and crank legislation according to a Henry George or some other half-educated apostle of the millennium, in which everybody is to have everything for nothing by recognizing and securing to him the gifts of God—as if the world bore any evidence that God had made it to be a paradise for everybody without any trouble. Everybody applauds denunciations of plutocracy or of democracy according to his adopted standpoint and pet notions. Everybody dreams of a victory for his pet ideas "in the twentieth century." They will all be disappointed. They will produce great strife and confusion and loss, but the bigger force will prevail over the smaller in 2001 just as surely as it does to-day. Now, what is the greater force—the man or the dollar (we should say the dinner)? There are those who say that the men are, and they wax indignantly eloquent at the idea of putting the dinner above the man.

Now note the facts of experience: (1) the cases of the tariff, the pensions, the socialistic devices, in short, all the cases in which men make friends with the steal when they get into it, prove the power of the dinner over the man, because they show the man repudiating his principles in favor of his interests. (2) All the achievements of the plutocrats which are denounced prove that they are men of transcendent ability, more powerful than thousands of other men put together simply by force of brains. Every disputant who enters the debate affirms these two facts. They are the foundation of the case of all who believe in numbers. Now put them together. Then we have the men of intellectual force, with the force of capital in their hands, and the very arena in which they have shown their power is that of "votes" and of the democratic legislature, where the orators of lunar political economy say that they expect to defeat them. What is the conclusion? That the plutocrats should be allowed to have their own way? Not by any means; but that the lunar politics should be discarded and not allowed to form the platform of attacks on property. Property is the strongest, deepest, most universal interest of mankind. It is the most fundamental condition of the struggle for existence; that is to say, of the welfare of mankind. It does not mean millions of dollars; it means cents. It must be aggregated in large masses under personal control or the work of society cannot go on. It is silly to get into states of excitement about "large aggregations of capital" or the "excessive wealth of individuals." If the legislature were pure and if it restricted itself to its proper business, it would have no trouble at all in regulating any arrogance of wealth whenever it showed itself. The contest of democracy and plutocracy is the contest between the economic power and opportunity mentioned at the outset and the political conditions under which it must be carried on.

In the history of the United States the conflict between democracy and plutocracy began when the protective system was adopted, and the protective system has been the origin of all the ramifications of the special abuses of legislation which have come in since, for the evil methods were invented in connection with tariff legislation, and the great device for forcing legislation on behalf of other special interests has been to threaten to break the steal if not admitted into it. The protectionists have necessarily been forced to help every other job. It has, therefore, become a question in regard to every "reform" whether it is a real contest against an abuse for the purpose of destroying it or only a means of forcing admission for another party into the profits of the abuse. The reforms all die, one after another, when the clamor ceases, and that comes when those who made the outcry have been appeased by a slice of the plunder. There are very few groups of reformers who have not succumbed to these bribes. The statesman who put into a formula the determination to fight the steal or get into it deserves the honors of the debate. The ship subsidy is the biggest and most shameless proposition to perpetrate a job and a steal in the face of the whole country which has yet been made. It may be taken as a landmark in political jobbery to show at the turning point of the century how far we have come. The pensions, the oleomargarine law, the attacks on trusts and department stores, and the formulated demands of populists and "organized labor" are only other incidents in the rising war inside of society between democracy and plutocracy.

The protective system is another problem which is bequeathed to the new century, not only as a part of plutocracy but as a positive device. Free trade is not a matter of political economy. It is a matter of common sense and enlightenment. As the great modern inventions draw the world together and consolidate the whole into one great economic unit, the state lines which mark off political control are found to break the prosperous action of the economic functions. The protective laws of the different states of the world are now a gigantic attempt to defeat the action of all the great modern industrial forces and in spite of them to give arbitrary form to the local industries of each separate state. Can it be done? No intelligent man can believe that it can be done for long. The attempt can produce only confusion and loss. Every interest which is staked on it is in peril every moment, for a new invention at any moment may make all the tariff apparatus futile and ridiculous. There must come a time when it is a question of life or death to all the interests inside of the protective system to take it down, and the problem how to take it down is a very serious one from any point of view. The generation which has to take it down will not see in it any reason to bless their fathers for building it. Already experience has shown us some of the contradictions between being a state with a stringent protective system and being a world power. The contradictions will work out a solution which the twentieth century will have to meet. It is no enviable task.

The summary of the line of thought in this paper is that while the outlook on the twentieth century from the industrial standpoint is in the highest degree encouraging, the outlook from the political stand-point is of the opposite character. It is essential to the interests of human society that its institutions should be developed harmoniously; its political institutions and methods must be adequate to perform in a healthful manner the functions which they are called on to perform in order to sustain the development of the industrial organization. Such is not now the case, and the consequence is that the nineteenth century bequeaths to the twentieth a great degree of social confusion, both in ideas and in institutions, which is due to the maladjustment between the industrial system and the political system. It is plain that each of these systems has a sphere of legitimate and independent activity. A victory either of democracy over plutocracy or of plutocracy over democracy would be disastrous to civilization. For the present and the immediate future the purification of political institutions is the most urgent task which demands our effort, and it seems that the most effective effort in that direction is to dispel the illusions and popular notions which now prevail in this domain.

# The Mores of the Present and the Future

In one of his last published essays, Sumner looked pessimistically at a rising tide of socialism that within three years gave Eugene Debs the largest socialist vote in an American presidential election. Divorce was up sharply, threatening the family. Immigrants and rural Americans thronged to the cities. Popular culture provided only sentimentalism and sensationalism. Offering little hope, the two major parties seemed bankrupt: the Democrats having run the populistic William Jennings Bryan unsuccessfully three times, the Republicans still under the cloud of the Theodore Roosevelt years. Playing the Jeremiah, Sumner insisted that current mores reflected a temporarily favorable balance in the land-man ratio, reasserting the Malthusianism that was a bedrock of his thought. Disaster awaited when the "exceptional period" passed. Originally published in the *Yale Review* 18 (1909), 233–245; reprinted in *War*, ed. Albert Galloway Keller, pp. 149–164.

The great utility of studying the origin and history of the mores would be to form judgments about their present status and future tendency. The future tendency can never be discussed beyond the immediate future without running into predictions which would always be vague and in a high degree uncertain. For instance, there is now more or less discussion about divorce, and it will unquestionably affect the mores about marriage. Whether the discussion properly reflects any movement of popular interest is an important question with regard to the present status and tendency. Also, if we could reach results with regard to the present drift of things, we might become convinced of the probable changes in the marriage institution, but more definite or far-reaching predictions about marriage would be unwise.

It will be well to begin with a restatement of the definition of the mores. When a number of men living in neighborhood have the same needs, each one of them attempts to satisfy his need as well as he can whenever it recurs. They notice each other's efforts and select the attempt which satisfies the need best with the least pain or exertion. A selection results by which one way becomes customary for all—a habit of each and a custom for society. This way is a folkway. It has the power of a habit and custom, and is carried on by tradition. It has the character originally of an experiment. It is established by selection and approved by experience. Here then we have some reflection and some judgment:

the reflection is caused by pleasure or pain, which the lowest savages experience and use for criticism; and the judgments are the most simple, consisting only in comparison of effort and satisfaction. From the reflection and judgment there arises at last an opinion as to the relation of the mode of satisfying needs to welfare. This is a moral opinion; namely, an opinion that a usage is favorable to welfare. When a folkway has this moral and reflective judgment added to it, it becomes a part of the mores. The moral inferences become wider and vaguer as they go on, but they constitute, when taken together, the best thinking men can do on human life and wisdom in it. The mores are the customs in which life is held when taken together with the moral judgments as to the bearing of the same on welfare.

The mores, in their origin, were immediately connected with ghost fear and religion, because they came down by tradition from ancestors. This gave them the sanction of a high and vague authority from the other world and created the first notion of duty. Together these elements made up the mental life of men for ages, when they were laying the foundation of all our mental operations and forming our first mental outfit.

I use the word "folkways" for ways of doing things which have little or no moral element. The greatest and best example is language. Language is habit and custom; its formation is made by acts of judgment, although the consideration is slight, the judgment is vague and unconscious, and the authority of tradition prevails. Uneducated people make or destroy a language, in their life, satisfying their interests and needs; expediency seems to be the highest motive. Abortion and infanticide are folkways which simply satisfy the desire to avoid care and toil. Children are a great trouble and adults try to shirk the burden; they adopt direct means to get rid of it. Religion sanctifies the acts and they become customary; then they are a law and beyond argument. In time, however, conditions change. If, for example, warriors are needed, then abortion and infanticide do not seem wise beyond question; the means of getting food may be easier, and affection has a chance to grow. Then these folkways are subjected to reflection again and a new judgment is formed, with the result that the customs are set aside by doubt and revolt. While they last they are mores, not folkways. The murder of children had a moral judgment of wisdom and right policy in it while it was practiced, and the same may be said of the custom of killing the old.

What now are some of the leading features in the mores of civilized society at the present time? Undoubtedly they are monogamy, antislavery, and democracy. All people now are more nervous than anybody used to be. Social ambition is great and is prevalent in all classes. The idea of class is unpopular and is not understood. There is a superstitious yearning for equality. There is a decided preference for a city life, and a stream of population from the country into big cities. These are facts of the mores of the time, and our societies are almost unanimous in their response if there is any question raised on these matters.

It is very difficult to discuss the mores; we can hardly criticise them, for they are our law of right. We are all in them, born in them, and made by them. How can we rise above them to pass judgment on them? Our mores are very different from those of the Middle Ages. Mediaeval people conceived of society under forms of status as generally as we think of it under forms of individual liberty. The mores of the Orient and the Occident differ from each other now as they apparently always have differed: the Orient is a region where time, faith, tradition, and patience rule, while the Occident forms ideals and plans and spends energy and enterprise to make new things with thoughts of progress. All details of life follow the leading ways of thought of each group. We can compare and judge ours and theirs, but independent judgment of our own, without comparison with other times or other places, is possible only within narrow limits.

Let us first take up the nervous desire and exertion which mark the men of our time in the Western civilized societies. There is a wide popular belief in what is called progress. The masses in all civilized states strain toward success in some adopted line. Struggling and striving are passionate tendencies which take possession of groups from time to time. The newspapers, the popular literature, and the popular speakers show this current and popular tendency. This is what makes the mores. A select minority may judge otherwise, and in time their judgment may be accepted and ratified and may make the mores of another age; but the mores are always the ways of the great masses at a time and place. The French were formerly thought to be mercurial, the English sober, and the Germans phlegmatic. The Germans have become nervous; they struggle feverishly for success and preeminence; the war of 1871 and the foundation of the German Empire have made them nationally proud, and made them feel on a level with any other state. Such a change was sure to produce great changes in the mores within two or three generations. Germany now has ambition for the first place among nations; she is sensitive and suspicious, and often seems quarrelsome. The English, in the Boer War, went through crises of excitement of which it was supposed they were insusceptible. The French, burdened by debt and taxes, feel some sense of losing ground in the rank of nations, and the national party is a product of this feeling. It seems to believe that a truculent and ferocious behavior will win adherents. Perhaps it is right, in view of the nervous temper of the age—certainly the old love of moderation and sobriety in politics seems to be diminishing. The United States is stimulated by its growth and prosperity to unlimited hope and ambition. Professor Giddings thinks that he has proved statistically that the "mental 'mode' of the American people as a whole is ideo-emotional to dogmatical-emotional," and that the market for books confirms this. The market for books could prove only the mental mode of that part of the public which reads books. What fraction is that? It would be most interesting and important to know. Of the books published, Professor Giddings finds that fifty per cent aim to please, and appeal to emotion or sentiment; forty per cent aim to convert, and appeal to belief, ethical emotion, or self-interest; eight per cent are critical and aim to instruct— they appeal to reason. This means that our literature is almost entirely addressed to the appetite for day-dreaming, romantic longings, and sentimentalism, to theoretical interest in crime, adventure, marital infelicity, family tragedies, and the pleasure of emotional excitement, while a large part of it turns upon ethical emotion and ignorant zeal in social matters. This literature reflects the mores and at the same time strengthens them. The people who are educated on it are trained either to Philistinism or to become the victims of suggestion. No question produced by the fall of silver could possibly be a proper political question. When it was proposed, in the United States, to make the adoption of the single silver standard a party issue and to take a vote on it, consequences were produced which were interesting for the mores. In the first place, there were interests at stake—those of the silver miners and the debtors. Interests dominate modern politics, but always more or less secretly, because it is not admitted in the mores to be right that they should dominate. Hence another pretext must be put forward to cover the interest. The best pretext is always an abstruse doctrine in the theory of public welfare. A protective tariff is never advocated because it will enable some citizens to win wealth by taxing others; it is always advocated as a prosperity policy for the country. Henry C. Carey elevated a protective tariff to a philosophy of society. When the New York courts held a law to be valid which forbade a saloon to be licensed within two hundred feet of a schoolhouse, the saloon-keepers attacked the schools as a nuisance detrimental to property. The advocates of a single silver standard put forward their proposition as a prosperity policy, and they elaborated a philosophy to serve as a major premise to it. Their ultimate philosophy was that gold is a mischief-maker to mankind, while silver is an agent of good. Obviously this is mythology, and is not capable of discussion. The silver question as a political issue was, therefore, a recent and very striking proof of the persistence in the mores of a great modern civilized state of the methods of mythology which have come down to us from prehistoric man. Mythology is in the popular mores.

There are mores corresponding to each of the great stages of the industrial organization—hunting, herding, and agricultural. When two groups which are on different stages are neighbors, or when one part of a group advances to another stage, while the remainder still practices the old form, conflicts arise. The Indian and Iranian branches of the Aryans separated under intense enmity and mutual contempt when the Iranians became tillers. All the ways of one people which conform to its industrial pursuits are an abomination to the other. The best explanation yet suggested of the statements of Caesar and Tacitus about the Germans is that the Germans were, at that period, between nomadism and settled agriculture. There is a deep contrast of mores between town and country, agriculture on the one side and manufactures, commerce, banking, etc., on the other, and this contrast may, at any time, rise to an antagonism. The antagonism is kept down if the two classes meet often; it is developed if they become strictly separated. The town looks upon the country as rustic and uncultivated; the country looks upon the town as vicious and corrupt. The individual interests of the two are antagonistic, and one may be subjected to the other, as is always the case under a protective tariff, for the protective system never can do anything but make the stronger form of industry carry the weaker. It is a characteristic of our time that in all civilized countries the population is moving from the country to the towns. This movement is not due to the same forces in all countries. Wherever agriculture is burdened by taxes to favor manufacturing, the legislation causes, or intensifies, the movement. It is not probable that the love of luxury, excitement, social intercourse, and amusement is any greater now than it always has been, but popular literature has spread the hunger for it to classes of people who never felt it formerly. The hunger enters into the mores and becomes a characteristic of the age.

The people in the slums and tenement houses will not give up the enjoyment of the streets for any amount of rural comfort. Other classes try to help them, assuming that, to them, crowds, noise, filth, contagious diseases, and narrow quarters, must be painful. The evidence is that they like the life, and are indifferent to what others consider its evils and discomforts. They like it because it satisfies the strongest desires in the mores of our time. The people in the slums feel the same desires as those other people who have clubs, balls, visitors, the park, opera, theater, and all the other means of excitement, gossip, and entertainment which make up fashionable city life.

In Germany it is said that the country population still increases rapidly by a high birth rate. When the land is all taken up this means that there is a surplus in the rural population which goes into the wages class, and a part of it seeks the towns to become unskilled laborers or handicraftsmen. It was formerly believed that great cities consume population; that there is a waste which would produce diminution if it were not for the influx from the country. City life exercises a selection on this immigration from the country; a part of it is consumed by vice and misery and disappears; another part advances to greater social power in two or three generations; another part settles into the tenement houses and recruits the city proletariat. Nowhere in the world, perhaps, are the effects of this migration from the country to the city so strikingly apparent as in New England, for here we see farms abandoned, houses torn down, and land returning to a state of nature. Cities, however, now have a number of institutions of rescue and protection, which are believed to redeem the old destruction, so that cities do not, nowadays, consume population. The migration affects the mores of both the rural and the urban population. Their ideas, standards, ways of looking at things, ambitions, appetites, concepts of right and wrong, and their judgments on all the policy of life are affected by the efflux and reflux between town and country.

One of the most noteworthy and far-reaching features in modern mores is the unwillingness to recognize a vow or to enforce a vow by any civil or ecclesiastical process, although vows have the full authority of Scripture. It is by the mores that vows have been judged wrong, and if they are made, neglect to fulfill them is regarded with indifference. In modern mores it is allowed that a man may change his mind as long as he lives. This view is produced by the doctrine of liberty. At the most he may incur liability for damages, if his vow causes damage to somebody else. The marriage vow is the only one which remains in our mores, and no doubt the leniency of divorce has been largely due to the unwillingness to enforce a vow by which it may appear later that one's life career has been injured. It does not at all lie in the mores to give the vow prominence as the aspect of marriage which determines what it is. On the contrary, the wedding ceremony is a striking case of ritual, since people attach importance to the ceremony, not to the rational sense of what is said and done.

The mores of the latter half of the nineteenth century were marked by the decline of the dominion of the classical culture which had prevailed since the Renaissance. In art it was marked by a return to nature as the only model and an abandonment of the classical models. In architecture it was marked by a revival of Gothic and Renaissance forms, but with a wide electicism, the outcome of which is not yet reached. In religion two tendencies were developed, one to mediaevalism, the other to agnosticism. What was most important for the mores was the toleration of each other, with which these opposite tendencies in religion existed side by side. Militant infidelity, or religion, was regarded as bad form, and heresy hunting became ridiculous. The popular philosophy became realistic, and the tests of value which were accepted were more and more frankly commercial; "ideal good" lost esteem and "material good" controlled. This was nothing new in the history of mankind, but the opportunities of wealth, comfort, and luxury never before were offered to the whole of society in any such manner and degree, and the utilities of wealth for all purposes of mankind never were so obvious and immediate. The classical culture and the religious philosophy had offered ideals which were no longer highly valued, and the way was clear for the dominion of materialistic standards and ideals. They spread everywhere, in spite of all protests and denials. The state won greatly in importance, and political institutions extended their operations over the field of the mores. Political institutions took the place of ecclesiastical institutions as adjuncts of the economic struggle for existence. The eighteenth century had bequeathed to the nineteenth a great mass of abstract notions about rights and about the ultimate notions of political philosophy, and in the nineteenth century many of these notions were reduced to actuality in constitutions, laws, and judicial rulings. The masses in all civilized nations were led to believe that their welfare could be obtained by dogmatic propositions if such propositions were enacted into constitutions and laws. This faith has entered into the mores of all civilized men and now rules their discussion of social questions. Rights, justice, liberty, and equality are the watchwords instead of the church, faith, heaven, and hell. The amount of superstition is not much changed, but it now attaches to politics, not to religion.

The grand controlling fact in modern society is that the earth is underpopulated on the existing stage of the arts. As a consequence men are in demand. The human race is going through a period of enlargement with ease and comfort; accordingly a philosophy of optimism prevails, and the world-beatifiers reign in philosophy. Since, as a fact, the struggle for existence and competition of life are not severe, the philosophy prevails that so they always ought to be. An ethical ideal is carried into nature. It is a fact that the great masses of the human race get on very well with a minimum of education, for the conditions favor most, proportionately, those who are worst off—the unskilled laborers. Hence we find it preached as a doctrine that men, if in crowds, know the truth, feel virtuously, and act wisely by intuition, without education or training.

All modern economic developments have tended to level classes and ranks, and therefore to create democracy, and to throw political power into the hands of the most numerous class; the courtiers of power, therefore, turn to the masses with the same flattery and servility which they used to pay to kings, prelates, and nobles. At every boundary line at which the interests of individuals or groups meet in the competition of life, there is strife and friction, and at all such points there are rights which are in the mores or the laws and which have been produced by the need to solve the collisions of power and interest in peace. There is, therefore, always another resource for the party which has been defeated in the competition of life; they can appeal to rights and fight over again, on the political domain, what they have lost on the economic domain. Inasmuch as the masses cannot win on the economic domain because their opponents, though few in number, have talent, knowledge, craft, and capital, and inasmuch as the masses have political power, this appeal from the field of economic effort to that of politics is characteristic of the age. It now gives form and color to both the economic and political effort, and it is dominating all the mores which have to do with either. The master of industry dare not neglect political power; the statesman cannot maintain an independent footing against capitalistic interest. Primarily, we see a war between plutocracy and democracy. Secondarily, we see a combination of the two loom up in the future—the apostles of socialism, state socialism, municipalization, etc., are all working for it. In the combination the strongest element will rule, and the strongest element is capital. The defeat and decline of the Democratic political party in the United States within forty years, its incompetence as an opposition party, its chase after any captivating issue, its evolution into populism, coupled with administrative folly, the fear and distrust which it has consequently inspired in all who have anything, so that they turn to the ruling party for security at the sacrifice of everything else, the more and more complete surrender, at the same time, of the Republican party to the character of a conspiracy to hold power and use it for plutocractic ends, are phenomena already observable of the coming consolidation of political and monetary power. The more industrial and pecuniary functions are confided to the State or city, the more rapidly will this result be brought about. The place to watch to see whether the result will be arrested or not is in the mores. Do the people show strong political sense? Do they show real insight into their own institutions and the spirit of the same, so that they cannot be deceived by political fallacies? Do they resist the allurements of glory and cling to the genuine forces which make for national health and strength? Are they cynical about political corruption, or honestly outraged by it? Is their world-philosophy ignoble? Do they resist a steal because it is a steal or because they are not in it? Are they captivated by appeals to national vanity or do they turn aside from such appeals with contempt? These are the questions which decide the trend of institutions and the destiny of states, and the answer to them must be sought in the mores.

Parties formed on interests invent dogmas which will serve as major premises for the especial inferences which will suit their purposes. These are the "great principles" of history which are always preached as eternal and immutable. John of Salisbury, the friend of Thomas à Becket, taking part in the quarrel of the prelate with the king, which really was a quarrel of the Roman law concept of the State with the Church, developed, in his *Polycraticus*, notions of the sovereignty of the people and of republican self-government. Guelphs argued the sovereignty of the people to get the alliance of the middle class against the emperor, in Italy; while Ghibellines used the same argument to get the alliance of the middle class against the popes, in Germany. St. Augustine thought that the State was due to sin, while Gregory VII said that it was the work of the devil. This was in order to exalt the Church. The "two sword" doctrine furnished a dogmatic basis for mediaeval society: Pope and Emperor side by side, with the Pope above. The Church was due to God, the State was a human invention. Hence arose the doctrine that the State was based on a contract between ruler and ruled, and the inference that tyrannicide was justifiable, an inference which was so frequently put into practice in the sixteenth century that its fallacy was demonstrated. Any ruler of whose acts anybody disapproved was a tyrant. Then the doctrine of contract was changed into the later "social compact" of the democratic republican form with natural rights, which ran from Grotius to Rousseau. This doctrine was used by Mariana and other Jesuits against the absolute kings (at first, of Spain); it was thoroughly destructive of the mediaeval doctrines of political authority and of rights.

When the Americans, in 1776, revolted against the colonial policy of England, they found a great number of principles afloat, and had great trouble to select the one which would suit their purpose without suggesting other inferences which would be unwelcome. The first paragraph of the Declaration of Independence contains a number of these great principles which were supposed to be axioms of political philosophy. In 1898, when we forced our rule on the Philippine Islands, some of these principles were very inconvenient. In time we shall have to drop others of them. There are no dogmatic propositions of political philosophy which are universally and always true; there are views which prevail, at a time, for a while, and then fade away and give place to other views. Each set of views colors the mores of a period. The eighteenth century notions about equality, natural rights, classes, etc., produced nineteenth century states and legislation, all strongly humanitarian in faith and temper; at the present time the eighteenth century notions are disappearing, and the mores of the twentieth century will not be tinged by humanitarianism as those of the last hundred years have been. If the State should act on ideas of every man's duty, instead of on notions of natural rights, evidently institutions and usages would undergo a great transformation.

While the views of rights are thus afloat on the tide of interests and carry with them, in the ebb and flow, a great mass of corollaries, it does not appear that the doctrine and institutions of constitutional government are being more thoroughly understood or more firmly established. Yet constitutional government is the guarantee of interests and welfare. It is a product of experience, it contains institutions by which collisions of interest can be adjusted and rights can be secured. Yet it does not offer any definitions or dogmatic statements about rights and interests. If men turn from the institutions and put faith in abstract propositions, evidently the chances of welfare will be greatly changed. At the present time constitutional institutions are the great reliance for rights and justice and the great ground of hope and confidence in the future. Nevertheless, constitutional government can never overcome the mores. We have plenty of cases of experiment to prove that constitutional institutions of the best type fall into corruption and decay unless the virtues of political self-control exist in high vigor and purity in the mores of the society.

We see, then, in the status and outlook of the present time, these facts: underpopulation of the globe and increasing control of natural forces give easier conditions for the struggle for existence. This means the most to those who have inherited the least. It is, however, obviously a temporary advantage, for the human race will, in a few generations, find itself face to face with overpopulation and harder conditions. In the meantime philosophies and notions win general acceptance which are relatively true in the exceptional period. They are broadly stated and confidently accepted in the mores and in legislation. Rights are changed in popular opinion and in constitutions, and the location of political power is shifted, especially as between classes; notions about property, marriage, family, inheritance, and so on, change to suit facts and faiths about the struggle for existence. Then groups and parties will form and war will occur between them. Great dogmas will be put forth at all stages of these movements and appropriate watchwords will never be wanting.

# Index

The text of this book was set in Melior, a typeface designed in 1948/49 by the German type designer and calligrapher Hermann Zapf. Originally designed for metal-cast type, Melior was redrawn by Zapf in 1966 for photocomposition, by commission from the Mergenthaler Linotype Company of New York. "To understand the general principle of Melior please study the story about Piet Hein's *Superellipse*, a mathematical construction of 1959, in *Scientific American*, September 1965," Zapf noted on his layout for the redesign of this typeface.

Editorial services by BooksCraft, Inc., Indianapolis, Indiana
Book design by Hermann Strohbach, New York, New York
Typesetting by Weimer Typesetting Company, Inc., Indianapolis, Indiana
Index by Shirley Kessel, Primary Sources Research, Chevy Chase, Maryland
Printed and bound by Worzalla Publishing Company, Stevens Point, Wisconsin